Lecture Notes in Control and Information Sciences

Edited by A. V. Balakrishnan and M. Thoma

Vol. 1: Distributed Parameter Systems: Modelling and Identification
Proceedings of the IFIP Working Conference, Rome, Italy, June 21–26, 1976
Edited by A. Ruberti
V, 458 pages. 1978

Vol. 2: New Trends in Systems Analysis
International Symposium, Versailles, December 13–17, 1976
Edited by A. Bensoussan and J. L. Lions
VII, 759 pages. 1977

Vol. 3: Differential Games and Applications
Proceedings of a Workshop, Enschede, Netherlands, March 16–25, 1977
Edited by P. Hagedorn, H. W. Knobloch, and G. J. Olsder
XII, 236 pages. 1977

Vol. 4: M. A. Crane, A. J. Lemoine
An Introduction to the Regenerative Method for Simulation Analysis
VII, 111 pages. 1977

Vol. 5: David J. Clements, Brian D. O. Anderson
Singular Optimal Control: The Linear Quadratic Problem
V, 93 pages. 1978

Vol. 6: Optimization Techniques
Proceedings of the 8th IFIP Conference on Optimization Techniques, Würzburg, September 5–9, 1977
Part 1
Edited by J. Stoer
XIII, 528 pages. 1978

Vol. 7: Optimization Techniques
Proceedings of the 8th IFIP Conference on Optimization Techniques, Würzburg, September 5–9, 1977
Part 2
Edited by J. Stoer
XIII, 512 pages. 1978

Vol. 8: R. F. Curtain, A. J. Pritchard
Infinite Dimensional Linear Systems Theory
VII, 298 pages. 1978

Vol. 9: Y. M. El-Fattah, C. Foulard
Learning Systems:
Decision, Simulation, and Control
VII, 119 pages. 1978

Vol. 10: J. M. Maciejowski
The Modelling of Systems with Small Observation Sets
VII, 241 pages. 1978

Vol. 11: Y. Sewaragi, T. Soeda, S. Omatu
Modelling, Estimation, and Their Applications for Distributed Parameter Systems
VI, 269 pages. 1978

Vol. 12: I. Postlethwaite, A. G. J. McFarlane
A Complex Variable Approach to the Analysis of Linear Multivariable Feedback Systems
IV, 177 pages. 1979

Vol. 13: E. D. Sontag
Polynomial Response Maps
VIII, 168 pages. 1979

Vol. 14: International Symposium on Systems Optimization and Analysis
Rocquentcourt, December 11–13, 1978;
IRIA LABORIA
Edited by A. Bensoussan and J. Lions
VIII, 332 pages. 1979

Vol. 15: Semi-Infinite Programming
Proceedings of a Workshop, Bad Honnef, August 30 – September 1, 1978
V, 180 pages. 1979

Vol. 16: Stochastic Control Theory and Stochastic Differential Systems
Proceedings of a Workshop of the „Sonderforschungsbereich 72 der Deutschen Forschungsgemeinschaft an der Universität Bonn"
which took place in January 1979 at Bad Honnef
VIII, 615 pages. 1979

Vol. 17: O. I. Franksen, P. Falster, F. J. Evans
Qualitative Aspects of Large Scale Systems
Developing Design Rules Using APL
XII, 119 pages. 1979

Vol. 18: Modelling and Optimization of Complex Systems
Proceedings of the IFIP-TC 7 Working Conference
Novosibirsk, USSR, 3–9 July, 1978
Edited by G. I. Marchuk
VI, 293 pages. 1979

Vol. 19: Global and Large Scale System Models
Proceedings of the Center for Advanced Studies (CAS)
International Summer Seminar
Dubrovnik, Yugoslavia, August 21–26, 1978
Edited by B. Lazarević
VIII, 232 pages. 1979

Vol. 20: B. Egardt
Stability of Adaptive Controllers
V, 158 pages. 1979

Vol. 21: Martin B. Zarrop
Optimal Experiment Design for Dynamic System Identification
X, 197 pages. 1979

For further listing of published volumes please turn over to inside of back cover.

Lecture Notes in Control and Information Sciences

Edited by A.V. Balakrishnan and M.Thoma

IFIP

49

Theory and Application of Random Fields

Proceedings of the IFIP-WG 7/1 Working Conference
held under the joint auspices of the Indian Statistical Institute
Bangalore, India, January 1982

Edited by G. Kallianpur

Springer-Verlag Berlin Heidelberg GmbH 1983

Editor
G. Kallianpur
Center for Stochastic Processes
Department of Statistics
Univ. of North Carolina at Chapel Hill
Chapel Hill, N.C. 27514
USA

ISBN 978-3-540-12232-6 ISBN 978-3-540-39564-5 (eBook)
DOI 10.1007/978-3-540-39564-5

Originally published by Springer-Verlag Berlin Heidelberg New York in 1983.

2061/3020-543210

Preface

The Conference on the Theory and Applications of Random Fields was held in January 1982 at the Bangalore Centre of the Indian Statistical Institute (ISI) under the joint auspices of IFIP and the ISI. It was also included as part of the Golden Jubilee celebrations of the ISI.

The conference was organized primarily to bring together scientists working in different areas of random field theory and its applications. As a result, the papers in these Proceedings range over a wide variety of topics -- from stochastic differential equations and Markov fields to quantum mechanics. Many outstanding probabilists working in random fields and closely related areas participated in the conference. An important feature of the latter was the opportunity for young scholars to have informal discussions with them and the time available for a free exchange of ideas among all participants.

I should like to thank the other members of the International Program Committee, the Organizing Committee and its chairman, Professor A.V. Balakrishnan (who first had the idea of holding such a working conference in Bangalore) for valuable assistance.

The constant encouragement and material help given by Dr. B.P. Adhikari, Director of the ISI made it possible to hold the conference in India. The devoted efforts of the faculty and staff of the Bangalore, Calcutta and Delhi campuses of the ISI, and of the local organizing committee under the able guidance of Mr. N. Srinivasan contributed greatly to its success. It is a pleasure to express my gratitude to all these friends and former colleagues of mine.

Finally, my thanks are due to another of my ISI colleagues, Dr. R.L. Karandikar for editorial and other assistance in preparing this volume for publication.

G. Kallianpur

Chapel Hill, N.C.
December 20, 1982

CONTENTS

* To be published elsewhere

RANDOM MEASURES AND STOCHASTIC INTEGRATION

K. BICHTELER and J. JACOD

Starting from the well-known and very important fact that a semimartingale on a space $(\Omega,\underline{\underline{F}},(\underline{\underline{F}}_t)_{t\geq 0},P)$ may be viewed as a σ-additive measure on the space $\Omega\times\mathbb{R}_+$ with values in L^0, we introduce a random measure as being a σ-additive measure on $\Omega\times\mathbb{R}_+\times E$, where E is an auxiliary space, with values in L^0. This apparently includes all usual notions of random measures and vector-valued semimartingales.

1 - INTRODUCTION : SEMIMARTINGALES AS VECTOR-VALUED MEASURES.

§1-a. Let $(\Omega,\underline{\underline{F}},\underline{F}=(\underline{\underline{F}}_t)_{t\geq 0},P)$ be a filtered probability space, $\underline{F}$ is right-continuous, $\underline{\underline{F}}$ is P-complete, $\underline{\underline{F}}_0$ contains all P-null sets of $\underline{\underline{F}}$. We denote by $\underline{\underline{S}}$ the space of all semimartingales, by $\underline{\underline{V}}$ the space of all adapted right-continuous processes with finite variation over finite intervals, by $\underline{\underline{M}}_{loc}$ the space of all local martingales, and by $\underline{\underline{L}}^c$ the space of all continuous local martingales that are null at time $t=0$.

The predictable and optional σ-fields on $\Omega\times\mathbb{R}_+$ are respectively denoted by $\underline{\underline{P}}$ and $\underline{\underline{O}}$; and $b\underline{\underline{P}}$ (resp. $b\underline{\underline{O}}$, ..) denotes the set of all bounded functions that are predictable (resp. optional,..) If $X\in\underline{\underline{S}}$ and if H is a predictable process that is integrable with respect to X, we denote by $H\bullet X$ the stochastic integral process (which may happen to be a pathwise "Stieltjes" integral if $X\in\underline{\underline{V}}$).

If X is a càdlàg process (i.e. with right-continuous and left-hand limited paths), X_- is the process of left-hand limits (and $X_{0-}=0$), and $\Delta X=X-X_-$ (hence $\Delta X_0=X_0$). For all other unexplained (but standard) notations, we refer to [4] or [9] or [17].

Finally, we endow the space $L^p(\Omega,\underline{\underline{F}},P)$ with the usual quasi-norm $\|.\|_p$, a norm if $p\geq 1$, and $\|Z\|_0=E(|Z|\wedge 1)$ if $p=0$.

§1-b. It is only recently that Dellacherie and Mokobodzki, and Bichteler [2], proved the following fundamental result. But the idea of considering, first quasimartingales as L^1-valued measures, then semimartingales as L^0-valued measures, is much older and due to Métivier and Pellaumail: [18],[14],[15].

We will recall the essentials of vector-valued measures in the next section. To understand the following theorem, it suffices to know that an

L^0-<u>valued finite measure</u> on a measurable space $(Y,\underline{\underline{Y}})$ is a linear mapping $\eta: b\underline{\underline{Y}} \longrightarrow L^0(\Omega,\underline{\underline{F}},P)$ which satisfies the following: if (f_n) is a sequence of measurable functions, all bounded by 1, and which converges pointwise to 0, then $\eta(f_n) \longrightarrow 0$ in L^0. Then we have:

(1.1) THEOREM: <u>There is a bijective correspondance between</u> $\underline{\underline{S}}$ (with the convention that we identify two processes that are indistinguishable), <u>and the set of all families</u> $\eta = (\eta_t)_{t\geq 0}$ <u>satisfying</u>

(i) <u>each</u> η_t <u>is a finite measure on</u> $(\Omega\times\mathbb{R}_+,\underline{\underline{P}})$ <u>with values in</u> $L^0(\Omega,\underline{\underline{F}}_t,P)$;

(ii) $\eta_s(H) = \eta_t(H 1_{[0,s]})$ <u>for all</u> $H\in b\underline{\underline{P}}$, $s\leq t$;

(iii) $\eta_t(H 1_{A\times I}) = 1_A \eta_t(H 1_{\Omega\times I})$ <u>for all</u> $H\in b\underline{\underline{P}}$, $t\geq 0$, <u>if</u> $A\in\underline{\underline{F}}_0$ <u>and</u> $I = \mathbb{R}_+$, <u>or if</u> $A\in\underline{\underline{F}}_s$ <u>and</u> $I = (s,s']$ <u>with</u> $s<s'$.

<u>Moreover, the correspondance is as follows:</u>

$$\eta_t(H) = H\bullet X_t \quad \text{for } H\in b\underline{\underline{P}}, \qquad X_t = \eta_t(1). \tag{1.2}$$

Hence, we will <u>identify</u> a family η satisfying the above conditions, with the corresponding (class of) semimartingale X given by $X_t = \eta_t(1)$.

This theorem asserts that, as far as we want to integrate all bounded predictable processes, the largest "reasonnable" class of integrators is the class of semimartingales. Similarly, consider the following situation: $(E,\underline{\underline{E}})$ is an auxiliary measurable space, and set

$$\tilde{\Omega} = \Omega\times\mathbb{R}_+\times E, \quad \tilde{\underline{\underline{P}}} = \underline{\underline{P}}\otimes\underline{\underline{E}}, \quad \tilde{\underline{\underline{O}}} = \underline{\underline{O}}\otimes\underline{\underline{E}}. \tag{1.3}$$

A natural problem (which occurs when considering multi-dimensional semimartingales, vector-valued semimartingales, random point processes,...) consists in integrating functions that are $\tilde{\underline{\underline{P}}}$-measurable on $\tilde{\Omega}$. So the largest "reasonnable" class of integrators will be the class of L^0-valued measures on $(\tilde{\Omega},\tilde{\underline{\underline{P}}})$.

2 - <u>L^p-VALUED σ-FINITE MEASURES</u>.

<u>§2-a</u>. For all details (and proofs) concerning vector-valued measures, we refer to Bichteler [1] or Schwartz [20]. Here we only give ad-hoc definitions and recall some well-known properties. We choose $p\in[0,\infty)$.

(2.1) DEFINITION: <u>A σ-finite</u> L^p-<u>valued random measure</u> is a family $\theta = (\theta_t)_{t\geq 0}$ that satisfies the following:

(i) For each $t\geq 0$, θ_t is a σ-finite measure on $(\tilde{\Omega},\tilde{\underline{\underline{P}}})$ with values in $L^p(\Omega,\underline{\underline{F}}_t,P)$: which means that there is a strictly positive $\tilde{\underline{\underline{P}}}$-measurable function V such that, if $\tilde{\underline{\underline{P}}}_V = \{\varphi: \tilde{\underline{\underline{P}}}\text{-measurable}, \varphi/V \text{ bounded}\}$, we have:

(i-1) θ_t is a linear mapping from $\tilde{\underline{\underline{P}}}_V$ into $L^p(\Omega,F_t,P)$;

(i-2) if (φ_n) is a sequence in $\tilde{\underline{\underline{P}}}_V$, bounded by V and converging pointwise to 0, then $\theta_t(\varphi_n) \longrightarrow 0$ in L^p.

(ii) $\theta_s(\varphi) = \theta_t(\varphi 1_{[0,s]})$ for all $\varphi \in \tilde{\underline{\underline{P}}}_V$, $s \leq t$.

(iii) $\theta_t(\varphi 1_{A\times I\times E}) = 1_A \theta_t(\varphi 1_{\Omega\times I\times E})$ for all $\varphi \in \tilde{\underline{\underline{P}}}_V$, $t \geq 0$, if $A \in \underline{\underline{F}}_0$ and $I = \mathbb{R}_+$, or if $A \in \underline{\underline{F}}_s$ and $I = (s,s']$ with $s < s'$.

Moreover, when $V \equiv 1$, θ is called a <u>finite</u> L^p-<u>valued random measure</u>. ∎

We shall denote by $\tilde{\underline{\underline{S}}}^p_\sigma$ (resp. $\tilde{\underline{\underline{S}}}^p$) the space of all σ-finite (resp. finite) L^p-valued random measures.

Owing to the special structure of spaces L^p, we can easily extend a measure $\theta \in \tilde{\underline{\underline{S}}}^p_\sigma$ to a much larger class of integrands than $\tilde{\underline{\underline{P}}}_V$. More precisely if φ is any $\tilde{\underline{\underline{P}}}$-measurable function we set

$$(2.2) \qquad \|\varphi\|_{L^{1,p}(\theta)} = \sum_{n\geq 1} 2^{-n} \left[1 \wedge \sup_{\psi \in \tilde{\underline{\underline{P}}}_V,\ |\psi| \leq |\varphi|} \|\theta_n(\psi)\|_p\right].$$

(2.3) DEFINITION: $L^{1,p}(\theta)$ is the set of <u>all</u> $\tilde{\underline{\underline{P}}}$-<u>measurable functions</u> φ for which there is a sequence $(\varphi_n) \subset \tilde{\underline{\underline{P}}}_V$ with $\|\varphi_n - \varphi\|_{L^{1,p}(\theta)} \longrightarrow 0$. ∎

Then each θ (or rather, each θ_t) can be extended to $L^{1,p}(\theta)$: if $\varphi \in L^{1,p}(\theta)$, pick any sequence $(\varphi_n) \subset \tilde{\underline{\underline{P}}}_V$ with $\|\varphi_n - \varphi\|_{L^{1,p}(\theta)} \longrightarrow 0$; then for each $t \geq 0$, $\theta_t(\varphi_n)$ tends in $L^p(\Omega, \underline{\underline{F}}_t, P)$ to a limit which does not depend on the particular choice of (φ_n), and is denoted by $\theta_t(\varphi)$. Then each $\varphi \in L^{1,p}(\theta)$ satisfies properties (ii) and (iii) of Definition (2.1).

(2.4) <u>Important Remark</u>. So far it may appear to the reader that the definitions of $\|\cdot\|_{L^{1,p}(\theta)}$ and of $L^{1,p}(\theta)$ depend on the choice of V. But this is actually not so, since it turns out that:

1) If $(V', \theta' = (\theta'_t)_{t \geq 0})$ also satisfies the conditions of (2.1) and if $\theta'_t(\varphi) = \theta_t(\varphi)$ for all $\varphi \in \tilde{\underline{\underline{P}}}_V \cap \tilde{\underline{\underline{P}}}_{V'}$, then $\|\cdot\|_{L^{1,p}(\theta)} = \|\cdot\|_{L^{1,p}(\theta')}$ and $L^{1,p}(\theta) = L^{1,p}(\theta')$ and $\theta_t(\varphi) = \theta'_t(\varphi)$ for all $\varphi \in L^{1,p}(\theta)$.

2) Any strictly positive function V' belonging to $L^{1,p}(\theta)$ also satisfies the conditions of Definition (2.1). ∎

This induces to set:

$$(2.5) \qquad \tilde{\underline{\underline{S}}}^p_V = \{\theta \in \tilde{\underline{\underline{S}}}^p : V \in L^{1,p}(\theta)\}$$

and we have $\tilde{\underline{\underline{S}}}^p = \tilde{\underline{\underline{S}}}^p_1$, that is, $\theta \in \tilde{\underline{\underline{S}}}^p_\sigma$ is a <u>finite</u> measure if and only if $1 \in L^{1,p}(\theta)$. Another way of stating property (2.1,i-2), combined with (2.4,2), is the <u>dominated convergence Theorem</u>:

(2.6) If a sequence (φ_n) of $\tilde{\underline{\underline{P}}}$-measurable functions converges pointwise to φ and $|\varphi_n| \leq V$ for some $V \in L^{1,p}(\theta)$, then $\varphi_n, \varphi \in L^{1,p}(\theta)$ and $\theta_t(\varphi_n) \longrightarrow \theta_t(\varphi)$ in L^p and $\|\varphi_n - \varphi\|_{L^{1,p}(\theta)} \longrightarrow 0$.

Now we state some properties of random measures.

(2.7) $L^{1,p}(\theta)$ is a complete vector lattice under the quasi-norm $\|\cdot\|_{L^{1,p}(\theta)}$

(2.8) $L^{1,p}(\theta) = \{\varphi : \tilde{\underline{\underline{P}}}\text{-measurable}, \ \lim_{r\downarrow 0} \|r\varphi\|_{L^{1,p}(\theta)} = 0\}$.

(2.9) If $p \leq q$ and $\theta \in \tilde{\underline{\underline{S}}}^q_\sigma$ (resp. $\tilde{\underline{\underline{S}}}^q$), then $\theta \in \tilde{\underline{\underline{S}}}^p_\sigma$ (resp. $\tilde{\underline{\underline{S}}}^p$) and $L^{1,q}(\theta) \subset L^{1,p}(\theta)$.

Let W be a finite-valued $\tilde{\underline{\underline{P}}}$-measurable function. Then we define a measure $W.\theta \in \tilde{\underline{\underline{S}}}^p_\sigma$ by putting

(2.10) $$W.\theta_t(\varphi) = \theta_t(W\varphi) \qquad \text{if } W\varphi \in L^{1,p}(\theta).$$

Note that if $V \in L^{1,p}(\theta)$, then $W.\theta \in \tilde{\underline{\underline{S}}}^p_{V'}$ for $V' = V/(|W| \wedge 1)$. We have

(2.11) $$W.\theta \in \tilde{\underline{\underline{S}}}^p \iff W \in L^{1,p}(\theta).$$

(2.12) $$L^{1,p}(W.\theta) = \{\varphi : \tilde{\underline{\underline{P}}}\text{-measurable}, \ \varphi W \in L^{1,p}(\theta)\}.$$

(2.13) PROPOSITION: $L^{1,0}(\theta)$ <u>is stable by localization, i.e. if</u> (T_n) <u>is a sequence of stopping times with</u> $\sup T_n = \infty$ <u>and if</u> $\varphi 1_{[\![0,T_n]\!]\times E} \in L^{1,0}(\theta)$ <u>for all</u> n, <u>then</u> $\varphi \in L^{1,0}(\theta)$ (this is false in general for $L^{1,p}$, $p>0$).

<u>Proof</u>. Let $S_n = \sup_{m<n} T_m$ and $\varphi_n = |\varphi| 1_{[\![0,S_n]\!]\times E}$. We have $\varphi_n \in L^{1,0}(\theta)$, so by (2.1,ii) we have for $r>0$:

$$\sup_{\psi\in\tilde{\underline{\underline{P}}}_{V'},\,|\psi|\leq|r\varphi|} \|\theta_t(\psi)\|_0 \leq \sup_{\psi\in\tilde{\underline{\underline{P}}}_{V'},\,|\psi|\leq r\varphi_p} \|\theta_t(\psi)\|_0 + P(S_p<t);$$

hence

$$\|r\varphi\|_{L^{1,0}(\theta)} \leq \|r\varphi_p\|_{L^{1,0}(\theta)} + \textstyle\sum_{n\geq 1} 2^{-n} P(S_p<n).$$

Then applying twice (2.8) and $\lim_{(p)} P(S_p<n) = 0$ yield the result. ∎

§2-b. <u>Finite measures</u>. The most natural topology to endow $\tilde{\underline{\underline{S}}}^p$ with is the topology of the <u>semi-variation</u> (or: of uniform convergence on the unit ball of $b\tilde{\underline{\underline{P}}}$). Since a θ in $\tilde{\underline{\underline{S}}}^p$ is actually a family $(\theta_t)_{t\geq 0}$ of measures, one may define the topology through the following quasi-norm:

(2.14) $$\|\theta\|_{\tilde{S}^p} = \textstyle\sum_{n\geq 1} 2^{-n} \left[1 \wedge \sup_{\varphi\in b\tilde{\underline{\underline{P}}},\,|\varphi|\leq 1} \|\theta_n(\varphi)\|_p\right].$$

Then $\tilde{\underline{\underline{S}}}^p$ is <u>complete</u> under this quasi-norm, and we have:

(2.15) $$W \in L^{1,p}(\theta),\ \theta \in \tilde{\underline{\underline{S}}}^p_\sigma \longrightarrow \|W\|_{L^{1,p}(\theta)} = \|W.\theta\|_{\tilde{S}^p}.$$

One of the main results about finite measures is the Maurey-Rosenthal Theorem ([11],[19],[2]). If $\theta \in \tilde{\underline{\underline{S}}}^0_\sigma$ and T is a stopping time, we call θ^T the random measure "stopped at time T", that is $\theta^T = 1_{[\![0,T]\!]\times E}.\theta$. If Q is another probability measure that is equivalent to P, then $L^0(\Omega,\underline{\underline{F}}_t,P) = L^0(\Omega,\underline{\underline{F}}_t,Q)$, hence the space $\tilde{\underline{\underline{S}}}^0$ is the same for P and for Q. But $\underline{\underline{S}}^p(P) \neq \underline{\underline{S}}^p(Q)$ if $p>0$.

(2.16) THEOREM (Maurey-Rosenthal): Let $\theta\in \underline{\underline{S}}^0(P)$ and let $t\geq 0$. Then there is a probability measure Q that is equivalent to P, such that the Radon-Nikodym derivative $\frac{dQ}{dP}$ is bounded, and that $\theta^t\in \underline{\underline{S}}^2(Q)$ (Q may of course depend on θ and on t).

§2-c. Random measures and semimartingales.

1) Instead of considering measures on $(\tilde{\Omega},\tilde{\underline{\underline{P}}})$, we might have introduced measures on $(\Omega\times\mathbb{R}_+,\underline{\underline{P}})$, which would amount to look at the case when E contains only one point. In this case, Theorem (1.1) asserts that $\tilde{\underline{\underline{S}}}^0$ may be identified to the set $\underline{\underline{S}}$ of all (real-valued) semimartingales, while $\tilde{\underline{\underline{S}}}^0_\sigma$ is the class of "formal semimartingales" of Schwartz [20]. Moreover,

(2.17) The topology of the semi-variation, defined by (2.14) (and the corresponding quasi-norm is denoted by $\|\cdot\|_S$) is exactly the topology introduced by Emery [6] (cf. also Mémin [12]).

(2.18) If $X\in\underline{\underline{S}}=\tilde{\underline{\underline{S}}}^0$, then $L^{1,0}(X)$ is exactly the space of all predictable processes that can be integrated with respect to X, as introduced in [8] (cf. also [3]).

(2.19) REMARK: Similarly, for $p>0$, $\tilde{\underline{\underline{S}}}^p$ may be identified with a subspace of $\underline{\underline{S}}$ called $\underline{\underline{S}}^p$, and the corresponding quasi-norm is written $\|\cdot\|_{S^p}$: this space has been introduced and studied by Emery [5] under the name "$\underline{\underline{H}}^p$-space of semimartingales" (more accurately, the space $\underline{\underline{S}}^p$ defined above coincide with the space $\underline{\underline{H}}^p$ when the time interval is finite). ∎

2) Now we turn back to the general case where $(E,\underline{\underline{E}})$ is any measurable space. Let $\theta\in\tilde{\underline{\underline{S}}}^0_\sigma$ and $\varphi\in L^{1,0}(\theta)$. If we set

(2.20)
$$(\varphi\times\theta)_t(H) = \theta_t[\varphi(H\otimes 1)] \qquad \text{for } H\in b\underline{\underline{P}},$$

it follows from (2.6) that the family $\varphi\times\theta=\{(\varphi\times\theta)_t\}_{t\geq 0}$ satisfies all conditions of Theorem (1.1): thus we have defined a semimartingale, also denoted by $\varphi\times\theta$. By definition, this semimartingale $\varphi\times\theta$ is called the stochastic integral process of φ with respect to θ, and by (1.2) we have

(2.21)
$$\varphi\times\theta_t = (\varphi\times\theta)_t(1) = \theta_t(\varphi).$$

For any stopping time T, we have

(2.22)
$$(\varphi\times\theta)^T = \varphi\times\theta^T = (\varphi 1_{[\![0,T]\!]\times E})\times\theta.$$

If in addition $\theta\in\tilde{\underline{\underline{S}}}^p_\sigma$ and $\varphi\in L^{1,p}(\theta)$, then $\varphi\times\theta\in\underline{\underline{S}}^p$ (see (2.19)) and

(2.23)
$$\|\varphi\times\theta\|_{S^p} \leq \|\varphi\|_{L^{1,p}(\theta)},$$

an inequality which may be strict.

Example: Let again E be reduced to one point, and consider $X \in \underline{\underline{S}}$ and $H \in L^{1,0}(X)$ (see (2.18)). Then $H \bullet X = H \times X$. ∎

§2-d. Construction of a random measure. A priori, a random measure may not be defined on the whole set $\tilde{\underline{\underline{P}}}_V$ associated to a strictly positive function V; exactly like a finite real-valued measure is sometimes defined on a σ-field (or even, a semi-algebra) and thereafter extended to all bounded measurable functions. So we seek for a "minimal" characterization of σ-finite L^p-valued random measures. The proofs are in [1].

(2.24) DEFINITION: An Integration Lattice is a vector lattice $\mathcal{S}$ of functions on $\tilde{\Omega}$ with: (i) $\mathcal{S}$ is stable under the mapping: $\varphi \rightsquigarrow 1 \wedge \varphi$;

(ii) there is a sequence $(\varphi_n) \subset \mathcal{S}$ such that: $\sup \varphi_n = 1$;

(iii) $\mathcal{S}$ generates the σ-field $\tilde{\underline{\underline{P}}}$;

(iv) $\mathcal{S}$ is stable under the mappings: $\varphi \rightsquigarrow \varphi 1_{A \times I \times E}$, for $A \in \underline{\underline{F}}_0$ and $I = \mathbb{R}_+$, and for $A \in \underline{\underline{F}}_s$ and $I = (s,s']$, with $s < s'$. ∎

(2.25) THEOREM: Let $\mathcal{S}$ be an integration lattice, and $\theta = (\theta_t)_{t \geq 0}$ be such that: (i) each θ_t is a linear mapping: $\mathcal{S} \longrightarrow L^p(\Omega, \underline{\underline{F}}_t, P)$ and for any sequence $(\varphi_n) \subset \mathcal{S}$ converging pointwise to 0, with $|\varphi_n| \leq \varphi$ for some $\varphi \in \mathcal{S}$, then $\theta_t(\varphi_n) \longrightarrow 0$ in L^p.

(ii) Conditions (ii) and (iii) of (2.1) are satisfied for all $\varphi \in \mathcal{S}$.

Then, θ has a unique extension as a σ-finite L^p-valued random measure.

Note that if $\theta \in \tilde{\underline{\underline{S}}}^p_\sigma$, then $L^{1,p}(\theta)$ is an integration lattice, and it is the largest one on which θ is defined.

If we construct a random measure from an integration lattice $\mathcal{S}$, it may be useful to characterize $\|.\|_{L^{1,p}(\theta)}$ and $L^{1,p}(\theta)$ in terms of $\mathcal{S}$ alone. This goes as follows:

$$\mathcal{S}_+^\uparrow = \{\varphi : \varphi = \sup \varphi_n, \ \varphi_n \in \mathcal{S}, \ \varphi_n \geq 0\}$$

$$\theta_t^{*p}(\varphi) = \sup\{\|\theta_t(\psi)\|_p : \psi \in \mathcal{S}, \ |\psi| \leq \varphi\} \qquad \text{for } \varphi \in \mathcal{S}_+^\uparrow$$

$$\text{(2.26)} \quad \|\varphi\|_{L^{1,p}(\theta)} = \sum_{n \geq 1} 2^{-n} \left[1 \wedge \inf_{\psi \in \mathcal{S}_+^\uparrow, \ \psi \geq |\varphi|} \theta_n^{*p}(\psi)\right]$$

for any $\tilde{\underline{\underline{P}}}$-measurable φ. And $L^{1,p}(\theta)$ is the set of all $\tilde{\underline{\underline{P}}}$-measurable φ for which there ewists a sequence $(\varphi_n) \subset \mathcal{S}$ with $\|\varphi_n - \varphi\|_{L^{1,p}(\theta)} \longrightarrow 0$.

§2-e. Examples. The following shows that nearly all processes or random measures with respect to which one usually defines stochastic integration may be fitted into the above framework. However, we do not claim that the most general space of integrands with respect to some $\theta \in \tilde{\underline{\underline{S}}}^0_\sigma$ is $L^{1,0}(\theta)$: it is actually quite the opposite, as we shall see in the next section.

Example 1. $E=\{1\}$ is reduced to one point. We have already described $\underset{=}{\tilde{S}}^0$ and $\underset{=}{\tilde{S}}^0_\sigma$. Moreover if $X\in \underset{=}{S}$, then $L^{1,0}(X)$ is the biggest possible class of predictable integrands (for instance, the set $\{H\times X : H\in L^{1,0}(X)\}$ is closed in $\underset{=}{S}$), so there is no further extension. ∎

Example 2. $E=\{1,..,n\}$. Then $\underset{=}{\tilde{S}}^0$ is identified with the set of n-dimensional semimartingales. If $X=(X^i)_{i\le n}\in \underset{=}{\tilde{S}}^0$ it is immediate to check that:

$$L^{1,0}(X) \;=\; \{H=(H^i)_{i\le n} :\; H^i\in L^{1,0}(X^i) \;\text{ for } 1\le i\le n\}. \tag{2.27}$$

However, the set $\{H\times X=\sum_{i\le n} H^i\times X^i : H\in L^{1,0}(X)\}$ is not closed in $\underset{=}{S}$, and one may define stochastic integrals for processes H not in $L^{1,0}(X)$ [10]. ∎

Example 3. $E=\mathbb{N}$. Then $\underset{=}{\tilde{S}}^0$ may be identified with the set of all sequences $X=(X^n)_{n\in\mathbb{N}}$ of semimartingales. Here again,

$$L^{1,0}(X) \;=\; \{H=(H^n)_{n\in\mathbb{N}} :\; H^n\in L^{1,0}(X^n) \;\text{ for all } n\in\mathbb{N}\}. \tag{2.28}$$ ∎

Example 4, semimartingales with values in the dual F' of a separable vector space F. Let X be an F'-valued semimartingale, and $(e_n)_{n\in\mathbb{N}}$ be a total sequence in F. Then X is characterized by its "coordinates" $X^n=\langle X,e_n\rangle$ and we are back to the previous example. ∎

In [9] we have introduced another sort of random measures:

(2.29) DEFINITION: A strict random measure is a signed transition kernel $\mu(\omega;dt\times dx)$ from $(\Omega,\underset{=}{F})$ into $(\mathbb{R}_+\times E,\underset{=}{\mathbb{R}}_+\otimes\underset{=}{E})$, such that:

(i) there is a strictly positive $\underset{=}{\tilde{P}}$-measurable function V such that the variable: $\omega \rightsquigarrow \int V(\omega,t,x)\,|\mu|(\omega;dt\times dx)$ is integrable;

(ii) for each $\underset{=}{\tilde{O}}$-measurable function φ such that φ/V is bounded, the following process is optional:

$$(\varphi*\mu)_t(\omega) \;=\; \int_{[0,t]\times E} \varphi(\omega,tx)\mu(\omega;dt\times dx)\,. \tag{2.30}$$ ∎

More generally, for each $\underset{=}{\tilde{O}}$-measurable function φ we define the process $\varphi*\mu$ by (2.30), letting $\varphi*\mu_t(\omega)=+\infty$ whenever the right-hand side in (2.30) does not converge.

Example 5, strict random measures. Let μ be a strict random measure and V be associated to it like in (2.29,i). We trivially associate to μ a σ-finite L^0-valued random measure, denoted again $\mu=(\mu_t)_{t\ge 0}$, by putting $\mu_t(\varphi)=\varphi*\mu_t$ for $\varphi\in\underset{=}{\tilde{P}}_V$. This measure is finite if and only if $1*\mu\in\underset{=}{V}$ (or equivalently, if $1*|\mu|\in\underset{=}{V}$). If φ is $\underset{=}{\tilde{P}}$-measurable, we have

$$\varphi*\mu\in\underset{=}{V} \;\Longrightarrow\; \varphi\in L^{1,0}(\mu) \quad\text{and}\quad \varphi\times\mu=\varphi*\mu \tag{2.31}$$

As we presently see, if μ is a signed measure a description of $L^{1,0}(\mu)$

is difficult to obtain. However, we obviously have:

(2.32) If μ is positive, then $L^{1,0}(\mu) = \{\varphi: \tilde{\underline{\underline{P}}}\text{-measurable}, \varphi*\mu \in \underline{\underline{V}}\}$.

Then, by (2.31) we have $L^{1,0}(|\mu|) \subset L^{1,0}(\mu)$ in all cases. ∎

Example 6, integer-valued random measures. We suppose that E is a Lusin space with its Borel σ-field $\underline{\underline{E}}$, and that

$$(2.33) \qquad \mu(\omega, dt\times dx) = \sum_{s>0} 1_D(\omega,s)\, \varepsilon_{(s,\beta_s(\omega))}(dt\times dx)$$

where D is an optional thin random set and β is an E-valued optional process: see [9] for all facts about this type of strict random measures. In particular let ν be its dual predictable projection, which is another positive strict random measure, and from (2.32) we deduce $L^{1,0}(\nu) \subset L^{1,0}(\mu)$.

We also recall that we set

$$\tilde{\varphi}_t(\omega) = \int_E [\mu(\omega;\{t\}\times dx) - \nu(\omega;\{t\}\times dx)]\, \varphi(\omega,t,x) ,$$

with $\tilde{\varphi}_t(\omega) = +\infty$ whenever this expression diverges; then set

$$G^1_{loc}(\mu) = \{\varphi : \tilde{\underline{\underline{P}}}\text{-measurable}, (\textstyle\sum_{s\leq .} (\tilde{\varphi}_s)^2)^{1/2} \text{ is locally integrable}\}$$

and if $\varphi \in G^1_{loc}(\mu)$ one may define the stochastic integral $\varphi*(\mu-\nu)$ as the only purely discontinuous local martingale such that $\Delta[\varphi*(\mu-\nu)] = \tilde{\varphi}$. Of course this expression coincides with the integral (2.30) when the latter is finite. It is elementary to check that

$$(2.34) \qquad \varphi \in G^1_{loc}(\mu) \cap L^{1,0}(\mu-\nu) \longrightarrow \varphi*(\mu-\nu) = \varphi\times(\mu-\nu) .$$

(2.35) PROPOSITION: Let $\mathcal{L} = \{\varphi : \tilde{\underline{\underline{P}}}\text{-measurable}, (\varphi^2 \wedge |\varphi|)*\nu \in \underline{\underline{V}}\}$.

(i) We have $\mathcal{L} \subset L^{1,0}(\mu-\nu) \cap G^1_{loc}(\mu)$.

(ii) If μ is quasi-left-continuous, then $\mathcal{L} = L^{1,0}(\mu-\nu) = G^1_{loc}(\mu)$.

(quasi-left-continuous means that $\mu(\{T\}\times E) = 0$ a.s. on $\{T<\infty\}$ for each predictable time, or equivalently that ν has a version satisfying identically $\nu(\omega;\{t\}\times E) = 0$).

Proof. i) Let $\varphi \in \mathcal{L}$, $\varphi' = \varphi 1_{\{|\varphi|\leq 1\}}$, $\varphi'' = \varphi - \varphi'$. We have $|\varphi''|*\nu \in \underline{\underline{V}}$, hence $\varphi'' \in L^{1,0}(\nu)$, hence $\varphi'' \in L^{1,0}(\mu-\nu)$.

We have $\varphi'^2*\nu \in \underline{\underline{V}}$. By localization, and using (2.13), we may assume that $a := E(\varphi'^2*\nu_\infty)$ is finite. Let $V>0$ be like in (2.29,i), and $r>0$. Let $\psi \in \tilde{\underline{\underline{P}}}_V$, $|\psi| \leq r|\varphi'|$. Then $M = \psi*(\mu-\nu)$ is a square-integrable martingale, and its brackett $\langle M,M\rangle$ is smaller than $\psi^2*\nu$ [9], hence $\|M_t\|_0 \leq \|M_t\|_2 \leq \|\psi^2*\nu_t\|_1 \leq r\,a$. Then by (2.2) we obtain $\|r\varphi'\|_{L^{1,0}(\mu-\nu)} \leq r\,a$, and (2.8) yields $\varphi' \in L^{1,0}(\mu-\nu)$. Finally $\varphi \in G^1_{loc}(\mu)$ is known [9].

ii) Similarly, it is known that $\mathcal{L} = G^1_{loc}(\mu)$ when μ is quasi-left-continuous. Let $\varphi \in L^{1,0}(\mu-\nu)$. Then φ' and φ'' defined as above are also in $L^{1,0}(\mu-\nu)$. By hypothesis $X = \varphi''\times(\mu-\nu)$ is a semimartingale, and $\Delta X_t(\omega) =$

$\int_E \mu(\omega;\{t\}\times dx)\varphi''(\omega,t,x)$, hence either $|\Delta X_t|>1$ or $\Delta X_t = 0$. Thus $\varphi''*\mu_t = \sum_{s\leq t}\Delta X_s$ is in $\underline{\underline{V}}$ and $\varphi''\in L^{1,0}(\mu)$, thus $\varphi''\in L^{1,0}(\nu)$, thus $\varphi''*\nu\in\underline{\underline{V}}$.

Let $\varphi_n = \varphi' 1_{\{|\varphi'|\leq n V\}}$, and $X^n = \varphi_n x(\mu-\nu)$. By (2.6), $X^n \longrightarrow X := \varphi' x(\mu-\nu)$ in $\underline{\underline{S}}$. Moreover all X^n's are local martingales with $|\Delta X^n|\leq 1$, hence X is also a local martingale with $|\Delta X|\leq 1$ [12]. Thus it follows from [9] that $\varphi'^2 *\nu\in\underline{\underline{V}}$, and we have shown that $\varphi = \varphi' + \varphi''\in\mathcal{L}$. ∎

In the non-quasi-left-continuous case, the inclusion $\mathcal{L}\subset L^{1,0}(\mu-\nu)$ is in general strict: take for instance μ to be predictable, so $\nu = \mu$ and each $\underline{\underline{\tilde{P}}}$-measurable function is in $L^{1,0}(\mu-\nu)$.

3 - A FURTHER EXTENSION OF L^p-VALUED RANDOM MEASURES.

§3-a. So far, the product structure $\tilde{\Omega} = \Omega\times\mathbb{R}_+\times E$ has been very little exploited, except for the definition of $\varphi\times\theta$. In the further extension to come now, we essentially use this structure, under the form $\tilde{\Omega} = (\Omega\times\mathbb{R}_+)\times E$.

The idea is that we may define a semimartingale, or more generally a formal semimartingale, $\varphi\times\theta$ by (2.20) even though φ is not in $L^{1,0}(\theta)$; a natural way to do it is to set for $\theta\in\underline{\underline{\tilde{S}}}^p_\sigma$:

(3.1) $L^p_\sigma(\theta) = \{\varphi$: $\underline{\underline{\tilde{P}}}$-measurable, there is a strictly positive predictable process K such that $(K\otimes 1)\varphi\in L^{1,p}(\theta)\}$.

Then if $\varphi\in L^p_\sigma(\theta)$ and if K is as above, put

(3.2) $$(\varphi\times\theta)_t(H) = \theta_t((H\otimes 1)\varphi) \quad \text{for } H \text{ predictable, } H/K \text{ bounded.}$$

This clearly defines a σ-finite L^p-valued random measure on $(\Omega\times\mathbb{R}_+,\underline{\underline{P}})$, i.e. a formal semimartingale, denoted by $\varphi\times\theta$. We obviously have:

(3.3) $L^p_\sigma(\theta)$ is a vector lattice and contains $L^{1,p}(\theta)$; $L^p_\sigma(\theta)\subset L^0_\sigma(\theta)$.

(3.4) If φ and ψ are $\underline{\underline{\tilde{P}}}$-measurable, we have $\psi\in L^p_\sigma(\varphi.\theta)$ if and only if $\varphi\psi\in L^p_\sigma(\theta)$, in which case $\psi\times(\varphi.\theta) = (\varphi\psi)\times\theta$ (use (2.12)).

(3.5) If $\varphi\in L^p_\sigma(\theta)$ and if H is a predictable process with $H\otimes 1\in L^{1,p}(\varphi.\theta)$ we have $H\in L^{1,p}(\varphi\times\theta)$ and $(\varphi\times\theta)_t(H) = \theta_t((H\otimes 1)\varphi)$.

Now, a more interesting class is the set of all $\varphi\in L^p_\sigma(\theta)$ for which $\varphi\times\theta$ is a finite measure, or equivalently is associated to a semimartingale, of course still denoted by $\varphi\times\theta$. So we set:

(3.6) $$\hat{L}^p(\theta) = \{\varphi\in L^p_\sigma(\theta) : \varphi\times\theta\in\underline{\underline{S}}^p\}.$$

The point is that the trivial inclusion $L^{1,p}(\theta)\subset\hat{L}^p(\theta)$ is usually <u>strict</u> as we shall see in examples. A practical criterion is the next one:

(3.7) PROPOSITION: <u>Let</u> $\theta\in\underline{\underline{\tilde{S}}}^p_\sigma$ <u>and let</u> φ <u>be a</u> $\underline{\underline{\tilde{P}}}$<u>-measurable function. Then</u> φ

<u>belongs to</u> $\hat{L}^p(\theta)$ <u>if and only if there is an increasing sequence</u> (A_n) <u>of predictable random sets satisfying:</u>

(i) $\bigcup A_n = \Omega\times\mathbb{R}_+$;

(ii) <u>for each</u> n, <u>we have</u> $\varphi 1_{A_n\times E}\in L^{1,p}(\theta)$;

(iii) $(\varphi 1_{A_n\times E})\times\theta$ <u>converges to a limit in</u> $\underline{\underline{S}}^p$.

<u>Then any increasing sequence</u> (A_n) <u>of predictable random sets satisfying (i) and (ii) will also satisfy (iii), and the limit is always</u> $\varphi\times\theta$.

<u>Proof</u>. a) We first prove that $\varphi\in L^p_\sigma(\theta)$ if and only if there is an increasing sequence $(A_n)\subset\underline{\underline{P}}$ with (i) and (ii). For the necessary condition, take $A_n=\{K\geq 1/n\}$, where K is like in (3.1). Conversely suppose $(A_n)\subset\underline{\underline{P}}$ is increasing and satisfies (i) and (ii). For each n pick $a_n\in(0,2^{-n}]$ with $\|a_n\varphi 1_{A_n\times E}\|_{L^{1,p}(\theta)}\leq 2^{-n}$. Then $K_n=\sum_{p\leq n}a_p 1_{A_p\times E}$ is in $L^{1,p}(\theta)$ and increases to a limit K that is predictable and strictly positive, and

$$\|\varphi(K\otimes 1)-\varphi(K_n\otimes 1)\|_{L^{1,p}(\theta)}\leq\sum_{p>n}\|a_p\varphi 1_{A_p\times E}\|_{L^{1,p}(\theta)}\leq 2^{-n}.$$

It follows that $\varphi(K\otimes 1)\in L^{1,p}(\theta)$, hence $\varphi\in L^p_\sigma(\theta)$.

b) Suppose $\varphi\in\hat{L}^p(\theta)$ and $(A_n)\subset\underline{\underline{P}}$ satisfies (i) and (ii). Let $X=\varphi\times\theta$. By (3.5), $(\varphi 1_{A_n\times E})\times\varphi=1_{A_n}\cdot X$; by (i) and (2.6), $1_{A_n}\cdot X\longrightarrow X$ in $\underline{\underline{S}}^p$.

c) Finally assume (i),(ii),(iii), and denote by X the limit in (iii). $\varphi\in L^p_\sigma(\theta)$ by (a), so let K be like in (3.1). If H is predictable and H/K bounded, we have $H\cdot X_t=\lim_{(n)}H\cdot[(\varphi 1_{A_n\times E})\times\theta]_t$, which by (3.5) equals $\lim_{(n)}\theta_t((H\otimes 1)\varphi 1_{A_n\times E})$, which by (2.6) equals $\theta_t((H\otimes 1)\varphi)=(\varphi\times\theta)_t(H)$. Hence $X=\varphi\times\theta$, and we deduce that $\varphi\times\theta\in\underline{\underline{S}}^p$. ∎

Here are some properties of $\hat{L}^p(\theta)$:

(3.8) $\hat{L}^p(\theta)$ is a vector space containing $L^{1,p}(\theta)$: $\hat{L}^p(\theta)\subset\hat{L}^0(\theta)$.

(3.9) If $\varphi\in\hat{L}^p(\theta)$ it might exist a $\tilde{\underline{\underline{P}}}$-measurable ψ with $|\psi|\leq|\varphi|$, and $\psi\notin\hat{L}^p(\theta)$ (contrarily to what happens for $L^{1,p}(\theta)$).

<u>§3-b</u>. <u>Examples</u>. Let us consider again some of the examples of §2-e.

<u>Example 1</u>. If $X\in\underline{\underline{S}}$ (or even $X\in\underline{\underline{S}}_\sigma$), then $\hat{L}^0(X)=L^{1,0}(X)$. ∎

<u>Example 2</u>. Let $X=(X^i)_{i\leq n}$ with $X^i\in\underline{\underline{S}}$. We introduced in [10] a set $L(X)$ of predictable processes $H=(H^i)_{i\leq n}$, with the following property: if we set $H(m)=H1_{\{|H|\leq m\}}$, then H belongs to $L(X)$ if and only if the real-valued semimartingales $H(m)\cdot X=\sum_{i\leq n}H(m)^i\cdot X^i$ converge to a limit in $\underline{\underline{S}}$. That is, $L(X)$ is exactly $\hat{L}^0(X)$. Moreover, Mémin [12] has shown that the set $\{H\cdot X: H\in L(X)\}$ is closed in $\underline{\underline{S}}$: here again, we have thus achieved the largest "reasonnable" set of predictable integrands. ∎

Examples 3 and 4. Let $X=(X^n)_{n\in\mathbb{N}}$ with $X^n \in \underline{\underline{S}}$. Here again the inclusion $L^{1,0}(X)\subset \hat{L}^0(X)$ is usually strict. However it is possible to define stochastic integrals for processes $H=(H^n)_{n\in\mathbb{N}}$ that are not even in $\hat{L}^0(X)$. For instance Métivier and Pistone [16] have considered Hilbert-valued square-integrable martingale, which amounts here to considering for each $n\in\mathbb{N}$ a square-integrable martingale X^n; then there is an increasing predictable process A and a predictable process $(c^{nm})_{n,m\in\mathbb{N}}$ with values in the set of (infinite) symmetric nonnegative matrices, with $\langle X^n,X^m\rangle = c^{nm}\bullet A$. Then

a) If $H\in\hat{L}^0(X)$ we have a sequence $(B_k)\subset\underline{\underline{P}}$ with $\bigcup B_k=\Omega\times\mathbb{R}_+$ and $[(H^n)^2 1_{B_k} c^{nn}]\bullet A\in\underline{\underline{V}}$ for all $n,k\in\mathbb{N}$;

b) while H is integrable in the sense of [16] if and only if (loosely speaking!) $(\sum_{n,m\in\mathbb{N}} H^n c^{nm} H^m)\bullet A\in\underline{\underline{V}}$; this condition is obviously much more general than (a) (see also Métivier [13] for similar considerations).∎

Example 6. In the situation of Example 6, we have:

(3.10) PROPOSITION: We have $G^1_{loc}(\mu)\subset\hat{L}^0(\mu-\nu)$ and if $\varphi\in G^1_{loc}(\mu)$ we have $\varphi*(\mu-\nu)=\varphi\times(\mu-\nu)$ (the inclusion $G^1_{loc}(\mu)\subset\hat{L}^0(\mu-\nu)$ is in general strict, as shown by a counter-example in Stricker [21], with only one point in E).

Proof. Let (T_n) be a sequence of predictable times with pairwise disjoint graphs, such that $\bigcup[\![T_n]\!]=J:=\{(\omega,t):\nu(\omega;\{t\}\times E)>0\}$. Let $\varphi\in G^1_{loc}(\mu)$, and $\varphi'=\varphi 1_{J^c\times E}$, $\varphi_n=\varphi 1_{[\![T_n]\!]\times E}$. By [9] we have $(\varphi'^2\wedge|\varphi'|)*\nu\in\underline{\underline{V}}$ and $|\varphi_n|*\nu\in\underline{\underline{V}}$. Thus if $A_n=(\bigcup_{p\leq n}[\![T_p]\!])\cup J^c$ we have $\varphi 1_{A_n\times E}=\varphi'+\sum_{p\leq n}\varphi_p \in L^{1,0}(\mu-\nu)$ by (2.35). Moreover $\bigcup A_n=\Omega\times\mathbb{R}_+$, and if $X=\varphi*(\mu-\nu)$ we have $(\varphi 1_{A_n\times E})\times(\mu-\nu)=(\varphi 1_{A_n\times E})*(\mu-\nu)=1_{A_n}\bullet X$; hence we also have (3.7,iii), and φ belongs to $\hat{L}^0(\mu-\nu)$.∎

4 - DECOMPOSITIONS OF RANDOM MEASURES.

§4-a. We first recall some basic facts about semimartingales.

(4.1) If $X\in\underline{\underline{S}}$ there is a unique $X^c\in\underline{\underline{L}}^c$ such that if $X=M+A$ is any decomposition with $M\in\underline{\underline{M}}_{loc}$, $A\in\underline{\underline{V}}$, then X^c is the "continuous local martingale part" of M.

(4.2) A semimartingale X is called special if it has the form

$$X=M(X)+A(X):\quad M(X)\in\underline{\underline{M}}_{loc},\quad A(X)\in\underline{\underline{P}}\cap\underline{\underline{V}},\quad A(X)_0=0.$$

($\underline{\underline{P}}\cap\underline{\underline{V}}$ is the set of all predictable processes in $\underline{\underline{V}}$). This decomposition is unique, and called the canonical decomposition. Any $X\in\underline{\underline{P}}\cap\underline{\underline{S}}$ (predictable semimartingale) or $X\in\underline{\underline{S}}^p$ with $p\geq 1$, is a special semimartingale.

(4.3) Let $X\in\underline{\underline{S}}$ and let D be an optional discrete random set: discrete means that all sections $D_\omega\cap[0,t]=\{s:0<s\leq t,\ (\omega,s)\in D\}$ are finite.

Then if $\{|\Delta X|>1\}\subset D$ there is a unique decomposition:

$$X_t = X_0 + \sum_{0<s\leq t} 1_D(s)\Delta X_s + M_t + A_t : \; M\in \underline{\underline{M}}_{loc}, \; A\in \underline{\underline{P}}\cap\underline{\underline{V}}, \; A_0=0 .$$

Since the measures in $\underline{\underline{\tilde{S}}}^p_\sigma$ constitute a natural generalization of semimartingales, we wish to examine whether they share the same properties as above. For this, the following continuity results are fundamental (see [6], [12]).

(4.4) $X \rightsquigarrow X^c$ is continuous from $\underline{\underline{S}}^p$ into $\underline{\underline{L}}^c\cap\underline{\underline{S}}^p$ (endowed with the topology of $\underline{\underline{S}}^p$), and $\underline{\underline{L}}^c\cap\underline{\underline{S}}^p$ is closed in $\underline{\underline{S}}^p$ for $p\geq 1$ and $p=0$.

(4.5) $\underline{\underline{P}}\cap\underline{\underline{S}}^p$ and $\underline{\underline{P}}\cap\underline{\underline{V}}\cap\underline{\underline{S}}^p$ are closed in $\underline{\underline{S}}^p$, for $p\geq 1$ and $p=0$.

(4.6) $\underline{\underline{M}}_{loc}\cap\underline{\underline{S}}^p$ is closed in $\underline{\underline{S}}^p$ for $p\geq 1$.

(4.7) $X \rightsquigarrow M(X)$ and $X \rightsquigarrow A(X)$ are continuous for the topology of $\underline{\underline{S}}^p$ in the following cases: (a) when $p\geq 1$, on the set $\underline{\underline{S}}^p$;
(b) when $p=0$, on the set $\underline{\underline{P}}\cap\underline{\underline{S}}^p$.

(4.8) $X \rightsquigarrow (\sum_{0<s\leq .} 1_D(s)\Delta X_s)$ is continuous for the topology of $\underline{\underline{S}}^p$ in the following cases: (a) D is an optional discrete set and $p=0$;
(b) $D=\bigcup_{1\leq q\leq N}[\![T_q]\!]$ for $T_1,\dots,T_N$ stopping times, and $p\geq 1$.

§4-b. <u>Some classes of random measures</u>. We put:

$$PV\text{-}\underline{\underline{\tilde{S}}}^p_\sigma = \{\theta\in\underline{\underline{\tilde{S}}}^p_\sigma : \exists V\in L^{1,p}(\theta),\ V>0 \text{ and } \varphi\times\theta\in\underline{\underline{P}}\cap\underline{\underline{V}} \text{ for all } \varphi\in\underline{\underline{\tilde{P}}}_V\}$$

$$P\text{-}\underline{\underline{\tilde{S}}}^p_\sigma = \{\theta\in\underline{\underline{\tilde{S}}}^p_\sigma : \exists V\in L^{1,p}(\theta),\ V>0 \text{ and } \varphi\times\theta\in\underline{\underline{P}}\cap\underline{\underline{S}}^p \text{ for all } \varphi\in\underline{\underline{\tilde{P}}}_V\}$$

$$L^c\text{-}\underline{\underline{\tilde{S}}}^p_\sigma = \{\theta\in\underline{\underline{\tilde{S}}}^p_\sigma : \exists V\in L^{1,p}(\theta),\ V>0 \text{ and } \varphi\times\theta\in\underline{\underline{L}}^c \text{ for all } \varphi\in\underline{\underline{\tilde{P}}}_V\}$$

$$M\text{-}\underline{\underline{\tilde{S}}}^p_\sigma = \{\theta\in\underline{\underline{\tilde{S}}}^p_\sigma : \exists V\in L^{1,p}(\theta),\ V>0 \text{ and } \varphi\times\theta\in\underline{\underline{M}}_{loc} \text{ for all } \varphi\in\underline{\underline{\tilde{P}}}_V\}.$$

(4.9) PROPOSITION: a) <u>Let</u> $\theta\in PV\text{-}\underline{\underline{\tilde{S}}}^p_\sigma$ (<u>resp</u>. $P\text{-}\underline{\underline{\tilde{S}}}^p_\sigma$, <u>resp</u>. $L^c\text{-}\underline{\underline{\tilde{S}}}^p_\sigma$). <u>Then</u> $\varphi\times\theta$ <u>belongs to</u> $\underline{\underline{P}}\cap\underline{\underline{V}}$ (<u>resp</u>. $\underline{\underline{P}}\cap\underline{\underline{S}}$, <u>resp</u>. $\underline{\underline{L}}^c$) <u>for all</u> $\varphi\in\hat{L}^0(\theta)$.
b) <u>Let</u> $\theta\in M\text{-}\underline{\underline{\tilde{S}}}^p_\sigma$ <u>for some</u> $p\geq 1$. <u>Then</u> $\varphi\times\theta\in\underline{\underline{M}}_{loc}$ <u>for all</u> $\varphi\in\hat{L}^1(\theta)$.

Note that $\varphi\times\theta$ may not be a local martingale for all $\varphi\in L^{1,0}(\theta)$ when $\theta\in M\text{-}\underline{\underline{\tilde{S}}}^p_\sigma$: see an example in [21] with E containing only one point.

<u>Proof</u>. Let $V\in L^{1,0}(\theta)$, $V>0$, $q\leq p$. Then $\underline{\underline{\tilde{P}}}_V$ is an integration lattice and by the results of §2-d and by (3.7), for each $\varphi\in\hat{L}^q(\theta)$ there is a sequence $(\varphi_n)\subset\underline{\underline{\tilde{P}}}_V$ such that $\varphi_n\times\theta \longrightarrow \varphi\times\theta$ in $\underline{\underline{S}}^q$. Hence the results follow from (4.5) and (4.4) for (a), from (4.6) for (b). ∎

We have the following representation theorem for $PV\text{-}\underline{\underline{\tilde{S}}}^0_\sigma$; recall the definition (2.29) of a strict random measure μ, called <u>predictable</u> if $\varphi*\mu$ is predictable for each $\underline{\underline{\tilde{P}}}$-measurable φ such that $|\varphi|*|\mu|\in\underline{\underline{V}}$.

(4.10) THEOREM: <u>Suppose that</u> E <u>is a Lusin space with its Borel</u> σ<u>-field</u> $\underline{\underline{E}}$.

<u>There is a bijective correspondance between random measures</u> θ <u>in</u> PV-$\underline{\underline{\tilde{S}}}^0_\sigma$, <u>and predictable strict random measures</u> μ (we identify two strict random measures that agree outside a P-null set), <u>through the following</u>:

$$(4.11)\quad \begin{cases} L^{1,0}(\theta) = \{\varphi : \underline{\underline{\tilde{P}}}\text{-measurable}, \ |\varphi| * |\mu| \in \underline{\underline{V}}\} = L^{1,0}(|\mu|) \\ \varphi \in L^{1,0}(\theta) \longrightarrow \varphi \times \theta = \varphi * \mu . \end{cases}$$

<u>Proof</u>. a) Let μ be a predictable strict random measure. By example 5 (§2-e) $|\mu|$ and μ may be considered as elements of $\underline{\underline{\tilde{S}}}^0_\sigma$, obviously in PV-$\underline{\underline{\tilde{S}}}^0_\sigma$. Then (4.11) follows from (2.31) and (2.32) and from the Jordan-Hahn decomposition $\mu = \mu^+ - \mu^-$, $|\mu| = \mu^+ + \mu^-$ (see [9,(3.14)]).

b) Conversely, let $\theta \in$ PV-$\underline{\underline{\tilde{S}}}^0_\sigma$. Everything in the theorem being "local", we may suppose that $\theta = \theta^t$ for some $t > 0$. Everything in the theorem being invariant under an equivalent change of measure, if we consider a strictly positive $V \in L^{1,0}(\theta)$ and apply Theorem (2.16) to the measure $V.\theta = V.\theta^t$, we may assume that $V.\theta \in \underline{\underline{\tilde{S}}}^1$.

For each $\varphi \in b\underline{\underline{\tilde{P}}}$ we put $m(\varphi) = E[\theta_t(\varphi V)]$: this defines a real-valued measure m on $(\tilde{\Omega}, \underline{\underline{\tilde{P}}})$, with finite variation because

$$\sup_{\varphi \in b\underline{\underline{\tilde{P}}},\ |\varphi| \le 1} |m(\varphi)| = \sup_{\varphi \in \underline{\underline{\tilde{P}}}_V,\ |\varphi| \le V} \|\theta_t(\varphi)\|_1 = \|V.\theta^t\|_{\tilde{S}^1} < \infty .$$

We extend m as a signed measure with finite variation on $(\tilde{\Omega}, \underline{\underline{F}} \otimes \underline{\underline{R}}_+ \otimes \underline{\underline{E}})$ by putting $m(H \otimes f) = m({}^pH \otimes f)$ for $H \in b(\underline{\underline{F}} \otimes \underline{\underline{R}}_+)$ and $f \in b\underline{\underline{E}}$, where ${}^pH$ denotes the predictable projection of the process H. From [9,(3.11)] there is a strict predictable random measure μ' such that, for each $\varphi \in b\underline{\underline{\tilde{P}}}$, we have $|\varphi| * |\mu'| \in \underline{\underline{V}}$ and $E(\varphi * \mu'_t) = m(\varphi)$. Hence if $\varphi \in b\underline{\underline{\tilde{P}}}$ and $H \in b\underline{\underline{P}}$, we have

$$E[H \bullet (\varphi * \mu')_t] = E[((H \otimes 1)\varphi) * \mu'_t] = m[(H \otimes 1)\varphi] = E[\theta_t((H \otimes 1)\varphi V)] = E[H \bullet (\varphi V \times \theta)_t],$$

by (2.20). Thus the two predictable processes $\varphi * \mu'$ and $(\varphi V) \times \theta$ in $\underline{\underline{V}}$ have the same Doléans-measure in restriction to the σ-field $\underline{\underline{P}}$, so they are equal. It remains to put $\mu = \frac{1}{V} \cdot \mu'$, which is again a predictable strict random measure, with $\varphi * \mu = \varphi \times \theta$ for all $\varphi \in \underline{\underline{\tilde{P}}}_V$. So we may identify μ and θ, and the theorem is proved. ∎

The following result, of the same vein, is much easier. A random measure $\theta \in \underline{\underline{\tilde{S}}}^0_\sigma$ is called <u>positive</u> if $\theta_t(\varphi) \ge 0$ for every nonnegative φ belonging to some integration lattice, and then of course $\varphi \times \theta$ is a nonnegative increasing process for every nonnegative $\varphi \in \hat{L}^0(\theta)$.

(4.12) THEOREM: <u>Suppose that</u> E <u>is a Lusin space with its Borel</u> σ<u>-field</u> $\underline{\underline{E}}$. <u>There is a bijective correspondance between positive random measures</u> $\theta \in \underline{\underline{\tilde{S}}}^0_\sigma$, <u>and positive strict random measures</u> μ, <u>through (4.11).</u>

<u>Proof</u>. The only non-trivial assertions is that one may associate to a positive $\theta \in \underline{\underline{\tilde{S}}}^0_\sigma$ a positive strict measure μ, with the second half of (4.11).

Let $V \in L^{1,0}(\theta)$, $V>0$. For each $f \in b\underline{\underline{E}}$ put $A^f = (1 \otimes f V) \times \theta$, and $A = A^1$. If $0 \leq f \leq 1$, then $A = A^f + A^{1-f}$ and A^f and A^{1-f} are increasing processes: so there is $K^f \in b\underline{\underline{O}}$ with $0 \leq K^f \leq 1$ and $A^f = K^f \bullet A$. Moreover if $f = \sum f_n$ is bounded by 1, then by (2.6) we have $A_t^f = \sum A_t^{f_n}$ a.s., hence $K^f = \sum K^{f_n}$ outside a set $B \in \underline{\underline{O}}$ with $1_B \bullet A = 0$ a.s. Then by a classical result about Lusin spaces (see [7] for instance) there is a positive transition kernel $N(\omega,t;dx)$ from $(\Omega \times \mathbb{R}_+, \underline{\underline{O}})$ into $(E, \underline{\underline{E}})$ with $N1 = 1$ and $A^f = (Nf) \bullet A$ for all $f \in b\underline{\underline{E}}$, $0 \leq f \leq 1$. Then $\tilde{\mu}(\omega; dt \times dx) = dA_t(\omega)\, N(\omega,t;dx)$ defines a positive strict random measure, as well as $\mu = \frac{1}{V} \cdot \tilde{\mu}$. Finally, μ satisfies (4.11) because for all $H \in b\underline{\underline{P}}$, $f \in b\underline{\underline{E}}$, $0 \leq f \leq 1$, we have:

$$V(H \otimes f) \times \theta = H \bullet A^f = [H\, N(f)] \bullet A = (H \otimes f) * \tilde{\mu} = V(H \otimes f) * \mu . \blacksquare$$

§4-c. First decompositions. The first result below extends (4.1).

(4.13) THEOREM: Let $\theta \in \tilde{\underline{\underline{S}}}^p_\sigma$ with $p \geq 1$ or $p = 0$. Then there is a unique decomposition $\theta = \theta^c + \theta'$ with $\theta^c \in L^c\text{-}\tilde{\underline{\underline{S}}}^p_\sigma$, such that $L^{1,p}(\theta) \subset L^{1,p}(\theta^c)$ and that $(\varphi \times \theta)^c = \varphi \times \theta^c$ for all $\varphi \in L^{1,p}(\theta)$.

Moreover, $\hat{L}^0(\theta) \subset \hat{L}^0(\theta^c)$ and $(\varphi \times \theta)^c = \varphi \times \theta^c$ for all $\varphi \in \hat{L}^0(\theta)$.

Proof. Let $V \in L^{1,p}(\theta)$, $V>0$. For φ in the integration lattice $\mathcal{S} = \tilde{\underline{\underline{P}}}_V$, we set $\theta^c_t(\varphi) = (\varphi \times \theta)^c_t$. Then $\theta^c = (\theta^c_t)_{t \geq 0}$ obviously satisfies (2.25,ii), and also (2.25,i) by (4.4): hence we obtain a $\theta^c \in \tilde{\underline{\underline{S}}}^p_\sigma$, which clearly belongs to $L^c\text{-}\tilde{\underline{\underline{S}}}^p_\sigma$. We have seen in the proof of (4.9) that if $\varphi \in \hat{L}^0(\theta)$, there is a sequence $(\varphi_n) \subset \tilde{\underline{\underline{P}}}_V$ such that $\varphi_n \times \theta \longrightarrow \varphi \times \theta$ in $\underline{\underline{S}}^p$, hence the last statement again comes from (4.4), and the uniqueness of θ^c is trivial. $\blacksquare$

Then, similar proofs using (4.7) and (4.5) yield:

(4.14) THEOREM: Let $\theta \in \tilde{\underline{\underline{S}}}^p_\sigma$ with $p \geq 1$. Then there is a unique decomposition $\theta = \theta' + \theta''$ with $\theta' \in M\text{-}\tilde{\underline{\underline{S}}}^p_\sigma$, $\theta'' \in PV\text{-}\tilde{\underline{\underline{S}}}^p_\sigma$, such that $L^{1,p}(\theta) \subset L^{1,p}(\theta') \cap L^{1,p}(\theta'')$ and that $\varphi \times \theta = \varphi \times \theta' + \varphi \times \theta''$ is the canonical decomposition of $\varphi \times \theta$ for all $\varphi \in L^{1,p}(\theta)$.

Moreover, $\hat{L}^1(\theta) \subset \hat{L}^1(\theta') \cap \hat{L}^1(\theta'')$ and $\varphi \times \theta = \varphi \times \theta' + \varphi \times \theta''$ is the canonical decomposition of $\varphi \times \theta$ for all $\varphi \in \hat{L}^1(\theta)$.

(4.15) THEOREM: Let $\theta \in P\text{-}\tilde{\underline{\underline{S}}}^p_\sigma$ with $p \geq 1$ or $p = 0$. Then $\theta' = \theta - \theta^c$ belongs to $PV\text{-}\tilde{\underline{\underline{S}}}^p_\sigma$ and $\hat{L}^0(\theta) \subset \hat{L}^0(\theta^c) \cap \hat{L}^0(\theta')$ and $\varphi \times \theta = \varphi \times \theta^c + \varphi \times \theta'$ is the canonical decomposition of $\varphi \times \theta$ for all $\varphi \in \hat{L}^0(\theta)$.

§4-d. Jumps of a random measure. D being an optional discrete random set, put

$$\tilde{\underline{\underline{S}}}^p_\sigma(D) = \{ \theta \in \tilde{\underline{\underline{S}}}^p_\sigma : \exists V \in L^{1,p}(\theta), V>0, \text{ and } (\varphi \times \theta)_t = \textstyle\sum_{s \leq t} 1_D(s) \Delta(\varphi \times \theta)_s \text{ for all } \varphi \in \tilde{\underline{\underline{P}}}_V \}.$$

A proof similar to that of (4.9), using (4.8), yields:

(4.16) PROPOSITION: If $\theta \in \underset{\approx}{\tilde{S}}^{p}_{\sigma}(D)$ for some optional discrete random set D, we have for all $\varphi \in \hat{L}^0(\theta)$:

(4.17) $$(\varphi \times \theta)_t = \sum_{s \leq t} 1_D(s)\, \Delta(\varphi \times \theta)_s .$$

If $X \in \underset{=}{S}$ and if D is as above, $X_t - \sum_{s \leq t} 1_D(s) \Delta X_s$ is also a semimartingale, that is continuous on the set D. Similarly,

(4.18) PROPOSITION: Let $\theta \in \underset{\approx}{\tilde{S}}^{p}_{\sigma}$ and D be an optional discrete random set. Suppose either that $p = 0$, or that $p \geq 1$ and $D = \bigcup_{1 \leq q \leq N} [\![T_q]\!]$ for N stopping times T_q. Then there is a unique decomposition $\theta = 1_D.\theta + 1_{D^c}.\theta$ with: a) $1_D.\theta \in \underset{\approx}{\tilde{S}}^{p}_{\sigma}(D)$;

b) if $\varphi \in L^{1,p}(1_{D^c}.\theta)$, then $\Delta(\varphi \times 1_{D^c}.\theta) = 0$ on D.

Moreover, we have:

(i) $L^{1,p}(\theta) \subset L^{1,p}(1_D.\theta) \bigcap L^{1,p}(1_{D^c}.\theta)$, and $\hat{L}^0(\theta) \subset \hat{L}^0(1_D.\theta) \bigcap \hat{L}^0(1_{D^c}.\theta)$, and if $\varphi \in \hat{L}^0(\theta)$,

(4.19) $$[\varphi \times (1_D.\theta)]_t = \sum_{s \leq t} 1_D(s)\, \Delta(\varphi \times \theta)_s .$$

(ii) If $D \in \underset{=}{P}$, then $1_D.\theta$ and $1_{D^c}.\theta$ are the measures defined by (2.10).

(iii) If V is a $\underset{=}{\tilde{P}}$-measurable function, then $1_D.(V.\theta) = V.(1_D.\theta)$.

Proof. Let $V \in L^{1,p}(\theta)$, $V > 0$. For φ in the integration lattice $\mathcal{J} = \underset{=}{\tilde{P}}_V$ we set $(1_D.\theta)_t(\varphi) = [\varphi \times (1_D.\theta)]_t$ by formula (4.19). Then $1_D.\theta = [(1_D.\theta)_t]_{t \geq 0}$ satisfies (2.25,ii) trivially, and also (2.25,i) by (4.8), hence $1_D.\theta \in \underset{\approx}{\tilde{S}}^{p}_{\sigma}$. By construction, we have $1_D.\theta \in \underset{\approx}{\tilde{S}}^{p}_{\sigma}(D)$, and we set $1_{D^c}.\theta = \theta - 1_D.\theta$. The same proof as in (4.16), again based upon (4.8), shows (i). Then (b) is trivial, as well as the uniqueness of the decomposition satisfying (a,b).

Assume that $D \in \underset{=}{P}$ and consider the measure $\eta = 1_{D \times E}.\theta$ defined by (2.10). If $\varphi \in L^{1,p}(\theta)$ we have

$$\eta_t(\varphi) = \theta_t(\varphi 1_{D \times E}) = (\varphi \times \theta)_t(1_D) = [1_D \cdot (\varphi \times \theta)]_t = \sum_{s \leq t} 1_D(s)\, \Delta(\varphi \times \theta)_s$$

because D is discrete. But this is equal to $(\varphi \times 1_D.\theta)_t = (1_D.\theta)_t(\varphi)$ by (4.17). Hence $\eta = 1_D.\theta$ and we have (ii).

Finally let $\varphi \in L^{1,p}(1_D.(V.\theta)) \bigcap L^{1,p}(V.(1_D.\theta))$. Then by (4.17),

$$\varphi \times [1_D.(V.\theta)]_t = \sum_{s \leq t} 1_D(s) \Delta[\varphi \times (V.\theta)]_s = \sum_{s \leq t} 1_D(s) \Delta[(\varphi V) \times \theta]_s$$

because $(\varphi V) \times \theta = \varphi \times (V.\theta)$; similarly $\varphi \times (V.(1_D.\theta)) = (\varphi V) \times (1_D.\theta)$, hence

$$\varphi \times [V.(1_D.\theta)]_t = (\varphi V) \times (1_D.\theta)_t = \sum_{s \leq t} 1_D(s) \Delta[(\varphi V) \times \theta]_s .$$

Thus $\varphi \times [1_D.(V.\theta)] = \varphi \times [V.(1_D.\theta)]$, and we have (iii). ∎

(4.20) REMARK: Let $D = [\![T]\!]$ for a stopping time T. Then $1_{[\![T]\!]}.\theta$ represents the "jump" of θ at time T: it is again a random measure; one may show that it charges only the set $[\![T]\!] \times E$, so it may be identified to a measure on $(E, \underset{=}{E})$, but this measure is itself an L^0-valued measure. ∎

Now we obtain an extension of (4.3):

(4.21) THEROEM: Let $\theta \in \underset{=\sigma}{\tilde{S}^0}$. For any strictly positive $V \in L^{1,0}(\theta)$ one can find a discrete optional random set D_0 such that, if D is any discrete optional random set with $D \supset D_0$, we have a decomposition

$$\theta = 1_D . \theta + \theta' + \theta'',$$

with $1_D . \theta$ defined in (4.16), and $\theta' \in M\text{-}\underset{=\sigma}{\tilde{S}^0}$ with $\varphi \times \theta' \in \underline{\underline{M}}_{loc}$ for all $\varphi \in \underline{\underline{\tilde{P}}}_V$, and $\theta'' \in PV\text{-}\underset{=\sigma}{\tilde{S}^0}$ with $V \in L^{1,0}(\theta'')$.

Moreover, for a given D, this decomposition is unique.

Proof. Everything in the theorem being "local", we may assume that $\theta = \theta^s$ for some $s > 0$. By (2.16) there is a probability measure Q that is equivalent to P, such that $Z_\infty = \frac{dQ}{dP}$ is bounded, and that $V.\theta \in \underline{\underline{S}}^2(Q)$, thus $\theta \in \underset{=\sigma}{\tilde{S}^2}(Q)$. Call Z the right-continuous martingale $Z_t = E_P(Z_\infty | \underline{\underline{F}}_t)$. Then Z and Z_- never vanish, so $Z' = 1/Z$ is a càdlàg positive process (and a Q-martingale) and $D_0 = \{|\Delta Z'| > 1\}$ is a discrete optional random set.

Now we choose another discrete optional random set $D \supset D_0$. There is a strictly increasing sequence (T_n) of stopping times such that $D = \bigcup [\![T_n]\!]$. Using again the local character of the theorem, we may and will assume that $\theta = \theta^{T_n}$ for some $n \in \mathbb{N}$: then if we consider $1_D . \theta$ we obviously have $1_D . \theta = 1_{D_n} . \theta$ where $D_n = \bigcup_{q \leq n} [\![T_q]\!]$, so Proposition (4.16) implies that $1_D . \theta \in \underset{=\sigma}{\tilde{S}^2}(D,Q)$ and that $V \in L^{1,2}(1_D . \theta, Q)$.

Let $\eta = 1_{D^c} . \theta$; we have $\eta \in \underline{\underline{S}}^2(Q)$, $V \in L^{1,2}(\eta, Q)$, and $\Delta(\varphi \times \eta) = 0$ on D for all $\varphi \in \underline{\underline{\tilde{P}}}_V$. It remains to prove that $\eta = \eta' + \eta''$ for some $\eta' \in M\text{-}\underset{=\sigma}{\tilde{S}^0}(P)$, $\eta'' \in PV\text{-}\underset{=\sigma}{\tilde{S}^0}(P)$, $V \in L^{1,0}(\eta', P) \cap L^{1,0}(\eta'', P)$, and $\varphi \times \eta' \in \underline{\underline{M}}_{loc}(P)$ for $\varphi \in \underline{\underline{\tilde{P}}}_V$.

We apply Theorem (4.14): we have $\eta = \eta^1 + \eta^2$ with $\eta^1 \in M\text{-}\underset{=\sigma}{\tilde{S}^2}(Q)$, $\eta^2 \in PV\text{-}\underset{=\sigma}{\tilde{S}^2}(Q)$, $V \in L^{1,2}(\eta^i, Q)$ and $\varphi \times \eta^1 \in \underline{\underline{M}}_{loc}(Q)$ for $\varphi \in \underline{\underline{\tilde{P}}}_V$. Let then $\varphi \in \underline{\underline{\tilde{P}}}_V$. The quadratic covariation of $\varphi \times \eta^1$ with Z' is

$$[\varphi \times \eta^1, Z'] = [\varphi \times \eta, Z'] - [\varphi \times \eta^2, Z'];$$

since $\varphi \times \eta^2 \in \underline{\underline{P}} \cap \underline{\underline{V}}(Q)$ and $Z' \in \underline{\underline{M}}_{loc}(Q)$, the process $[\varphi \times \eta^2, Z']$ has a Q-locally integrable variation [9]; since $\Delta(\varphi \times \eta) = 0$ on D and $|\Delta Z'| \leq 1$ outside D, we have $|\Delta(\varphi \times \eta) \Delta Z'| \leq |\Delta(\varphi \times \eta)|$, while $\varphi \times \eta$ is a Q-special semimartingale: hence $[\varphi \times \eta, Z']$ has also a Q-locally integrable variation, and so has $[\varphi \times \eta^1, Z']$. Therefore the latter admits a Q-dual predictable projection $A(\varphi) = {}^Q\langle \varphi \times \eta^1, Z' \rangle$. Finally we set

$$(4.22) \qquad \varphi \times \eta' = \varphi \times \eta^1 - (1/Z'_-) \bullet A(\varphi) \quad ; \quad \varphi \times \eta'' = \varphi \times \eta^2 + (1/Z'_-) \bullet A(\varphi)$$

(recall that Z'_- never vanishes) and we know by Girsanov Theorem [9] that $\varphi \times \eta' \in \underline{\underline{M}}_{loc}(P)$, while $\varphi \times \eta'' \in \underline{\underline{P}} \cap \underline{\underline{V}}$ by construction.

Therefore, since $\eta \in \underset{=\sigma}{\tilde{S}^0}(P)$ and $V \in L^{1,0}(\eta, P)$, it remains to prove that the formula $\eta'_t(\varphi) = (\varphi \times \eta')_t$ defines a measure η' in $\underset{=\sigma}{\tilde{S}^0}(P)$, with

$V \in L^{1,0}(\eta',P)$. For this, we consider the integration lattice $\mathcal{J} = \tilde{\underline{\underline{P}}}_V$ and apply Theorem (2.25), whose condition (ii) is trivially fulfilled.

In order to prove (2.25,1), consider a sequence $(\varphi_n) \subset \tilde{\underline{\underline{P}}}_V$ that converges pointwise to 0 and that satisfies $|\varphi_n| \leq V$. We know that $\varphi_n * \eta^1$ tends to 0 in $\underline{\underline{S}}^2(Q)$, hence in $\underline{\underline{S}}(P) = \underline{\underline{S}}(Q)$, and in view of (4.22) it thus suffices to prove that $A(\varphi_n) \longrightarrow 0$ in $\underline{\underline{S}}(P)$. Set $B_t = \sum_{s \leq t} 1_D(s)\Delta Z'_s$, that has Q-locally integrable variation, and call $\tilde{B}$ its Q-dual predictable projection, and set $M = Z' - B + \tilde{B}$. We have $M \in \underline{\underline{M}}_{loc}(Q)$ and $|\Delta M| \leq 2$ because $|\Delta Z'| \leq 1$ outside D. A simple computation shows that

$$A(\varphi_n) = {}^Q\!\langle \varphi_n * \eta^1, M\rangle + {}^Q\!\langle \varphi_n * \eta, B\rangle - {}^Q\!\langle \varphi_n * \eta^2, B\rangle - {}^Q\!\langle \varphi_n * \eta^1, \tilde{B}\rangle .$$

M and $\varphi_n * \eta^1$ are Q-locally square-integrable martingales, and for each finite t the process $(\varphi_n * \eta^1)^t$ stopped at time t tends to 0 in $\underline{\underline{S}}^2(Q)$, hence also in the Hilbert space $\underline{\underline{H}}^2(Q)$ of square-integrable martingales [5]; then ${}^Q\!\langle \varphi_n * \eta^1, M\rangle$ tends to 0 in $\underline{\underline{S}}$. By construction $[\varphi_n * \eta, B] = 0$, hence ${}^Q\!\langle \varphi_n * \eta, B\rangle = 0$. We have $[\varphi_n * \eta^2, B] = [\Delta(\varphi_n * \eta^2)] \bullet B$ and $\varphi_n * \eta^2$ is predictable, so ${}^Q\!\langle \varphi_n * \eta^2, B\rangle = [\Delta(\varphi_n * \eta^2)] \bullet \tilde{B}$; but the convergence $\varphi_n * \eta^2 \longrightarrow 0$ in $\underline{\underline{S}}^2(Q)$ implies that: $\sup_{s \leq t} |\varphi_n * \eta^2_s| \longrightarrow 0$ in Q-measure for each $t > 0$, thus yielding ${}^Q\!\langle \varphi_n * \eta^2, B\rangle \longrightarrow 0$ in $\underline{\underline{S}}$ [9]. Finally $\varphi_n * \eta^1 \in \underline{\underline{M}}_{loc}(Q)$ and $\tilde{B} \in \underline{\underline{P}} \cap \underline{\underline{V}}$, so $[\varphi_n * \eta^1, \tilde{B}] \in \underline{\underline{M}}_{loc}(Q)$ and ${}^Q\!\langle \varphi_n * \eta^1, \tilde{B}\rangle = 0$. Putting all those results together implies that $A(\varphi_n) \longrightarrow 0$ in $\underline{\underline{S}}$, and we are finished. ∎

The last result is of secondary importance.

(4.23) PROPOSITION: Let $\theta \in \tilde{\underline{\underline{S}}}^p_\sigma$ and assume that $\underline{\underline{E}}$ is a separable σ-field.

a) There is a sequence $(X^n)_{n \geq 1} \subset \underline{\underline{S}}$ such that the set $\{\varphi * \theta : \varphi \in \hat{L}^p(\theta)\}$ lies in the closure in $\underline{\underline{S}}^p$ of the linear space spanned by the sets $\{H \bullet X^n : H \in L^{1,p}(X^n)\}$.

b) There is a unique (up to evanescence) thin optional random set D with
(i) $\Delta(\varphi * \theta) = 0$ outside D for all $\varphi \in \hat{L}^0(\theta)$;
(ii) there is a sequence $(\varphi_n) \subset L^{1,p}(\theta)$ with $D = \bigcup_{(n)} \{\Delta(\varphi_n * \theta) \neq 0\}$.

Proof. a) Let $(A_n)_{n \geq 1}$ be a countable algebra generating the σ-field $\underline{\underline{E}}$. Let $V \in L^{1,p}(\theta)$, $V > 0$, and set $\varphi_n = V 1_{\Omega \times \mathbb{R}_+ \times A_n}$ and $X^n = \varphi_n * \theta$. Then $\mathcal{J} = \{\sum_{1 \leq n \leq N} V(H^n \otimes 1_{A_n}) : N \in \mathbb{N}^*, H^n \in b\underline{\underline{P}}\}$ is an integration lattice and if $\varphi = \sum_{1 \leq n \leq N} V(H^n \otimes 1_{A_n}) \in \mathcal{J}$ then $\varphi * \theta = \sum_{1 \leq n \leq N} H^n \bullet X^n$: hence the result.

b) This is trivial: just take $D = \bigcup_{n \geq 1} \{\Delta X^n \neq 0\}$. ∎

REFERENCES

1 K. BICHTELER: Integration Theory. Lect. Notes in Math. 315, Springer Verlag: Berlin, 1973.

2 K. BICHTELER: Stochastic integration and L^p-theory of semimartingales. Annals of Probab. 9, 49-89, 1981.

3 C.S. CHOU, P.A. MEYER, C. STRICKER: Sur les intégrales stochastiques de processus prévisibles non bornés. Sém. Proba. XIV, Lect. Notes in Math. 784, 128-139; Springer Verlag, Berlin: 1980.

4 C. DELLACHERIE, P.A. MEYER: Probabilités et potentiel, tome II, 2ième édition, Hermann, Paris: 1980.

5 M. EMERY: Stabilité des solutions des équations différentielles stochastiques, applications aux intégrales multiplicatives stochastiques. Z. für Wahr. 41, 241-262, 1978.

6 M. EMERY: Une topologie sur l'espace des semimartingales. Sém. Proba. XII, Lect. Notes in Math. 721, 260-280; Springer Verlag, Berlin: 1979.

7 R.K. GETOOR: On the construction of kernels. Sém. Proba. IX, Lect. Notes in Math. 465, 443-463; Springer Verlag, Berlin: 1975.

8 J. JACOD: Sur la construction des intégrales stochastiques et les sous-espaces stables de martingales. Sém. Proba. XI, Lect. Notes in Math. 581, 390-410; Springer Verlag, Berlin: 1977.

9 J. JACOD: Calcul stochastique et problèmes de martingales. Lect. Notes in Math. 714; Springer Verlag, Berlin: 1979.

10 J. JACOD: Intégrale stochastique par rapport à une semimartingale vectorielle et changements de filtration. Sém. Proba. XIV, Lect. Notes in Math. 784, 161-172; Springer Verlag, Berlin: 1980.

11 B. MAUREY: Théorèmes de factorisation pour les opérateurs linéaires à valeurs dans les espaces L^p. Astérisque, 11, 1-163, 1974.

12 J. MEMIN: Espaces de semimartingales et changements de probabilité. Z. für Wahr. 52, 9-41, 1980.

13 M. METIVIER: Stability Theorems for Stochastic Integral Equations driven by random Measures and Semimartingales. J. of Integral Equa. 3, 109-135, 1981.

14 M. METIVIER, J. PELLAUMAIL: Mesures stochastiques à valeurs dans les espaces L_0. Z. für Wahr. 40, 101-114, 1977.

15 M. METIVIER, J. PELLAUMAIL: Stochastic Integration. Acad. Press, New York: 1980.

16 M. METIVIER, G. PISTONE: Une formule d'isométrie pour l'intégrale stochastiques hilbertienne. Z. für Wahr. 33, 1-18, 1975.

17 P.A. MEYER: Un cours sur les intégrales stochastiques. Sém. Proba. X, Lect. Notes in Math. 511, 245-400; Springer Verlag, Berlin: 1976.

18 J. PELLAUMAIL: Sur l'intégrale stochastiques et la décomposition de Doob-Meyer. Astérisque 9, 1973.

19 H. ROSENTHAL: On subspaces of L^p. Ann. Math. 97/2, 344-373, 1973.

20 L. SCHWARTZ: Les semi-martingales formelles. Sém. Proba. XV, Lect. Notes in Math. 850, 413-489; Springer Verlag, Berlin: 1981.

21 C. STRICKER: Quelques remarques sur la topologie des semimartingales, applications aux intégrales stochastiques. Sém. Proba. XV, Lect. Notes in Math. 850, 499-522, 1981.

K. Bichteler: Department of Mathematics, University of Texas
AUSTIN, Texas, 78712, USA

J. Jacod: Département de Mathématiques et Informatique, Campus de Beaulieu
35042 - RENNES - Cedex, France

A TOPOLOGICAL INVARIANT FOR LINEAR SYSTEMS DESCRIBING SOME RANDOM FIELDS*

T. E. Duncan**

1. INTRODUCTION

In recent years random fields have been important in the mathematical models that describe some problems in picture processing and seismic data processing. Besides these two areas of applications random fields appear naturally in other mathematical areas. From the experience with stochastic processes whose index sets are $\mathbb{N}$ or $\mathbb{R}_+$ an important subclass of random fields should be those fields that are obtained as the output of a multi-time parameter linear system whose input is white noise. Many properties of such random fields are closely associated with the system theory of these multi-time parameter linear systems. Unfortunately the system theory of such linear systems is still in its infancy and some basic questions need to be resolved before the theory is comparable to the well known system theory for linear systems with one time parameter.

In this paper some topological properties of families of linear systems with two time parameters will be given. In particular the number of topological components in the space of a natural family of two time parameter linear systems will be calculated by defining an index that separates the path components. This space is a smooth manifold. In addition it is shown that some of these components are homeomorphic to Euclidean space. Since the results in this paper are described in terms of transfer functions they are applicable to linear systems where each of the two time parameters are $\mathbb{N}$ or $\mathbb{R}_+$. The extension of these results to more than two time parameters is straightforward.

To gain some perspective of the methods and the results in this paper it is useful to have a brief review of linear systems in one time parameter or equivalently transfer functions in one variable. A linear system viewed as an input-output device has three important descriptions in system theory. The transfer function describes the system by the Laplace transform. The Hankel matrix description of a linear system is an infinite matrix whose elements can be determined from the expansion of the transfer function at infinity. Finally the orbit space description of a linear system is the family of minimal state space

*Research Supported by NSF Grant ECS-8024917

**Department of Mathematics
University of Kansas
Lawrence, KS 66045 USA

realizations of the system modulo the action of the general linear group as the automorphism group of the state space. State space realization is the method which determines a minimal state space realization from a transfer function or a Hankel matrix. Not only are these three descriptions of one linear system equivalent but also topologies can be introduced on these three descriptions so that these descriptions are equivalent for families of linear systems [3]. Thus the study of the topology of families of linear systems can be viewed as the study of transfer functions. In this study of transfer functions of one variable Brockett [1] showed that the space of scalar transfer functions of McMillan degree n has n+1 topological components and Byrnes-Duncan [3] showed that the space of symmetric multivariable transfer functions of McMillan degree n has n+1 topological components that are separated by the Cauchy-Maslov index. In addition, Byrnes-Duncan have obtained results for other transfer function symmetries, e.g., Hamiltonian [2]. The space of multivariable transfer functions without symmetries of fixed McMillan degree is path connected [3].

An important problem in system theory is the identification of linear systems, that is, the construction of a state space model from some input-output data. Typically the identification methods are adaptive, that is, the state space realization changes as more data are available. The existence of a continuous identification algorithm with certain global convergence properties severely restricts the topology of the space. For scalar one variable transfer functions it has been shown [3] that most topological components do not possess such identification algorithms. Another difficulty in an identification procedure can occur because there is more than one topological component. If a continuous algorithm starts in one component then it cannot leave this component. Thus the initial guess in the procedure is very important. Clearly these identification questions are important for multi-time parameter linear systems. The results that are obtained here are applicable to some of these questions.

2. Two Variable Transfer Functions

In the well known linear system theory many of the results do not depend on whether the state evolves in discrete or continuous time. In particular the transfer function description is formally the same in discrete or continuous time. The description of linear two time parameter systems in this paper will be in terms of transfer functions so that the results are applicable for both discrete and continuous time linear systems. However, since discrete time is much more important in actual applications the state space models that yield these transfer functions will be given in discrete time. While a number of state space models exist for two discrete time parameter linear systems it seems that the most popular model was proposed by Roesser [8]. In fact this model includes many of the other proposed models. Before explicitly describing this model it is useful to explain briefly the notion of state. This model will describe the evolution of the local state. While this local state is finite dimensional, in general, the global state is an infinite dimensional object. For example the global initial condition would be data at all the positive integer points along the two coordinate axes for $t \in \mathbb{N} \times \mathbb{N}$. The local state consists of a horizontal state x^h of dimension n_1 and a vertical state x^v of dimension n_2. The local state satisfies the discrete time linear equations

$$\begin{bmatrix} x^h(i+1,j) \\ x^v(i,j+1) \end{bmatrix} = \begin{bmatrix} A_1 & A_2 \\ A_3 & A_4 \end{bmatrix} \begin{bmatrix} x^h(i,j) \\ x^v(i,j) \end{bmatrix} + \begin{bmatrix} B_1 \\ B_2 \end{bmatrix} u(i,j) \tag{1}$$

$$y(i,j) = [C_1 \; C_2] \begin{bmatrix} x^h(i,j) \\ x^v(i,j) \end{bmatrix} \tag{2}$$

where $i,j \in \mathbb{N}$

Let

$$A = \begin{bmatrix} A_1 & A_2 \\ A_3 & A_4 \end{bmatrix}$$

$$B = \begin{bmatrix} B_1 \\ B_2 \end{bmatrix}$$

$$C = [C_1 \; C_2]$$

Assuming zero initial conditions the transfer function of this two time parameter system (A,B,C) is

$$G(s_1,s_2) = C[(s_1 I_{n_1} \oplus s_2 I_{n_2}) - A]^{-1} B \tag{3}$$

A random field on $\mathbb{N} \times \mathbb{N}$ can be generated by letting the input u in (1) be a discrete white noise. The analogous two continuous time parameter system can describe random fields on $\mathbb{R}_+ \times \mathbb{R}_+$. For example the infinite dimensional

Ornstein-Uhlenbeck process [5] can be described by such a linear system where the input is the formal derivative of the two parameter Brownian motion.

To formulate the problems in this paper it is necessary to define some notions of transfer functions.

Definition 1. A scalar two variable transfer function $G(s_1,s_2) = p(s_1,s_2)/q(s_1,s_2)$ is the ratio of two relatively prime polynomials in $\mathbb{R}[s_1,s_2]$ such that $\deg_i p < \deg_i q$ $i = 1,2$ where $\deg_i$ is the degree of the polynomial in the indeterminate s_i.

The concepts of reachability and observability occupy a central role in the theory of linear systems with one time parameter. For linear systems with two time parameters or equivalently two variable transfer functions a number of definitions of reachability and observability have been introduced. None of these definitions seems to have all or even many of the properties that the definitions have for linear systems with one time parameter. A comparison of some of these definitions is given in [6,7].

Given a scalar two variable transfer function G the problem of state space realization is to find a state space model (1-2) of minimal state space dimension whose transfer function is G. For one variable transfer functions there is a simple, constructive solution to this problem. However for two variable transfer functions the solution is not complete. Specifically the minimal state space dimension that is required in the realization of an arbitrary two variable transfer function is not known. This situation motivates the following definition.

Definition 2. A separable scalar two variable transfer function $G(s_1,s_2) = p(s_1,s_2)/q(s_1,s_2)$ is a scalar two variable transfer function whose denominator polynomial q is the product q_1q_2 where $q_i \in R[s_i]$ $i = 1,2$ with leading coefficients one.

For a separable scalar transfer function it is known [7] that there is a minimal state space realization of dimension $n_1 + n_2$ where $n_i = \deg q_i$ $i = 1,2$. In addition, there are algorithms for such realizations.

It seems to be particularly useful to refine the class of separable scalar transfer functions that are considered here. This class is given in the following definition.

Definition 3. Let $G(s_1,s_2) = p(s_1,s_2)/q_1(s_1)q_2(s_2)$ be a separable, scalar transfer function where $\deg q_i = n_i$ $i = 1,2$. Let λ_{ij} be the jth root of q_i with multiplicity m_{ij}. G is a regular, separable, scalar transfer function if each of the rational functions in $\mathbb{C}(s_i)$ for $i = 1,2$ and all j formed by

$$\left. \frac{(s_i - \lambda_{ij})^{m_{ij}} \, p(s_1,s_2)}{q_1(s_1)\, q_2(s_2)} \right|_{s_i = \lambda_{ij}}$$

has McMillan degree n_i.

This definition is somewhat redundant but it is stated as above to appear symmetric in the two indeterminates.

This notion of regularity is related to properties of reachability and observability for linear systems with one time parameter. This relation should partially justify that regularity is a natural system theoretic property for two variable transfer functions. Consider a regular, separable two variable transfer function G_o whose denominator polynomials q_1 and q_2 have all real, distinct roots. Express G_o in a partial fraction expansion in one of the variables, say s_1. In this form G_o is represented as a sum of a cascade of linear systems in each of the time parameters separately. The regularity property requires that the linear system in the s_2 variable in cascade with the elementary first order system in the s_1 variable is a minimal system of state space dimension n_2, that is, it is reachable and observable. Clearly the roles of s_1 and s_2 can be interchanged in the preceding construction.

The family of regular, separable scalar two variable transfer functions is formalized in the following definition.

<u>Definition 4</u>. $Rat(n_1,n_2)$ is the family of regular, separable, scalar two variable transfer functions $G(s_1,s_2) = p(s_1,s_2)/q_1(s_1)q_2(s_2)$ such that deg q_i = n_i
$i = 1,2$.

<u>Proposition 1</u>. $Rat(n_1,n_2)$ is a smooth manifold of dimension $n_1n_2 + n_1 + n_2$.

<u>Proof</u>. Let $G = p/q_1q_2 \in Rat(n_1,n_2)$. Since the prime factors of q_1,q_2,p are continuous functions of the coefficients of the polynomials q_1,q_2,p, a subset U of $Rat(n_1,n_2)$ that contains G is defined by an open subset of a Euclidean space whose coordinates are the coefficients of generic polynomials $\tilde{q}_1$, $\tilde{q}_2$, $\tilde{p}$ such that $\tilde{p}/\tilde{q}_1\tilde{q}_2 \in (Rat(n_1,n_2)$. Define this subset U of $Rat(n_1,n_2)$ as an open neighborhood of G. This construction provides a base for a topology on $Rat(n_1, n_2)$ and a local diffeomorphism of a subset of $Rat(n_1,n_2)$ with a subset of a Euclidean space. This local diffeomorphism shows that $Rat(n_1,n_2)$ with this topology is a smooth manifold and that the subset of transfer functions of $Rat(n_1,n_2)$ whose denominator polynomials have distinct roots is dense in $Rat(n_1,n_2)$. Let G be in the dense subset of $Rat(n_1,n_2)$. Apply a partial fraction expansion of G in the indeterminates s_1 and s_2 and count the parameters. This count shows that the dimension of $Rat(n_1,n_2)$ is $n_1n_2 + n_1 + n_2$. ∎

3. A Topological Index for Two Variable Transfer Functions

An index will be associated with each element in $Rat(n_1,n_2)$. This index is called the two parameter Cauchy index because it generalizes the Cauchy index [4] of transfer functions of one time parameter scalar input-output linear systems.

Initially it will be defined on the dense subset of $Rat(n_1,n_2)$ of transfer functions with distinct poles. Let $G \in Rat(n_1,n_2)$ have distinct poles. Represent G in a partial fraction expansion in the two variables. The two parameter Cauchy index of G is defined as the sum of the signatures of the residues of the pairs of roots of (q_1,q_2) that are both real. For one variable transfer functions with distinct poles this procedure is one method to compute the (one parameter) Cauchy index [3].

The two parameter Cauchy index will be extended to an arbitrary element of $Rat(n_1,n_2)$. Specifically it must be defined for each G $Rat(n_1,n_2)$ that has poles with multiplicity greater than one. The procedure shows that this extension is consistent with the previous definition. For such a G it will be shown that there is a neighborhood $U \subset Rat(n_1,n_2)$ of G such that if $G_1,G_2 \in U$ have distinct poles then the two parameter Cauchy indices of G_1 and G_2 are the same. From the subsequent procedure it will be clear that it suffices to consider each pole with multiplicity greater than one individually. If such a pole λ_o is complex then there is a neighborhood of G determined from the coefficients of the polynomials p, q_1, q_2 as in the proof of Proposition 1 such that this complex pole decomposes into distinct complex poles. In the partial fraction expansion of these transfer functions with distinct complex poles the contribution to the index from these poles is zero. Thus the contribution of the index of G from λ_o will be defined as zero. Now assume that λ_o is a real pole of G with multiplicity $m(\lambda_o) > 1$. Any neighborhood of G will contain transfer functions where λ_o decomposes into all real distinct poles or to (possibly) both distinct real and complex poles. It is necessary to verify that the contribution to the index of such poles of any of these transfer functions in a neighborhood of G is the same. It suffices to show that for transfer functions where the pole λ_o decomposes into distinct real poles $\lambda_1 < \lambda_2 < \ldots < \lambda_{m(\lambda_o)}$ that the contribution to the index from these real poles is determined from the parity of $m(\lambda_o)$. For the discussion assume that λ_o is a root of q_1. Let $r_1, \ldots, r_{m(\lambda_o)}$ be the residues of the poles $\lambda_1, \ldots, \lambda_{m(\lambda_o)}$ in $\mathbb{R}[s_2]$ from a partial fraction expansion in the indeterminant s_1. The residue r_j is approximately $(-1)^{j+1}r_1$ so that the contribution to the index from these real poles is $m(\lambda_o) \bmod (2)$.

This extension of the index along with its definition on transfer functions with distinct poles ensures that the index is a continuous function. This result is recorded in the following proposition.

Proposition 2. The two parameter Cauchy index is continuous on $Rat(n_1,n_2)$ where $n_1,n_2 \in \mathbb{N}$.

The following result represents the main result of this paper.

Theorem 3. The manifold $Rat(n_1,n_2)$ has $n_1n_2 + 1$ path components that are separated by the two parameter Cauchy index.

Proof. Let $G_1, G_2 \in Rat(n_1,n_2)$. It suffices to assume that G_1 and G_2 are transfer functions with distinct poles. Let $m \in \{-n_1n_2, -n_1n_2 + 2, \ldots, n_1n_2\}$. It is elementary to construct a G $Rat(n_1,n_2)$ such that the two parameter Cauchy index is m. Thus to complete the proof it suffices to show that if G_1 and G_2 have the same two parameter Cauchy index then G_1 can be continuously deformed into G_2 through a path in $Rat(n_1,n_2)$. Initially it will be shown that there is a continuous path in $Rat(n_1,n_2)$ connecting G_1 to $\tilde{G}_1 \in Rat(n_1,n_2)$ that has all real, distinct poles. Represent G_1 in a partial fraction expansion in (s_1,s_2) as

$$G(s_1,s_2) = \sum_{i,j} \frac{A_{ij}}{(s_1 - \alpha_i)(s_2 - \beta_j)}$$

The complex roots in $(\alpha_1, \alpha_2, \ldots, \alpha_{n_1})$ and $(\beta_1, \beta_2, \ldots, \beta_{n_2})$ occur in conjugate pairs and the corresponding residues (A_{ij}) are complex conjugates. For the complex poles it is possible to choose a continuous path in $Rat(n_1,n_2)$ that connects G_1 to a $\tilde{G}_1 \in Rat(n_1,n_2)$ that has all real, distinct poles. This is clear because the path in $\mathbb{C} \times \mathbb{C}$ only has to avoid a finite set. The path can be constructed as a composition of paths each of which takes one pair of complex conjugate roots into real, distinct roots. Thus it suffices to assume that G_1 and G_2 have only real, distinct poles. Since the two parameter Cauchy indices for G_1 and G_2 are the same, each of these transfer functions has the same number of positive and negative residues. It is elementary to find a path in $Rat(n_1,n_2)$ that maps continuously the poles of G_1 with positive (respectively negative) residues into the poles of G_2 with positive (resp. negative) residues. Clearly a residue can be continuously deformed in $Rat(n_1,n_2)$ into another residue with the same signature. ∎

As a computational property for the Cauchy index the condition of regularity ensures that no residue in the partial fraction expansion for transfer functions with distinct poles is allowed to become zero.

For certain components of $Rat(n_1,n_2)$ the topology can be precisely described.

Proposition 4. The components of $Rat(n_1,n_2)$ that have the two parameter Cauchy indices of $\pm n_1n_2$ are homeomorphic to Euclidean space.

Proof. To have the extreme two parameter Cauchy indices of $\pm n_1n_2$ it is necessary and sufficient that all the poles are real and distinct and that the residues are all positive or are all negative. Let $G = p/q_1q_2 \in Rat(n_1,n_2)$ have the two parameter Cauchy index n_1n_2. Let $\alpha_1 < \alpha_2 < \ldots < \alpha_{n_1}$ be the roots of q_1 and $\beta_1 < \beta_2 < \ldots < \beta_{n_2}$ be the roots of q_2. G can be represented as

$$G(s_1,s_2) = \sum_{i,j} \frac{A_{ij}}{(s_1-\alpha_i)(s_2-\beta_j)}$$

where $A_{ij} > 0$ for all i,j. The orderings of the poles in this manner and an ordering of the residues from these orderings of the poles provide a homeomorphism of this component of $Rat(n_1,n_2)$ with the Euclidean space, $R^2 \times (\mathbb{R}_+)^{n_1n_2 + n_1 + n_2-2}$. ∎

This result shows that the identification problem in these topological components has a simple topological structure and this structure would admit the existence of locally and globally convergent vector fields.

REFERENCES

1. R.W. Brockett, Some geometric questions in the theorem of linear systems, IEEE Trans. Aut. Control 21 (1976) 449-455.

2. C.I. Byrnes and T.E. Duncan, A note on the topology of spaces of Hamiltonian transfer functions, Algebraic and Geometric Methods in Linear System Theory, AMS Lectures in Appl. Math. 18 (1970) 7-26.

3. C.I. Byrnes and T.E. Duncan, On certain topological invariants arising in system theory, New Directions in Applied Mathematics, P. Hilton and G.S. Young, eds., 29-71 Springer-Verlag, 1982.

4. A Cauchy, Calcul des indices des fonctions, J. L'École Polytechnique (1835) 196-229.

5. T.E. Duncan, Some methods of integration in function space for use in control and filtering, Proc. 20th Conf. on Decision and Control (1981), 575-578, San Diego.

6. R. Eising, 2-D Systems, An Algebraic Approach, Mathematical Centre Tracts 125 Amsterdam 1980.

7. S.Y. Kung, B.C. Lévy, M. Morf and T. Kailath, New results in 2-D systems theory, Part II, 2-D state space models - realization and the notions of controllability, observability and minimality, Proc. IEEE 65(1977) 945-961.

8. R.P. Roesser, A discrete state space model for linear image processing, IEEE Trans. Aut. Control, AC-20 (1975), 1-10.

GAUSSIAN RANDOM FIELDS AND GAUSSIAN EVOLUTIONS

E.B. Dynkin

1. Introduction.

During the last decade a number of fundamental examples of random fields have been investigated whose role in the formation of a general theory of multiparameter stochastic processes might be comparable with that of the Brownian motion in the case of one parameter.

Motivated by quantum field theory Nelson [5] introduced the so called free Markov field. It belongs to a class of Gaussian random fields associated with symmetric Markov processes studied in [1]. Another important Gaussian field - the Brownian sheet has been investigated by Yeh, Orey, Pruitt, Cairoli, Walsh, Wong, Zakai and others. The Brownian sheet can be interpreted as the Brownain motion in the Wiener space and it is closely related to the Ornstein-Uhlenbeck process in the same space. The latter is the base of Malliavin's calculus which provides tools for the probabilistic study of hypo-elliptic partial differential equations.

In this survey we outline a unified approach to all these classes of random fields and we discuss the relation between Gaussian fields and a sort of generalized stochastic processes in Hilbert space which we call Gaussian evolutions.

2. Covariance operator of a Gaussian random field

2.1. Intuitively, a random field over a space E is a family of random variables ϕ_x, $x \in E$. However in many important cases the values of the field at fixed points are not defined but it is possible to use measures on E and functions on E as indices.

Let Φ be a linear space of real-valued measurable functions on a probability space $(\Omega, \mathcal{F}, P)$ (we do not distinguish P-equivalent functions). We say that Φ is a Gaussian random field over a measurable space $(E, \mathcal{B})$ if every $\phi \in \Phi$ has a normal probability distribution and if there are given two linear mappings:

(i) a map $\mu \to \phi_\mu$ from a cone M of σ-finite measures on $\mathcal{B}$ to Φ ;

(ii) a map $h \to \mu^h$ of a linear space H of measurable functions on E onto Φ (M-equivalent functions are identified).

We assume that:

Research partially supported by NSF Grant MCS 77-03543.

2.1.A. The cone M is complete, i.e., it contains with every measure its restriction to any set $B \in \mathcal{B}$.

2.1.B. For all $\mu \in M$, $h \in H$,

$$E\phi_\mu \phi^h = \mu(h) .$$

To simplify formulas, we assume, in addition, that

$$E\phi = 0 \quad \text{for all} \quad \phi \in \Phi .$$

2.2. We write $h = G_\mu$ if $\mu \in M$, $h \in H$, $\phi_\mu = \phi^h$ and we call G <u>the covariance operator of the field</u> Φ. This is a linear mapping from M into the space $S(M)$ whose elements are classes of M-equivalent $\mathcal{B}$-measurable functions. Properties 2.1.A, B, imply that elements $\phi_\mu - \phi_\nu$ are everywhere dense in Φ in the topology of $L^2(P)$ and that

$$E\phi_\mu\phi_\nu = \mu(G\nu) = \nu(G\mu) \quad \text{for all} \quad \mu, \nu \in M. \tag{1}$$

If G is given, then covariance of ϕ_μ and ϕ_ν is determined by (1) and the covariance of ϕ_μ and ϕ^h is determined by 2.1.B. There is some degree of freedom in the choice of the space H. It must contain the set H_0 of all differences $G\mu - G\nu$, $\mu, \nu \in M$ and it must be a part of the space H_1 defined by the condition: $h \in H_1$ if $\mu(h)/\sqrt{\mu(G\mu)}$, $\mu \in M$ is bounded. There is a unique way to extend the mapping $h \to \phi^h$, $h \in H_0$ to H_1 preserving 2.1.B. The set $\{\phi^h, h \in H_0\}$ is an everywhere dense subset of $\{\phi^h, h \in H_1\}$ and therefore $E\phi^h\phi^f, h, f \in H_1$ is determined uniquely by the operator G. We get all Gaussian fields Φ with the covariance operator G by specifying an arbitrary linear space H such that $H_0 < H < H_1$. The minimal field corresponding to H_0 and the maximal field corresponding to H_1 are the extremal choices.

The formula

$$(h,f)_H = E\phi^h\phi^f \tag{2}$$

defines an inner product on H_1. H is a Hilbert space if and only if the set Φ is closed in $L^2(P)$. In this case $H = H_1$.

2.3. A linear mapping G from a complete cone M of σ-finite measures into $S(M)$ is a covariance operator of a Gaussian field if and only if

$$(\mu,\nu)_M = \mu(G\nu)$$

satisfies the conditions:

2.3.A. $(\mu,\nu)_M = (\nu,\mu)_M$.

2.3.B. $(\mu,\nu)_M \leq [(\mu,\mu)_M(\nu,\nu)_M]^{1/2}$

An important class of covariance operators is described by the formula

$$G_\mu(y) = \int_E \mu(dx)\ g(x,y) \tag{3}$$

where $g(x,y)$ is a positive symmetric $\mathcal{B} \times \mathcal{B}$-measurable function. For the corresponding field Φ ,

$$E\phi_\mu\phi_\nu = \int_E \int_E \mu(dx)\ g(x,y)\ \nu(dy) \tag{4}$$

In particular, if the measures $\delta_x(B) = 1_B(x)$ belong to M then setting $\phi_x = \phi_{\delta_x}$, we have

$$E\phi_x\ \phi_y = g(x,y).$$

This cannot happen if $g(x,x) = \infty$. However (4) is consistent with the heuristic formula

$$\phi_\mu = \int_E \phi_x\ \mu(dx)$$

even if the values ϕ_x are not defined. We say that Φ is a <u>Gaussian field with the covariance function $g(x,y)$</u>.

A more general concept of a covariance kernel is intorduced as follows. We say that $g(x,B)$ is <u>the covariance kernel for a Gaussian field</u> Φ if for every $\mu \in M$, $G\mu$ is equal M-a.e. to the Radon-Nikodym derivative of the measure

$$\hat{\mu}(B) = \int_E \mu(dx)\ g(x,B)$$

with respect to a reference measure m. Condition 2.3.A is satisfied if g is symmetric relative to m, i.e., if

$$\int_A m(dx)\ g(x,B) = \int_B m(dx)\ g(x,A) \quad \text{for all} \quad A,B \in \mathcal{B} .$$

If $g(x,y)$ is a covariance function for Φ , then $g(x,dy)=g(x,y)m(dy)$ with an arbitrary measure m is a covariance kernel.

2.4. The standard Brownian motion B_t, $t \geq 0$ on the real line can be viewed as a Gaussian field over $R^+ = [0,+\infty)$ with the covariance function $g(s,t) = s \wedge t$. The cone M consists of all measures μ for which

$$\int_{R^+} \mu(t,\infty)^2 dt < \infty ,$$

and H consists of all absolutely continuous functions h such that $h(0) = 0$ and

$$\int_{R^+} h'(t)^2 dt < \infty .$$

Note that $H_0 = H_1 = H$. We have

$$\phi_\mu = \int_{R^+} B_t \, \mu(dt),$$

$$\phi^h = \int_{R^+} h'(t) \, dB_t .$$

The Ornstein-Uhlenbeck process on the real line R is a Gaussian random field over R with the covariance function

$$g(s,t) = e^{-\lambda|t-s|} .$$

2.5. The next example is a Gaussian random field over an arbitrary measure space $(E,\mathcal{B},m)$ with the covariance kernel $g(x,B) = 1_B(x)$. The cone M consists of measures $\mu(dx) = \rho(x)\, m(dx)$ with $\rho \in L^2(m)$ and $H = L^2(m)$. We have

$$G\mu = \frac{d\mu}{dm} ,$$

$$(\mu,\nu)_M = \int_E \frac{d\mu}{dm} \frac{d\nu}{dm} \, dm .$$

Obviously 2.3.A,B holds and $H_0=H_1=H$. The corresponding Gaussian field can be expressed by the formula

$$\phi^h = \int_E h(x) \, W(dx)$$

where $W(B)$ is the Gaussian random measure such that

$$E\, W(A)W(B) = m(A \cap B) .$$

It is natural to write

$$\phi_\mu = \int_E \frac{dW}{dm}(x) \, \mu(dx)$$

and to interpret Φ as the white noise over $(E, \mathcal{B}, m)$.

2.6. Suppose that Φ^i is a Gaussian field over $(E^i,\mathcal{B}^i)$ with the covariance operator G^i, $i=1, 2$. We consider the product space

$(E^1\times E^2, \mathcal{B}^1\times \mathcal{B}^2)$, the cone M spanned by measures $\mu^1\times\mu^2, \mu^1 \varepsilon M^1, \mu^2\varepsilon M^2$ and the linear space H spanned by functions $h^1(x^1)\ h^2(x^2)$, $h^1\varepsilon H^1$, $h^2\varepsilon H^2$. There exists one and only one linear mapping G from M to $S(M)$ such that $G(\mu^1\times\mu^2) = G^1(\mu^1)G^2(\mu^2)$. The operator G is the covariance operator of a Gaussian field which we denote by $\Phi^1\times\Phi^2$ and call <u>the tensor product</u> of Φ^1 and Φ^2.

If Φ^i is a Gaussian field with the covariance function $g^i(x^i,y^i)$, then $\Phi^1\times\Phi^2$ is a Gaussian field with the covariance function

$$g(x,y) = g^1(x^1,y^1)\ g^2(x^2,y^2) \text{ for } x=(x^1,x^2), y=(y^1,y^2).$$

The Brownian sheet is the tensor product of two standard Brownian motions and the Ornstein-Uhlenbeck process in the Wiener space (used in Malliavin's calculus) is the tensor product of the standard Brownian motion and the one-dimensional Ornstein-Uhlenbeck process described in Subsection 2.4.

2.7. The Brownian motion in a d-dimensional Euclidean space killed exponentially with rate λ has the transition density

$$p_t(x,y) = e^{-\lambda t}(2\pi t)^{-d/2}e^{-|x-y|^2/2t} .$$

Its Green's function

$$g(x,y) = \int_0^\infty p_t(x,y)\ dt$$

is positive, symmetric and the operator G defined by (3) satisfies conditions 2.3.A,B. Nelson's free field is a Gaussian field with the covariance function $g(x,y)$. The cone M consists of all σ-finite measures such that

$$\int_E \int_E \mu(dx)\ g(x,y)\ \mu(dy) < \infty$$

and H is the Sobolev space of all square integrable functions with square integrable weak partial derivatives.

In general, Green's function of any symmetric Markov process X is the covariance function of a Gaussian field Φ. Properties of Φ can be investigated using the following expression established in [1]

$$E\ \phi_\mu\ \phi_\nu = P_\mu \int_0^\infty \frac{d\nu}{dm}\ (X_t) \tag{5}$$

where P_μ is the measure in the paths space corresponding to the initial measure μ, m is the reference measure and the integral of a generalized function $\frac{d\nu}{dm}(X_t)$ is defined by an appropriate passage to the limit.

2.8. If $p_t(x,B)$ is a Markov transition function symmetric relative to a measure m, then

$$g(x,B) = \int_0^\infty p_t(x,B)dt$$

is the covariance kernel of a Gaussian field. The cone M is a complete metric space with respect to the metric

$$d(\mu,\nu) = ((\mu,\mu)_M + (\nu,\nu)_M - 2(\mu,\nu)_M)^{1/2}$$

and the space H is a Hilbert space (it is called the Dirichlet space associated with $p_t(x,B)$).

If $g(x,B)$ is absolutely continuous with respect to m, then we have the situation described in Subsection 2.7. Formula (6) has been extended to the general case in [3].

3. Subfields, conditioning and Markov property

3.1. Let Φ be a Gaussian field over $(E,\mathcal{B})$. To define a subfield Φ_B of Φ on a set $B \in \mathcal{B}$ we start from the minimal closed linear subspace $\overline{\Phi}_B$ of $L^2(P)$ which contains all $\tilde{\phi}_\mu$, $\mu \in M_B$ where $M_B = \{\mu:\mu \in M, \mu(E\setminus B) = 0\}$. The map $\mu \to \tilde{\phi}_\mu$ from M_B to $\overline{\Phi}_B$ is the restriction of the map $\mu \to \tilde{\phi}_\mu$ to the set M_B.

Functions $f \in H$ for which $\phi^f \in \Phi_B$ are called <u>harmonic</u> in $E\setminus B$. We put $h \in H_B$ if there exists an f which is harmonic in $E\setminus B$ and such that $f = h$ M-a.e. on B. We note that, if $h = 0$, then $E\phi_\mu\phi^f = \mu(f) = \mu(h) = 0$ for all $\mu \in M_B$; hence $\phi^f = 0$ and $f = 0$. Therefore f is defined uniquely by h and we put $f = j_B(h)$. We set

$$\tilde{\phi}^h = \phi^{j_B(h)} \quad \text{for} \quad h \in H_B, \ \Phi_B = \{\phi^h, h \in H_B\}.$$

It is easy to check that conditions 2.1.A, B are satisfied and that the covariance operators of Φ and Φ_B are related by the formula

$$G_B\mu = (G\mu)^B, \quad \mu \in M_B$$

where f^B is the restriction of f to B. We note that

$$j_B(G_B\mu) = G\mu \quad \text{for} \quad \mu \in M_B .$$

3.2. For every $h \in H$,

$$E\{\phi^h | \mathfrak{F}_B\} = \pi_B\phi^h = \phi^{j_B(h^B)}$$

where π_B means the orthogonal projection on ϕ_B.

The Gaussian fields considered in Section 2 satisfy the following condition:

3.2.A. The set $\{\phi_\mu, \mu \in M$ is invariant with respect to the operators π_B, $B \in \mathcal{B}$.

This is easy to check directly for the Brownian motion, the Brownian sheet, the Ornstein-Uhlenbeck process and the white noise and it follows from an explicit formula for fields associated with Markov processes. Namely if τ is the first hitting time of a set B by a path of the process, then

$$F\{\phi_\mu | \mathcal{F}_B\} = \phi_{\tilde{\mu}} \tag{6}$$

where $\tilde{\mu}(A) = P_\mu\{X_\tau \in A\}$. Formula (6) has been deduced from (5) in [1].

3.3. We say that Φ has the Markov property on a pair of sets A, B if the subfields Φ_A, Φ_B are conditionally independent given $\Phi_{A\cap B}$. Using formula (6), we proved in [1] and [2] that this property holds for a field associated with a Markov process if and only if a path cannot reach B from A without crossing $A \cap B$ (we assume that the process if fine and that $A \cup B = E$).

4. Gaussian evolutions

4.1. Suppose that a Gaussian field Φ_t over a measurable space $(E_t, \mathcal{B}_t)$ is given for every t of an interval I and let all these fields be defined on the same probability space $(\Omega, \mathcal{F}, P)$. We say that Φ_t is a Gaussian evolution if, for all $t_1, \ldots, t_n \in I$ and all $\phi_1 \in \Phi_{t_1}, \ldots, \phi_n \in \Phi_{t_n}$, the joint probability distribution of $\phi_1, \ldots, \phi_n$ is normal. If the random variable

$$E\{\phi | \Phi_u, u \leq s\} \tag{6}$$

belongs to Φ_s for every $s < t \in I, \phi \in \Phi_t$, then Φ_t is called a Markovian evolution.

4.2. Let Φ be a Gaussian field over a measurable space $(\mathcal{E}, \mathcal{B}_\mathcal{E})$ and let ρ be a measurable map from $(\mathcal{E}, \mathcal{B}_\mathcal{E})$ onto an interval I. Denote by Φ_t the subfield of Φ on the set $\{\rho = t\}$. We call the Gaussian evolution Φ_t, $t \in I$ a Gaussian wave (Φ, ρ). Suppose that Φ is the free field. The results formulated in Subsection 3.3 imply that (Φ, ρ) is a Markovian evolution for every continuous function ρ. Applying the results of [4], W. S. Yang evaluated the infinitesimal generator of Φ_t in the case of a smooth function ρ.

If Φ is the Brownian sheet and $\rho(s,t) = t$, then the Gaussian wave (Φ,ρ) is known as the Brownian motion in the Wiener space.

4.3. Under broad assumptions, a Gaussian evolution Φ_t, $t \in I$ can be viewed as a Gaussian wave. We assume that, for every $t \in I$, Φ_t is closed in $L^2(P)$ and there exist a measurable space $(\mathcal{E},\mathcal{B}_{\mathcal{E}})$ and a measurable mapping ρ from $\mathcal{E}$ onto I such that the set $\{\rho = t\}$ is isomorphic, as a measurable space, to $(E_t,\mathcal{B}_t)$. We identify this set with E_t.

We denote by $\pi_t\phi$ the orthogonal projection of ϕ on Φ_t.

Suppose that Φ_t is given by maps ϕ^t_μ, $\mu \in M_t$ and ϕ^h_t, $h \in H_t$. We have

$$\pi_s\phi^h_t = \phi_s^{V_{st}h}$$

where V_{st} is a linear operator from H_t to H_s. Let $\overline{\Phi}$ be the minimal closed linear subspace of $L^2(P)$ which contains all Φ_t. For every function h on $\mathcal{E}$, we denote by h^t its restriction to E_t.

We put $h \in H$, $\phi^h = \phi$ if h is $\mathcal{B}_{\mathcal{E}}$-measurable, $\phi \in \overline{\Phi}$ and $h^t \in H_t$, $\phi_t^{h^t} = \pi_t\phi$ for every $t \in I$.

We consider measures on $\mathcal{B}_{\mathcal{E}}$ of the form

$$\mu(dx) = \int_I \hat{\mu}(dt)\mu_t(dx)$$

where $\hat{\mu}$ is a σ-finite measure on I and μ_t is a σ-finite measure on $\mathcal{E}$ concentrated on E_t such that, for every $B \in \mathcal{B}_{\mathcal{E}}$, $\mu_.(B)$ is a Borel function. We put $\mu \in M$ if $\mu_t \in M_t$ and $\phi^t_{\mu_t}$ is a Pettis integrable $L^2(P)$-valued function (with respect to $\hat{\mu}$). For $\mu \in M$, we set

$$\phi_\mu = \int_I \hat{\mu}(dt)\phi^t_{\mu_t} .$$

It is easy to check that $E\phi_\mu\phi^h = \mu(h)$ and that, for every $\mu \in M$, $\phi_\mu = \phi^h$, where

$$h^s = \int_I V_{st}G_t\mu_t\hat{\mu}(dt).$$

This formula described $h = G\mu$ in terms of the covariance operators G_t and the projection operators V_{st}.

4.4. Now we suppose that an evolution Φ_t is Markovian. Then the operators V_{st} satisfy the equation

$$V_{st}V_{tu} = V_{su} \quad \text{for all} \quad s < t < u \in I \tag{7}$$

and the difference $\delta^h_{st} = \phi^h_t - \phi_s^{V_{st}h}$ is independent of Φ_u, $u \le s$; therefore

$$E\{(\delta^h_{st})^2 | \Phi_u, u \le s\} = E(\delta^h_{st})^2 = F_{st}(h) \text{ a.s. } P$$

where F_{st} is a positive semi-definite quadratic form on H_t. In terms of the inner product defined by (2)

$$F_{st}(h) = (h,h)_{H_t} - (V_{st}h, V_{st}h)_{H_s} \tag{8}$$

and therefore

$$F_{su}(h) = F_{st}(V_{tu}h) + F_{tu}(h) \quad \text{for all} \quad s < t < u \in I. \tag{9}$$

4.5. We investigate in more detail Gaussian Markovian evolutions on the interval $I = (0,\infty)$ for which $(E_t, \mathcal{B}_t)$ and H_t are independent of t. An evolution Φ_t is <u>stationary</u> if the probability distribution of $\phi_{t_1}^{h_1}, \dots, \phi_{t_k}^{h_k}$ does not change under the shifts $t \to t+u$ and it is <u>symmetric</u> if this distribution is invariant under reflections $t \to 2u-t$. An evolution Φ_t is stationary if and only if the covariance operator G_t does not depend on t. An evolution Φ_t is symmetric if and only if it is stationary and if, for every $0 < s < t$, the joint probability distribution of ϕ_s^f, ϕ_t^h is identical with the joint probability distribution of ϕ_s^h, ϕ_t^f.

We say that Φ_t is <u>time homogeneous</u> if the topology in H generated by the inner product $(f,h)_t = E\phi_t^f\phi_t^h$ does not depend on t and if V_{st} and F_{st} depend only on $t-s$. We put $V_{st} = V_{t-s}$, $F_{st} = F_{t-s}$. Obviously, $V_t h$ and $F_t(h)$ are continuous in h. By (7) and (9), V_t is a semi-group and

$$F_{s+t}(h) = F_s(V_t h) + F_t(h) \quad \text{for all} \quad s,t > 0. \tag{10}$$

We use an abbreviation GHM for Gaussian time homogeneous Markovian evolutions.

4.6. We say that an evolution Φ_t is L^2-<u>continuous</u> if, for every $h \in H$, ϕ_t^h is a continuous mapping from $(0,\infty)$ to $L^2(P)$. This property implies that V_t is strongly continuous in t and therefore its generator A has a domain D_A which is everywhere dense in H.

Let

$$F_t(f,h) = \frac{1}{2}(F_t(f+h) - F_t(f) - F_t(h)).$$

We prove that, for every $f, h \in D_A$,

$$C(f,h) = \lim_{t\to 0} \frac{F_t(f,h)}{t}$$

exists and has a representation

$$C(f,h) = C_0(f,h) + C_1(Af,h) + C_1(f,Ah) \tag{11}$$

where C_0 and C_1 are continuous bilinear forms on H. It follows from (10) that

$$F_t(h) = \int_0^t C(V_u h, V_u h)du \quad \text{for} \quad h \in D_A. \tag{12}$$

We say that $\Phi_0 = \{\phi^h\}$ is <u>the initial state of the evolution</u> Φ_t, if

$$\lim_{t\to 0} \phi_y^h = \phi^h \quad \text{in} \quad L^2(P) \quad \text{for all} \quad h \in H.$$

Passing to the limit in (8) as $s \to 0$, we get

$$(h,h)_t = F_t(h)+R(V_t h, V_t h) \tag{13}$$

where $R(f,h) = E\phi^f\phi^h$ is a positive semi-definite form on H. Hence

$$E\phi_s^f\phi_t^h = \int_0^{s\wedge t} C(V_{s-u}f, V_{t-u}h)du+R(V_s f, V_t h). \tag{14}$$

4.6. It follows from (14) that a GHM evolution is determined by parameters A, C, R. We call A <u>the drift operator</u>, C <u>the diffusion form</u> and R <u>the initial form</u>. If Φ_0 is a Gaussian field with the covariance kernel $g(x,B)$, then $R(f,h) = \int_E m(dx)f(x)\int_E g(x,dy)h(y)$.

A GHM evolution Φ_t is stationary if and only if

$$-C(f,h) = R(Af,h) + R(f,Ah) \tag{15}$$

It is symmetric if and only if, in addition to (15),

$$R(Af,h) = R(f,Ah). \tag{16}$$

An important example of a symmetric GHM evolution is <u>the Ornstein-Uhlenbeck evolution</u> for which $A = -\lambda I$ and $C = 2\lambda R$. In particular, we get the Ornstein-Uhlenbeck process in the Wiener space described in Subsection 2.6 by taking the space H defined in Subsection 2.4 and putting

$$R(f,h) = \int_0^\infty f'h' \, dt.$$

If $A=0$, then

$$E\phi_s^f \phi_t^h = s \wedge t \; C(f,h) + R(f,h) .$$

We call such an evolution <u>the Brownian motion</u>. If H is the Hilbert space defined in the last paragraph and if $C(f,h) = R(f,h) = (h,h)$, then we have the Brownian motion in the Wiener space mentioned in Subsection 4.2.

Suppose that $\Phi_t = \{\phi_t^h, h \in H\}$ is a Gaussian evolution with the drift operator A. Then the formula

$$\psi_t^h = \phi_t^h - \int_0^t \phi_s^{Ah}\, ds \qquad (17)$$

determines a Brownian motion ψ with the same diffusion form as Φ.

Let $U \xrightarrow{\alpha} H \xrightarrow{\beta} W$ be a rigging of H which means: U and W are Banach spaces in duality relative to a form $\langle u,w\rangle$, α is a continuous injection of U into H with the range everywhere dense in H, β is an analogous injection of H into W and $\langle u,h\rangle = (u,h)$ for $u \in U$, $h \in H$. Suppose that, for every $h \in U$, $\phi_t^h = \langle h,X_t\rangle$, $\psi_t^h = \langle h,W_t\rangle$ where X_t and W_t are W-valued stochastic processes. If U is invariant with respect to the semi-group V_t, then the equation (17) is equivalent to

$$W_t = X_t - \int_0^t A^* X_s\, ds$$

where A^* is the operator in W adjoint to the restriction of A to U. We write this equation in the form

$$dX_t = dW_t + A^*X_t\, dt \qquad (18)$$

and we interpret the evolution Φ_t as a solution of the stochastic differential equation (18).

4.7. Let $\Phi_0 = \{\phi_0^h, h \in H\}$ be a Gaussian field over a measurable space $(E,\mathcal{B})$. We assume that Φ is closed in $L^2(P)$. Hence H is a Hilbert space with the inner product $(f,h)_H = E\phi_0^f\,\phi_0^h$. Suppose that V_t is a strongly continuous semi-group of bounded operators in H with a generator A and C is a positive semi-definite form on D_A which has a representation (11). Then there exists an L^2-continuous GHM evolutions with drift operator A, diffusion form C and initial value Φ_0.

For instance, we can start from the white noise Φ_0 on $(E,\mathcal{B},M)$ in which case $H = L^2(m)$. Let V_t be a Markov semi-group in $(E,\mathcal{B})$ symmetric relative to m and let $C(h,h) = -\frac{1}{2}(Ah,h)$. The GHM evolution with drift A, diffusion C and initial value Φ_0 can be described by the formula

$$E\phi_s^f\phi_t^h = (f,V_{t-s}h).$$

REFERENCES

1. E.B. Dynkin, Markov processes and random fields, Bull. Amer. Math. Soc. 3,3 (1980), 975-999.
2. E.B. Dynkin, Markov processes, random fields and Dirichlet spaces, Physics Reports 77, 3 (1981), 239-247.
3. E.B. Dynkin, Green's and Dirichlet spaces associated with fine Markov processes, J. Functional Analysis (1982).
4. E.B. Dynkin and R.J. Vanderbei, Stochastic Waves, Trans. Amer. Math. Soc. (1983).
5. E. Nelson, The free Markov field, J. Functional Analysis 12 (1973), 211-227.

Department of Mathematics
Cornell University
Ithaca, NY 14853
USA

Remarks on Convergence of Feynman Path Integrals

By

Daisuke Fujiwara

Department of Mathematics, Tokyo Institute of Technology

Ohokayama, Meguro, Tokyo 152, Japan

§1. Introduction.

We consider the initial value problem of the Schrödinger equation

$$(1.1)\qquad \{\frac{\partial}{\lambda\partial t} + \frac{1}{2}\sum_{j=1}^{n}(\frac{\partial}{\lambda\partial x_j})^2 + V(x)\}\ u(\lambda,t,x) = 0,$$

$$u(\lambda,0,x) = \psi(x),\quad x \in R^n,$$

where $\lambda=2\pi i h^{-1}$ with the Planck constant h. We denote by $k(\lambda,t,x,y)$ the kernel function of the fundamental solution $U(\lambda,t)$ of the problem (1.1), i.e.,

$$(1.2)\qquad u(\lambda,t,x) = U(\lambda,t)\ \psi(x)$$

$$= \int_{R^n} K(\lambda,t,x,y)\ \psi(y)\ dy.$$

Feynman's path integral is a method to construct the function $K(\lambda,t,x,y)$. Let

$$L(x,x) = \frac{1}{2}|x|^2 - V(x)$$

be the Lagrangian. Let Ω be the totality of paths starting from a point $y \in R^n$ at time 0 and reaching another point x at time t. Then Feynman stated that

$$(1.3)\qquad K(\lambda,t,x,y) = \int_{\Omega} e^{\lambda\int L(\gamma)d\tau}\ \mathcal{D}(\gamma).$$

Here $\mathcal{D}(\gamma)$ is the so-called "Feynman measure", which does not exists. (cf. [6] and [7]).

Feynman defined the right hand side of (1.3) as follows. Let γ: $[0,\ t]\ \tau \longrightarrow \gamma(\tau) \in R^n$ be the classical path with $\gamma(0)=y$ and $\gamma(t)=x$. Once x and y are given and if $|t|$ is very small, then such a path exists uniquely. So let us define

(1.4) $$S(t,x,y) = \int_0^t \{ \gamma(\tau)^2 - V(\gamma(\tau))\} d\tau.$$

$S(t,x,y)$ is the classical action along $\gamma(\tau)$. We introduce

(1.5) $$e_o(\lambda,t,x,y) = (\frac{-\lambda}{2\pi t})^{n/2} e^{\lambda S(t,x,y)}.$$

We define the integral transform:

(1.6) $$E_o(\lambda,t) f(x) = \int_{R^n} e_o(\lambda,t,x,y) f(y)dy.$$

Let $\Delta : 0 = t_o < t_1 <\ldots < t_L = t$ be an arbitrary subdivision of the interval $[0, t]$. Consider the product of operators:

(1.7) $$E(\Delta|\lambda,t)=E_o(\lambda,t-t_{L-1})E_o(\lambda,t_{L-1}-t_{L-2})\ldots E_o(\lambda,t_1-t_0).$$

Let $I(\Delta|\lambda,t,x,y)$ denote its kernel function, that is,

$$E(\Delta|\lambda,t) f(x) = \int_{R^n} I(\Delta|\lambda,t,x,y) f(y) dy.$$

Then we clearly have

$$I(\Delta|\lambda,t,x,y)$$
$$=\prod_{j=1}^{L}(\frac{-\lambda}{2\ (t_j-t_{j-1})})^{n/2}\int_{R^n}\int_{R^n} \exp\lambda\sum_j S(t_j-t_{j-1},x^j,x^{j-1})\prod_{j=1}^{L-1} dx^j,$$

where $x^j \in R^n$, $x^o=y$ and $x^L=x$. Now we can state Feynman's definition of (1.3):

Let $|\Delta| = \max_j |t_j- t_{j-1}|$ be the size of the subdivision Δ. Then

(1.8) $$K(\lambda,t,x,y) = \lim_{|\Delta|\to 0} I(\Delta|\lambda,t,x,y).$$

This is the kernel function of the fundamental solution of the Schrodinger equation (1.1).

There are many ways to give sense to (1.3) or (1.8). For instance one may refer to [1], [2], [3], [5], [8], [9], [10], [11], [12], [14], [15], [17], [18] and their references. In particular Nelson [15] gave sense to the right hand side of (1.3) for a very wide class of potentials which may admit local singularity like $|x|^{-2}$. However the topology of convergence is very weak in

Nelson's theory. He did not prove pointwise convergence of the right hand side of (1.8).

W. Pauli discussed (1.8) in his famous lecture on Physics [16]. He treated convergence of the right hand side of (1.8) under the assumption that there exists a positive constant C satisfying

(1.9) $$|\text{grad } V(x)| < C(|x| + 1)$$

Pauli's discussion depends heavily on physical intuition. So one may ask the following question: "Can one give mathematically rigorous proof of Feynman's conjecture (1.8) under the assumption (1.9) of Pauli?"

This problem is still open. In [8] and in [9] convergence of (1.8) was proved under a little stronger assumption (see also [12]):

(A) $V(x)$ is a real valued infinitely differentiable function of x such that for any multi-index α with $|\alpha| \geq 2$

$$C_\alpha = \text{Sup}_x \left|\left(\frac{\partial}{\partial x}\right)^\alpha V(x)\right| < \infty.$$

It was shown in [9] that the fundamental solution $K(\lambda,t,x,y)$ is a very good function under the assumption (A). This will be reviewed in §2. Starting from this good potential, we can discuss perturbation of it. In particular convergence of the Dyson series will be discussed in §3.

§2. Path integral for smooth potentials.

Under the assumption (A) there exists a positive number T such that for any $t\in[-T, T]$ and any $x, y\in R^n$, the classical action $S(t,x,y)$ is uniquely determined and is of the form:

$$S(t,x,y)=\frac{|x-y|^2}{2t} + t\omega(t,x,y). \tag{2.1}$$

Here $\omega(t,x,y)$ is infinitely differentiable in x,y and it statisfies the estimate

$$\sup_{x,y}\left|\left(\frac{\partial}{\partial x}\right)^{\alpha}\left(\frac{\partial}{\partial y}\right)^{\beta} \omega(t,x,y)\right| = C_{\alpha\beta} < \infty$$

for any pair of multi-indices α and β with $|\alpha+\beta| \geq 2$. We may suppose that T is small enough to guarantee

$$T\Sigma_{|\alpha+\beta|=2} \sup_{x,y} \left|\left(\frac{\partial}{\partial x}\right)^{\alpha}\left(\frac{\partial}{\partial y}\right)^{\beta} \omega(t,x,y)\right| < 2^{-1}. \tag{2.2}$$

As in [9], we write

$$I(\Delta|\lambda,t,x,y)=\left(\frac{-\lambda}{2\pi t}\right)^{n/2}a(\Delta|\lambda,t,x,y)\ e^{\lambda S(t,x,y)}.$$

The function $a(\Delta|\lambda,t,x,y)$ belongs to the space $\mathcal{B}(R^n_x\times R^n_y)$ of Schwartz as a function of (x,y) if $t<T$. Feynman's path integral exists in the following sense.

<u>Theorem 1.</u> ([9]). Let $V(x)$ be a potential satisfying assumption (A). Assume $t < T$. Then the function $a(\Delta|\lambda,t,x,y)$ converges to a function $k(\lambda,t,x,y)$ in the space $\mathcal{B}(R^n_x\times R^n_y)$ as $|\Delta| \longrightarrow 0$. Moreover for any pair of multi-indices α and β there exists a positive constant $C_{\alpha\beta}$ such that

$$\sup_{x,y}\left|\left(\frac{\partial}{\partial x}\right)^{\alpha}\left(\frac{\partial}{\partial y}\right)^{\beta} \{a(\Delta\ \lambda,t,x,y)-k(\lambda,t,x,y)\}\right| < C_{\alpha\beta}|\Delta|$$

if $t < T$ and $\lambda > 1$.

The fundamental solution $K(\lambda,t,x,y)$ of the schrödinger equation (1.1) is of the form

$$K(\lambda,t,x,y) =\left(\frac{-\lambda}{2\pi t}\right)^{n/2}k(\lambda,t,x,y)\ e^{\lambda S(t,x,y)}. \tag{2.3}$$

The amplitude function $k(\lambda,t,x,y)$ satisfies the estimate

$$\left|\left(\frac{\partial}{\partial x}\right)^{\alpha} \left(\frac{\partial}{\partial y}\right)^{\beta}k(\lambda,t,x,y)\right| < C_{\alpha\beta}$$

for any multi-indices α and β. See [9] for more details.

§3 Convergence of Born series for singular potentials.

Let us begin with the Coulomb potential:

(3.1) $$V(x) = -e\,|x|^{-1},$$

where e is a positive constant. Theorem 1 does not apply to this potential, because (3.1) is singular at the origin.

Let $\chi(x) \in C_0^\infty(R^n)$ such that $\chi(x) = 1$ near the origin $x=0$. Then we have

(3.2) $$V(x) = V_0(x) - V_1(x)$$

with

(3.3) $$V_0(x) = -(1-\chi(x))V(x) \quad \text{and} \quad V_1(x) = \chi(x)\,V(x).$$

Corresponding Schrödinger equation is of the form

(3.4) $$\{\frac{\partial}{\lambda\partial t} + \frac{1}{2}\Sigma_j(\frac{\partial}{\lambda\partial x_j})^2 + V_0(x) + V_1(x)\}\,u(\lambda,t,x) = 0.$$

Since $V_0(x)$ satisfies the assumption (A), we can construct the fundamental solution $U_0(\lambda,t)$ of the Schrödinger equation;

(3.5) $$\{\frac{\partial}{\lambda\partial t} + \frac{1}{2}\sum_{j=1}^{n}(\frac{\partial}{\lambda\partial x_j})^2 + V_0(x)\}\,u(\lambda,t,x) = 0.$$

We consider $V_1(x)$ as a perturbation of this and treat the Born series (cf.[7]):

(3.6) $$U(\lambda,t) = U_0(\lambda,t) + U_1(\lambda,t) + U_2(\lambda,t) + \ldots.$$

where

(3.7)
$$U_1(\lambda,t) = -\lambda\int_0^t U_0(\lambda,t-\sigma)\,V_1\,U_0(\lambda,\sigma)\,d\sigma,$$
$$U_2(\lambda,t) = -\lambda\int_0^t U_0(\lambda,t-\sigma)\,V_1\,U_1(\lambda,\sigma)\,d\sigma,$$
$$\cdots\cdots\cdots\cdots$$
$$U_k(\lambda,t) = -\lambda\int_0^t U_0(\lambda,t-\sigma)\,V_1\,U_{k-1}(\lambda,\sigma)\,d\sigma.$$

Slightly generalizing the situation, we can prove the following

<u>Thorem 2.</u> Let $V(x)$ be a real valued potential of the form

$$V(x) = V_0(x) + V_1(x).$$

Assume that $V_0(x)$ satisfies the assumption (A) and that

$V_1(x) \in L^q(R^n)$, where $\frac{n}{2} < q \leq \infty$. Let T be the positive number of Theorem 1 for the potential $V_o(x)$. Then fc $|t| < T$ the Born series (3.6) converges with respect to the norm operators of $L^r(R^n)$ to $L^{r'}(R^n)$, where $\frac{1}{r} = \frac{1}{2} + \frac{1}{2q}$ and $\frac{1}{r} + \frac{1}{r'} =$

To prove Theorem 2 we need an inequality, which is a generalization of the Hausdorff-Young inequality for Fourier transform.

Lemma 3.1. (cf. Theorem 4.2 of |4|.) Let p be any positive number satisfying $1 \leq p \leq 2$. Then there exists a positive constant γ such that for any $f \in L^2(R^n) \cap L^1(R^n)$,

$$\| U_o(\lambda,t) f \|_{p'} < \gamma^{\theta} \left|\frac{\lambda}{t}\right|^{n\theta/2} \| f \|_p ,$$

where $\frac{1}{p} + \frac{1}{p'} = 1$, $\frac{1}{p} = \frac{1-\theta}{2} + \frac{\theta}{1}$ and $\| \ \|_p$ denotes the standard norm in the space $L^p(R^n)$.

Proof. We write as in §2

$$U_o(\lambda,t) f(x) = \left(\frac{-\lambda}{2\pi t}\right)^{n/2} \int_{R^n} k(\lambda,t,x,y)\, e^{\lambda S(t,x,y)} f(y)\, dy.$$

Since $U_o(\lambda,t)$ is a unitary operator, we have

$$\| U_o(\lambda,t) f \|_2 = \| f \|_2.$$

Let $\sup_{x,y} |k(\lambda,t,s,y)| = \gamma_o$. Then we have

$$\| U_o(\lambda,t) f \|_{\infty} \leq \gamma_o \left|\frac{\lambda}{2\pi t}\right|^{n/2} \| f \|_1.$$

This and Riesz' interpolation theorem proves Lemma.

Now we majorize $\| U_1(\lambda,t)f \|_{r'}$. Note that

$$\|U_1(\lambda,t)f\|_{r'} \leq |\lambda| \int_0^t \|U_o(\lambda,t-\sigma)\, V_1\, U_o(\lambda,\sigma)f\|_{r'}\, d\sigma.$$

We define $\varepsilon > 0$ by $\frac{1}{q} = \frac{2}{n}(1-\varepsilon)$. Applying Lemma 3.1 with $\theta = \frac{2}{n}(1-\varepsilon)$, we have

$$\|U_o(\lambda,t)g\|_{r'} < \gamma^{\theta} \left|\frac{\lambda}{\sigma}\right|^{1-\varepsilon} \| g \|_r. \tag{3.8}$$

Putting $g = V_1\, U_o(\lambda,\sigma)f$, we have

(3.9) $\quad \|U_o(\lambda, t-\sigma)V_1U_o(\lambda,\sigma)f\|_{r'} \leq \gamma^{\theta}\left|\frac{\lambda}{t-\sigma}\right|^{1-\varepsilon} \|V_1U_o(\lambda,\sigma)f\|_r.$

Since $\frac{1}{r} = \frac{1}{q} + \frac{1}{r'}$, Holder's inequality gives

(3.10) $\quad \|V_1U_o(\lambda, t-\sigma)\, f\|_r \leq \|V_1\|\ \|U_o(\lambda,\sigma)f\|_{r'}.$

Applying (3.8) once more and using (3.9) and (3.10), we have

$$\|U_o(\lambda,t-\sigma)V_1U_o(\lambda,\sigma)f\|_{r'} \leq \gamma^{2\theta}\left|\frac{\lambda}{t-\sigma}\right|^{1-\varepsilon}\left|\frac{\lambda}{\sigma}\right|^{1-\varepsilon}\|V_1\|\ \|f\|_r.$$

This and (3.7) prove

(3.11) $\quad \|U_1(\lambda,t)f\|_{r'} \leq \gamma^{2\theta}\|V_1\|\ \|f\|_r\ |\lambda|^{3-2\varepsilon}\frac{\Gamma(\varepsilon)^2}{\Gamma(2\varepsilon)}|t|^{2\varepsilon-1}.$

Lemma 3.2. Let $\gamma_1 = \gamma^{\theta}$, then for $k=1,2,3,\ldots$, we obtain

(3.12) $\quad \|U_k(\lambda,t)f\|_{r'}$

$$\leq \gamma_1^{k+1}|\lambda|^{(2-\varepsilon)k+1-\varepsilon}\|V_1\|^k\ \frac{\Gamma(\varepsilon)^{k+1}}{\Gamma((k+1)\varepsilon)}\ t^{(k+1)\varepsilon-1}\ \|f\|_r$$

for any $f \in L^2(R^n) \cap L^1(R^n)$, where $\gamma_1=\gamma^{\theta}$.

Proof. We prove Lemma 3.2 by induction on k. Estimate (3.12) for k=1 is nothing but (3.11). Assume that (3.12) holds for k=k. Then

(3.13) $\quad \|U_{k+1}(\lambda,t)f\|_{r'} \leq |\lambda|\int_0^t \|U_o(\lambda,t-\sigma)V_1U_k(\lambda,\sigma)f\|_{r'}\,d\sigma.$

Applying (3.8) and Holder's inequality, we have

$$\|U_o(\lambda,t-\sigma)V_1U_k(\lambda,\sigma)f\|_{r'} \leq \gamma_1\left|\frac{\lambda}{t-\sigma}\right|^{1-\varepsilon}\|V_1U_k(\lambda,\sigma)f\|_r$$

$$\leq \gamma_1\left|\frac{\lambda}{t-\sigma}\right|^{1-\varepsilon}\|V_1\|\ \|U_k(\lambda,\sigma)f\|_{r'}.$$

By using induction hypothesis (3.12) for k, we obtain

$$\|U_o(\lambda,t-\sigma)V_1U_k(\lambda,\sigma)f\|_{r'}$$

$$\leq \gamma_1^{k+2}|\lambda|^{(2-\varepsilon)(k+1)-\varepsilon}\|V_1\|^{k+1}\frac{\Gamma(\varepsilon)^{k+1}}{\Gamma((k+1)\varepsilon)}\|f\|_r(t-\sigma)^{\varepsilon-1}\sigma^{(k+1)\varepsilon-1}.$$

This and (3.13) give the estimate

$$\|U_{k+1}(\lambda,t)f\|_{r'}$$

$$\leq \gamma_1^{k+2}|\lambda|^{(2-\varepsilon)(k+1)+1-\varepsilon}\|V_1\|^{k+1}\frac{\Gamma(\varepsilon)^{k+1}}{\Gamma((k+1)\varepsilon)}\|f\|_r\ B(\varepsilon,(k+1)\varepsilon)\,|t|^{(k+2)\varepsilon-1}.$$

This proves (3.12) for k=k+1. Lemma 3.2 has been proved.

Theorem 2 is a direct consequence of Lemma 3.2.

References

[1] Albeverio,S. - Høegh-Krohn,R.J., Mathematical theory of Feynman path integrals, Lecture notes in Math. 523, Springer, Berlin, 1976.

[2] Albeverio,S.-Hoegh Krohn,R.J., Oscillatory integrals and the method of stationary phase in infinitely many dimensions, with applications to the classical limit of quantum mechanics, I., Inv. Math. 40 (1977), 59-106.

[3] Albeverio,S.A., (ed) , Feynman path integrals, Proc. Marseille 1978, Lecture notes in Physics 196, Springer (1979).

[4] Asada, K.-Fujiwara,D., On some oscillatory integral transformations in $L^2(R^n)$, Japanese J. Math. vol.4(1978), 299-361.

[5] Elworthy,K.D.-Truman,A., Classical mechanics, the diffusion (heat) equations, Schrodinger equation on Riemannian manifolds,Preprint, Univ. Warwick, 1979.

[6] Feynman, R.P., Space time approach to non-relativistic quantum mechanics, Rev. Modern Physics, 20 (1948), 367-387.

[7] Feynman,R.P.- Hibbs A.R., Quantum mechanics and path integrals. Mcgraw-Hill New York (1965).

[8] Fujiwara,D., A construction of the fundamental solution for the Schrodinger equations. J. d'Analyse Math. 35 (1979), 41-96.

[9] Fujiwara,D., Remarks on convergence of some Feynman path integrals., Duke Math. J. 47 (1980), 559-600.

[10] Ito,K., Generalized uniform complex measure in Hilbert space and its application to the Feynman path integrals,

Proc. 5th Berkeley symposium on Math.Statistics and Probability, vo.2, part 1,145-161, Univ. California Press, Berkeley (1967).

[11] Kallianpur,G., Generalized Feynman integrals using analytic continuation in several complex variables, to appear in "Advances in Probability" Vol. 7 (ed. M. Pinsky) (1982).

[12] Kitada, H., A construction of the fundamental solution for Schrodinger equations. J.Fac. Sci. Univ. Tokyo .vol. 27, (1980), 193-226.

[13] Maslov, V.P., Théorie des perturbations et méthodes asymptotiques, Dunod, Paris (1970).

[14] Morette, C., On the definition and approximation of Feynman path integrals, Physical Rev. 81 (1951), 848-852.

[15] Nelson,E., Feynman integrals and Schrodinger equation, J. Math. Phys., 5 (1964), 332-343.

[16] Pauli,W., (Enz,C. ed.), Pauli lecture on Physics, vol.6. MIT Press,1977.

[17] Truman, A., Feynman path integrals and quantum mechanics as $h \to 0$, J. Math. Physics, 17 (1976), 1852-1862.

[18] Truman,A., Classical mechanics, the diffusion (heat) equation and Schrodinger equation, J. Math. Physics, 18 (1977),2308-2315.

STOCHASTIC EVOLUTION EQUATIONS AND DENSITIES OF THE CONDITIONAL DISTRIBUTIONS

B.Grigelionis, R.Mikulevičius

Introduction

One of the possible approaches to the problem of existence and smoothness of the density with respect to the Lebesgue measure for the conditional distribution $P(\theta_t \in \Gamma / \mathcal{F}_t^Y)$, $t \geq 0$, $\Gamma \in \mathcal{B}(R^d)$, where (θ_t, Y_t), $t \geq 0$, is a d+m-dimensional $(P, \hat{\mathbb{F}})$ - semimartingale*), is the following (see [2]-[5]). Under reasonable assumptions consider suitable reference measure $\widetilde{P}$ such that $P|\hat{\mathcal{F}}_t \sim \widetilde{P}|\hat{\mathcal{F}}_t$, $Z_t = \frac{dP}{d\widetilde{P}}|\hat{\mathcal{F}}_t$. Noting that for each $f \in C_0^\infty(R^d)$

$$E(f(\theta_t)|\mathcal{F}_t^Y) = \widetilde{E}(f(\theta_t)Z_t|\mathcal{F}_t^Y)/\widetilde{E}(Z_t|\mathcal{F}_t^Y), \quad t \geq 0,$$

and using stochastic nonlinear filtering equations, we identify $\widetilde{E}(f(\theta_t)Z_t|\mathcal{F}_t^Y)$ with $(v_t, f)_0 = \int v_t(\theta)f(\theta)d\theta$, where v_t is a $L_2(R^d)$-valued unique solution to the defined stochastic evolution equation. Here we need the existence, uniqueness and stability conditions for the solutions to the stochastic evolution equations of the following form:

$$X_t = X_0 + \int_0^t A(s, X_{s-})dN_s + \int_0^t B(s, X_{s-}) \circ dM_s, \quad t \geq 0,$$

where X is a H-valued process, N is an increasing predictable process, M is an E-valued locally square integrable martingale, H is a Hilbert space, E is a separable Fréchet space, A and B are operators, satisfying some continuity, coercitivity and monotonicity assumptions (for

---

*) for terminology see e.g. [1]; $\hat{\mathbb{F}} = (\hat{\mathcal{F}}_t)_{t \geq 0}$ is a right continuous increasing family of σ-algebras in the probability space, $\mathbb{F} = (\mathcal{F}_t^Y = \sigma(Y_s, s \leq t))_{t \geq 0}$.

detailed formulation see § 3). The theory of such evolution equations in the case of the continuous Hilbert space valued local martingale M is reviewed in [6]. The related results in the discontinuous case are contained in [7]-[8].

In this paper we start with the definition of stochastic integrals for the operator valued functions with respect to the E-valued local martingales (cf.[9]-[10]). We use essentially the theory of Hilbert subspaces of E and their reproducing kernels (see [11]). In § 2 a version of the important Ito's formula for the square of the norm of a Hilbert space valued semimartingale is given which can be proved analoguously to [8]. The main results concerning stochastic evolution equations are obtained in § 3. After investigation of some properties of the predictable and optional projections of stochastic processes and stochastic integrals, in § 5 we apply the results from § 3 to the mentioned above problem of stochastic nonlinear filtering. The results contained in [5] are generalized in several aspects.

§ 1. Stochastic integrals with respect to the Fréchet valued local martingales

We shall recall some standard notations (see [1]). Let $(\Omega, \mathcal{F}, P)$ be a probability space with a right continuous filtration $\mathbb{F} = (\mathcal{F}_t)_{t\geq 0}$ of sub-σ-algebras of $\mathcal{F}$, $\mathcal{T}(\mathbb{F})$ be a class of all $\mathbb{F}$-stopping times, $\mathcal{T}^p(\mathbb{F})$ be a class of $\mathbb{F}$-predictable stopping times, $\mathcal{P}(\mathbb{F})$ be a σ-algebra of $\mathbb{F}$-predictable subsets of $R_+ \times \Omega$, $R_+ = [0, \infty)$, $\mathcal{O}(\mathbb{F})$ be a σ-algebra of $\mathbb{F}$-optional subsets of $R_+ \times \Omega$, $\mathcal{M}(P, \mathbb{F})$ be a class of uniformly integrable $(P, \mathbb{F})$-martingales, $\mathcal{M}^2(P, \mathbb{F}) = \{M \in \mathcal{M}(P, \mathbb{F}) :$

$E \sup_t |M_t|^2 < \infty\}$, $\mathcal{A}^+(P, \mathbb{F})$ be a class of increasing right continuous $\mathbb{F}$-adapted processes A, $A_0=0$, $EA_\infty < \infty$, $\mathcal{A}(P, \mathbb{F}) = \mathcal{A}^+(P, \mathbb{F}) - \mathcal{A}^+(P, \mathbb{F})$. For an arbitrary class $\mathcal{C}(P, \mathbb{F})$ we shall denote $\mathcal{C}_0(P, \mathbb{F})$ a subclass of processes $\mathcal{C}$ such that $\mathcal{C}_0 = 0$, $\mathcal{C}^c(P, \mathbb{F})$ a subclass of continuous processes of $\mathcal{C}(P, \mathbb{F})$ and $\mathcal{C}_{loc}(P, \mathbb{F})$ a class of processes $\mathcal{C}$ such that there exists a sequence $T_n \in \mathcal{T}(\mathbb{F})$, $n \geq 1$, $T_n \uparrow \infty$ satisfying $\mathcal{C}_{\cdot \wedge T_n} - \mathcal{C}_0 \in \mathcal{C}(P, \mathbb{F})$ for each n. We shall usually drop P and $\mathbb{F}$ in the notations when it is not danger of misunderstanding.

Let now E be a separable Fréchet space, i.e. E be a separable metrisable locally convex vector space, E′ be a topological dual space with the canonical bilinear form $\langle y', x\rangle$, $x \in E$, $y' \in E$ (for terminology see e.g. [12]), $\mathcal{L}^+(E)$ be a class of all linear mappings $Q: E' \to E$ such that for each $y', y'' \in E'$ $\langle y', Qy''\rangle = \langle y'', Qy'\rangle$ and $\langle y', Qy'\rangle \geq 0$, H_Q be a Hilbert subspace of E corresponding to Q, i.e. H_Q be a completion of QE' with respect to the inner product $(Qy', Qy'')_{H_Q} = \langle y', Qy''\rangle$, $\mathcal{B}(\mathcal{L}^+(E))$ be a σ-algebra of Borel subsets of $\mathcal{L}^+(E)$ equipped with the weak topology. Remark that all subspaces H_Q are separable. Indeed, it is well known that if E is separable, then E′ is weakly separable. Thus if a subset $K \subset E'$ is denumerable and dense in E′, then QK is dense in H_Q (for details see [11]).

Denote $\mathcal{M}_{loc}(E)(\mathcal{M}^2_{loc}(E))$ a class of E-valued processes M such that $\langle y', M\rangle \in \mathcal{M}_{loc}(\mathcal{M}^2_{loc})$ for each $y' \in E'$.

Let $N \in \mathcal{A}^+_{loc} \cap \mathcal{P}$, $M \in \mathcal{M}^2_{loc}(E)$ and assume that there exists $Q: R_+ \times \Omega \to \mathcal{L}^+(E)$ such that Q $(=Q^M)$ is $(\mathcal{B}(\mathcal{L}^+(E)), \mathcal{P})$ - measurable and for each $y', y'' \in E'$ $\{\langle y', M_t\rangle \langle y'', M_t\rangle - \int_0^t \langle y', Q_s y''\rangle\, dN_s,\ t \geq 0\} \in \mathcal{M}_{loc}$. Denote $H_{Q_s} = H_s$, L(Q) a class of all vector fields $f = \{f(s, \omega),$

$(s, \omega) \in R_+ \times \Omega$) such that $f_s \in H_s$, $(f_s, Q_s y')_{H_s}$ are $\mathcal{P}$-measurable for each $y' \in E'$. The pair $(H_s, L(Q))$ will be a $\mathcal{P}$-measurable field of Hilbert spaces (see [13]). Let $L^2(Q) = \{ f \in L(Q): E\int_0^\infty |f_s|^2_{H_s} dN_s < \infty \}$ and $L^2_{loc}(Q) = \{ f \in L(Q): \int_0^t |f_s|^2_{H_s} dN_s < \infty$ P - a.e., $t \geq 0 \}$. Using notations from [4] $L^2(Q)$ is a Hilbert space $\int^\oplus H_s dN_s dP$ with the inner product

$$(f, g) = E \int_0^\infty (f_s, g_s)_{H_s} dN_s .$$

Let $K = \{ e_1', e_2', \dots \}$ be dense in E'. Define

$$e_s^1 = \begin{cases} Q_s e_1' / |Q_s e_1'|_{H_s}, & \text{if } |Q_s e_1'|_{H_s} \neq 0 \\ 0 & \text{, other wise} \end{cases}$$

....

$$e_s^{n+1} = \begin{cases} \dfrac{Q_s e_{n+1}' - \sum_{k=1}^n (Q_s e_{n+1}', e_s^k)_{H_s} e_s^k}{\left| Q_s e_{n+1}' - \sum_{k=1}^n (Q_s e_{n+1}', e_s^k)_{H_s} e_s^k \right|}, & \text{if } \left| Q_s e_{n+1}' - \sum_{k=1}^n e_s^k (Q_s e_{n+1}', e_s^k)_{H_s} e_s^k \right| \neq 0 \\ 0, & \text{otherwise} \end{cases}$$

It is easy to check that for each $f \in \int^\oplus H_s dN_s dP$ $f_s = \sum_k (f_s, e_s^k)_{H_s} e_s^k$ and $|f_s|^2_{H_s} = \sum_k (f_s, e_s^k)^2_{H_s}$.

Using this property now for each $f \in L^2_{loc}(Q)$ we can define stochastic integrals $\mathcal{J}_t(f) = \int_0^t f_s dM_s$ having the following properties:

1) $\int_0^t Q_s y' dM_s = \langle y', M_t \rangle$, $y' \in E'$, $t \geq 0$,

2) $\mathcal{J}(f) \in \mathcal{M}^2_{loc}$,

3) $\langle \mathcal{J}(f) \rangle_t = \int_0^t |f_s|^2_{H_s} dN_s$,

4) for each bounded $\mathcal{P}$-measurable process φ and $f \in L^2_{loc}(Q)$

$$\int_0^t \varphi(s) \, d\, \mathcal{J}_s(f) = \mathcal{J}_t(\varphi f).$$

Let H be a separable Hilbert space, $L_2(H, H_s)$ be a space of Hilbert-Schmidt operators, $L(H, Q)$ be a class of all vector fields B such that $B_s \in L_2(H, H_s)$ and $Bh \in L(Q)$ for each $h \in H$,

$L^2(H, Q) = \{B \in L(H, Q) : E \int_0^\infty |B_s|^2_{L_2(H,H_s)} dN_s < \infty\}$, i.e.

$L^2(H, Q) = \int^{\oplus} L_2(H, H_s) dN_s dP$, $L^2_{loc}(H, Q) = \{B \in L(H, Q) :$

$\int_0^t |B_s|^2_{L_2(H,H_s)} dN_s < \infty$ P-a.e., $t \geq 0\}$.

For each $B \in L^2_{loc}(H, Q)$ define stochastic integrals $\mathcal{J}_t(B) = \int_0^t B_s \circ dM_s$ taking values in H, Skorohod[x)] in the strong topology of H, by means of the assumption that for each $h \in H$, $t \geq 0$

$$\int_0^t B_s h dM_s = (\mathcal{J}_t(B), h)_H.$$

The existence and uniqueness of $\mathcal{J}(B)$ with this property can be easily checked.

We have from these definitions that for each $B \in L^2_{loc}(H, Q)$ $|\mathcal{J}_t(B)|^2_H = \int_0^t |B_s|^2_{L_2(H,H_s)} dN_s + L_t(B)$, where $L(B) \in \mathcal{M}_{loc}$ and for each orthonormal basis (h_n) in H

$$|B(s)|^2_{L_2(H,\, H_s)} = \sum_n |B_s h_n|^2_{H_s}.$$

§ 2. Ito's formula

For $L \in \mathcal{M}^2_{loc}(H)$ we shall denote the continuous and the pure jump parts of L by L^c and L^d correspondingly, $[L]_t = \langle L^c \rangle_t + \sum_{s \leq t} |\Delta L_s|^2_H$ [xx)], where $\langle L^c \rangle$ is the continuous increasing part of the Doob-Meyer decomposition of $|L^c|^2_H$. For a normed vector space E we shall denote $\mathcal{V}(E)$ a class of $\mathbb{F}$-adapted Skorohod E-valued processes, having P-a.e. finite variation on each finite time interval.

Let now V be a separable reflexive Banach space, which is a dense subset of H assuming that H is identified with H' and imbeddings

---

x) i.e. right continuous with left hand limits.

xx) $\Delta L_s = L_s - L_{s-}$.

$V \subset H = H' \subset V'$ are continuous. For $N \in \mathcal{A}^+_{loc}$ denote $\mathcal{N} = \{(t,\omega): \Delta N_t(\omega) = 0\}$, $\mathcal{N}^d = R_+ \times \Omega \setminus \mathcal{N}$, for two normed vector spaces $E_1 \supset E_2$ and $e \in E_1$ denote $|e|_{E_2}$ a norm of e in E_2, if $e \in E_2$ and $= \infty$ if $e \notin E_2$.

Theorem 1 (Ito's formula). Let $Y \in \mathcal{V}(V')$, $Z \in \mathcal{V}(H)$, $X_0 \in H$, $L \in \mathcal{M}^2_{loc,\,0}(H)$, $X_t = X_0 + Y_t + Z_t + L_t$ and $\int_0^t |X_s|_V d|Y|_s < \infty$ P-a.e., $t \geq 0$. Then X is P-a.e. H - valued Skorohod in the strong topology of H and

$$|X_t|^2_H = |X_0|^2 + 2\int_0^t X_s dY_s + 2\int_0^t X_{s-} dZ_s + 2\int_0^t Q^L_s X_{s-} dL_s + [L]_t + 2[L, Z]_t + \\ + [Z]_t - \sum_{s \leq t} |\Delta Y_s|^2_H, \quad t \geq 0.$$

Proof of this formula is analoguous to the proof of the similar formula in [8] and we shall omit it.

We shall need later the following inequality.

Lemma 1. Let X be H-valued Skorohod process such that

$$X_t = X_0 + \int_0^t v'(s) dN_s + L_t, \quad t \geq 0,$$

where $N \in \mathcal{A}_{loc} \cap \mathcal{P}$, v' be a V'-valued $(\mathcal{B}(V'), \mathcal{P})$-measurable process and

$$E\left[\int_0^\infty (|v'_s|^2_{V'} \chi_{\mathcal{N}} + |v'_s|^2_H \chi_{\mathcal{N}^d} + |X_{s-}|^2_V + \Delta N_s |v'_s|^2_H) dN_s + |X_0|^2_H + \langle L \rangle_\infty\right] < \\ < \infty .$$

Then there exists an absolute constant $C > 0$ such that

$$E \sup_t |X_t|^2_H \leq C\Big\{E\left[\int_0^\infty \Delta N_s |v'_s|^2_H dN_s + |X_0|^2_H + \langle L \rangle_\infty\right] + (E \int_0^\infty |X_{s-}|^2_V dN_s)^{1/2} \\ (E \int_0^\infty |v'_s|^2_{V'} dN_s)^{1/2}\Big\} \tag{1}$$

Proof. Denote $T_k = \inf(t: |X_t|_H > k)$, $X^k_t = X_{t \wedge T_k}$, $L^k_t = L_{t \wedge T^k}$, $N^k_t = N_{t \wedge T^k}$, $Y^k_t = 2\int_0^t Q^{L^k}_s X^k_{s-} dL^k_s$, $t \geq 0$. Then applying Ito's formula to X^k with $Y_t = \int_0^{t \wedge T_k} v'_s dN^c_s$, $Z_t = \int_0^{t \wedge T_k} v'_s dN^d_s$, $t \geq 0$, we find that

$$|X^k_t|^2_H = |X_0|^2_H + 2\int_0^t \langle v'_s, X_{s-} \rangle \, dN^k_s + \int_0^t \Delta N_s |v'_s|^2_H \, dN^k_s + Y^k_t + 2\sum_{s \leq t} \Delta N^k_s \times$$

$\times(v_s, \Delta L^k_s)_H + [L^k]_t$ (2)

It is easy to check that $E\left[\sup_t |X^k_t|^2_H\right] < \infty$. Using Burkholder's inequality (see [14]) we have that

$$E \sup_t |Y^k_t| \leq 3E(\langle Y^k \rangle^{1/2}_\infty).$$

But for each $\varepsilon > 0$

$$E\left[\langle Y^k \rangle^{1/2}_\infty\right] \leq 2E\left[\sup_t |X^k_t|_H \langle L^k \rangle^{1/2}_\infty\right] \leq 2(E[\sup_t |X^k_t|^2_H])^{1/2} \times$$

$$\times (E[\langle L^k \rangle_\infty)^{1/2} \leq \frac{1}{\varepsilon^2} E[\langle L^k \rangle_\infty] + \varepsilon^2 E\left[\sup_t |X^k_t|^2_H\right].$$

From these estimations and (2) the inequality (1) now follows trivially.

§ 3. Stochastic evolution equations

We shall consider stochastic evolution equation

$$X_t = X_0 + \int_0^t A(s, X_{s-})dN_s + \int_0^t B(s, X_{s-}) \circ dM_s, \quad t \geq 0, \tag{3}$$

where $X_0 \in H$, $N \in \mathcal{A}^+_{loc} \cap \mathcal{P}$, $M \in \mathcal{M}^2_{loc}(E)$, $A: R_+ \times \Omega \times V \to V'$ is $(\mathcal{B}(V'), \mathcal{P} \otimes \mathcal{B}(V))$ - measurable, for each $v \in V$ $B(\cdot, v) \in L^2_{loc}(H, Q)$ and for for each $y' \in E'$ $(B(s, v), Q_s y')_{H_s}$ is $\mathcal{P} \otimes \mathcal{B}(V)$- measurable.

A solution to (3) is called a H-valued stochastic process X which is Skorohod in the strong topology of H, $X_{t-} \in V$ dNdP-a.e.,
$\int_0^t |B(s, X_{s-})|^2_{L_2(H, H_s)} dN_s < \infty$, $\int_0^t |A(s, X_{s-})|_{V'} dN_s < \infty$ P - a.e., $t \geq 0$, and equation (3) is satisfied.

Let (X^n) be a sequence of solutions to the following stochastic evolution equations

$$X^n_t = X^n_0 + \int_0^t A_{n,1}(s, X^n_{s-})\, dN_s + \int_0^t B_n(s, X^n_{s-}) \circ dM_s, \quad t \geq 0,$$

such that there exist a subsets $V_n \subset V$, $\overline{\bigcup_n V_n} = V$, $X^n_{t-} \in V_n$ dNdP- a.e., $t \geq 0$, $n \geq 1$.

We shall use the following assumptions:

I. For each $v, v_1, v_2 \in V$, $t \geq 0$, $\langle A(t, v_1+\lambda v_2), v\rangle$ is continuous with respect to $\lambda \in R^1$;

II. There exist $A_{n,2}: R_+ \times \Omega \times V \to V'$ such that $A_{n,2}$ $(\mathcal{B}(V'), \mathcal{P} \otimes \mathcal{B}(V))$ - measurable and for each $v_1, v_2 \in V_n$

$$\langle A_{n,1}(t, v_1), v_2\rangle = \langle A_{n,2}(t, v_1), v_2\rangle \quad , t \geq 0, n \geq 1 ;$$

III. For each $v_1, v_2 \in V$, $t \geq 0$

$$2 \langle A_{n,2}(t, v_1)-A_{n,2}(t, v_2), v_1-v_2\rangle + |A_{n,1}(t, v_1)-A_{n,1}(t,v_2)|_H^2 \Delta N_t + |B_t(t, v_1)-B_n(t, v_2)|^2_{L_2(H,H_t)} + \mathcal{E}_0 |v_1-v_2|_V^2 \leq l_t |v_1-v_2|_H^2 ,$$

where $\mathcal{E}_0 \geq 0$, $l \in \mathcal{P}^+$ and $\int_0^t l_s dN_s < \infty$ P - a.e., $t \geq 0$;

IV. For each $v \in V$, $t \geq 0$

$$2 \langle A_{n,2}(t, v), v\rangle + |A_{n,1}(t, v)|_H^2 \Delta N_t + |B_t(t, v)|^2_{L_2} + \mathcal{E} |v|_V^2 \leq$$
$$\leq g_t (1+|v|_H^2),$$

where $\mathcal{E} > 0$, $g \in \mathcal{P}^+$ and $\int_0^t g_s dN_s < \infty$ P - a.e., $t \geq 0$;

V. For each $v \in V$, $t \geq 0$

$$|A_{n,j}(t, v)|_{V'}^2 \chi_{\mathcal{N}} + |A_{n,j}(t, v)|_H^2 \chi_{\mathcal{N}^d} \leq g_t (1+|v|_H^2) + R|v|_V^2 ,$$

$j = 1, 2$, $R > 0$;

VI. Assume that $dNdP$ - a.e. for each $v \in V$

$$A_{n,2}(t, v) \xrightarrow{V'} A(t, v), \; B_n(t, v) \xrightarrow{L_2(H,H_t)} B(t, v) \text{ as } n \to \infty ,$$

$dN^d dP$-a.e. for each $v \in V$ $A_{n,1}(t, v) \xrightarrow{H} A(t, v)$ as $n \to \infty$ and $X_0^n \xrightarrow{H} X_0$ as $n \to \infty$ in probability.

Theorem 2. Under assumptions I-VI there exist a unique solution X to the equation (3) and a sequence $T_m \in \mathcal{T}$, $T_m \uparrow \infty$, such that for each $m \geq 1$, $\sigma \leq T_m$, $\sigma \in \mathcal{T}$

$$E|X_\sigma^n - X_\sigma|_H^2 \to 0, \; E\left[\int_0^{T_m} (|X_t^n - X_t|_H^2 + (|X_{t-}^n - X_{t-}|_H^2) \, dN_t\right] \to 0 \text{ as } n \to \infty .$$

If $\mathcal{E}_0 > 0$ then there exists a sequence $T_m \in \mathcal{T}$, $T_m \uparrow \infty$ such that for each m

$$\lim_n E\Big[\sup_{t\le T_m} |X_t^n-X_t|_H^2+\int_0^{T_m} |X_{t-}^n-X_{t-}|_V^2\, dN_t\Big] = 0.$$

Remarks. 1^0. From the assumptions II-V it follows that the operators A and B satisfy the assumptions II-V.

2^0. From III-V we find that

$$|B_n(t,v)|^2_{L_2(H,H_t)} \le 2|v|_V|A_{n,2}(t,v)|_{V'}+g_t(1+|v|_H^2) \le (R+1)|v|_V^2+ +2g_t(1+|v|_H^2),$$

$$|A_{n,1}(t,v)|_H^2\, \Delta N_t \le (R+1)|v|_V^2+ 2g_t(1+|v|_H^2),$$

$$|B_n(t,v_1)-B_n(t,v_2)|^2_{L_2(H,H_t)} \le l_t|v_1-v_2|_H^2+2|v_1-v_2|_V|A_{n,2}(t,v_1)- - A_{n,2}(t,v_2)|_{V'}$$

and

$$|A_{n,1}(t,v_1)-A_{n,1}(t,v_2)|_H^2\, \Delta N_t \le l_t|v_1-v_2|_H^2+ 2|v_1-v_2|_V|A_{n,2}(t,v_1)- -A_{n,2}(t,v_2)|_{V'}$$

3^0. Taking a sequence $\sigma_m \in \mathcal{T}, \sigma_m\uparrow\infty$ such that N_{σ_m}, $\int_0^{\sigma_m} g_s dN_s$, $\int_0^{\sigma_m} l_s dN_s$ are bounded, $|X_0^n|_H$, $n\ge 1$, are bounded on the set $\{\sigma_m<\infty\}$ and replacing N_t, M_t to $N_{t\wedge T_m}$, $M_{t\wedge T_m}$ with $T_m=\sigma_m\wedge m$ we can reduce the proof of the theorem 1 to the case when N_∞, $\int_0^\infty g_s dN_s$, $\int_0^\infty l_s dN_s$, $|X_0^n|_H$, and $|X_0|_H$ are bounded by some constant K and all processes are defined on $[0,\infty]$.

We shall use later the following lemmas.

Lemma 2. Let a function f be nonnegative F-adapted right continuous with left hand limits, $Z\in\mathcal{A}^+\cap\mathcal{P}$, $Z_\infty\le K$, $U\in\mathcal{A}$ and for each $\tau\in\mathcal{T}$, $\sigma\in\mathcal{T}^p$

$$E\big[f^\tau(\sigma-)\big]\le a\, E\Big[\int_0^{\sigma-} f(s-)dZ_s^\tau\Big] +E\big[U^\tau_{\sigma-}\big] \qquad (4)$$

where $h^\tau(t)=h(t\wedge\tau)$, a and K be constants.

Then

$$E\left[\int_0^\infty f(s-)dZ_s\right] \le e^{aK} \int_0^K e^{-as} E U_{\sigma_{s-}}\, ds,$$

where $\sigma_s = \inf(t: Z_t \geq s)$.

Proof. Let $\tau_n = \inf(t: f(t) > n)$. Then from (4) with $\sigma = \sigma_s$ and $\tau = \tau_n$ we find that

$$E\left[f^{\tau_n}(\sigma_{t-})\right] \le aE\left[\int_0^\infty f^{\tau_n}(s-)\chi\{s < \sigma_t\}\, dZ_s\right] + E\left[U^{\tau_n}_{\sigma_{t-}}\right].$$

Denoting $g_n(t) = E\left[f^{\tau_n}(\sigma_{t-})\right]$ and $b_n(t) = E\left[U^{\tau_n}_{\sigma_{t-}}\right]$ we have that

$$E\left[\int_0^\infty f^{\tau_n}(s-)\chi\{s<\sigma_t\} dZ_s\right] = E\left[\int_0^\infty f^{\tau_n}(\sigma_{s-})\chi\{\sigma_s < \sigma_t\}\chi\{\sigma_s < \infty\}\, ds\right] \le$$

$$\le \int_0^t g_n(s)ds.$$

Thus

$$g_n(t) \le a \int_0^t g_n(s)ds + b_n(t)$$

and

$$e^{-at}\int_0^t g_n(s)ds = \int_0^t e^{-as}\left[g_s(s) - a\int_0^s g_n(u)du\right] ds \le \int_0^t e^{-as} b_n(s)ds.$$

Finally

$$E\left[\int_0^\infty f(s-)dZ_s^{\tau_n}\right] \le \int_0^K g_n(s)ds \le e^{aK}\int_0^K e^{-as} E\left[U^{\tau_n}_{\sigma_{s-}}\right]ds.$$

The following two propositions are obvious.

Lemma 3. Let f be a nonnegative $\mathbb{F}$-adapted Skorohod function, $g \in \mathcal{A}$, $L \in \mathcal{M}_{loc,0}$ and

$$f(t) \le g(t) + L_t.$$

Then

$$\sup_{\sigma\in\mathcal{T}} E\left[f(\sigma)\right] \le \sup_{\sigma\in\mathcal{T}} E\left[g(\sigma)\right]$$

and

$$\sup_{\sigma\in\mathcal{T}^p} E\left[f(\sigma-)\right] \le \sup_{\sigma\in\mathcal{T}^p} E\left[g(\sigma-)\right].$$

Lemma 4. Let $(f_n)_{n\geq 0}$ be a sequence of nonnegative measurable functions on $R_+ \times \Omega$, $Z \in \mathcal{A}^+$, $Z_\infty \le K$.

Then

$$E\left[\int_0^\infty f_0(s)dZ_s\right] \le K \sup_{\sigma\in\mathcal{T}} E\left[f_0(\sigma)\right].$$

If besides $Z \in \mathcal{A}^+ \cap \mathcal{P}$,

$$\sup_n \sup_{\sigma\in\mathcal{T}^p} E\left[f_n(\sigma)\right] < \infty$$

and for each $\sigma\in\mathcal{T}^p$

$$\lim_n E\left[f_n(\sigma)\right] = 0$$

then

$$E\left[\int_0^\infty f_0(s)\, dZ_s\right] \le K \sup_{\sigma\in\mathcal{T}^p} E\left[f_0(\sigma)\right]$$

and

$$\lim_n E\left[\int_0^\infty f_n(s)dZ_s\right] = 0.$$

Really, it is enough to note that

$$E\left[\int_0^\infty f_n(s)dZ_s\right] = E\left[\int_0^\infty \chi_{\{\sigma_s<\infty\}}\; f_n(\sigma_s)ds\right] \le \int_0^K \left[E\, f_n(\sigma_s)\right]ds.$$

Proof of theorem 2. We shall accept further the boundedness assumption from remark 3^0. Uniqueness. Let $X_t^{(j)}$, $j = 1, 2$, be two solutions to the equation (3). Applying Ito's formula and assumption III we find that

$$\left|X_t^{(1)}-X_t^{(2)}\right|_H^2 = \int_0^t \Big\{2\left\langle A(s, X_{s-}^{(1)}) - A(s, X_{s-}^{(2)}),\ X_{s-}^{(1)}-X_{s-}^{(2)}\right\rangle +$$

$$+\left|A(s, X_{s-}^{(1)})-A(s, X_{s-}^{(2)})\right|_H^2 \Delta N_s+\left|B(s, X_{s-}^{(1)}) - B(s,X_{s-}^{(2)})\right|_{L_2(H,H_s)}^2\Big\}\times$$

$$\times dN_s+L_t \le \int_0^t 1_s\left|X_{s-}^{(1)} - X_{s-}^{(2)}\right|_H^2 dN_s+L_t, \quad t \ge 0,$$

where $L\in \mathcal{M}_{loc,\,0}$.

From lemma 2 with $U = 0$ we obtain that P - a.e.

$$\int_0^\infty 1_s\left|X_{s-}^{(1)} - X_{s-}^{(2)}\right|_H^2 dN_s = 0.$$

Then the inequality

$$0 \le \left|X_t^{(1)} - X_t^{(2)}\right|_H^2 \le L_t, \quad t \ge 0$$

implies that $X^{(1)} = X^{(2)}$ P - a.e.

Existence. Denoting $L^n_t = \int_0^t B_n(s, X^n_{s-}) \circ dM_s$ we have that

$$|X^n_t|^2_H = |X^n_0|^2_H + \int_0^t \Big\{ 2 \langle A_{n,2}(s, X^n_{s-}), X^n_{s-} \rangle + \Delta N_s \, |A_{n,1}(X^n_{s-})|^2_H +$$

$$+ |B_n(s, X^n_{s-})|^2_{L_2(H, H_s)} \Big\} dN_s + [L^n]_t - \langle L^n \rangle_t + 2 \int_0^t Q^{L^n} X^n_{s-} dL^n_s +$$

$$+ \sum_{s \le t} \Delta N_s \, (A_{n,1}(s, X^n_{s-}), \Delta L^n_s)_H .$$

Using assumption IV and remark 3° we find that

$$|X^n_t|^2_H + \varepsilon \int_0^t |X^n_{s-}|^2_V \, dN_s \le 2K + \int_0^t |X^n_{s-}|^2_H \, g_s \, dN_s + Y^n_t$$

where $Y^n \in \mathcal{M}_{loc,0}$.

From here and lemmas 2-4 it follows that

$$E \Big[\int_0^\infty |X^n_{s-}|^2_H \, g_s dN_s \Big] \le 2K(e^K - 1),$$

$$E \Big[\int_0^\infty |X^n_{s-}|^2_V \, dN_s \Big] \le 2K \, e^K,$$

$$\sup_{\sigma \in \mathcal{T}} E |X^n_\sigma|^2_H \le 2K \, e^K$$

and

$$E \Big[\int_0^\infty |X^n_s|^2_H \, dN_s \Big] \le 2Ke^K.$$

Applying assumption V and remark 2° we obtain that

$$\sup_n E \Big\{ \int_0^\infty \Big[|A_{n,1}(s, X^n_{s-})|^2_{V'} + |A_{n,2}(s, X^n_{s-})|^2_{V'} + |B_n(s, X^n_{s-})|^2_{L_2(H, H_s)} +$$

$$+ \Delta N_s |A_{n,1}(s, X^n_{s-})|^2_H \, \chi_{N^d} \Big] dN_s \Big\} < \infty .$$

For $\mathcal{G} \subset \mathcal{B}(R_+) \otimes \mathcal{F}$ and some Banach space W denoting $L^2_{\mathcal{G},W}$ the Banach space of $\mathcal{G}$-measurable dNdP-square integrable W-valued functions and $\hat{L}^2_{\mathcal{G},W}$ the Banach space of $\mathcal{G}$-measurable $dN^d dP$-square integrable

W-valued functions, remark that if W is reflexive, then $L^2_{\mathcal{G},W}$ and $\hat{L}^2_{\mathcal{G},W}$ are also reflexive. Having in mind the above estimations we can assume that the following weak limits exist:

$$A_{n,j}(X^n_-) \to A_{\infty,j} \quad \text{in } L^2_{\mathcal{P},V'},\ j = 1, 2,$$
$$X^n_- \to X^- \quad \text{in } L^2_{\mathcal{P},V},$$
$$X^n \to X \quad \text{in } L^2_{\mathcal{O},H},$$
$$B^n(X^n_-) \to B_\infty \quad \text{in } \int^{\oplus} L_2(H,H_s)dN_s dP$$

and

$$A_{n,1}(X^n_-) \to \hat{A}_\infty \quad \text{in } \hat{L}^2_{\mathcal{P},H}\ .$$

From the assumption that $\overline{\bigcup_n V_n} = V$ we have that $A_{\infty,1} = A_{\infty,2} = A_\infty dNdP$ - a.e. Because ΔN is $\mathcal{P}$-measurable, then $\hat{A}_\infty = A_\infty dN^d dP$ - a.e.

Define $\Phi^{\pm}_1 : \int^{\oplus} L_2(H,H_s)\, dN_s dP \to L^2_{\mathcal{O},H}$ and $\Phi^{\pm}_2 : L^2_{\mathcal{P},V'} \to L^2_{\mathcal{O},V}$ by means of the formulas:

$$\Phi^{\pm}_1(f)(t) = \int_0^{t\pm} f(s) \circ dM_s$$

$$\Phi^{\pm}_2(v')(t) = \int_0^{t\pm} v'(s)\, dN_s$$

It is easy to check that these mappings are strongly continuous. For example,

$$E\left[\int_0^\infty \left|\int_0^t f(s) \circ dM_s\right|^2_H dN_s\right] \leq K\, E\left[\sup_t \left|\int_0^t f(s) \circ dM_s\right|^2_H\right] \leq$$

$$\leq 4K\, E\left[\int_0^\infty |f(s)|^2_{L_2(H,H_s)} dN_s\right].$$

From the rexlexivity of the spaces under consideration we have that $\Phi^{\pm}_1$ and $\Phi^{\pm}_2$ are weakly continuous. Thus dNdP - a.e.

$$X_t = X_0 + \int_0^t A_\infty(s)\, dN_s + \int_0^t B_\infty(s) \circ dM_s$$

and $X^- = X_-$;

(According to the theorem 1 we shall consider a Skorohod modification of X.) Then

$$|X_t^n - X_t|_H^2 = |X_0^n - X_0|_H^2 + \int_0^t \Big\{ 2\langle A_{n,1}(s, X_{s-}^n) - A_\infty(s),$$

$$X_{s-}^n - X_{s-}\rangle + |A_{n,1}(s, X_{s-}^n) - A_\infty(s)|_H^2 \,\Delta N_s + |B_n(s, X_{s-}^n) -$$

$$- B_\infty(s)|^2_{L_2(H,H_s)}\Big\}\, dN_s + Y_t^{n,\infty} \quad , t \geq 0 , \qquad (5)$$

where

$$Y_t^{n,\infty} = 2 \int_0^t (X_{s-}^n - X_{s-})\, dL_s^{n,\infty} + [L^{n,\infty}]_t - \langle L^{n,\infty}\rangle_t +$$

$$+ \sum_{s \leq t} \Delta N_s (A_{n,1}(s, X_{s-}^n) - A_\infty(s),\ \Delta L_s^{n,\infty})_H,$$

$$L_t^{n,\infty} = \int_0^t \big[B_n(s, X_{s-}^n) - B_\infty(s)\big] \circ dM_s .$$

From lemma 1 it follows that $\sup_n E\,(\sup_t |X_t^n|_H^2 + \sup_t |X_t|_H^2) < \infty$ and $\sup_n E(\sup_t |Y_t^{n,\infty}|^2) < \infty$ Using assumption II and III from (5) we have, that

$$|X_t^n - X_t|_H^2 + \varepsilon_0 \int_0^t |X_{s-}^n - X_{s-}|_V^2\, dN_s \leq \int_0^t |X_{s-}^n - X_{s-}|_H^2\, l_s dN_s + U_t^n + Y_t^{n,\infty}, \qquad (6)$$

where

$$U_t^n = \int_0^t \Big\{ \Big[2 \langle A_{n,2}(s, X_{s-}^n) - A_{n,1}(s, X_{s-}^n),\ X_{s-}\rangle +$$

$$+ 2\langle A_{n,2}(s, X_{s-}),\ X_{s-}^n - X_{s-}\rangle - 2\langle A_\infty(s),\ X_{s-}^n - X_{s-}\rangle +$$

$$+ 2(B_n(s, X_{s-}^n),\ B_n(s, X_{s-}))_{L_2(H,H_s)} - |B_n(s, X_{s-})|^2_{L_2(H,H_s)} -$$

$$- 2(B_n(s, X_{s-}^n),\ B_\infty(s))_{L_2(H,H_s)} + |B_\infty(s)|^2_{L_2(H,H_s)}\Big] +$$

$+ \Delta N_s \left[2(A_{n,1}(s, X^n_{s-}), A_{n,1}(s, X_{s-}))_H - 2(A_{n,1}(s, X^n_{s-}), A_\infty(s))_H - \right.$

$\left. - |A_{n,1}(s, X_{s-})|^2_H + |A_\infty(s)|^2_H \right] \Big\} dN_s.$

Note that $\sup_n E(|U^n|_\infty) < \infty$. App lying VI and the Lebesgue theorem on the dominated convergence we find that as $n \to \infty$

$$A_{n,2}(t, X_{t-}) \to A(t, X_{t-}) \quad \text{in } L^2_{\mathcal{P},V'},$$

$$B_n(t, X_{t-}) \to B(t, X_{t-}) \quad \text{in } \int^{\oplus} L_2(H,H_s) dN_s dP, \tag{7}$$

$A_{n,1}(t, X_{t-}) \to A(t, X_{t-})$ in $L^2_{\mathcal{P},H}$ strongly and for each $\sigma \in \mathcal{T}^p$

$$\lim_{n\to\infty} E\, U^n_{\sigma-} = -E \int_0^{\sigma-} \Big[|B_\infty(s) - B(s, X_{s-})|^2_{L_2(H,H_s)} + \Delta N_s\, |A_\infty(s) - A(s, X_{s-})|^2_H \Big] dN_s.$$

From (6), (7) and lemmas 2-4 it is easy to obtain that

$$\lim_n E\Big[\int_0^\infty |X^n_s - X_s|^2_H\, dN_s\Big] = 0, \quad \lim_n E\Big[\int_0^\infty |X^n_{s-} - X_{s-}|^2_H\, dN_s\Big] = 0$$

and $\forall\ \sigma \in \mathcal{T}$

$$\lim_n E\, |X^n_\sigma - X_\sigma|^2_H = 0.$$

Then we shall have the equality

$$\lim_n E\, U^n_\infty = 0,$$

which implies that $A_\infty(s) = A(s, X_{s-})$ $dN^d dP$ - a.e. and $B_\infty(s) = B(s, X_{s-}) dN dP$ - a.e.

In the case when $\varepsilon_0 > 0$ from (6) we find that

$$\lim_n E\Big[\int_0^\infty |X^n_{t-} - X_{t-}|^2_V\, dN_s\Big] = 0.$$

Now applying remark 1° and (7) it follows that as $n \to \infty$

$$E\Big[\int_0^\infty |A_{n,1}(t, X^n_{t-}) - A(t, X_{t-})|^2_H\, \Delta N_t dN_t\Big] \to 0$$

and

$$B_n(t, X^n_{t-}) \to B(t, X_{t-}) \text{ in } \int^{\oplus} L_2(H,H_s)\, dN_s dP \text{ strongly.}$$

From here and lemma 1 we obtain that

$$\lim_n E\left[\sup_t |X_t^n - X_t|_H^2\right] = 0.$$

It remains to identify $A_\infty(s)$ with $A(s, X_{s-})$ dNdP - a.e.

Let $u \in L^2_{\mathcal{P},V}$ and $\lambda > 0$. From assumption III we have that

$$I_n = E\left[\int_0^\infty \{2\langle A_{n,2}(t, X_{t-}^n) - A_{n,2}(X_{t-} - \lambda u(t)),\right.$$

$$X_{t-}^n - X_{t-} + \lambda u(t)\rangle + \Delta N_t |A_{n,1}(t, X_{t-}^n) - A_{n,1}(t, X_{t-} - \lambda u(t))|_H^2 +$$

$$\left. + |B_n(t, X_{t-}^n) - B_n(t, X_{t-} - \lambda u(t))|^2_{L_2(H,H_t)}\} dN_t\right] \leq$$

$$\leq E\left[\int_0^\infty |X_{t-}^n - X_{t-} + \lambda u(t)|_H^2 l_t dN_t\right]$$

and

$$\lim_n I_n \leq \lambda^2 E\left[\int_0^\infty |u(t)|_H^2 \, l_t dN_t\right]. \tag{9}$$

From other hand

$$\lim_n I_n = \lim_n E\left[\int_0^\infty \{2\langle A_{n,1}(t, X_{t-}^n) - A_\infty(t), X_{t-}^n - X_{t-}\rangle + \right.$$

$$+ 2\lambda\langle A_{n,2}(t, X_{t-}^n) - A_{n,2}(t, X_{t-} - \lambda u(t)), u(t)\rangle + 2\langle A_\infty(t) -$$

$$- A_{n,2}(t, X_{t-} - \lambda u(t)), X_{t-}^n - X_{t-}\rangle + \langle A_{n,1}(t, X_{t-}^n) - A_{n,2}(t, X_{t-}^n), X_{t-}\rangle +$$

$$+ |B_n(t, X_{t-}^n) - B(t, X_{t-})|^2_{L_2(H,H_t)} + 2(B_n(t, X_{t-}^n) - B(t, X_{t-}), B(t, X_{t-}) -$$

$$- B_n(t, X_{t-} - \lambda u(t)))_{L_2(H,H_t)} + |B_n(t, X_{t-} - \lambda u(t))|^2_{L_2(H,H_t)} + \Delta N_t \left[|A_{n,1}(t, X_{t-}^n) -\right.$$

$$- A(t, X_{t-})|_H^2 + 2(A_{n,1}(t, X_{t-}^n) - A(t, X_{t-}), A(t, X_{t-}) - A_{n,1}(t, X_{t-} - \lambda u(t)))_H +$$

$$+\left|A_{n,1}(t,X_{t-}-\lambda u(t))\right|_H^2\Big]\Big\}\, dN_t\Big] = \lim_n E\left|X^n_\infty - X_\infty\right|_H^2 +$$

$$+ E\Big[\int_0^\infty \Big\{2\lambda\langle A_\infty(t) - A(t,X_{t-}-\lambda u(t)),\, u(t)\rangle +$$

$$+\left|B(t,X_{t-}-\lambda u(t))\right|^2_{L_2(H,H_t)} + \Delta N_t\left|A(t,X_{t-}-\lambda u(t))\right|_H^2\Big\}\, dN_t\Big]. \qquad (9')$$

Thus from (9) and (9') it follows, that

$$2E\Big[\int_0^\infty \langle A_\infty(t)-A(t,X_{t-}-\lambda u(t)),\, u(t)\rangle\, dN_t\Big] \le$$

$$\le \lambda\, E\Big[\int_0^\infty |u(t)|_H^2 1_t\, dN_t\Big].$$

Using assumption I and taking $\lambda \to 0$ we find that for each $u \in L^2_{\mathcal{P},V}$ the inequality

$$E\Big[\int_0^\infty \langle A_\infty(t) - A(t,X_{t-}),\, u(t)\rangle\, dN_t\Big] \le 0$$

holds which implies that $A_\infty(t) = A(t,X_{t-})$ $dNdP$ - a.e. The proof of theorem 2 is complete.

We shall need later the following version of the theorem 2. Consider stochastic evolution equation (3), assuming that $A: V \to V'$, $B: V \to L^2_{loc}(H,Q)$ on the set $\mathcal{N}$, $A: H \to H$, $B: H \to L^2_{loc}(H, Q)$ on the set $\mathcal{N}^d$ and satisfying analoguous measurability properties as in the previous case. Now we call a H-valued stochastic process X which is Skorohod in the strong topology of H a solution to (3) if $X_t \in V$ $dN^c dP$ - a.e., $\int_0^t |A(s,X_{s-})|_{V'}\, dN_s < \infty$, $\int_0^t |B(s,X_{s-})|^2_{L_2(H,H_s)}\, dN_s < \infty$ P - a.e., $t \ge 0$, and equation (3) is satisfied.

Let $(X^n)_{n\ge 1}$ be a sequence of solutions to the stochastic evolution equations

$$X^n_t = X^n_0 + \int_0^t A_{n,1}(s,X^n_{s-})\, dN_s + \int_0^t B_n(s,X^n_{s-}) \circ dM_s$$

such that there exist a subsets $V_n \subset V$, $\overline{\bigcup_n V_n} = V$, $X^n_{t-} \in V_n$ $dN^c dP$ - a.e.,

$n \geq 1$.

We shall use the following versions of the assumptions II-VI under agreement that $0 \cdot \infty = 0$.

II'. There exist $A_{n,2} : \mathcal{N} \times V \to V'$ such that $A_{n,2}$ is $(\mathcal{B}(V'), \mathcal{P} \cap \mathcal{N} \otimes \mathcal{B}(V))$ - measurable, for each $v_1, v_2 \in V_n$ on the set $\mathcal{N}$

$$\langle A_{n,1}(t,v_1), v_2 \rangle = \langle A_{n,2}(t, v_1), v_2 \rangle , n \geq 1.$$

Let $A_{n,2} = A_{n,1}$ on the set $\mathcal{N}^d \times H$, $n \geq 1$.

III'. For each $v_1, v_2 \in V$ on the set $\mathcal{N}$ and for each $v_1, v_2 \in H$ on the set $\mathcal{N}^d$

$$2 \langle A_{n,2}(t,v_1) - A_{n,2}(t,v_2), v_1 - v_2 \rangle + |B_n(t,v_1) - B_n(t,v_2)|^2_{L_2(H,H_t)} +$$

$$+ \varepsilon_0 \chi_{\mathcal{N}} |v_1 - v_2|^2_V \leq l_t |v_1 - v_2|^2_H ,$$

where $\varepsilon_0 \geq 0$, $l \in \mathcal{P}^+$ and $\int_0^t l_s dN_s < \infty$ P - a.e.;

IV'. For each $v \in V$ on the set $\mathcal{N}$ and for each $v \in H$ on the set $\mathcal{N}^d$

$$2 \langle A_{n,2}(t,v), v \rangle + |A_{n,1}(t,v)|^2_H \Delta N_t + |B_n(t,v)|^2_{L_2(H,H_t)} +$$

$$+ \varepsilon \chi_{\mathcal{N}} |v|^2_V \leq g_t(1 + |v|^2_H),$$

where $\varepsilon > 0$, $g \in \mathcal{P}^+$ and $\int_0^t g_s \, dN_s < \infty$ P - a.e.;

V'. For each $v \in V$ on the set $\mathcal{N}$ and for each $v \in H$ on the set $\mathcal{N}^d$

$$|A_{n,j}(t,v)|^2_{V'} \chi_{\mathcal{N}} + |A_{n,j}(t,v)|^2_H \chi_{\mathcal{N}^d} \leq g_t(1 + |v|^2_H) + R \chi_{\mathcal{N}} |v|^2_V,$$

$j = 1, 2$, $R > 0$;

VI'. Assume that $dN^c dP$ - a.e. for each $v \in V$ $A_{n,2}(t,v) \xrightarrow{V'} A(t,v)$, $B_n(t,v) \xrightarrow{L_2(H,H_t)} B(t,v)$ as $n \to \infty$, $dN^d dP$ - a.e. for each $v \in H$ $A_{n,1}(t,v) \xrightarrow{H} A(t,v)$, $B_n(t,v) \xrightarrow{L_2(H,H_t)} B(t,v)$ as $n \to \infty$ and $X_0^n \xrightarrow{H} X_0$ as $n \to \infty$ in probability.

Theorem 2'. Under assumptions I, II' - VI' there exist a unique solution X to the equation (3) and a sequence $T_m \in \mathcal{T}$, $T_m \uparrow \infty$, such that for each m, $\sigma \le T_m$, $\sigma \in \mathcal{T}$

$$E\,|X^n_\sigma - X_\sigma|^2_H \to 0, \quad E\Big[\int_0^{T_m} |X^n_t - X_t|^2_H\, dN_t + |X^n_{t-} - X_{t-}|^2_H\, dN_t\Big] \to 0 \text{ as}$$

$n \to \infty$.

If $\varepsilon_0 > 0$, then there exists a sequence $T_m \in \mathcal{T}$, $T_m \uparrow \infty$, such that for each m

$$\lim_n E\Big[\sup_{t \le T_m} |X^n_t - X_t|^2_H + \int_0^{T_m} |X^n_t - X_t|^2_V\, dN^c_t\Big] = 0.$$

The proof is analoguous to the proof of the theorem 2 and we shall omit it.

Remark 1. In the case, when V is a Hilbert space, A and B satisfy the assumptions I, III-V (or I, III$'$ - V$'$), using Galerkin's approximation method and the finite dimensional results from [7], it is easy to prove that there exists a unique solution to (3) in the corresponding sense.

§ 4. Some properties of the optional and predictable projections

Denote $\mathcal{J}$ a set of all sequences of P - a.e. finite stopping times (T_m), $T_n \uparrow \infty$, as $n \to \infty$, $\mathcal{J}^P$ a subset of $\mathcal{J}$ consisting the sequences of predictable stopping times. Foll owing C. Dellacherie it is easy to extend the notions of the optional and predictable projections to the following classes of random processes

$$\mathcal{O}\!\mathcal{L}^W = \{Y \mid \exists (T_n) \in \mathcal{J}: \forall \sigma \in \mathcal{T}\ E|Y_{\sigma \wedge T_n}| < \infty,\ n \ge 1\},$$

$$\mathcal{O}\!\mathcal{L}^P = \{Y \mid \exists (T_n) \in \mathcal{J}^P: \forall \sigma \in \mathcal{T}^P\ E|Y_{\sigma \wedge T_n}| < \infty,\ n \ge 1\}.$$

Lemma 5. Let $Y \in \mathcal{O}\!\mathcal{L}^W$ ($\mathcal{O}\!\mathcal{L}^P$). Then there exists unique $\mathcal{O}$ ($\mathcal{P}$) measurable ${}^1Y$ (${}^3Y$) such that for each $\sigma \in \mathcal{T}$ ($\mathcal{T}^P$) satisfying $E[|Y_\sigma| \chi_{\{\sigma < \infty\}}] < \infty$

we have that

$$E\left[Y_\sigma \chi_{\{\sigma<\infty\}}\right] = E\left[{}^1Y_\sigma \chi_{\{\sigma<\infty\}}\right] \left(= E\left[{}^3Y_\sigma \chi_{\{\sigma<\infty\}}\right]\right).$$

Proof is obvious.

Lemma 6. Let Y be Skorohod. If there exists $(T_n) \in \mathcal{J}^P$ such that $E\left[\sup_t |Y_{t\wedge T_n}|^2\right] < \infty$, $n \geq 1$, then

$$E\left[\sup_t |{}^1Y_{t\wedge T_n}|^2\right] \leq 4\, E\,(\sup_t |Y_{t\wedge T_n}|^2),\ n \geq 1.$$

If $E\left[\sup_t |Y_{t\wedge T_n}|\right] < \infty$, $n \geq 1$, then ${}^1Y$ is Skorohod and under assumption that $(T_n) \in \mathcal{J}^P$ P - a.e. ${}^1Y_{t-} = {}^3(Y_-)_t$, where $(Y_-)_t = Y_{t-}$.

Proof. We have that

$$\chi_{[0,T_n]} |{}^1Y_t| \leq {}^1(\chi_{[0,T_n]} |Y|)_t \leq$$

$$\leq {}^1(\sup_u |Y_{u\wedge T_n}|)_t = E\left[\sup_u |Y_{u\wedge T_n}| \,\middle|\, \mathcal{F}_t\right].$$

Now it is enough to apply Doob's inequality.

The proof that ${}^1Y$ is Skorohod is analoguous to the proof of theorem IV - T28 in [15].

Let now $\sigma \in \mathcal{T}^P$, $\sigma \leq T_n$, $\sigma_n \uparrow \sigma$, $\sigma_n < \sigma$ P - a.e.

Then we find, that for each n

$$E\left[{}^1Y_{\sigma_n}\right] = E\left[Y_{\sigma_n}\right]$$

and thus

$$E\left[{}^1Y_{\sigma-}\right] = E\left[Y_{\sigma-}\right] = E\left[({}^3Y_-)_\sigma\right].$$

This equality implies that ${}^1Y_- = {}^3(Y_-)$.

Lemma 6 is proved.

Assume that Y takes values in a Polish space $\mathfrak{X}$ and denote $D(\mathfrak{X})$ a space of $\mathfrak{X}$-valued Skorohod functions with $\mathcal{J}_1$-topology. The proof of the following assertion is standard (see, e.g. [17]).

Lemma 7. There exists a family of $\mathcal{B}(R_+)\otimes\mathcal{F}$-measurable positive measures $E^t(dw)$ on $D(\mathfrak{X})$ such that $E^t(D(\mathfrak{X})) = 1$ for $t < \zeta$, $= 0$ for $t \geq \zeta$, $P(\zeta < \infty) = 0$, E^t is Skorohod in the topology of weak convergence and for each continuous bounded function Z on $D(\mathfrak{X})$ $E^t(Z)$ is the Skorohod version of $E(Z(Y)|\mathcal{F}_t)$.

If f is bounded and $\mathcal{O} \otimes \mathcal{B}(R_+) \otimes \mathcal{B}(D(\mathfrak{X}))$ - measurable, then

$$\int f(t,\omega,t,w)E^t(dw) = E^t(f_t) = {}^1(f(Y))_t.$$

If f is bounded and $\mathcal{P} \otimes \mathcal{B}(R_+) \otimes \mathcal{B}(D(\mathfrak{X}))$ - measurable, then

$$E^{t-}(f_t) = {}^3(f(Y))_t.$$

Corrolary 1. If $f_t = f_t(Y) \in \mathcal{O}^w(\mathcal{O}^p)$ then $E^t(f_t) = {}^1f_t$ and $E^{t-}(f_t) = {}^3f_t$ correspondingly*).

Let N be increasing and $\mathcal{P}$ -measurable, $\Pi(dt, dx) = \pi(t,dx)dN_t$ be a random positive measure on $R_+ x G$, where $\pi(t,dx)$ be $\mathcal{P}$ -measurable and $(G, \mathcal{G})$ be a measurable space.

Lemma 8. 1) Let $a_t(w)$ be $\mathcal{P} \otimes \mathcal{B}(R_+) \otimes \mathcal{B}(D(\mathfrak{X}))$ - measurable function and there exists $(T_n) \in \mathcal{J}$ such that for each n

$$E\left[\int_0^{T_n} |a_s(Y)|\, dN_s\right] < \infty .$$

Then

$${}^1\left(\int a_s(Y)dN_s\right)_t = \int_0^t E^{s-}(a_s)dN_s.$$

2) Let $f_t(w,x)$ be $\mathcal{P} \otimes \mathcal{B}(D(\mathfrak{X})) \otimes \mathcal{G}$ - measurable and there exists $(T_n) \in \mathcal{J}$ such that for each n

$$E\left[\int_0^{T_n}\int |f_s(Y,x)|\, \Pi(ds,dx)\right] < \infty .$$

Then

---

*) We suppose here and later that $E^t(g) = 0$, if the integral does not exists.

$$^{1}\left(\int\int f_s(Y,x)\,\Pi(ds,\,dx)\right)_t = \int_0^t\int E^{s-}(f_s(\cdot\,,x))\,\Pi(ds,\,dx).$$

Proof. Using localization we can assume, that $T_n = \infty$. Approximating a_s by means of the bounded processes $(a_s \vee (-n)) \wedge n$ the assertion 1) we derive from the definition of the optional projection.

In order to check 2) it is enough to note that

$$E\left[\int_0^\infty \int_G |f_s(Y,x)|\,\Pi(s,dx)\,dN_s\right] =$$

$$= E\left[\int_0^\infty \int_G E^{t-}\left(\int_G |f_s(Y,x)|\,\Pi(s,dx)\,dN_s\right]\right) < \infty$$

and apply Fubini's theorem.

Let $\hat{\mathbb{F}} = (\hat{\mathcal{F}}_t)_{t\geq 0}$, $\hat{\mathcal{F}}_t \supset \mathcal{F}_t$, $t \geq 0$, $\hat{\mathcal{O}}$ ($\hat{\mathcal{P}}$) be a σ-algebra $\hat{\mathbb{F}}$-optional (predictable) subsets, $dP = \alpha\, d\tilde{P}$, $\alpha > 0$, $\alpha_t = E(\alpha\,|\mathcal{F}_t)$ be the Skorohod version $\tilde{^1Y}$ ($\tilde{^3Y}$) be the $(\tilde{P},\, \mathbb{F})$ - optional (predictable) projection of Y.

Lemma 9. If Y is bounded and $\hat{\mathcal{O}}$- measurable, then $\tilde{^1}(Y\alpha) = \tilde{^1}\alpha\,{}^1Y$. If Y is bounded and $\hat{\mathcal{P}}$- measurable, then $\tilde{^3}(Y\alpha_-) = \tilde{^3}(\alpha_-)\,{}^3Y$.

Proof. Let $T \in \mathcal{T}(\mathbb{F})$, $P(T<\infty) = 1$. Then

$$\tilde{E}\left[\tilde{^1}(\alpha Y)_T\right] = \tilde{E}\left[\alpha_T Y_T\right] = EY_T = E\,{}^1Y_T = \tilde{E}\left[\alpha_T\,{}^1Y_T\right] = \tilde{E}\left[\tilde{^1}\alpha_T\,{}^1Y_T\right].$$

Analoguously if $T \in \mathcal{T}^p(\mathbb{F})$, $P(T<\infty) = 1$, then

$$\tilde{E}\left[\tilde{^3}(\alpha_- Y)_T\right] = \tilde{E}\left[\alpha_{T-} Y_T\right] = EY_T = E\,{}^3Y_T = \tilde{E}\left[\alpha_{T-}\,{}^3Y_T\right] = \tilde{E}\left[\tilde{^3}(\alpha_-)_T\,{}^3Y_T\right].$$

Lemma 9 is proved.

Define $H^n(R^1) = \left\{ f: R^1 \to R^1 \;\middle|\; \sum_{|\beta|\leq n} r_n^\beta\, |\partial^\beta f|_0^2 = |f|_n^2 < \infty \right\}$, where $\beta = (\beta_1, \ldots, \beta_l) \in \mathbb{N}^l$, $\partial^\beta = \partial_1^{\beta_1} \ldots \partial_l^{\beta_l}$, $\partial_i = \frac{\partial}{\partial x_i}$, $\partial_i^0 f = f$,

$|f|_0^2 = \int |f(x)|^2\,dx$, $|\beta| = \beta_1 + \ldots + \beta_l$, $r_n^\beta = \dfrac{n!}{\beta!\,(n-|\beta|)!}$, $\beta! = \beta_1! \ldots \beta_l!$. We shall denote $(\ ,\ )_n$ the inner product of the Hilbert space $H^n(R^l)$. Let θ be R^d-valued Skorohod process and E^t be a system of measures corresponding to $\tilde{P}$ and (θ, α).

Lemma 10. Let there exists $(T_n) \in \mathcal{T}$ such that $\tilde{E}\left[\sup_t |\alpha_{t\wedge T_n}|^2\right] < \infty$ for each n. Then there exists a σ - measurable $H^{[d/2]}(R^d)$-valued function Ψ_t which is Skorohod in t in the weak topology of $H^{[d/2]}(R^d)$ and P - a.e.

$$\tilde{E}^t(\varphi(\theta_t)\alpha_t) = (\Psi_t, \varphi)_{[d/2]} = \Psi_t(\varphi),$$

$$\tilde{E}^{t-}(\varphi(\theta_{t-})\alpha_{t-}) = \Psi_{t-}(\varphi), \forall\ \varphi \in H^{[d/2]}(R^d),$$

and

$$\tilde{E}(\sup_t |\Psi_{t\wedge T_n}|^2_{[d/2]}) < \infty .$$

Proof. For $\varphi \in C_0^\infty(R^d)$ from the Sobolev's inequality we have that

$$|\tilde{E}^t(\varphi(\theta_t)\alpha_t)|^2 \le \sup_\theta |\varphi(\theta)|^2 \,[\tilde{E}^t(\alpha_t)]^2 \le$$
$$\le \text{const}.|\varphi|^2_{[d/2]}\,(\tilde{E}^t(\alpha_t))^2.$$

Using corrolary 1 and lemma 6 we find that $\tilde{E}\left[\sup_{t\le T_n}(\tilde{E}^t(\alpha_t))^2\right] < \infty$.

Thus there exists σ-measurable $H^{[d/2]}(R^d)$-valued function Ψ_t such that for each $\varphi \in C_0^\infty(R^d)$

$$\tilde{E}^t(\varphi(\theta_t)\alpha_t) = (\Psi_t, \varphi)_{[d/2]}$$

and

$$|\Psi_t|^2_{[d/2]} \le \text{const}\,(\tilde{E}^t(\alpha_t))^2.$$

From lemma 6 we have that for each $\varphi \in C_0^\infty(R^d)$ $C_t^\varphi = (\Psi_t, \varphi) = E^t(\varphi(\theta_t)\alpha_t)$ is Skorohod and $C_{t-}^\varphi = \tilde{E}^{t-}(\varphi(\theta_{t-})\alpha_{t-})$. Using separability of $C_0^\infty(R^d)$ we can find a subset $\tilde{\Omega} \subset \Omega$ does not depending on φ, $\tilde{P}(\tilde{\Omega}) = 1$, and such that on $\tilde{\Omega}$ C_t^φ is Skorohod, $C_t^\varphi = \tilde{E}^t(\varphi(\theta_t)\alpha_t)$ and $C_{t-} = \tilde{E}^{t-}(\varphi(\theta_{t-})\alpha_{t-})$. As $\sup_{u\le t}|\Psi_u|^2_{[d/2]} < \infty$

for each $t \geq 0$ $\tilde{P}$ - a.e., then Ψ_t is Skorohod in the weak topology of $H^{[d/2]}(R^d)$, $\tilde{P}$ - a.e. $\Psi_t(\varphi) = \tilde{E}^t(\varphi(\theta_t)\alpha_t)$ and $\Psi_{t-}(\varphi) = \tilde{E}^{t-}(\varphi(\theta_{t-})\alpha_{t-})$ for each $\varphi \in H^{[d/2]}(R^d)$ considering the continuous modifications of φ.

Consider now two filtrations $\hat{\mathbb{F}} \supset \mathbb{F}$ and $M \in \mathcal{M}^2_{loc}(P, \mathbb{F}, E) \cap \mathcal{M}^2_{loc}(P, \hat{\mathbb{F}}, E)$ satisfying the assumptions of § 1. Denote $\hat{L}^2_{loc}$ a class of all vector fields $f = (f_s)$ such that $f_s \in H_s, (f_s, Q_s y')_{H_s}$ are $\hat{\mathcal{P}}$-measurable for each $y' \in K$ and there exists $(T_n) \in \mathcal{S}$ such that $E\left[\int_0^{T_n} |f_s|^2_{H_s} dN_s\right] < \infty$ (Q, N are $\mathcal{P}$-measurable).

Lemma 11. Let $f \in \hat{L}^2_{loc}$ and (T_n) be a localizing sequence. Then there exists unique $\check{f} \in L^2_{loc}(Q, P, \mathbb{F})$ such that for each $g \in L^2_{loc}(Q,P,\mathbb{F})$

$$^1\left(\int (f_s, g_s)_{H_s} dN_s\right)_t = \int_0^t (\check{f}_s, g_s)_{H_s} dN_s .$$

If $f_s^m = \sum_{k=1}^m (f_s, e_s^k) e_s^k$, then

$$\check{f}_s^m = \sum_{k=1}^m \overline{(f_s, e_s^k)} e_s^k$$

and for each n

$$\lim_m E\left[\int_0^{T_n} |\check{f}_s - f_s^m|^2_{H_s} dN_s\right] = 0.$$

It is true, that dNdP - a.e.

$$|\check{f}(s)|^2_{H_s} \leq \overline{|f(s)|^2_H} ,$$

where $\overline{Z}$ denotes a conditional mean value of Z with respect to $(\mathcal{P}, dN\ dP)$.

Proof. It is enough to consider the case when $T_n = \infty$ P - a.e., $n \geq 1$, and $E\left[\int_0^\infty |g_s|^2_{H_s} dN_s\right] < \infty$. Noting that

$$\left|\int (f_s, g_s)_{H_s}\, dN_s dP\right|^2 \leq \int |f_s|^2_{H_s}\, dN_s dP \cdot \int |g_s|^2_{H_s}\, dN_s dP$$

and using Riesz theorem we have that there exists unique $\mathcal{P}$-measurable field Cf such that

$$\int (f_s, g_s)_{H_s}\, dN_s dP = \int (Cf_s, g_s)_{H_s}\, dN_s dP$$

and

$$\int |Cf_s|^2_{H_s}\, dN_s\, dP \leq \int |f|^2_{H_s}\, dN_s\, dP.$$

The last inequality implies that $|Cf_s|^2_{H_s} \leq \overline{|f|^2_{H_s}}$ $dNdP$ - a.e.

Further

$$\int (f^m_s, g_s)_{H_s} dN_s dP = \sum_{k=1}^{m} \int (f_s, e^k_s)_{H_s} (g_s, e^k_s)_{H_s}\, dN_s dP =$$

$$= \sum_{k=1}^{m} \int \overline{(f(s), e^k_s)}_{H_s} (g_s, e^k_s)_{H_s}\, dN_s dP = \int (Cf^m_s, g_s)_{H_s}\, dN_s dP,$$

i.e. $Cf^m_s = \sum_{k=1}^{m} \overline{(f_s, e^k_s)}_{H_s}\, e^k_s$.

Using continuity of C we find that

$$\lim_m \int |Cf^m_s - Cf_s|^2_{H_s}\, dN_s dP \leq \lim_m \int |f^m_s - f_s|^2_{H_s}\, dN_s dP = 0,$$

i.e. $Cf = \check{f}$.

(R) Assume that for each bounded $(P, \mathbb{F})$-martingale $L(L_0 = 0)$ there exists unique $g \in L^2_{loc}(Q, P, \mathbb{F})$ such that $L_t = \int_0^t g_s dM_s$.

Lemma 12. Under assumption (R) for each $f \in \hat{L}^2_{loc}$

$$^1(\int f_s dM_s)_t = \int_0^t \check{f}_s dM_s\ .$$

If $L \in \mathcal{M}^2_0(P, \hat{\mathbb{F}})$ and L is orthogonal to $\int g_s dM_s$ for each $g \in L^2_{loc}(Q,P,\mathbb{F})$ then $^1L = 0$.

Proof. Let L be bounded $(P, \mathbb{F})$-martingale $L_t = \int_0^t g_s dM_s$, and $T \in \mathcal{T}(\mathbb{F})$. We can assume that $\int |f_s|^2_{H_s}\, dN_s dP < \infty$ and $\int |g_s|^2_{H_s}\, dN_s dP < \infty$ Then

$$E\left[{}^{1}\left(\int f_s dM_s\right)_T L_T\right] = E\left[\int_0^T f_s dM_s L_T\right] = E\left[\int_0^T (f_s, g_s)_{H_s} dN_s\right] =$$

$$= E\left[\int_0^T (\check{f}_s, g_s)_{H_s} dN_s\right] = E\left[\int_0^T \check{f}_s dM_s L_T\right].$$

The last assertion of lemma 12 as obvious.

Consider now a Skorohod process Y taking values in the Polish space $\mathcal{Y}$ and corresponding class of measures E^t. We shall calculate $\check{f}$ in two important cases.

1. Let $(U, \mathcal{B}(U))$ be a separable measurable space, $p(dt, dx)$ be $\mathbb{F}$-optional point process on $[0, \infty) \times U$, $\Pi(dt, dx) = \pi(t, dx)\, dN_t$ - $(\hat{\mathbb{F}}, P)$ - dual predictable projection of p, N be $\mathcal{P}$-measurable. Let then exists $U_n \in \mathcal{B}(U)$, $U_n \uparrow U$, $\Pi([0,t] \times U_m) < \infty$, $n \geq 1$, $t \geq 0$ and $\bar{\mathcal{K}}$ be a countable subset of $\mathcal{B}(U)$, $\mathcal{B}(U) = \sigma(\bar{\mathcal{K}})$ and such that for each $A \in \bar{\mathcal{K}}$, $A \subset U_m$ for some m. Denote $\mathcal{K} = \{\chi_A, A \in \bar{\mathcal{K}}\}$.

Let E' be a vector space generated by $\mathcal{K}$, $E = E'^{*}$ (algebraic dual space), $a_s = \Pi(\{s\} \times U) \leq 1$. It is obvious, that $(E, \sigma(E, E'))$ is a separable Frechet space.

For each $f, g \in E'$ we have that

$$q_t(f) = p(\chi_{[0,t]} \otimes f) - \Pi(\chi_{[0,t]} \otimes f)$$

is in $\mathcal{M}^2_{loc}(P, \mathbb{F})$ and

$$\langle q(f), q(g)\rangle_t = \int_0^t (f(x) - \hat{f}(s))\, g(x)\, \pi(s, dx)\, dN_s,$$

where $\hat{f}(s) = \int_U f(x)\, \Pi(\{s\} \times dx)$.

The kernel Q in this case can be obtained from the formula

$$\langle g, Q_t f\rangle = \int_U (f - \hat{f})\, g\, \pi(t, dx).$$

Let $L^2_s = L^2_{s,\omega}$ be a Hilbert space of $\pi(s, dx)$ square integrable functions f with a norm

$$|f|^2_{L_s} = \int_U (f - \hat{f})\, f\, \pi(s, dx) \text{ if } a_s < 1,$$

and be Hilbert space of $\pi(s, dx)$ square integrable functions f, such that $\hat{f} = 0$ with the norm $|f|^2_{L_s} = \int_U f^2 \pi(s, dx)$, if $a_s = 1$. Define isometries $Q_s E' \to L^2_s$: $Q_s f \to f$, if $a_s < 1$, $Q_s f \to f - \hat{f}$, if $a_s = 1$.

Noting that $\overline{Q_s E'} = H_s$ it is clear that H_s is isometric to L^2_s.

Thus $\int^{\oplus} h_s dN_s dP = \{ f : f_s \in L^2_s,\ (g, f_s)_{L_s}$ is $\hat{\mathcal{P}}$-measurable for each $g \in E'$ and $\int |f_s|^2_{L_s} dN_s\, dP < \infty \}$, assuming that $f^{(1)}$ and $f^{(2)}$ are identified if $\int |f^{(1)}_s - f^{(2)}_s|^2_{L^2_s} dN_s dP = 0$.

Let F be a $\mathcal{P} \otimes \mathcal{B}(R_+) \otimes \mathcal{B}(D(\mathcal{X})) \otimes \mathcal{B}(U)$ - measurable function, $\widetilde{F}(t,x) = F(t, \omega, t, Y, x)$.

Lemma 13. If $\widetilde{F} \in \hat{L}^2_{loc}$ then $d\Pi\, dP$ - a.e.

$$\check{F}_t = E^{t-}(F_t) = \int F(t, \omega, t, w, x)\, E^{t-}(dw).$$

Proof. As $E^{t-}(1) \leq 1$, it is easy to note using lemma 11 that $dNdP$ - a.e.

$$|E^{t-}(F_t)|^2_{L^2_t} \leq E^{t-}(|F_t|^2_{L^2_t}) = \overline{|\widetilde{F}_t|^2_{L^2_t}} .$$

Thus $E^{t-}(F_t) \in L^2_{loc}(Q,P,F)$ and from lemma 11 we find that $\check{F} = E^{t-}(F_t)$.

2\. Let $M = (M^1, \dots, M^n)$, $M^j \in \mathcal{M}^c_{loc}(P, F) \cap \mathcal{M}^c_{loc}(P, \hat{F})$, $d\langle M^i, M^j\rangle_t = a_{ij}(t) dN_t$, $A(t) = (a_{ij})$, $1 \leq i, j \leq n$, A and N be $\mathcal{P}$-measurable. In this case $\int^{\oplus} H_s dN_s dP = \{ f_s = (f^1_s, \dots, f^n_s) : A_s f_s$ is $\hat{\mathcal{P}}$-measurable and $\int (f_s, A_s f_s)\, dN_s dP < \infty \}$, assuming that f and g are identified if $\int (f_s - g_s, A_s(f_s - g_s))\, dN_s dP = 0$.

Let f be a n-dimensional $\mathcal{P} \otimes \mathcal{B}(R_+) \otimes \mathcal{B}(D(\mathcal{X}))$ - measurable function, $\widetilde{f}_s = f(s, \omega, s, Y)$. From the definitions and lemma 11 we have the following statment.

Lemma 14. If $f \in \widehat{L}^2_{loc}$, then

$$\check{\tilde{f}}_t = E^{t-}(f_t) = \int f(t, \omega, t, w)\, E^{t-}(dw) =$$
$$= \left(\int f^1(t, \omega, t, w)\, E^{t-}(dw), \ \ldots, \ \int f^n(t, \omega, t, w)\, E^{t-}(dw)\right).$$

§ 5. Densities of the conditional distribution

Let us consider a d-dimensional $(\tilde{P}, \hat{\mathbb{F}})$-semimartingale θ and a filtration $\mathbb{F} \subset \hat{\mathbb{F}}$. Let $(U^i, \mathcal{B}(U^i))$, $i = 1, 2$, be separable measurable spaces, p^i be $\hat{\mathbb{F}}$-optional point processes on $R_+ \times U^i$, $\Pi^i(dt, dx) = \pi^i(t, dx)\, dN_t$ be the corresponding $(\tilde{P}, \hat{\mathbb{F}})$-dual predictable projections, M^1 be continuous m-dimensional $(\tilde{P}, \hat{\mathbb{F}})$-local martingale, M^2 be continuous p- dimensional $(\tilde{P}, \hat{\mathbb{F}})$-local martingale, $d\langle M^{ik}, M^{ij}\rangle_t = a^i_{kj}(t)dN_t$, $A^i = (a^i_{kj})$, assuming that M^1, p^1 are $\mathcal{O}$-measurable and N, π^i, A^i, $i = 1, 2$ are $\mathcal{P}$-measurable.

We shall use later the following assumption.

A1. Assume, that p^1 and p^2 have no common jump times, $a^1_s a^2_s = 0$, $d\Pi^i d\tilde{P}$ - a.e. $\sum_{s \le t} a^i_s < \infty$, where $a^i_s = \Pi^i(\{s\} \times U^i)$, $i = 1, 2$, and there exists $U^i_n \uparrow U^i$ such that $\Pi^i([0, t], U^i_n) < \infty$ for each n, $t \geq 0$.

A2. Assume that $\langle M^{1k}, M^{2j}\rangle = 0$, $k = 1, \ldots, m$, $j = 1, \ldots, p$.

Denoting $\tilde{\Omega} = R_+ \times \Omega$, $p_1 = m$, $p_2 = p$, $L(R^{p_i}, R^d)$ a set of $p_i \times d$-dimensional matrixes, define $\mathcal{P} \otimes \mathcal{B}(R^d)$ - measurable functions $a: \tilde{\Omega} \times R^d \to R^d$, $h: \tilde{\Omega} \times R^d \to R^d$, $\sigma^i: \tilde{\Omega} \times R^d \to L(R^{p_i}, R^d)$, $i = 1, 2$, $\mathcal{P} \otimes \mathcal{B}(R^d) \otimes \mathcal{B}(U^i)$ - -measurable functions $\rho^i: \tilde{\Omega} \times R^d \times U^i \to R^1$, $i = 1, 2$, and $\mathcal{P} \otimes \mathcal{B}(U^i)$- -measurable functions $F^i: \tilde{\Omega} \times U^i \to R^d$, $G^i: \tilde{\Omega} \times U^i \to R^d$, $i=1, 2$, such that $F^i = F^i \chi_{U^{i\,c}_\ell}$, $G^i = G^i \chi_{U^i_\ell}$, $i = 1, 2$ for some integer l.

Denote $H^i = F^i + G^i$, $\tilde{\rho}^i = \rho^i - 1$, $\tilde{\rho}^i_t(\theta) = \tilde{\rho}^i_t(\theta, \cdot)$

B1. Assume that the distribution

$$\tilde{P}(\theta_0 \in \Gamma \mid \mathcal{F}_0), \quad \Gamma \in \mathcal{B}(R^d),$$

has a density $f_0(x)$ with respect to the Lebesgue measure and $f_0 \in H^L(R^d)$ for some integer $L \geq 0$.

B2. Assume that

$$a_t(\theta_{t-}) \Delta N_t = \sum_{i=1}^{2} \int_{U^i} F_t^i(y) \Pi^i(\{t\}, dy) \quad \tilde{P}\text{ - a.e.}$$

and

$$|a_t(\theta) - a_t(\theta')| \leq \delta_t |\theta - \theta'|,$$

where δ is $\mathcal{P}$-measurable and $\int_0^t \delta_s dN_s < \infty$.

B3. Assume that a_t, h_t, $\rho_t^i \in C^L(R^d)$, $\sigma^i \in C^{L+1}(R^d)$, $i = 1, 2$, as functions of θ, $\int_0^t \gamma_s dN_s < \infty$, where

$$\gamma_t = \sup_{\theta, i} \sup_{|\beta| \leq L} \Big(|\partial^\beta a_t| + |\partial^\beta h_t A_t^i \partial^\beta h_t^*| +$$

$$+ \int_{U^i} (\partial^\beta \tilde{\rho}^i - \widehat{\partial^\beta \tilde{\rho}_t^i}) \partial^\beta \tilde{\rho}_t^i \pi^i(t, dy) + \sum_{i=1}^{2} \int |F_t^i(y)|^2 \pi^i(t, dy) +$$

$$+ \sup_{\theta, i} \sup_{|\beta| \leq L+1} |\partial^\beta \sigma_t^i A_t^i \partial^\beta \sigma_t^{i*}|, \text{*)}$$

and, denoting $\Delta_t^{i,\beta}(\theta, \theta') = \partial^\beta \tilde{\rho}_t^i(\theta) - \partial^\beta \tilde{\rho}_t^i(\theta')$,

$$\lim_{\theta' \to \theta} \int_{U^i} (\Delta_t^{i,\beta}(\theta, \theta') - \widehat{\Delta_t^{i,\beta}(\theta, \theta')}) \Delta_t^{i,\beta}(\theta, \theta') \pi^i(t, dy) = 0$$

for each $\theta \in R^d$, $i = 1, 2$, $|\beta| \leq L$, $t \geq 0$.

Recall that we denote $\mathcal{N} = \{(t, \omega) : \Delta N_t = 0\}$.

B4. Assume that for each l there exist a sequence of $\mathbb{F}$-stopping times (T_n), $T_n \uparrow \infty$, the sequences (C_n), (k_n), k_n^l of strictly posi-

---

*) $*$ denotes the sighn of transposing

tive constants such that

a) $\lim\limits_{\ell\to\infty} \sup\limits_{[0,T_n]\cap \mathcal{N}} \int_{U_1^{ic}} |F_t^i(y)|^2 \pi^i(t, dy) = 0, \ i = 1,2;$

b) $\gamma_t \le k_n, \ \pi^i(t, U_1^i) \le k_n^\ell$, $i = 1, 2$, on the set $[0,T_n]\cap \mathcal{N}$;

c) on the set $[0,T_n]\cap \mathcal{N} \times R^d$ for each $\lambda \in R^d$ $\lambda \Gamma_t^i \lambda^* \ge c_n |\lambda|^2$,

where $\Gamma_t^i = \sigma_t^i A_t^i \sigma_t^{i*}$, $i = 1, 2$.

C. Suppose, that

$$d\theta_t = a_t(\theta_{t-})dN_t + \sum_{i=1}^{2} \Big[\sigma_t^i(\theta_{t-})dM_t^i + \int_{U^i} F_t^i(y)q^i(dt, dy) +$$

$$+ \int_{U^i} G_t^i(y)p^i(dt, dy)\Big],$$

$$d\alpha_t = \alpha_{t-}h_t(\theta_{t-})dM_t^1 + \sum_{i=1}^{2} \alpha_{t-} \int_{U^i} \tilde{\rho}_t^i(\theta_{t-}, y)q^i(dt, dy)$$

and each bounded $(\tilde{P}, \mathbb{F})$ martingale can be represented as a sum of stochastic integrals with respect to M^1 and q^1 where $q^i = p^i - \Pi^i$.

From Ito's formula for $f \in C_0^\infty(R^d)$ we find that

$$d(f(\theta_t)\alpha_t) = \alpha_{t-}df(\theta_t) + f(\theta_{t-})d\alpha_t + [f(\theta), \alpha]_t =$$

$$= \alpha_{t-}C_t f(\theta_{t-})dN_t + \sum_{i=1}^{2} \Big[b_t^{ci} f(\theta_{t-})dM_t^i + \int_{U^i} b_t^{di} f(\theta_{t-}, y)q^i(dt, dy)\Big],$$

where $C_t f(\theta) = \bar{C}_t^f(\theta) + \sum_{i=1}^{2} \int_{U^i} C_t^{if}(\theta, y)\pi^i(t, dy)$,

$$\bar{C}_t^f(\theta) = f'(\theta)a_t(\theta) + f'(\theta)\sigma_t^1(\theta)A_t^1 h_t^*(\theta) +$$

$$+ \sum_{i=1}^{2} \sum_{k,j=1}^{d} \partial_{kj}^2 f(\theta)\Gamma_{tkj}^i(\theta),$$

$$C_t^{if}(\theta, y) = f(\theta + H_t^i(y)) - f(\theta) - f'(\theta) F_t^i(y) + (f(\theta + H_t^i(y)) -$$

$-f(\theta))(\tilde{\rho}^{i}_{t}(\theta)-\widehat{\tilde{\rho}^{i}_{t}(\theta)}$, $b^{ci}_{t}f(\theta) =$ ~~$e'(\theta)$~~ $f'(\theta)\sigma^{i}_{t}(\theta)+f(\theta)h^{i}_{t}(\theta)$,

$h^1 = h,\ h^2 = 0,$

$$b^{di}f(\theta,y) = f(\theta + H^{i}_{t}(y))-f(\theta)+f(\theta)\tilde{\rho}^{i}_{t}(\theta,\ y)+(f(\theta+H^{i}_{t}(y))-f(\theta)) \times$$

$$\times(\tilde{\rho}^{i}_{t}(\theta,\ y) - \widehat{\tilde{\rho}^{i}_{t}(\theta)}).$$

Let $\tilde{E}^t$ be a family of measures defined in lemma 7 for $\mathfrak{X} = R^{d+1}$ and $Y = (\theta, \alpha)$. Using lemmas 8, 12, 13, 14 and the assumptions A-C we find that

$$\tilde{E}^t(f(\theta_t)\alpha_t) = \tilde{E}^0(f(\theta_0)) + \int_0^t \tilde{E}^{s-}(\alpha_{s-}\tilde{c}^f_s(\theta_{s-}))dN_s + \sum_{i=1}^{2}\int_0^t \tilde{E}^{s-}(\alpha_{s-} C^{if}_s(\theta_{s-},\ y))\pi^i(s,\ dy)dN_s + \int_0^t \int_{U^1} \tilde{E}^{s-}(\alpha_{s-}b^d_s\, f(\theta_{s-}, y))q^1(ds,\ dy) +$$

$$+ \int_0^t \tilde{E}^{s-}(\alpha_{s-}b^c_s f(\theta_{s-}))dM^1_s\ , \qquad (10),$$

where $b^c = b^{c1}$, $b^d = b^{d1}$.

Lemma 15. Let the assumptions A-C be fulfilled with $L = d+3$. Then there exists σ-measurable $H^0(R^d)$ valued Skorohod process λ such that $\int_0^t |\lambda_s|^2_1\, dN^c_s < \infty$, $t \geq 0$, and for each $\varphi \in C_0^\infty(R^d)$

$$\tilde{E}^t(\varphi(\theta_t)\alpha_t) = (\lambda_t, \varphi)_0.$$

Proof. Let $n = [d/2]+1$, $H = H^n(R^d)$, $V = H^{n+1}(R^d)$, $\Lambda = (1-\Delta)^{-1}$, where Δ is the Laplace operator in R^d. It is known that $\Lambda H^n = H^{n+2}$, $\Lambda: H^n \to H^{n+2}$ is continuous and for each $v \in H^k$, $\eta \in H^{n+k} \cap H^k$

$$(\Lambda^n v, \eta)_{n+k} = (v, \eta)_k.$$

From lemma 10 and the assumptions it follows that there exists σ-measurable H^{n-1} valued process $\bar{\Psi}_t$ which is Skorohod in the weak topology and such that for each $\varphi \in H^{n-1}$

$$\tilde{E}^t(\varphi(\theta_t)\alpha_t) = (\bar{\Psi}_t, \varphi)_{n-1},\quad \tilde{E}^{t-}(\varphi(\theta_{t-})\alpha_{t-}) = (\bar{\Psi}_{t-}, \varphi)_{n-1}.$$

Thus denoting $\psi_t = \Lambda \overline{\psi}_t$ from (10) it follows that

$$(\psi_t, f)_n = (\psi_0, f)_n + \int_0^t (\psi_{s-}, C_s f)_n dN_s + \int_0^t (\psi_{s-}, b_s^c f)_n dM_s^1 +$$

$$+ \int_0^t \int_{U^1} (\psi_{s-}, b_s^d f(\cdot, y))_n q^1(ds, dy). \qquad (12)$$

For $h \in R^1$ and $k: R^d \to R^d$ denote $\delta_h^i k(\theta) = (k(\theta + he_i) - k(\theta))/h$, $\tau_h^i k(\theta) = k(\theta + he_i)$ where e_i is the i-th unit vector. Then

$$(\delta_\varepsilon^i \psi_t, g)_n = \int_0^t (\delta_\varepsilon^i \psi_{s-}, C_s g)_n dN_s + \int_0^t (\delta_\varepsilon^i \psi_{s-}, b_s^c g) dM_s^1 +$$

$$+ \int_0^t \int_{U^1} (\delta_\varepsilon^i \psi_{s-}, b_s^d g(\cdot, y))_n q^1(ds, dy) + \int_0^t (\psi_{s-}, \delta_{-\varepsilon}^i (C_s g) -$$

$$- C_s \delta_{-\varepsilon}^i g)_n dN_s + \int_0^t (\psi_{s-}, \delta_{-\varepsilon}^i (b_s^c g) - b_s^c \delta_{-\varepsilon}^i g)_n dM_s^1 +$$

$$+ \int_0^t \int_{U^1} (\psi_{s-}, \delta_{-\varepsilon}^i (b_s^d g(\cdot, y)) - b_s^d \delta_{-\varepsilon}^i g(y))_n q^1(ds, dy).$$

Let $\overline{V} = C_0^\infty(R^d)$, $\overline{V}^*$ be the algebraic dual of $\overline{V}$. Define mappings $A_t : \overline{V} \to \overline{V}^*$, $A_t^\varepsilon \psi_{t-} : \overline{V} \to R^1$ by means of formulas:

$$\langle A_t f, g \rangle = \sum_{i=1}^2 \int_{U^i} (f, C_t^{ig}(\cdot, y))_n \pi^i(t, dy) + (f, \overline{C}_t g)_n =$$

$$= (f, C_t g)_n,$$

$$\langle A_t^\varepsilon \psi_{t-}, g \rangle = (\psi_{t-}, \delta_{-\varepsilon}^i (C_t g) - C_t \delta_{-\varepsilon}^i g)_n, \quad f, g \in C_0^\infty(R^d).$$

On the set $\mathcal{N}_2^d = \{\Delta N \neq 0\}$ we have that

$$|\langle A_t f, g \rangle| \leq \sum_{k=1}^2 \Big| \int_{U^k} [(g(\cdot + H_t^k(y)) - g(\cdot), f)_n +$$

$$+ ((g(\cdot + H_t^k(y)) - g(\cdot))(\tilde{\rho}_t^k(\cdot, y) - \widehat{\tilde{\rho}}_t^k), f)_n] \pi^k(t, dy)$$

and denoting $\tilde{g}_t^k = g(\theta + H_t^k) - g(\theta)$, $\check{\rho}^k = \tilde{\rho}^k - \widehat{\tilde{\rho}}^k$ for $|\alpha| \leq n$, $\beta + \gamma = \alpha$

find that

$$\Big|\int_{U^k}(\partial^\beta\tilde{g}^k\partial^\gamma\check{\rho}^k,\ \partial^\alpha f)_0\ \pi^k(t,\ dy)\Big| \le \Big|\Big(\int_{U^k}\partial^\beta\tilde{g}^k\partial^\gamma\check{\rho}^k\ \pi^k(t,\ dy),\ \partial^\alpha f\Big)_0\Big| . \tag{13}$$

But

$$\Big|\int_{U^k}\partial^\beta\tilde{g}^k\partial^\gamma\check{\rho}^k\ \pi^k(t,\ dy)\Big| \le \Big(\int_{U^k}|\partial^\beta\tilde{g}^k|^2\ \pi^k(t,dy)\Big)^{1/2}\gamma_t^{1/2}. \tag{14}$$

Thus

$$|\langle A_t f,\ g\rangle| \le \text{const}\sum_k\Big[\ |f|_n\ |g|_n\Big(a_t^k\ \frac{1}{\Delta N_t}+\gamma_t\Big)\Big] .$$

Similarily

$$|\langle A_t^\varepsilon\psi_{t-},\ g\rangle| \le \sum_k\Big|\int_{U^k}(\tau_{-\varepsilon}^i\ \tilde{g}^k\delta_{-\varepsilon}^i\ \check{\rho}^k,\ f)_n\ \pi^k(t,\ dy)$$

and

$$|\langle A_t^\varepsilon\psi_{t-},\ g\rangle| \le \text{const}\,|\psi_{t-}|_n\ |g|_n\sum_k\Big(a_t^k\ \frac{1}{\Delta N_t}+\gamma_t\Big).$$

Further we estimate A_t, A_t^ε on the $\mathcal{N}=\{\Delta N=0\}$.

As on a set $U_r^k(r\ge 1)$

$$g(\theta+H^k)-g(\theta)-g'(\theta)F^k = \int_0^1(1-s)F^k\partial^2 g(\theta+sF^k)F^{k*}ds$$

we have that

$$\Big|\int_{U^k}(\partial^\alpha\tilde{g}_t^k-\partial^\alpha g'F^k,\ \partial^\alpha f)_n\ \pi^k(t,\ dy)\Big| \le \text{const}\Big[|f|_n|g|_{n+1}\Big(\gamma_t +$$

$$+\pi^k(t,\ U_r^k)\Big)+|f|_{n+1}|g|_{n+1}\int_{U_r^{kc}}|F_t^k|^2\ \pi^k(t,\ dy)\Big] .$$

For $|\beta|\le n$ it follows that

$$\int_{U^k}|\partial^\beta\tilde{g}_t^k|^2\ \pi^k(t,\ dy) \le \int_{U_1^k}|\partial^\beta\tilde{g}_t^k|^2\ \pi^k(t,\ dy) +$$

$$+\int_{U^k}\Big(\int_0^1|\partial^\beta g'(\theta+sF^k)|\,|F^k|^2\ ds\Big)\ \pi^k(t,\ dy) .$$

Thus from (13), (14) we find, that

$$\Big|\int_{U^k}(\tilde{g}_t^k\ \check{\tilde{\rho}}_t,\ f)_n\ \pi^k(t,\ dy)\Big| \le \text{const}|g|_{n+1}\ |f|_n\big(\gamma_t+\pi^k(t,\ U_1^k)\big).$$

Similarily

$$\left|\int_{U^k}(\tau^i_{-\varepsilon}\bar{g}^k_t\,\delta^i_{-\varepsilon}\check{\rho}\,,\Psi_{t-})_n\,\pi^k(t,\,dy)\right| \le \mathrm{const}|g|_{n+1}|\Psi_{t-}|_n(\gamma_t +$$
$$+\pi^k(t,\,U^k_1).$$

Let

$$A^k_t(f,\,g) = \sum_{|\alpha|=n}(\partial^\alpha f'\Gamma^k_t,\,\partial^\alpha g')_0,$$

$$B^k_t(f,\,g) = (\sum_{l,j}\partial^2_{kj}\,g\Gamma^k_{tlj},\,f)_n + A^k_t(f,\,g).$$

Then

$$\left|B^k_t\,(f,\,g)\right| \le \mathrm{const}\sum_{\substack{|\alpha|\le n\\ \beta+\gamma+\varkappa=\alpha\\ |\beta|<n}}\ \sum_{l,j}\,(\partial^\beta\partial^2_{lj}\,g(\partial^\gamma\sigma^k A^k\partial^\varkappa\sigma^{k*})_{lj},\partial^\alpha f)_0 \le$$

$$\le \mathrm{const}\ \gamma_t|g|_V|f|_H\ ,$$

as

$$|\partial^\gamma\sigma^k A^k\partial^\varkappa\sigma^{k*}| \le |\partial^\gamma\sigma^k A^k\partial^\gamma\sigma^{k*}|^{1/2}\ |\partial^\varkappa\sigma^k A^k\ \partial^\varkappa\sigma^{k*}|^{1/2}.$$

Analoguously for each $\alpha=\beta+\gamma+\varkappa$, $|\alpha|\le n$

$$|(\partial^\beta\partial^2_{lj}\,\tau^k_{-\varepsilon}g(\partial^\gamma\tau^k_{-\varepsilon}\,\sigma^k A^k\ \partial^\varkappa\tau^k_{-\varepsilon}\sigma^{k*})_{lj},\ \partial^\alpha\Psi_-)_0| \le$$
$$\le \mathrm{const}\ \ \gamma_t\,|\Psi_{t-}|_{n+1}\,|g|_{n+1}\ ,$$

$$|(g'a_t,\,f)_n| \le \gamma_t|g|_{n+1}|f|_n\ ,$$
$$|(\tau^k_{-\varepsilon}\,g'\,\delta^k_{-\varepsilon}a_t,\,\Psi_{t-})_n| \le \gamma_t|g|_{n+1}|\Psi_{t-}|_n,$$
$$|(g'\sigma^1_tA^1_th,\,f)_n| \le \mathrm{const}\ |g|_{n+1}|f|_n$$

and

$$|(\,\delta^k_{-\varepsilon}(g'\sigma^1_tA^1_th) - \delta^k_{-\varepsilon}g\,\sigma^1_tA^1_th,\ \Psi_{t-})_n| \le \mathrm{const}\,|g|_{n+1}\,|\Psi_{t-}|_n.$$

Define the mappings B^c_t, $B^{c,\varepsilon}_t : \bar{V}\longrightarrow L_2(H,\mathcal{H}_{Q^{M^1}_t})$ by means of the equalities

$$\langle B^c_tf,\,g\rangle = (f,\,\bar{b}^c_tg)_n,\quad \langle B^{c,\varepsilon}_t\Psi\,,\,g\rangle = (\Psi_{t-},\,\bar{b}^{c,\varepsilon}_t\,g)_n,$$

where $f,\,g\in C_0^\infty\,(R^d)$,

$\tilde{b}^c_t = u_t b^c_t$, $\tilde{b}^{c,\varepsilon}_t g = u_t(\delta^i_{-\varepsilon}(b^c_t g) - b^c_t\ \delta^i_{-\varepsilon} g)$, $u_t = (A^1_t)^{1/2}$.

For $\beta + \gamma = \alpha$, $|\beta| < |\alpha| = n$ we have that

$$|(\partial^\beta g' \partial^\gamma \sigma^1_t u_t, \partial^\alpha f)_0| \leq \gamma^{1/2}_t\ |g|_H |f|_H .$$

For $|\alpha| = |\beta| = n$

$$|(\partial^\alpha g' \sigma^1_t u^t, \partial^\alpha f)_0| \leq |g|_H\ (\partial^\alpha f' \Gamma_t, \partial^\alpha f')^{1/2}_0 + \gamma^{1/2}_t |f|_H |g|_H .$$

Thus for each $\varepsilon > 0$

$$|B^c_t f|^2_{L^2(H, \mathcal{H}_{Q^{M'}_t})} \leq (1+\varepsilon)\ A^1_t(f, f) + \text{const}(\varepsilon) \cdot \gamma_t |f|^2_n .$$

Analoguously

$$|B^{c,\varepsilon}_t \psi_{t-}|^2_{L^2(H, \mathcal{H}_{Q^{M'}_t})} \leq \text{const}\ \gamma_t |\psi_{t-}|_{n+1} .$$

Define now the mappings $B^d_t : \tilde{V} \to L_2(H, \mathcal{H}_{Q^{q}_t 1})$, $B^{d,\varepsilon}_t : \tilde{V} \to$

$\to L_2(H, \mathcal{H}_{Q^{q}_t 1})$ by means of the equalities

$$\langle B^d_t f, g \rangle = (f, b^d_t g)_n, \quad \langle B^{d\varepsilon}_t f, g \rangle = (\psi_{t-}, \delta^i_{-\varepsilon}\ b^d_t g)_n -$$

$$-b^d_t\ \delta^i_{-\varepsilon} g)_n,\ f, g\ \ C^\infty_0(R^d).$$

For $\beta + \gamma = \alpha$, $|\alpha| \leq n$, we have that

$$|(\partial^\beta \tilde{g}^1_t\ \partial^\gamma \check{\tilde{\rho}}^1_t, \partial^\alpha f)_0|^2 \leq \text{const}\ \ |g|^2_n |\partial^\gamma \check{\tilde{\rho}}^1 \partial^\alpha f|^2_0 ,$$

$$|(\partial^\beta g\ \widehat{\partial^\gamma \tilde{\rho}^1}, \partial^\alpha f)_0|^2 \leq \text{const}\ |g_n|^2\ \ |\partial^\alpha f\ \widehat{\partial^\gamma \tilde{\rho}^1}|^2_0$$

and for each $r \geq 1$

$$|(\partial^\alpha f, \partial^\gamma \tilde{g}^1)_0|^2 \leq \text{const}\Big[\chi_{U^{1c}_r}(y)\ |F^k_t(y)|^2 |f|^2_{n+1} |g|^2_n +$$

$$+ \chi_{U^1_r}(y)\ |f|^2_n\ |g|^2_n\Big],\ \text{denoting}\ U^1_\infty = U^1.$$

Thus

$$|B_t^d f|^2_{L^2(H,\mathcal{R}_{Q_t^{q'}})} \le \text{const}\Big[\chi_{\mathcal{N}}{}^d |f|_n^2 \ a_t^1 \ \frac{1}{\Delta N_t} + \chi_{\mathcal{N}}(|f|^2_{n+1}\int_{U_r^{1c}} |F_t^1|^2 \times$$

$$\times \pi^1(t, dy) + |f|_n^2 (\pi^1(t, U_2^1) + \gamma_t))\Big] \ .$$

Analoguously

$$|B_t^{d,\varepsilon} f|^2_{L^2(H,\mathcal{X}_{Q_t^{q'}})} \le \text{const}\ \gamma_t |\Psi_{t-}|_n \ .$$

Using inequality

$$|ab| \le \frac{\varepsilon}{2} a^2 + \frac{1}{2} b^2, \quad a, b \in R^1, \ \varepsilon > 0$$

from the assumptions of lemma and the above estimations it foll ows that $\delta_\varepsilon^i \Psi_t$ satisfies the assumptions of theorem 2′ with $\varepsilon_0 > 0$, $H = H^n$, $V = H^{n+1}$. So we conclude that there exists $\partial_i \Psi_t$ which is Skorohod in H, $\int_0^t |\partial_i \Psi_s|_V^2 \, dN_s^c < \infty$ and $\partial_i \Psi_t$ is defined by the equation:

$$(\partial^\alpha \Psi_t, g)_n = \int_0^t (\partial^\alpha \Psi_{s-}, C_s g)_n \, dN_s + \int_0^t (\partial^\alpha \Psi_{s-}, b_s^c g)_n \, dM_s^1 +$$

$$+ \int_0^t \int_{U^1} (\partial^\alpha \Psi_{s-}, b_s^d g(\cdot, y))_n q^1(ds, dy) + (-1)^{|\alpha|} \int_0^t (\Psi_{s-}, C_s \partial^\alpha g -$$

$$- \partial^\alpha (C_s g))_n dN_s + \int_0^t (\Psi_{s-}, b_s^c \partial^\alpha g - \partial^\alpha (b_s^c g))_n \, dM_s^1 +$$

$$+ \int_0^t \int_{U^1} (\Psi_{s-}, b_s^d \partial^\alpha g(\cdot, y) - \partial^\alpha (b_s^d g(\cdot, y))_n q^1(ds, dy) \ , \qquad (15)$$

$g \in C_0^\infty(R^d)$, $\alpha = e_i$.

Using analoguous approximations and applying induction we obtain that there exist derivatives $\partial^\alpha \Psi_t$ for each α, $|\alpha| \le [\frac{d}{2}] + 1$, which are Skorohod in H, $\int_0^t |\partial^\alpha \Psi_{t-}|_V^2 \, dN_s < \infty$ and satisfy (15).

Noting that

$$(\Psi_t, f)_n = \sum_{|\alpha| \le n} r_n^\alpha (\partial^\alpha \Psi_t, \partial^\alpha f)_0 = \sum_{|\alpha| \le n} r_n^\alpha (-1)^{|\alpha|} (\partial^{2\alpha} \Psi_t, f)_0$$

we find that $\lambda_t = \sum_{|\alpha|\le n} r_n^{\alpha}(-1)^{|\alpha|}\partial^{2\alpha}\psi_t$ satisfy (11).

Lemma 15 is proved.

Remark, that λ is defined by the equation (12) with n = 0.

Theorem 3. Under assumptions A-C there exists $\mathcal{O}$-measurable H^L-valued Skorohod process Ψ such that $\int_0^t |\Psi_{s-}|^2_{H^{L+1}}\, dN_s^c < \infty$ and for each $f \in C_0^{\infty}(R^d)$ ${}^1(f(\theta)\alpha)_t = (\Psi_t, f)_0$.

Proof. Denoting f_0^{ε}, a^{ε}, $\sigma^{k\varepsilon}$, h^{ε}, $\rho^{k\varepsilon}$ the convolutions of f_0, a, σ^k, h, ρ^k with the function

$\omega_{\varepsilon}(\theta) = C(\varepsilon)\exp\{-\frac{|\theta|^2}{\varepsilon^2-|\theta|^2}\}$, if $|\theta|<\varepsilon$, $= 0$, if $|\theta|\ge\varepsilon$, $C(\varepsilon) = (\int \omega_{\varepsilon}(\theta)d\theta)^{-1}$,

define the corresponding stochastic process θ^{ε} and α^{ε} which will satisfy the assumptions of lemma 15. According to this lemma there exist $\mathcal{O}$-measurable H^0 valued Skorohod process λ^{ε} such that $\int_0^t |\lambda^{\varepsilon}_{s-}|_1^2\, dN_s^c < \infty$ and for each $f \in C_0^{\infty}(R^d)$ ${}^1(f(\theta^{\varepsilon})\alpha^{\varepsilon})_t =$

$= (\lambda^{\varepsilon}_t, f)_0$. It is obvious that λ^{ε}_t is defined by the equation

$$(\lambda^{\varepsilon}_t, f)_0 = (\lambda^{\varepsilon}_0, f)_0 + \int_0^t (\lambda^{\varepsilon}_{s-}, C_s^{\varepsilon} f)_0\, dN_s +$$

$$+ \int_0^t (\lambda^{\varepsilon}_s, b_s^{c\varepsilon} f)_0 dM_s^1 + \int_0^t \int_{U^1} (\lambda^{\varepsilon}_{s-}, b_s^{d\varepsilon} f(\cdot, y))_0\, q^1(ds, dy), \quad (16)$$

where C_s^{ε}, $b_s^{c\varepsilon}$, $b_s^{d\varepsilon}$ are obtained from the expressions for C_s, b_s^c, b_s^d by changing a, σ^k, h, ρ^k to a, $\sigma^{k\varepsilon}$, h^{ε}, $\rho^{k\varepsilon}$. As in the case of lemma 15 it is not difficult to check that the assumptions of theorem 2' are satisfied for the equation (16). So there exist a H^0-valued process λ such that in probability

$$\lim_{\varepsilon\to 0} \sup_{t\le T} |\lambda^{\varepsilon}_t - \lambda_t|_0 = 0, \quad \lim_{\varepsilon\to 0} \int_0^T |\lambda^{\varepsilon}_s - \lambda_s|_1^2\, dN_s^c = 0, \ T \ge 0,$$

and λ satisfy (16) with C^{ε}, $b^{c\varepsilon}$, $b^{d\varepsilon}$ changed to C, b^c, b^d. Using theorem 2' again and taking approximations like in the proof of lemma 15, we obtain that λ is Skorohod in H^L and $\int_0^t |\lambda_s|^2_{L+1}\, dN_s^c < \infty$. From other hand it is easy to see that $\sup_{t\leq T} |\theta^{\varepsilon}_t - \theta_t| \to 0$, $\sup_{t\leq T}|\alpha^{\varepsilon}_t - \alpha_t| \to 0$ in probability as $\varepsilon \to 0$ 0, $T \geq 0$, and there exist a sequence (T_n), $T_n \in \mathcal{T}$, $T_n \uparrow \infty$, such that for each n $\sup_{\varepsilon>0} E\left[\sup_t |\alpha^{\varepsilon}_{t\wedge T_n}|^2\right] < \infty$ which to-gether with equality ${}^1(f(\theta^{\varepsilon})\alpha^{\varepsilon})_t = (\lambda^{\varepsilon}_t, f)_0$ give us that ${}^1(f(\theta)\alpha)_t = (\lambda_t, f)_0$, $f \in C_0^{\infty}(R^d)$. Theorem 3 is proved.

Institute of Mathematics and Cybernetics

Academy of Sciences of the Lithuanian SSR

University of Vilnius

References

1. Jacod J. Calcul stochastique et problèmes de martingales. - Lecture Notes in Math., 714 , Springer-Verlag, 1979.

2. Krylov N.V., Rozovskiĭ B.L. On the Cauchy problem for linear stochastic partial differential equations. - Math. USSR Izvestija, 1977, vol.11, p.1267-1284.

3. Krylov N.V., Rozovskiĭ B.L. On conditional distributions of diffusion processes. - Math. USSR Izvestija, 1978, vol.12, p.336-356.

4. Pardoux E. Stochastic partial differential equations and filtering of diffusion processes. - Stochastics, 1979, vol.3, p.127-167.

5. Tinfavičius E. On the conditional distributions of discontinuous processes. I, II. - Lietuvos matem.rinkinys, 1980, vol.20, No 1, p.175-191; No 4, p.187-199.

6. Krylov N.V., Rozovskiĭ B.L. On evolution stochastic equations. - Ser.Modern problems of mathematics, vol.14, VINITI, Moscow, 1979, p.71-146 (in Russian).

7. Gyöngy I., Krylov N.V. On stochastic equations with respect to semimartingales. I. - Stochastics, 1980, vol.4, No 1, p.1-21.

8. Gyöngy I., Krylov N.V. On stochastic equations with respect to semimartingales. II. Ito formula. - Stochastics, 1982, vol.6, No 3-4, p.153-173.

9. Duncan T.E. Fréchet-valued martingales and stochastic integrals. - Stochastics, 1975, vol.1, No 4, p.269-284.

10. Hitsuda M., Watanabe H. On stochastic integrals with respect to an infinite number of Brownian motions and its applications. - Proc. of Intern.Symp.SDE, Kyoto, 1976, p.57-74.

11. Schwartz L. Sous-espaces hilbertiens d'espaces vectoriels topologiques et noyaux associés (noyaux reproduisant). - Journal d'Analyse Mathématique, 1964, t.13, p.115-256.

12. Schaefer H.H. Topological vector spaces. The MacMillan Ca., New York, 1961.

13. Dixmier J. Les algèbres d'opérateurs dans l'espaces hilbertien. Paris, Gauthiers-Willars, 1957.

14. Yor M. Les inégalités de sous-martingales, comme conséquences de la relation de domination. - Stochastics , 1979, vol.3, Nol, p.1-15.

15. Dellacherie C. Capacités et processus stochastiques. - Ergebn. der Math., vol. 67, Springer, Berlin, 1972.

16. Bremaud P., Yor M. Changes of filtrations and of probability measures. - Z. Wahrscheinlichkeitstheorie verw.Geb., 1978, B.45, H.4, S.269-295.

17. Meyer P.A. La theorie de la prediction de F.Knight. - Sém.Probab., X, Lecture Notes in Math., 511, p.86-103, Springer-Verlag, 1976.

Generalized Brownian Functionals

Takeyuki HIDA
Department of Mathematics
Faculty of Science
Nagoya University
Chikusa-ku, Nagoya, 464 Japan

§0. Introduction

Let $\{B(t) ; t \in R^1\}$ be a standard Brownian motion. The time derivative $\frac{d}{dt}B(t) = \dot{B}(t)$ defines a white noise $\{\dot{B}(t) ; t \in R^1\}$. We shall consider complex-valued functionals such as

(1) $\varphi(\dot{B}(t) ; t \in R^1)$

and discuss their analysis. Those functionals are often called Brownian functionals. Realizations of them are obtained in terms of a Hilbert space $L^2(\mathcal{S}^*, \mu)$, where $\mathcal{S}^*$ and μ are the space of tempered distributions and the probability distribution of $\{\dot{B}(t) ; t \in R^1\}$, respectively. Such a background will be reviewed quickly in Section 1.

There were several motivations, as we explained in the papers [3], [4] and [5], in introducing the concept of a generalized Brownian functional, however the main idea is that the space of Brownian functionals should be extended so as the causal calculus to be carried out. By the causal calculus we mean the analysis of Brownian functionals, the development of time being always taken into account. The $\{\dot{B}(t)\}$ is naturally thought of as a variable system of functionals and the transformation $\dot{B}(s) \to \dot{B}(s+t)$ is a representation of the time shift.

There are, of course, many ways of introducing a class of generalized Brownian functionals, and the way of generalization would depend upon what one has in mind on the development of his analysis. Actually, while we were discussing an application of our calculus to Feynman path integrals, we saw that a Brownian bridge is taken to be fluctuation for trajectories of a particle. The acceleration is therefore involving the second derivative $\ddot{B}(t)$, the functionals of which would be our concern. The effect of bridge requires to use delta-function such as $\delta(B(t) - a)$ (see [7]), which belongs to another kind of generalized Brownian functionals.

On the other hand, observing a connection between the integral representation (see Section 1) of Brownian functionals and the classical theory of functionals on $L^2[0,1]$, we can think of a class of more general Brownian functionals. (See, specifically, P. Lévy [2].) We are thus led in Section 2 to provide a larger space of much generalized Brownian functionals involving polynomials in higher order derivatives of Brownian motion.

Some concluding remarks will be in order in the last section.

§1. Preliminaries

Our first step is to introduce the probability distribution μ of white noise $\{\dot{B}(t)\}$. Since almost all sample functions of $\dot{B}(t)$ are generalized functions, the distribution μ has to be supported by a space of generalized functions, say by $\mathcal{S}^*$ the dual space of the Schwartz space $\mathcal{S}$.

Start with the characteristic functional $C(\xi)$ of white noise :

$$(2) \qquad C(\xi) \equiv E\{\exp[i\dot{B}(\xi)]\} = \exp[-\tfrac{1}{2}\|\xi\|^2], \quad \xi \in \mathcal{S},$$

and appeal to the Bochner-Minlos theorem which guarantees the existence and the uniqueness of the measure μ on the measurable space $(\mathcal{S}^*, \mathcal{B})$ such that

$$(3) \qquad C(\xi) = \int_{\mathcal{S}^*} \exp[i\langle x, \xi\rangle]\, d\mu(x),$$

where $\mathcal{B}$ is the σ-field generated by cylinder sets. This measure μ obtained above is nothing but the probability distribution of $\{\dot{B}(t)\}$. With this μ almost every $x \in \mathcal{S}^*$ is viewed as a sample or a path function of $\dot{B}(t)$. Set $(L^2) \equiv L^2(\mathcal{S}^*, \mathcal{B}, \mu)$, the complex Hilbert space. Any $\varphi(x)$ in (L^2) is a realization of a Brownian functional of the form (1) with finite variance.

The Hilbert space (L^2) admits the direct sum decomposition :

$$(L^2) = \sum_{n=0}^{\infty} \oplus \mathcal{H}_n,$$

where $\mathcal{H}_n$ is the space of multiple Wiener integrals of degree n.

In order to have a visualized representation of (L^2)- or $\mathcal{H}_n$-functionals we introduce a transformation $\mathcal{T}$ that carries (L^2) to a space of functionals on $\mathcal{S}$. Namely

$$(4) \qquad (\mathcal{T}\varphi)(\xi) = \int_{\mathcal{S}^*} \exp[i\langle x, \xi\rangle]\varphi(x)\,d\mu(x).$$

Theorem 1. If φ is an $\mathcal{H}_n$-functional, then there exists a unique function F in $\widehat{L^2}(R^n)$ (symmetric $L^2(R^n)$-functions) such that

$$(5) \qquad (\mathcal{T}\varphi)(\xi) = i^n C(\xi)U(\xi)$$

$$U(\xi) = \int_{R^n} F(u_1,\cdots,u_n)\xi(u_1)\cdots\xi(u_n)\,du^n.$$

The mapping $\varphi \to F$ from $\mathcal{H}_n$ to $\widehat{L^2(R^n)}$ is surjective and we have

(6') $$\|\varphi\|_{(L^2)} = \sqrt{n!}\,\|F\|_{L^2(R^n)}.$$

(Integral Representation.)

It should now be reminded that any φ in (L^2) is $\mathcal{B}$-measurable, namely φ is a realization of not a function of $\dot{B}(t)$'s themselves but a function of $\dot{B}(\xi)$'s the smeared variables. In the next section we shall go one step further to deal with functionals, the variable system of which is taken to be $\{\dot{B}(t)\}$.

§2. Generalized Brownian functionals.

We are interested, as was briefly mentioned in Section 1, in developing a causal calculus of Brownian functionals, where the evolution in time is taken into account explicitly. The basic idea is to take $\{\dot{B}(t)\}$ to be the variable system of Brownian functionals. The system $\{\dot{B}(t)\}$ is a continuous analogue of a sequence of i.i.d. (independent identically distributed) random variables. It is therefore quite natural to take

i) polynomials in $\dot{B}(t)$'s,

ii) exponential functions of $\dot{B}(t)$'s,

to be the basic functionals.

It is noted that each $\dot{B}(t)$ is a variable of Brownian functionals and at the same time $\dot{B}(t)$ itself should be viewed as a simplest generalized Brownian functional in the sense that the kernel of the integral representation is delta-function. As for the polynomials in $\dot{B}(t)$, in particular Hermite polynomials of degree n, they live in the class $\mathcal{H}_n^{(-n)}$ that is determined by the following diagram :

Diagram 1

$$\begin{array}{ccc} \mathcal{H}_n^{(-n)} & \cong & \sqrt{n!}\ \widehat{H^{-(n+1)/2}}(R^n) \\ \cup & & \cup \\ \mathcal{H}_n & \cong & \sqrt{n!}\ \widehat{L^2}(R^n) , \end{array}$$

where the lower isomorphism is a brief rephrasement of Theorem 1, $H^m(R^n)$ denotes the Sobolev space of order m over R^n, and $\widehat{\ }$ means "symmetric". With the $\mathcal{H}_n^{(-n)}$ as well as their sum, we are able to carry out the causal calculus (see [3],[4] and [5]).

Having been motivated by the applications to the Feynman path integrals and by the Lévy's work [2], we come to a position to discuss

i') polynomials in $\ddot{B}(t)$'s

iii) delta-functions such as $\delta(B(t) - a)$.

To invite Hermite polynomials in $\ddot{B}(t)$'s of degree n to a class of generalized Brownian functionals, the Sobolev space in the Diagram 1 should be replaced by $\widehat{H^{-(3n+1)/2}(R^n)}$, since, for instance, the kernel of the integral representation of $:\ddot{B}(t)^n: = n!H_n(\ddot{B}(t)\ ;\ 2/(dt)^3)$ is

(7) $\delta_t' \otimes \delta_t' \otimes \cdots \otimes \delta_t'$ (n-times tensor product),

where δ_t' is the derivative of delta-function δ_t.

Diagram 2

$$\begin{array}{ccc} \mathcal{H}_n^{(-n)} & \cong & \sqrt{n!}\ \widehat{H^{-(3n+1)/2}(R^n)} \\ \cup & & \cup \\ \mathcal{H}_n & \cong & \sqrt{n!}\ \widehat{L^2(R^n)}\ . \end{array}$$

We note that there is a freedom in how to sum up the spaces $\mathcal{H}_n^{(-n)}$ to form an entire space $(L^2)^-$ of generalized Brownian functionals. We may take a non-increasing sequence $\{a_n\}$ of positive numbers to form

(8) $$(L^2)^- = \sum_n \oplus\, a_n \mathcal{H}_n^{(-n)}.$$

The choice of the sequence, of course, depends upon what kind of generalized Brownian functionals are to be discussed.

Exponential functions, as we have discussed in [4], play a very important role in our calculus. We now prove

Theorem 2. Let $\mathcal{H}_n^{(-n)}$ be given by Diagram 2 and take $\{a_n\}$ in (8) to be

(9) $a_n = 1$.

Then the renormalized exponential function of $i\ddot{B}(t)$:

(10) $\varphi = :\exp[i\ddot{B}(t)]:$

belongs to the space $(L^2)^-$ of generalized Brownian functionals defined by (8). The $\mathcal{T}$-transform of φ is

(11) $\exp[\xi'(t)]$.

Proof. The renormalization of $\exp[i\ddot{B}(t)]$ can be done in a similar manner to $\exp[i\dot{B}(t)]$ in [7]. In fact,

$$\begin{aligned}\varphi = :\exp[i\ddot{B}(t)]: &= \exp[i\ddot{B}(t) + 1/dt^3] \\ &= \sum_{n=0}^{\infty} i^n H_n(\ddot{B}(t)\ :\ 2/dt^3)\end{aligned}$$

$$\equiv \Sigma \varphi_n,$$

where $H_n(x\ ;\ \sigma^2)$ is the Hermite polynomial of degree n with parameter σ^2. The above expression is of course a formal expression, however the exact meaning will be given in exactly the same manner as in [3, vol.II].

Now observe the $\mathcal{H}_n^{(-n)}$-norm of φ_n, which is $\sqrt{n!}\cdot H^{-(3n+1)/2}(R^n)$-norm of the kernel given by (7). Its actual value is proportional to $c^n n^{-3n/2}$ with $c > 1$. The rest of the proof is now straightforward.

A generalized Brownian functional which is expressed in the form

(12) $\varphi = \delta(B(t) - y)$, y real, δ the delta-function,

arose (see [7]) where the Feynman path integrals are discussed. Such a functional serves to give the effect of pinning a Brownian trajectories to y at instant t. There are several ways to give enough interpretation to φ in (12) so that φ is understood as a generalized Brownian functional. In fact, in the paper [7] we approximate the delta-function by the Gauss kernel and then let the variance tend to zero. An alternative way to give interpretation is to express the delta-function as the Fourier transform of a constant function. (See the paper by Professor H.-H. Kuo in this proceedings, and for related results see also Professor I.Kubo's paper.)

We now remind the results in [7] concerning the approximation to φ in (12), by the use of the Gauss kernel. For $\varepsilon > 0$, we set

$$\varphi_\varepsilon = \delta_\varepsilon(B(t) - y) \equiv (\pi\varepsilon)^{-1/2} \exp[-\tfrac{1}{\varepsilon}\{B(t) - y\}^2].$$

Then the $\mathcal{T}$-transform of φ_ε can be given explicitly :

$$(\mathcal{T}\varphi_\varepsilon)(\xi) = \{\pi(2t + \varepsilon)\}^{-1/2}C(\xi) \exp[\tfrac{1}{2t+\varepsilon}(\int_0^t \xi(s)ds)^2 + $$
$$+ \tfrac{2iy}{2t+\varepsilon}\int_0^t \xi(s)ds - \tfrac{y^2}{2t+\varepsilon}].$$

Note that the limit of this expression, as $\varepsilon \to 0+$, produces an admissible functional

$$f(\xi) = (2\pi t)^{-1/2}C(\xi) \exp[-\tfrac{1}{2t}\{y - i\int_0^t \xi(s)ds\}^2].$$

Divide it by $(\mathcal{T}\varphi)(0)$ (i.e. apply the multiplicative renormalization) to obtain the functional associated with $E\{\exp[i\dot{B}(\xi)]/B(t) = y\}$:

(13) $$\tilde{f}(\xi) = C(\xi) \exp[\tfrac{iy}{t}\int_0^t \xi(s)ds + \tfrac{1}{2t}(\int_0^t \xi(s)ds)^2].$$

The exact meaning of the Brownian functional φ given in (12) should now be understood as

(14) $\varphi = \mathcal{T}^{-1}(f(\xi))$, provided that $f \in \mathcal{T}(\sum_n \oplus a_n \mathcal{H}_n^{(-n)})$.

If we observe the expansion of $\tilde{f}(\xi)$.

(15) $$\tilde{f}(\xi) = C(\xi)\sum_{n=0}^{\infty} \frac{\pm^n}{n!} \frac{H_n(y/\sqrt{2t})}{(2t)^{n/2}} \int_0^t \cdots \int_0^t \xi(u_1)\cdots\xi(u_n)du^n,$$

we see that the n-th term corresponds to an ordinary $\mathcal{H}_n$-functional. The square of its $\mathcal{H}_n$-norm is

$$n!\cdot\frac{1}{(n!)^2}\cdot\frac{|H_n(y/\sqrt{2t})|^2}{(2t)^n}\ \|\chi_{[0,t]^n}\|^2$$

$$= \frac{1}{n!}\cdot\frac{|H_n(y/\sqrt{2t})|^2}{2^n}$$

$$= O(n^{-1/2}).$$

This means that the series in (15) does not correspond to a convergent series of $\mathcal{H}_n$-functionals. However the above computations prove

Theorem 3. The functional φ in (12) can be made to be a generalized Brownian functional living in the Hilbert space

(16) $$\sum_{n=0}^{\infty} \oplus\ a_n \mathcal{H}_n,$$

where a_n is taken so as the series $\sum_n a_n^2 \frac{|H_n(y/\sqrt{2t})|^2}{n!2^n}$ to be convergent, say $a_n = n^{-1}$.

§3. Concluding remarks.

Three remarks are now in order.

1) The first remark is concerned with how to define $(L^2)^-$ the space of generalized Brownian functionals. In order to introduce polynomials in $\ddot{B}(t)$'s in addition to those in $\dot{B}(t)$'s, we extend Diagram 1 to Diagram 2. If one wants further to introduce polynomials in higher order time derivatives $(\frac{d}{dt})^k B(t)$, $k \le p$, of a Brownian motion, then the order of the Sobolev space in the Diagram 1 or 2 should be replaced by that of order $-\{(2p - 1)n + 1\}/2$. Now, one may ask if we can choose a universal space, large enough, say $\mathcal{J}^*$ the subspace of the distributions $\mathcal{S}^*$ involving symmetric functions, in place of a symmetric Sobolev space in the diagrams. This might be a good idea, of course, although Hilbert space structure is missing. While the way done in the last section is rather economical, i.e. the extension of $\mathcal{H}_n$ is not too wide. In addition, it is convenient to form a weighted sum of the $\mathcal{H}_n^{(-n)}$ like (7). Once again, we say that the way of

generalization heavily depends upon what one has in mind on the development of his analysis.

ii) Multidimensional parameter white noise is a generalized Gaussian random field with the characteristic functional

$$C(\xi) = \exp[-\frac{1}{2}\|\xi\|^2], \quad \xi \in \mathcal{S}(R^d), \quad \|\ \| \text{ the } L^2(R^d)\text{-norm}.$$

Similar analysis can be established in this case, and we expect to discuss applications to constructive field theory.

iii) Important applications will be found in the field of nonlinear analysis of stochastic processes, in particular those processes determined by stochastic differential equations involving polynomials in the processes in question. Some results are obtained by Professor G. Kallianpur and the present author, in connection with nonlinear prediction problems, and they will be published elsewhere soon.

References

[1] P. Lévy, Problèmes concrets d'analyse fonctionnelle, Gauthier-Villars, Paris, 1951.

[2] ———, Fonctions de lignes et équations aux dérivées fonctionnelles, Proc. XIII International conference on History of Sciences, Moscow, 1971. Also in Oeuvres de Paul Lévy, I. pp.343-357.

[3] T. Hida, Analysis of Brownian functionals, Carleton Math. Lecture Notes no.13, 2nd ed. 1978,Carleton Univ. Ottawa; vol.II to appear 1982.

[4] ——— , Brownian motion, Springer-Verlag, New York 1980, Applications of Math. vol.11.

[5] ——— , Causal calculus of Brownian functionals, Statistics and Related Topics, ed.M. Csörgö et al. North-Holland Pub. Co., 1981, pp. 353-360.

[6] I.Kubo and S.Takenaka, Calculus on Gaussian white noise. I, II, Proc. Japan Academy. 56 (1980), 376-380, 411-416.

[7] L. Streit and T. Hida, Generalized Brownian functionals and the Feynman integrals, to appear in Stochastic Processes and their Applications.

TOWARDS A THEORY OF NONCOMMUTATIVE SEMIMARTINGALES ADAPTED TO BROWNIAN MOTION AND A QUANTUM ITO'S FORMULA

by

R.L. HUDSON, R.L. KARANDIKAR AND K.R. PARTHASARATHY

The University of Nottingham, Indian Statistical Institute, Calcutta, Indian Statistical Institute, Delhi

§ 1. Introduction : In order to develop a theory of 'stochastic differential equations' for noncommuting observables arising in quantum mechanics it seems desirable to introduce the notion of operator valued semimartingales in a continuous tensor product of Hilbert spaces over the interval $[0,\infty)$ and study their 'differentials'. Instead of plunging straightaway into such a programme we restrict ourselves to the special case when the Hilbert space under consideration is $L_2(P)$ where P is the probability measure of the standard Brownian motion process. Since Brownian motion has independent increments $L_2(P)$ can be viewed as a continuous tensor product over $[0,\infty)$. Even in this special case our theory is beset with many difficulties since all the operators of interest are unbounded. The main justification for presenting this somewhat brief and tentative account is a wealth of interesting examples leading to a natural conjecture which may justly be called a 'quantum mechanical Ito's formula'.

Using the concepts developed here it is, indeed, possible to construct specific examples of 'quantum diffusion processes' for canonical position and momentum operators $\{q(t), p(t); t \geq 0\}$, where $[q(t), p(t)] = i$ for all t. However, we postpone such an investigation to a separate article.

§ 2. Preliminaries : Let $\mathfrak{h}$ be a fixed complex separable Hilbert space and let $(\Omega, \mathcal{F}, P)$ be the probability space of the standard Brownian motion process. Thus Ω is the space of all real valued continuous functions on $[0,\infty)$ vanishing at 0. We write $\mathcal{F}_t = \sigma\{w(s), s \leq t\}$, $\mathcal{F}^t = \sigma\{w(s)-w(t), s > t\}$ respectively for the σ-algebras of the Brownian motion upto time t and its increments after time t. Define the Hilbert spaces

$$\mathcal{H} = L_2(\Omega, \mathcal{F}, P), \quad \mathcal{H}_t = L_2(\Omega, \mathcal{F}_t, P), \quad \mathcal{H}^t = L_2(\Omega, \mathcal{F}^t, P)$$

$$\tilde{\mathcal{H}} = \mathfrak{h} \otimes \mathcal{H}, \quad \tilde{\mathcal{H}}_t = \mathfrak{h} \otimes \mathcal{H}_t$$

and observe that $\tilde{\mathcal{H}}_t = \tilde{\mathcal{H}}_s \otimes \mathcal{H}(s,t)$, where $\mathcal{H}(s,t) \subset \mathcal{H}$ is the subspace of functions which are measurable with respect to the σ-algebra generated by the increments of the Brownian motion in the interval $[s,t]$ for each $s < t$. We shall view $\tilde{\mathcal{H}}$ as the

Hilbert space of $\mathfrak{h}$-valued 'square integrable' maps on $(\Omega, \mathcal{F}, P)$ and $\tilde{\mathcal{H}}_t$ as a subspace of $\tilde{\mathcal{H}}$ for every $t \geq 0$. For any $\rho \in L_2([0,\infty))$, let

$$e(\rho)(w) = \exp\left(\int_0^\infty \rho\, dw - \tfrac{1}{2}\int_0^\infty \rho^2\, dt\right), \quad w \in \Omega, \tag{2.1}$$

$$\rho_t(s) = \chi_{[0,t)}(s)\rho(s), \quad \rho^t(s) = \chi_{[t,\infty)}(s)\rho(s), \tag{2.2}$$

χ denoting indicator. An element $\rho \in L_2([0,\infty))$ is called simple if it can be expressed as $\rho = \Sigma\, \alpha_j\, \chi_{[a_j, b_j)}$ where the summation is over a finite number of j's, α_j's are constants and $a_1 < b_1 \leq a_2 < b_2 \ldots$. Let $\mathcal{S}$ denote the space of all such real valued simple functions and $\mathfrak{S}$ be the linear manifold generated by $e(i\rho)$ as ρ varies in $\mathcal{S}$. For any linear manifold $\mathfrak{D} \subset \mathfrak{h}$, let $\mathfrak{D} \underline{\otimes} \mathfrak{S}$ denote the linear manifold generated by elements of the form $u \otimes f$, $u \in \mathfrak{D}$, $f \in \mathfrak{S}$. Whenever $\mathfrak{D}$ is dense in $\mathfrak{h}$, $\mathfrak{D} \underline{\otimes} \mathfrak{S}$ is dense in $\tilde{\mathcal{H}}$. For any operator A, we denote by $\mathfrak{D}(A)$, its domain.

Lemma 2.1 Let ρ_j, u_j, $1 \leq j \leq n$ be such that $\rho_j \in L_2([0,\infty))$, $u_j \in \mathfrak{h}$ for all j, all the ρ_j's are distinct and all the u_j's are different from 0. Then $\{u_j \otimes e(\rho_j),\ 1 \leq j \leq n\}$ is a set of linearly independent elements in $\tilde{\mathcal{H}}$. For any $\rho_1, \rho_2 \in L_2([0,\infty))$,

$$E\, e(\rho_1)\, \overline{e(\rho_2)} = \exp \int_0^\infty \rho_1\, \bar{\rho}_2\, dt \quad .$$

Proof : We leave it to the reader.

Note that the element $u \otimes e(\rho) \in \mathfrak{h} \otimes \mathcal{H}$ can be written as $e(\rho)(w)u$, when viewed as an $\mathfrak{h}$-valued function of w. With this remark we introduce the following definition.

Definition 2.2 : Let $\mathfrak{D}_0 \subseteq \mathfrak{h}$ be a linear manifold. Suppose $\{M(t),\ t \geq 0\}$ is a family of operators in $\tilde{\mathcal{H}}$ such that

(i) $\mathfrak{D}(M(t)) \supseteq \mathfrak{D}_0 \underline{\otimes} \mathfrak{S}$

(ii) $M(t)\,[e(i\rho_t)u] \in \tilde{\mathcal{H}}_t$

(iii) $M(t)[e(i\rho)u] = e(i\rho^t)\, M(t)\, [e(i\rho_t)u]$

for all $t \geq 0$, $\rho \in \mathcal{S}$, $u \in \mathfrak{D}_0$, where the notations are as in (2.1), (2.2) and the subsequent paragraph. We call such a family of operators an adapted process and denote it by $M = \{\mathfrak{D}_0, M(t)\}$.

Roughly speaking, for an adapted process M, the operator M(t) restricted to the domain $\mathfrak{D}_0 \underline{\otimes} \mathfrak{S}$ factorises into $M_0(t) \otimes 1^t$ where $M_0(t)$ is an operator in the 'sector' $\tilde{\mathcal{H}}_t$ and 1^t is the identity operator in $\mathcal{H}^t$ for every $t \geq 0$.

Lemma 2.3 : Let $M = \{\mathcal{D}_0, M(t)\}$ be an adapted process. For any $u \in \mathcal{D}_0$, $\rho \in \mathcal{S}$, let

$$m_{\rho,u}(t) = e(i\rho)^{-1} M(t) [e(i\rho)u] . \qquad (2.3)$$

Then $m_{\rho,u}(t) \in \tilde{\mathcal{H}}_t$ for every t. Thus $\{m_{\rho,u}(t), t \geq 0\}$ is an $\mathfrak{h}$-valued nonanticipating Brownian functional.

Proof : For any $\rho \in \mathcal{S}$, $e(i\rho)^{-1}$ is bounded, $e(i\rho) = e(i\rho_t)e(i\rho^t)$ and $m_{\rho,u}(t) = e(i\rho_t)^{-1} M(t) [e(i\rho_t)u]$. The boundedness of $e(i\rho_t)^{-1}$ implies that $m_{\rho,u}(t) \in \tilde{\mathcal{H}}_t$. □

Definition 2.4 : Let $M = \{\mathcal{D}_0, M(t)\}$ be an adapted process such that for all $u \in \mathcal{D}_0$, $\rho \in \mathcal{S}$, the $\mathfrak{h}$-valued stochastic process $m_{\rho,u}$ defined by (2.3) admits the representation

$$m_{\rho,u}(t) = m_{\rho,u}(0) + \int_0^t \alpha_{\rho,u}(s)dw(s) + \int_0^t \beta_{\rho,u}(s)ds \qquad (2.4)$$

for all $t \geq 0$, where $\alpha_{\rho,u}$ and $\beta_{\rho,u}$ are $\mathfrak{h}$-valued nonanticipating Brownian functionals. Then M is called a semimartingale. If, in addition, there exist operators $\partial_w M(t)$ and $\partial_0 M(t)$ with domains containing $\mathcal{D}_0 \otimes \mathcal{S}$ and satisfying

$$\partial_w M(t) [e(i\rho)u] = \alpha_{\rho,u}(t) e(i\rho), \text{ a.e. } t \qquad (2.5)$$

$$\partial_0 M(t) [e(i\rho)u] = \beta_{\rho,u}(t) e(i\rho), \text{ a.e. } t \qquad (2.6)$$

for each $u \in \mathcal{D}_0$, $\rho \in \mathcal{S}$, we say that M is a smooth semimartingale.

Definition 2.5 : An adapted process $M = \{\mathcal{D}_0, M(t)\}$ is called a martingale if, for all $u,v \in \mathcal{D}_0$; $\rho, \tilde{\rho} \in \mathcal{S}$ and $0 \leq s \leq t$,

$$\langle M(t)[e(i\rho_s)u], e(i\tilde{\rho}_s)v\rangle = \langle M(s)[e(i\rho_s)u], e(i\tilde{\rho}_s)v\rangle. \qquad (2.7)$$

It is said to be smooth if, in addition, it is a smooth semimartingale.

Remark 2.6 : As mentioned at the beginning of this section the Hilbert space $\tilde{\mathcal{H}}(t)$ can be interpreted as $\tilde{\mathcal{H}}(s) \otimes \mathcal{H}(s,t)$. Let $1_{s,t}$ be the random variable identically equal to unity, considered as an element of $\mathcal{H}(s,t)$. Any bounded operator A on $\tilde{\mathcal{H}}(t)$ can be contracted to a bounded operator B on $\tilde{\mathcal{H}}(s)$ via the relation

$$\langle Bf,g\rangle = \langle A[f \otimes 1_{s,t}], g \otimes 1_{s,t}\rangle, \quad f,g \in \tilde{\mathcal{H}}(s).$$

Stretching this a lettle further we can interpret (2.7) as follows: M(t) viewed as an operator on $\tilde{\mathcal{H}}(t)$ when contracted to $\tilde{\mathcal{H}}(s)$ through the 'vacuum state' $1_{s,t}$ yields the operator M(s).

If $M_i = \{\mathcal{D}_i, M_i(t)\}$, $i = 1,2$ are martingales then $a_1M_1 + a_2M_2 = \{\mathcal{D}_1 \cap \mathcal{D}_2, a_1M_1(t) + a_2 M_2(t)\}$ is a martingale.

Proposition 2.7 : Let $M = \{\mathcal{D}_o, M(t)\}$ be a semimartingale so that $m_{\rho,u}$ defined by (2.3) satisfies (2.4). Then M is a martingale if and only if for every $a \geq 0$, $\rho \in \mathcal{S}$ satisfying $\rho(t) = 0$ for all $t \geq a$ and $u \in \mathcal{D}_o$,

$$\beta_{\rho,u}(t) = 0 \text{ a.e. } t \in [a,\infty) .$$

Proof : Since $\rho(t) = 0$ for all $t \geq a$,

$$m_{\rho,u}(t) = e(i\rho_a)^{-1} M(t) [e(i\rho)u] \quad \text{for } u \in \mathcal{D}_o,\ t \geq 0.$$

If M is a martingale, (2.7) implies

$$E(M(t)[e(i\rho)u] \mid \mathcal{F}_s) = M(s)[e(i\rho)u]$$

for all $u \in \mathcal{D}_o$, $a \leq s \leq t < \infty$. Hence $m_{\rho,u}(t)$ is an $\mathfrak{h}$-valued martingale in the interval $[a,\infty)$. Now (2.4) implies $\beta_{\rho,u}(s) = 0$ a.e. s in $[a,\infty)$.

Conversely, if $\beta_{\rho,u}(s) = 0$ a.e. s in $[a,\infty)$ whenever ρ has support in $[0,a)$, then $m_{\rho,u}(t)$ is a martingale in $[a,\infty)$ and

$$E(m_{\rho,u}(t) \mid \mathcal{F}_s) = m_{\rho,u}(s) = e(i\rho)^{-1} M(s)[e(i\rho)u] \text{ for } a \leq s \leq t < \infty.$$

Since $e(i\rho)^{-1} = e(i\rho_a)^{-1}$ is $\mathcal{F}_s$-measurable it follows that

$$E(M(t)[e(i\rho)u] \mid \mathcal{F}_s) = M(s)[e(i\rho)u] \quad \text{for } a \leq s \leq t < \infty.$$ This implies (2.7).

§ 3. Examples of Semimartingales and Martingales

Example 3.1 : Let $x(t,w)$ be a real or complex valued nonanticipating Brownian functional satisfying $dx = \varphi\, dw + \psi\, dt$ where

$$\int_0^t E(|\varphi(s,w)|^2 + |\psi(s,w)|^2)ds < \infty \quad \text{for all } t. \tag{3.1}$$

Define the multiplication operators

$$[M(t)f](w) = x(t,w)f(w) ,$$

$$[\partial_w M(t)f](w) = \varphi(t,w)f(w) ,$$

$$[\partial_o M(t)f](w) = \psi(t,w)f(w) , \quad f \in \tilde{\mathcal{H}}$$

with respective maximal domains. We may assume, without loss of generality, that the integrand in (3.1) is finite for all s. Then the maximal domains of the operators defined above include $\mathfrak{h} \underline{\otimes} \mathcal{S}$. Further

$$m_{\rho,u}(t) = e(i\rho)^{-1} x(t,w)e(i\rho)u = x(t,w)u ,$$

$$m_{\rho,u}(t) = m_{\rho,u}(0) + \int_0^t [\varphi(s,w)u]dw(s) + \int_0^t [\psi(s,w)u]ds .$$

Thus $M = \{\mathfrak{h}, M(t)\}$ is a smooth semimartingale. It is a martingale if and only if $\psi(s,\cdot) = 0$ a.e. s.

When $\psi \equiv 0$ we denote the smooth martingale by Q_φ. If $\varphi \equiv 1$, $\psi \equiv 0$, we denote the corresponding smooth martingale by Q and note that

$$Q(t)f = w(t)f, \ \partial_w Q(t)f = f, \ \partial_0 Q(t)f = 0 \tag{3.2}$$

with maximal domains. We call $\{\mathfrak{h}, Q(t)\}$ the <u>canonical position martingale</u>.

If we replace x,φ,ψ by $\mathfrak{h}$-operator valued nonanticipating Brownian functionals we can construct more general examples. An application of this idea was discussed in [2].

<u>Example 3.2</u> : Let $\varphi(t,w)$ be a real valued nonanticipating Brownian functional satisfying

$$\int_0^t E|\varphi(s,w)|^2 \, ds < \infty \quad \text{for all } t.$$

For each t define the functional

$$\Phi_t(s,w) = \int_0^{s\wedge t} \varphi(\tau,w)d\tau$$

where $s\wedge t = \min(s,t)$ and the operator $T_\varphi(t)$ by

$$[T_\varphi(t)f](w) = f(w+\Phi_t)$$

on the maximal domain. Define

$$(\partial_w T_\varphi)(t) = 0, \ \partial_0 T_\varphi(t)[e(i\rho)u] = i\rho(t)\varphi(t,w)T_\varphi(t)[e(i\rho)u]$$

for $u \in \mathfrak{h}$, $\rho \in \mathcal{S}$. Then

$$T_\varphi(t)[e(i\rho)u] = e^{i\int_0^t \rho\varphi\, ds} e(i\rho)u \in \tilde{\mathcal{H}} ,$$

$$m_{\rho,u}(t) = e(i\rho)^{-1} T_\varphi(t)[e(i\rho)u]$$

$$= e^{i\int_0^t \rho\varphi ds} u = m_{\rho,u}(0) + \int_0^t i\,\rho\varphi e^{i\int_0^s \rho\varphi d\tau} u \, ds$$

where the integrand in the last term vanishes whenever ρ vanishes. By Proposition 2.7, it follows that $T_\varphi = \{\mathfrak{h}, T_\varphi(t)\}$ is a smooth martingale. In defining the operators $\partial_0 T_\varphi(t)$ on $\mathfrak{h} \underline{\otimes} \mathcal{S}$ we make use of Lemma 2.1. We call T_φ a <u>translation martingale</u> since it is determined by translating the Brownian path w suitably.

<u>Example 3.3</u> : With the help of Exampln 3.2 we define the operators

$$[A_\varphi(t)f](w) = \frac{d}{d\varepsilon}[T_{\varepsilon\varphi}(t)f](w)\Big|_{\varepsilon=0}$$

where the differentiation is in the strong sense in $\tilde{\mathcal{H}}$. Then for $u \in \mathfrak{h}$, $\rho \in \mathcal{S}$

$$A_\varphi(t)[e(i\rho)u] = (\int_0^t i\rho\varphi\, ds)e(i\rho)u \in \tilde{\mathcal{H}} .$$

Define the operators

$$\partial_w A_\varphi(t) = 0, \quad \partial_0 A_\varphi(t)[e(i\rho)u] = i\rho(t)\varphi(t,w)e(i\rho)u$$

using Lemma 2.1. Then for the adapted process $A_\varphi = \{\mathfrak{h}, A_\varphi(t)\}$ we have

$$m_{\rho,u}(t) = [\int_0^t i\rho\varphi\, ds]u$$

and the integrand vanishes whenever ρ vanishes. Thus A_φ is a smooth martingale. When $\varphi \equiv 1$ we denote the corresponding martingale by A and call it the <u>canonical annihilation martingale</u>. For any $u \in \mathfrak{h}$, $\rho \in \mathcal{S}$ we have

$$\begin{aligned} &A(t)[e(i\rho)u] = (i\int_0^t \rho\, ds)\, e(i\rho)u , \\ &\partial_w A(t) = 0, \quad \partial_0 A(t)[e(i\rho)u] = i\rho(t)e(i\rho)u \end{aligned} \tag{3.3}$$

Define the martingales $A_\varphi^\dagger$ and $A^\dagger$ by putting

$$A_\varphi^\dagger(t) = Q_\varphi(t)-A_\varphi(t), \quad A^\dagger(t) = Q(t)-A(t)$$

where Q_φ and Q are as in Example 3.1. Then

$$\begin{aligned} &A^\dagger(t)[e(i\rho)u] = [w(t) - i\int_0^t \rho\, ds]e(i\rho)u \\ &\partial_w A^\dagger(t) = 1, \quad \partial_0 A^\dagger(t)[e(i\rho)u] = - i\rho(t)\, e(i\rho)u . \end{aligned} \tag{3.4}$$

We call $A^\dagger = \{\mathfrak{h}, A^\dagger(t)\}$ the <u>canonical creation martingale</u>.

Define the martingales P_φ and P by the equations

$$P_\varphi(t) = - i(A_\varphi(t)-A_\varphi^\dagger(t)), \quad P(t) = - i(A(t)-A^\dagger(t)).$$

Then

$$\begin{aligned} &P(t)[e(i\rho)u] = - i(2i\int_0^t \rho ds-w(t))e(i\rho)u \\ &\partial_w P(t) = i, \quad \partial_0 P(t)[e(i\rho)u] = (2\int_0^t \rho\, ds)e(i\rho)u \end{aligned} \tag{3.5}$$

We call $P = \{\mathfrak{h}, P(t)\}$ the <u>canonical momentum martingale</u>.

<u>Example 3.4</u> : Let φ, Φ_t be as in Example 3.2 and let $E \exp[-\int_0^t \varphi dw - \frac{1}{2}\int_0^t \varphi^2 ds] = 1$

for all t. Define the operators

$$[\tilde{T}_\varphi(t)f](w) = f(w+\Phi_t)\exp[-\tfrac{1}{2}\int_0^t \varphi\, dw - \tfrac{1}{4}\int_0^t \varphi^2\, ds] \tag{3.6}$$

for all $f \in \tilde{\mathcal{H}}$. It follows from Girsanov's theorem that $\tilde{T}_\varphi(t)$ is a unitary operator for every t. Then $\tilde{T}_\varphi = \{\mathfrak{h}, T_\varphi(t)\}$ is a unitary operator valued adapted process. It is a smooth semimartingale with

$$\begin{aligned} \partial_w \tilde{T}_\varphi(t)\,[e(i\rho)u] &= -\tfrac{1}{2}\,\varphi(t,w)\,\tilde{T}_\varphi(t)[e(i\rho)u] \\ \partial_0\, \tilde{T}_\varphi(t)[e(i\rho)u] &= [i\rho(t)\varphi(t,w) - \tfrac{1}{8}\,\varphi(t,w)^2]\,\tilde{T}_\varphi(t)[e(i\rho)u] \end{aligned} \tag{3.7}$$

provided φ is bounded. Define

$$[\tilde{A}_\varphi(t)f](w) = \frac{d}{d\varepsilon}[\tilde{T}_{\varepsilon\varphi}(t)f]\Big|_{\varepsilon=0}$$

where the differentiation is in the strong sense and the domain is maximal. Then

$$\tilde{A}_\varphi(t)[e(i\rho)u] = [i\int_0^t \rho\varphi\, ds - \tfrac{1}{2}\int_0^t \varphi\, dw]\, e(i\rho)u.$$

From Example 3.3 we have for $u \in \mathfrak{h}$, $\rho \in \mathcal{S}$

$$-2i\,\tilde{A}_\varphi(t)\,[e(i\rho)u] = P_\varphi(t)\,[e(i\rho)u]\,.$$

If $\varphi \equiv 1$, $\tilde{T}_{\varepsilon\varphi}(t)$ is a one parameter unitary group in the parameter ε and correspondingly $-2i\,\tilde{A}_\varphi(t)$ is a selfadjoint operator which is equal to $P(t)$ on $\mathfrak{h} \underline{\otimes} \mathcal{S}$. We denote this selfadjoint extension by $P(t)$ itself and call the corresponding martingale the <u>canonical momentum martingale</u>. An elementary computation yields

$$[Q(t), P(t)] = 2it, \; [A(t), A^\dagger(t)] = t \text{ for all } t \tag{3.8}$$

on their domains of definition.

<u>Example 3.5</u> : For any nonanticipating Brownian functional ψ, define

$$e(\psi)(w) = \exp(\int_0^\infty \psi\, dw - \tfrac{1}{2}\int_0^\infty \psi^2\, dt).$$

For any complex valued nonanticipating functional φ of modulus unity define the operator $\Gamma(\varphi)$ on $\tilde{\mathcal{H}}$ by putting

$$\Gamma(\varphi)\,[e(\rho)u] = e(\rho\varphi)u, \quad \rho \in L_2([0,\infty)),\; u \in \mathfrak{h}\,.$$

If $\eta(t) = e(\chi_{[0,t)}\psi)$ then

$$d|\eta|^2 = 2|\eta|^2\, \mathrm{Re}\,\psi\, dw + |\eta\psi|^2\, dt\,.$$

In particular, if $\psi = \rho\varphi$ we obtain

$$E|\eta(t)|^2 = e^{\int_0^t |\rho|^2 ds} \quad \text{for all } t.$$

Hence

$$||e(\rho\varphi)u||^2 = ||e(\rho)u||^2 \text{ for all } \rho \in L_2([0,\infty)),\ u \in \mathfrak{h} .$$

Since $\{e(\rho)u,\ \rho \in L_2([0,\infty)),\ u \in \mathfrak{h}\}$ is a spanning set for $\tilde{\mathcal{H}}$, it follows that $\Gamma(\varphi)$ is an isometry. Define

$$\hat{\varphi}_t = \chi_{[0,t)}\varphi + \chi_{[t,\infty)} ,$$

$$\Gamma_\varphi(t) = \Gamma(\hat{\varphi}_t) \quad \text{for each } t.$$

Then $\Gamma_\varphi = \{\mathfrak{h}, \Gamma_\varphi(t)\}$ is an adapted process and for $u \in \mathfrak{h}$, $\rho \in \mathcal{S}$,

$$m_{\rho,u}(t) = e(i\rho)^{-1}\,\Gamma_\varphi(t)[e(i\rho)u]$$

$$= \{\exp[i\int_0^t \rho(\varphi-1)dw + \int_0^t \rho^2/2\ (\varphi^2-1)ds]\}u .$$

This shows that Γ_φ is a semimartingale. Further, putting

$$\partial_w\Gamma_\varphi(t)f = (\varphi-1)\Gamma_\varphi(t)\ \partial_0 A(t)f ,$$

$$\partial_0\Gamma_\varphi(t)f = (\varphi-1)\Gamma_\varphi(t)\ (\partial_0 A)^2(t)f,$$

for all $f \in \mathfrak{h}\otimes\mathcal{S}$, makes Γ_φ smooth. Since $\partial_0\Gamma_\varphi(t)\ e(i\rho)u] = 0$ whenever $\rho(t) = 0$ it follows that Γ_φ is a smooth martingale.

If $\varphi(t,w) = \varphi(t)$ is independent of w then the operators $\Gamma_\varphi(t)$ are unitary. For two such φ,ψ we have $\Gamma_\varphi(t)\Gamma_\psi(t) = \Gamma_{\varphi\psi}(t)$. In other words, product of two smooth martingales can again be a smooth martingale.

Example 3.6 : Continuing with Example 3.2 define

$$T_\varphi^\dagger(t)f = e^{\int_0^t \varphi dw - \frac{1}{2}\int_0^t \varphi^2 ds}\ T_{-\varphi}(t)f . \tag{3.9}$$

For any two real valued bounded nonanticipating functionals φ,ψ define

$$\psi^\varphi(t,w) = \psi(t,w+\Phi_t) \tag{3.10}$$

Then

$$T_\varphi(t)T_\psi(t) = T_{\varphi+\psi^\varphi}(t) , \tag{3.11}$$

$$T_\varphi^\dagger(t)T_\psi^\dagger(t) = T^\dagger_{\varphi+\psi^{-\varphi}}(t) . \tag{3.12}$$

Further

$$T_\varphi^\dagger(t)T_\psi(t)[e(i\rho)u] = e^\gamma\, e(i\rho)u$$

where

$$\gamma(t,w) = \int_0^t \varphi dw - \tfrac{1}{2}\int_0^t \varphi^2\, ds + \int_0^t i\rho(-\varphi+\psi^{-\varphi})ds \ .$$

For the adapted process $T_\varphi^\dagger T_\psi = \{\mathfrak{h}, T_\varphi^\dagger(t)T_\psi(t)\}$, $m_{\rho,u}(t) = e^{\gamma(t,w)}u$. Hence $T_\varphi^\dagger T_\psi$ is a smooth semimartingale and

$$\partial_w\, T_\varphi^\dagger T_\psi = \varphi\, T_\varphi^\dagger T_\psi$$

$$\partial_0\, T_\varphi^\dagger T_\psi = (-\varphi+\psi^{-\varphi})T_\varphi^\dagger T_\psi\, \partial_0\, A$$

on the domain $\mathfrak{h} \underline{\otimes} \mathcal{S}$. The condition of Proposition 2.7 is fulfilled and $T_\varphi^\dagger T_\psi$ is a smooth martingale.

From (3.11) and (3.12) and the above discussions it follows that for real valued bounded nonanticipating functionals the process

$$T_{\varphi_1}^\dagger\, T_{\varphi_2}^\dagger \cdots T_{\varphi_k}^\dagger\, T_{\psi_1} \cdots T_{\psi_\ell} = \{\mathfrak{h}, T_{\varphi_1}^\dagger(t) \cdots T_{\varphi_k}^\dagger(t)T_{\psi_1}(t)\cdots T_{\psi_\ell}(t)\}$$

is a smooth martingale.

If all the φ_i, ψ_j are functions of t only, then we can change φ_i to $\varepsilon_i\, \varphi_i$ and ψ_j to $\delta_j\psi_j$ for each i,j and differentiate with respect to the real parameters ε_i, δ_j successively at 0 in the strong sense. This implies that for such functions

$$A_{\varphi_1}^\dagger\, A_{\varphi_2}^\dagger \cdots A_{\varphi_k}^\dagger\, A_{\psi_1} \cdots A_{\psi_\ell} = \{\mathfrak{h}, A_{\varphi_1}^+(t)\cdots A_{\varphi_k}(t)A_{\psi_1}(t) \cdots A_{\psi_\ell}(t)\}$$

is a martingale. We may call linear combinations of such martingales as Wick martingales.

Example 3.7 : For any two real valued bounded nonanticipating Brownian functionals φ,ψ define the operator

$$[W_{\varphi,\psi}(t)f](w) = e^{\gamma(t,w)}\, f(w+\Psi_t)$$

where

$$\Psi_t(s,w) = \int_0^{s\wedge t} \psi(\tau,w)d\tau \ ,$$

$$\gamma(t,w) = \frac{i}{2}\int_0^t \varphi\psi\, ds + i\int_0^t \varphi\, dw - \tfrac{1}{2}\int_0^t \psi\, dw - \tfrac{1}{4}\int_0^t \psi^2\, ds \ .$$

From Example 3.4 it follows that $W_{\varphi,\psi} = \{\mathfrak{h}, W_{\varphi,\psi}(t)\}$ is an adapted process of unitary operators constituting a smooth semimartingale. Further

$$W_{\varphi_1,\psi_1}(t)_{\varphi_2,\psi_2}(t) = e^{-\frac{i}{2}\int_0^t (\varphi_1\, \psi_2^{\psi_1} - \psi_1\varphi_2^{\psi_1})ds}\, W_{\varphi_1+\varphi_2^{\psi_1},\ \psi_1+\psi_2^{\psi_1}}(t)$$

where ψ^φ is defined by (3.10). If φ_i, ψ_i are functions of t only the above identity yields the Weyl representation of the Bose-Einstein field for the real Hilbert space

$L_2[0,t]$ for each t, when restricted to the linear manifold of bounded functions. In view of this property we call $W_{\varphi,\psi}$ a <u>Weyl semimartingale</u> .

<u>Example 3.8</u> : In all the examples discussed till now the role of the Hilbert space $\mathfrak{h}$ was passive. We now consider the case when $\mathfrak{h} = L_2(\mathbb{R})$. Let α,β,φ be bounded Borel functions of (t,x,w), $t \geq 0$, $x \in \mathbb{R}$, $w \in \Omega$, such that they are nonanticipating for each x. Let β,φ be real valued and

$$d\alpha = a\,dw + b\,dt \quad , \quad d\beta = p\,dw + q\,dt$$

where a,b,p,q are again bounded Borel functions of (t,x,w). Let $\mathfrak{D}_0 = \{u : u \in \mathfrak{h}$, u is twice continuously differentiable and has compact support$\}$. Define

$$[M_{\alpha,\beta,\varphi}(t)f]\,(x,w) = \alpha(t,x,w)f(\beta(t,x,w),\, w + \Phi_t)$$

where $\Phi_t(s,x,w) = \int_0^{s\wedge t} \varphi(\tau,x,w)d\tau$. This defines an adapted process and for $\rho \in \mathcal{S}$, $u \in \mathfrak{D}_0$,

$$m_{\rho,u}(t,x,w) = \alpha(t,x,w)e^{i\int_0^t \rho\varphi ds} u(\beta(t,x,w)).$$

Ito's formula implies that $M_{\alpha,\beta,\varphi}$ is a semimartingale.

A very useful example of such a process of unitary operators occurs in [3]. They play an important role in the construction of quantum diffusion processes.

§ 4. Integration of adapted processes with respect to a smooth semimartingale

Let $M = \{\mathfrak{D}_0, M(t)\}$ be a semimartingale and for $u \in \mathfrak{D}_0$, $\rho \in \mathcal{S}$, let the $\mathfrak{h}$-valued process $\{m_{\rho,u}(t), t \geq 0\}$ be as in Definition 2.4. For any simple adapted process $F = \{\mathfrak{h}, F(t)\}$ where $F(t) = \sum_{i=1}^{n} F(t_{i-1})\chi_{[t_{i-1},\, t_i)}$, $0 = t_0 < t_1 < \ldots < t_n$ and $F(t_0), F(t_1),\ldots,F(t_{n-1})$ are bounded operators, define

$$J(t) = \int_0^t F dM = \sum_{i=1}^{n} F(t_{i-1})\,[M(t\wedge t_i) - M(t\wedge t_{i-1})] .$$

Then $\mathfrak{D}(J(t)) \supseteq \mathfrak{D}_0 \underline{\otimes} \mathcal{S}$ and for $u \in \mathfrak{D}_0$, $v \in \mathfrak{h}$; $\rho,\tilde{\rho} \in \mathcal{S}$ we have

$$\langle J(t)[e(i\rho)u]\ ,\ e(i\tilde{\rho})v\rangle = \sum_{j=1}^{n} \langle e(i\rho)[m_{\rho,u}(t_j)-m_{\rho,u}(t_{j-1})], F^{\dagger}(t_{j-1})[e(i\tilde{\rho})v]\rangle \tag{4.1}$$

where $F^{\dagger}(t)$ is the adjoint of $F(t)$. Observe that

$$f^{\dagger}_{\tilde{\rho},v}(t) = e(i\tilde{\rho})^{-1}\,F^{\dagger}(t)\,[e(i\tilde{\rho})v]$$

is an $\mathfrak{h}$-valued nonanticipating Brownian functional and $m_{\rho,u}$ is an $\mathfrak{h}$-valued semimartingale. If M is smooth we can write (4.1) as

$$<J(t)[e(i\rho)u],\ e(i\tilde{\rho})v> = E\ e(i\rho)\overline{e(i\tilde{\rho})}[\int_0^t <\alpha_{\rho,u},\ f^{\dagger}_{\tilde{\rho},v}>_0\ dw + \int_0^t <\beta_{\rho,u}, f^{\dagger}_{\tilde{\rho},v}>_0\ ds] \tag{4.2}$$

where $<\cdot,\cdot>_0$ denotes inner product in $\mathfrak{h}$ and $\alpha_{\rho,u}$, $\beta_{\rho,u}$ are as in (2.4). Starting from (4.2) and using the classical Ito calculus it follows (from a rather tedious computation) that the operator J(t) satisfies

$$J(t)[e(i\rho)u] = e(i\rho)\{\int_0^t e(i\rho)^{-1}\ F(s)\partial_w M(s)[e(i\rho)u]dw(s) + \int_0^t e(i\rho)^{-1}\ F(s)\partial_0 M(s)[e(i\rho)u]ds\}.$$

In view of this relation we make the following definition.

<u>Definition 4.1</u> Let $M = \{\mathcal{D}_0, M(t)\}$ be a smooth semimartingale and let F be an adapted process such that for all $\rho \in \mathcal{S}$, $u \in \mathcal{D}_1 \subsetneq \mathcal{D}_0$, where $\mathcal{D}_1$ is a linear manifold, the following holds:

$$e(i\rho)u \in \mathcal{D}(F(t)\partial_w M(t)) \cap \mathcal{D}(F(t)\partial_0 M(t)),$$

$$\int_0^t [||F(s)\partial_w M(s)[e(i\rho)u]||^2 + ||F(s)\partial_0 M(s)[e(i\rho)u]||^2]ds < \infty ,$$

for all t. Then we say that $F \in \mathcal{L}_2(M, \mathcal{D}_1)$ and define the operator $J(t) = \int_0^t F\, dM$ by the equation

$$J(t)[e(i\rho)u] = e(i\rho)\{\int_0^t e(i\rho)^{-1}\ F(s)\partial_w M(s)[e(i\rho)u]\ dw(s) + \int_0^t e(i\rho)^{-1}\ F(s)\partial_0 M(s)[e(i\rho)u]ds\} ,$$

for all $\rho \in \mathcal{S}$, $u \in \mathcal{D}_0$. If $J = \{\mathcal{D}_1, J(t)\}$ is any adapted process such that

$J(t) = J(0) + \int_0^t F dM$ on $\mathcal{D}_1 \otimes \mathcal{S}$ then we write $dJ = F\, dM$.

<u>Remark 4.2</u> : If $F \in \mathcal{L}_2(M, \mathcal{D}_1)$ and $dJ = F\, dM$ then J is a smooth semimartingale satisfying $\partial_w J(t) = F(t)\partial_w M(t)$, $\partial_0 J(t) = F(t)\partial_0 M(t)$ on $\mathcal{D}_1 \otimes \mathcal{S}$.

<u>Example 4.3</u> : Let M = Q be the canonical position martingale. Then $F \in \mathcal{L}_2(Q, \mathcal{D}_1)$ if and only if

$$\int_0^t ||F(s)[e(i\rho)u]||^2 ds < \infty \quad \text{for all } u \in \mathcal{D}_1,\ \rho \in \mathcal{S}.$$

If $J(t) = \int_0^t F\, dQ$ then

$$J(t)[e(i\rho)u] = e(i\rho) \int_0^t e(i\rho)^{-1}\ F(s)[e(i\rho)u]\ dw(s)$$

for $u \in \mathcal{D}_1$, $\rho \in \mathcal{S}$, $t \geq 0$. Further $J = \{\mathcal{D}_1, J(t)\}$ is a smooth martingale.

Example 4.4 : Let $M = A$ be the canonical annihilation martingale. Then $F \in \mathcal{L}_2(A, \mathcal{D}_1)$ if and only if

$$\int_0^t ||F(s)[e(i\rho)u]||^2 \rho(s)^2 ds < \infty \quad \text{for} \quad u \in \mathcal{D}_1,\ \rho \in \mathcal{S} \quad .$$

If $J(t) = \int_0^t F\,dA$ then

$$J(t)[e(i\rho)u = \int_0^t i\rho(s)F(s)[e(i\rho)u]ds$$

for $u \in \mathcal{D}_1$, $\rho \in \mathcal{S}$. Further $J = \{\mathcal{D}_1, J(t)\}$ is a smooth martingale.

Remark 4.5 : Definition 4.1 and Examples 4.3 and 4.4 imply that for any smooth semimartingale $M = \{\mathcal{D}_0, M(t)\}$ and adapted process $F \in \mathcal{L}_2(M, \mathcal{D}_1)$, $\mathcal{D}_1 \subseteq \mathcal{D}_0$, the equation $dJ = F\,dM$ is equivalent to

$$F\,dM = F\partial_w M\, dQ + F\, \partial_0 M\, dt.$$

We may express this in the form

$$dM = \partial_w M\, dQ + \partial_0 M\, dt$$

where $\partial_w M \in \mathcal{L}_2(Q, \mathcal{D}_0)$, $\partial_0 M \in \mathcal{L}_2(L, \mathcal{D}_0)$, $L = \{\mathfrak{h}, L(t)\}$, $L(t) = tI$ for all t.

Theorem 4.6 : An adapted process $M = \{\mathcal{D}_0, M(t)\}$ is a smooth martingale if and only if there exist adapted processes $F_1 \in \mathcal{L}_2(A, \mathcal{D}_0)$, $F_2 \in \mathcal{L}_2(A^\dagger, \mathcal{D}_0)$ such that $dM = F_1\, dA + F_2\, dA^\dagger$, where A and $A^\dagger$ are the canonical annihilation and creation martingales.

Proof : Sufficiency is immediate from Example 4.3, 4.4 and the fact that $Q(t) = A(t) + A^\dagger(t)$. Let M be a smooth martingale. By Proposition 2.7, for $u \in \mathcal{D}_0$, $\rho \in \mathcal{S}$, $\beta_{\rho,u}(t) = e(i\rho)^{-1}\, \partial_0 M(t)[e(i\rho)u] = 0$ for a.e. $t > a$ whenever the the support of ρ is contained in $[0,a)$. Let $\rho = \sum_j \alpha_j\, \chi_{[a_j,b_j)}$ where $\alpha_j \neq 0$ for each j and $a_1 < b_1 \leq a_2 < b_2 \ldots$ and $t \in (b_j, a_{j+1})$. Then, in the notation (2.2), we have

$$\begin{aligned} m_{\rho,u}(t) &= e(i\rho)^{-1}\, M(t)[e(i\rho)u] \\ &= e(i\rho_{b_j})^{-1}\, M(t)[e(i\rho_{b_j})u] \\ &= m_{\rho',u}(t) \end{aligned}$$

where $\rho' = \rho_{b_j}$ has support in $[0,b_j)$. Hence $\beta_{\rho,u}(t) = \beta_{\rho',u}(t) = 0$ a.e. $t \in (b_j, a_{j+1})$. In other words we can write $\beta_{\rho,u}(t) = i\rho(t)\ \gamma_{\rho,u}(t)$ for all t. If we define $F(t)[e(i\rho)u] = e(i\rho)\gamma_{\rho,u}(t)$ then $\partial_0 M(t)[e(i\rho)u] = F(t)\partial_0 A(t)[e(i\rho)u]$. Since $dA = \partial_0 A(t)dt$ we conclude from Remark 4.5 that

$$dM = \partial_w M\, dQ + F(t)dA$$
$$= \partial_w M\, (dA+dA^\dagger) + FdA$$
$$= (\partial_w M+F)dA + \partial_w M\, dA^\dagger . \square$$

Theorem 4.7 : Let f_i, i = 1,2,3 be adapted processes such that $F_1 \in \mathcal{L}_2(A, \mathcal{D}_o)$, $F_2 \in \mathcal{L}_2(A^\dagger, \mathcal{D}_o)$, $F_3 \in \mathcal{L}_2(L, \mathcal{D}_o)$ where L(t) = tI for all t. Let

$$\lim_{||\rho-\tilde{\rho}||\to 0} ||F_1(s)[e(i\rho)-e(i\tilde{\rho})]u|| + ||F_3(s)[e(i\rho)-e(i\tilde{\rho})]u|| = 0 \quad \text{a.e.s}$$

for each $u \in \mathcal{D}_o$, where $||\rho-\tilde{\rho}||$ is the norm of $L_2([0,\infty))$. If

$$\left(\int_0^t F_1 dA + \int_0^t F_2 dA^\dagger + \int_0^t F_3\, ds\right)[e(i\rho)u] = 0 \tag{4.3}$$

for all $u \in \mathcal{D}_o$, $\rho \in \mathcal{S}$ then $F_1(s) = F_2(s) = F_3(s) = 0$ a.e.s on $\mathcal{D}_o \otimes \mathcal{S}$.

Proof : Since $dQ = dA+dA^\dagger$ we have from Example 4.3, 4.4 and (4.3)

$$e(i\rho) \int_0^t e(i\rho)^{-1} F_2(s)[e(i\rho)u]dw(s) + \int_0^t [i\rho(s)F_1(s)+F_3(s)-F_2(s)][e(i\rho)u]ds = 0.$$

The independence of the differentials dw and dt implies

$$\left.\begin{aligned} &F_2(s)[e(i\rho)u] = 0 \text{ a.e. } s, \\ &[i\rho(s)F_1(s)+F_3(s)](e(i\rho)u) = 0 \text{ a.e.s} \end{aligned}\right\} \tag{4.4}$$

for all $u \in \mathcal{D}_o$, $\rho \in \mathcal{S}$. For any ρ with support in [0,a) we conclude from (4.4),

$$F_3(s)[e(i\rho)u] = 0 \quad \text{a.e. } s > a.$$

In other words, for each $\rho \in \mathcal{S}$, $u \in \mathcal{D}_o$,

$$F_3(s)[e(i\rho_a)u] = 0 \quad \text{a.e.} \quad s > a.$$

By Fubini's theorem and the continuity of the left hand side in a we obtain $F_3(s)[e(i\rho_s)u] = 0$ a.e. s. Since F_3 is an adapted process it follows that $F_3(s)[e(i\rho)u] = 0$ a.e. s. Now (4.4) implies $\rho(s)\, F_1(s)[e(i\rho)u] = 0$ a.e. s. The continuity of $F_1(s)[e(i\rho)u]$ in the variable ρ implies $F_1(s)[e(i\rho)u] = 0$ a.e.s. $\square$

§ 5. Quantum Ito's formula in a special case

We begin with the special case when $\mathfrak{h} = \mathbb{C}$, the one dimensional Hilbert space so that $\tilde{\mathcal{H}} = \mathcal{H}$ and consider the unitary operators M(t) defined by

$$[M(t)f](w) = x(t,w)[\tilde{T}_\varphi(t)f](w), \qquad f \in \mathcal{H} \tag{5.1}$$

where

$$x(t,w) = \exp i\left(\int_0^t y\, dw + \int_0^t z\, ds\right) ,$$

y, z, φ are bounded real nonanticipating Brownian functionals and $\tilde{T}_\varphi(t)$ is defined as in Example 3.4. By the classical Ito calculus we obtain

$$\partial_w M = (iy - \tfrac{\varphi}{2})M, \quad \partial_o M = (iz - \tfrac{y^2}{2} - \tfrac{\varphi^2}{8} - iy\tfrac{\varphi}{2})M + \varphi M \partial_o A$$

where a function is interpreted as multiplication operator and A is the canonical annihilation martingale. By Remark 4.5 and the fact that $Q = A + A^\dagger$ it follows that $dM = F_1 dA + F_2 dA^\dagger + F_3 dt$ where $F_1 = (iy + \frac{\varphi}{2})M$, $F_2 = (iy - \frac{\varphi}{2})M$, $F_3 = (iz - \frac{y^2}{8} - \frac{\varphi^2}{8} - iy\frac{\varphi}{2})M$. We shall denote these coefficients F_1, F_2 and F_3 by $\bar{\partial}_A M$, $\bar{\partial}_{A^\dagger} M$ and $\bar{\partial}_o M$ respectively.

Let now M_j, $j = 1,2$ be two adapted processes of unitary operators of the form (5.1) determined by x_j, y_j, z_j, φ_j, $j = 1,2$. Then $M(t) = M_1(t)M_2(t)$, $t \geq 0$ determines an adapted process of the same kind with $x = x_1 x_2'$, $y = y_1 + y_2'$, $z = z_1 + z_2' + y_2'\varphi_1$, $\varphi = \varphi_1 + \varphi_2'$, where, for any nonanticipating functional ξ, we define $\xi'(t,w) = \xi(t,\tilde{w})$ and $\tilde{w}(s) = w(s) + \int_0^s \varphi_1(\tau,w)d\tau$. Then

$$\begin{aligned}
\bar{\partial}_A M &= (iy + \tfrac{\varphi}{2})M \\
&= [i(y_1+y_2') + \tfrac{1}{2}(\varphi_1+\varphi_2')]M_1M_2 \\
&= (iy_1+\tfrac{1}{2}\varphi_1)M_1M_2 + M_1(iy_2+\tfrac{1}{2}\varphi_2)M_2 \\
&= (\bar{\partial}_A M_1)M_2 + M_1(\bar{\partial}_A M_2). \qquad (5.2)
\end{aligned}$$

Similarly,

$$\bar{\partial}_{A^\dagger} M = (\bar{\partial}_{A^\dagger} M_1)M_2 + M_1(\bar{\partial}_{A^\dagger} M_2) \qquad (5.3)$$

Further

$$\begin{aligned}
\bar{\partial}_o M &= (iz - \tfrac{1}{2}y^2 - \tfrac{1}{8}\varphi^2 - \tfrac{i}{2}y\varphi)M \\
&= (iz_1 - \tfrac{1}{2}y_1^2 - \tfrac{1}{8}\varphi_1^2 - \tfrac{i}{2}y_1\varphi_1)M_1M_2 + M_1(iz_2 - \tfrac{1}{2}y_2^2 - \tfrac{1}{8}\varphi_2^2 - \tfrac{i}{2}y_2\varphi_2)M_2 \\
&\qquad + (iy_1+\tfrac{1}{2}\varphi_1)M_1(iy_2-\tfrac{1}{2}\varphi_2)M_2 \\
&= (\bar{\partial}_o M_1)M_2 + M_1(\bar{\partial}_o M_2) + (\bar{\partial}_A M_1)(\bar{\partial}_{A^\dagger} M_2). \qquad (5.4)
\end{aligned}$$

Combining (5.2) - (5.4) we obtain

$$d(M_1M_2) = (\bar{\partial}_A M_1)M_2 dA + (\bar{\partial}_{A^\dagger} M_1)M_2 dA^\dagger + (\bar{\partial}_o M_1)M_2 dt + M_1 dM_2 + (\bar{\partial}_A M_1)(\bar{\partial}_{A^\dagger} M_2)dt \quad (5.5)$$

For any adapted process $F \in \mathcal{L}_2(A, \mathcal{D}_o)$ or $\mathcal{L}_2(A^\dagger, \mathcal{D}_o)$, define

$$\int_0^t (dA)F = \int_0^t F\,dA \quad \text{or} \quad \int_0^t (dA^\dagger)F = \int_0^t F\,dA^\dagger.$$

This is only appropriate because, intuitively, dA and $dA^\dagger$ operate in the sector $\mathcal{H}(t,t+dt)$ of the continuous tensor product whereas $F(t)$ operates in the sector $\mathcal{H}(0,t)$. If $dM = F_1 dA + F_2 dA^\dagger + F_3\, dt$ then we define $\int_0^t (dM)F$ as

$\int_0^t F_1 F dA + \int_0^t F_2 F dA^\dagger + \int_0^t F_3 F\, dt$. With this convention (5.5) becomes

$$d(M_1M_2) = M_1 dM_2 + (dM_1)M_2 + (\bar\partial_A M_1)(\bar\partial_{A^\dagger} M_2)dt \qquad (5.6)$$

We now go back to the general case when $\tilde{\mathcal{H}} = \mathfrak{h} \otimes \mathcal{H}$. For any bounded operator m on $\mathfrak{h}$ and an adapted process M of unitary operators defined by (5.1) we construct the adapted process N = $\{\mathfrak{h}, N(t)\}$, where $N(t) = m \otimes M(t)$. Let $\mathcal{N}$ denote the set of all linear combinations of such processes. Then $\mathcal{N}$ is an algebra of smooth semimartingales. The discussions above and Theorem 4.7 lead easily to the following theorem.

Theorem 5.1 : Let $\mathcal{N}$ be the algebra of smooth semimartingales described above. Every $N \in \mathcal{N}$ admits the representation

$$dN = (\bar\partial_A N)dA + (\bar\partial_{A^\dagger} N)dA + \bar\partial_0 N\, dt \qquad (5.7)$$

where $\bar\partial_A N$, $\partial_{A^\dagger} N$ and $\bar\partial_0 N$ are determined uniquely. Further for any $N_1, N_2 \in \mathcal{N}$,

$$d(N_1N_2) = (dN_1)N_2 + N_1(dN_2) + (\bar\partial_A N_1)(\bar\partial_{A^\dagger} N_2)dt\ . \qquad (5.8)$$

Remark 5.2 : In defining the class $\mathcal{N}$ there is no necessity to restrict m to be bounded operator in $\mathfrak{h}$. Unbounded operators can be allowed. Then (5.7) and (5.8) will hold on more restricted domains.

Remark 5.3 : Fairly routine computations yield the following identities:

(i) $dA_\varphi = \varphi dA \ ; \quad dA^\dagger_\varphi = \varphi dA^\dagger$

(ii) $dT_\varphi = \varphi T_\varphi dA \ ; \quad dT^\dagger_\varphi = \varphi T^\dagger_\varphi dA^\dagger$

(iii) $d\tilde T_\varphi = \frac{i}{2}\varphi \tilde T_\varphi dP - \frac{1}{8}\varphi^2 \tilde T_\varphi dt$

(iv) $d\Gamma_\varphi = 2(\varphi-1)\Gamma_\varphi \partial_0 A dA + (\varphi-1)\Gamma_\varphi \partial_0 A\, dA^\dagger$

(v) $dW_{\varphi,\psi} = (i\varphi + \frac{\psi}{2})W dA + (i\varphi - \frac{\psi}{2})W dA^\dagger - \frac{1}{2}|i\varphi - \frac{\psi}{2}|^2 W dt$

where $\varphi = \varphi(t,w)$, $\psi = \psi(t,w)$ are real bounded nonanticipating functionals and the same symbols denote multiplication operators and $A, A^\dagger, A_\varphi, A^\dagger_\varphi, P, T_\varphi, T^\dagger_\varphi, \tilde T_\varphi, \Gamma_\varphi$ and $W_{\varphi,\psi}$ are the various smooth semimartingales described in Section 3. This also indicates how $T_\varphi, \tilde T_\varphi, \Gamma_\varphi, W_{\varphi,\psi}$ are solutions of certain 'quantum stochastic differential equations'.

References

[1] H.P.Mckean, Stochastic Integrals, London-New York : Academic Press, 1969.

[2] K.R.Parthasarathy and K.B. Sinha, A random Trotter-Kato product formula, Statistics and Probability: Essays in Honor of C.R. Rao (G.Kallianpur, P.R. Krishnaiah, J.K. Ghosh, eds.) 553-565, North Holland, 1982.

[3] K.R.Parthasarathy, On a class of Time Inhomogeneous Nonsingular Flows and Schrodinger Operators, Math. Z, 179, 123-133, 1981.

QUANTUM DIFFUSIONS

by

R.L. Hudson,
Mathematics Department,
University of Nottingham,
University Park,
Nottingham NG7 2RD,
England,

and

K.R. Parthasarathy,
Indian Statistical Institute,
7, S.J.S. Sansanwal Marg,
New Delhi 110029,
India.

Abstract

Stochastic evolutions governed by quantum Brownian motion are considered for quantum mechanical Boson systems of one degree of freedom. These give rise to semi-groups of completely positive maps and to non-commutative Feynman-Kac formulae upon taking time zero conditional expectations.

1. Stochastic evolutions

The quantum mechanical description of a Boson system of one degree of freedom is based on a canonical pair, that is essentially a pair of self-adjoint operators (p,q), which represent respectively the momentum and position observables, satisfying the Heisenberg commutation relation

$$[p,q] = -iI \tag{1.1}$$

where $[\ ,\ ]$ denotes the commutator,

$$[S,T] = ST - TS,$$

and I is the identity operator. An example of such a pair is provided by the Schrödinger operators, essentially

$$p^{(0)} = -i\frac{d}{dx}, \quad q^{(0)} = x,$$

which act by differentiation and multiplication by the variable x in $L^2(\mathbb{R})$. The von Neumann uniqueness theorem [5] states that an arbitrary canonical pair is unitarily equivalent to a direct sum of copies of the Schrödinger pair; in particular any pair (p,q) which acts irreducibly is unitarily equivalent to $(p^{(0)},q^{(0)})$, so that there exists a unitary operator U such that

$$Up_0 = pU, \quad Uq_0 = qU.$$

U is unique to within multiplication by a scalar of unit modulus or phase.

It is convenient to replace each canonical pair (p,q) by the pair of mutually adjoint annihilation and creation operators

$$a = 2^{-\frac{1}{2}}(q+ip), \quad a^{\dagger} = 2^{-\frac{1}{2}}(q-ip)$$

which, equivalently to (1.1), satisfy

$$[a,a^{\dagger}] = I. \tag{1.2}$$

In the Heisenberg picture of dynamical evolution, operators representing observables evolve in time while maintaining algebraic properties such as irreducibility or commutation relations like (1.2). Thus, for a system described in terms of $L^2(\mathbb{R})$ for which we assume that at time t = 0 position and momentum are the Schrödinger observables, there will exist, for each time t, a unitary operator U_t intertwining the annihilation and creation operators a_t, $a_t^{\dagger}$ at time t with the corresponding operators $a^{(0)}$, $a^{(0)\dagger}$ for the Schrödinger pair,

$$U_t a^{(0)} = a_t U_t, \qquad U_t a^{(0)\dagger} = a_t^{\dagger} U_t.$$

If it is assumed that time evolution is autonomous and deterministic, and continuous in an appropriate sense, then with an appropriate choice of phase the evolution operators U_t will form a continuous one-parameter unitary group, in particular

$$U_s U_t = U_{s+t}, \quad s,t \in \mathbb{R},$$

and by Stone's theorem there exists a self-adjoint operator $\mathcal{H}$, the Hamiltonian of the system, such that

$$U_t = e^{it\mathcal{H}}, \quad t \in \mathbb{R};$$

equivalently $(U_t : t \in \mathbb{R})$ is the solution of the differential equation

$$dU = (N\,dt)U \tag{1.3}$$

with $U_0 = I$, where $N = i\mathcal{H}$. Correspondingly a_t and $a_t^{\dagger}$ satisfy the Heisenberg equations of motion

$$da = H\,dt \tag{1.4}$$

$$da^{\dagger} = H^{\dagger}\,dt \tag{1.5}$$

with $(a_0,a_0^{\dagger}) = (a^{(0)},a^{(0)\dagger})$, where $H = i[\mathcal{H},a]$.

Our purpose in this work is to describe some stochastic evolutions generalising (1.4), (1.5) for a pair $(a,a^{\dagger})$ satisfying (1.2), of the form

$$da = F\,dA^{\dagger} + G\,dA + H\,dt \tag{1.6}$$

$$da^{\dagger} = G^{\dagger}\,dA^{\dagger} + F^{\dagger}\,dA + H^{\dagger}\,dt. \tag{1.7}$$

Here $(A,A^{\dagger})$ is the pair of annihilation and creation martingales [3], which is the quantum analog of Brownian motion. These equations generalise stochastic differential equations of the form

$$dY = \sigma(Y)dQ + m(Y)dt \tag{1.8}$$

where Q is classical Brownian motion. In particular the operator-valued coefficients F, G and H are "functions" of the non-commuting unknowns a and $a^{\dagger}$ in the following sense.

Let $F^{(0)}$, $G^{(0)}$, $H^{(0)}$ be fixed operators in $L^2(\mathbb{R})$. Provided (1.2) is always satisfied, by the von Neumann uniqueness theorem the operators a_t, $a_t^{\dagger}$, the solution of (1.6) and (1.7) at time t, are unitarily equivalent to a direct sum of copies of the Schrödinger operators $a^{(0)}$, $a^{(0)\dagger}$. By F_t, G_t and H_t we mean the preimages under this unitary equivalence of the corresponding direct sum of copies of $F^{(0)}$, $G^{(0)}$ and $H^{(0)}$ respectively; thus F_t is that "function" of $(a_t,a_t^{\dagger})$ that $F^{(0)}$ is of $(a_0,a_0^{\dagger})$. The universal validity of (1.2) is thus essential for the self-consistency of our programme.

Quantum Brownian motion is realised [3] in the Fock space $\Gamma(L^2(\mathbb{R}_{\geq 0}))$ over $L^2(\mathbb{R}_{\geq 0})$. The solutions of (1.6) and (1.7) are operators in a Hilbert space tensor product $h_0 \otimes \Gamma(L^2(\mathbb{R}_{\geq 0}))$. It is convenient to assume that the initial values of the solution are uncorrelated to the Brownian motion, and to take them to be essentially the Schrödinger operators in $L^2(\mathbb{R})$; thus we take $h_0 = L^2(\mathbb{R})$ and seek solutions of (1.6), (1.7) with

$$a_0 = a^{(0)} \otimes I, \qquad a_0^{\dagger} = a^{(0)\dagger} \otimes I.$$

A more correct but unwieldy notation for the stochastic differentials in (1.6) and (1.7) acknowledges that they are operators in $h_0 \otimes \Gamma(L^2(\mathbb{R}_{\geq 0}))$ rather than $\Gamma(L^2(\mathbb{R}_{\geq 0}))$ of the form $I \otimes dA^{\dagger}$, $I \otimes dA$.

Since neither pair of operators is irreducible, there is no apriori guarantee of existence of a unitary operator U_t intertwining the solutions a_t and $a_t^{\dagger}$ of (1.6) and (1.7) with their initial values,

$$U_t a_0 = a_t U_t, \qquad U_t a_0^{\dagger} = a_t^{\dagger} U_t, \tag{1.9}$$

and if such U_t does exist it will be far from unique, since its intertwining action is specified on only one of the infinitely many degrees of freedom carried by the Fock space. However we shall see that, in examples, such a family $(U_t\colon t \geq 0)$ does exist and can be uniquely chosen to satisfy a stochastic differential equation of form

$$dU = (LdA + MdA^{\dagger} + Ndt)U \tag{1.10}$$

with $U_0 = I$. Here L, M and N are "functions" of a_t and $a_t^{\dagger}$ in the same sense as are the coefficients occurring in (1.6) and (1.7). Because of the intertwining (1.9), and because the solution U is adapted and therefore commutes with the differentials dA and

$dA^\dagger$, (1.10) can also be expressed in the form

$$dU = U(L_0 dA + M_0 dA^\dagger + N_0 dt). \tag{1.11}$$

2. Consistency equations

We determine the conditions which must be satisfied by the coefficients F, G and H occurring in (1.6) and (1.7) in order that these equations admit solutions satisfying (1.2) at all times. In view of Theorems 4.6, 4.7 and 5.1 of [3] we assume that the solutions $(a_t, a_t^\dagger : t \geq 0)$ are smooth semimartingales satisfying (1.6) and (1.7) where products of stochastic differentials are evaluated by bilinear extension of the rules

$$(dA)^2 = (dA^\dagger)^2 = dA^\dagger dA = 0, \qquad dAdA^\dagger = dt. \tag{2.1}$$

Differentiating (1.2) we thus require that $d[a,a^\dagger] = 0$, that is,

$$\begin{aligned}
0 &= d[a,a^\dagger] \\
&= [da,a^\dagger] + [a,da^\dagger] + [da,da^\dagger] \\
&= [dA^\dagger F + GdA + Hdt,\ a^\dagger] + [a,\ dA^\dagger G^\dagger + F^\dagger dA + H^\dagger dt] \\
&\quad + [dA^\dagger F + GdA + Hdt,\ dA^\dagger G^\dagger + F^\dagger dA + H^\dagger dt] \\
&= dA^\dagger\{[F,a^\dagger] + [a,G^\dagger]\} + \{[G,a^\dagger] + [a,F^\dagger]\}\ dA \\
&\quad + \{[H,a^\dagger] + [a,H^\dagger] + GG^\dagger - F^\dagger F\}\ dt
\end{aligned}$$

where we use the fact that the smooth semimartingales a and $a^\dagger$ are adapted and therefore commute with the differentials dA and $dA^\dagger$ which point into the future. Equating to zero the coefficients of $dA^\dagger$ and dt (that of dA is the Hermitian conjugate of that of $dA^\dagger$) we thus obtain the consistency equations which limit the choice of F, G and H

$$[F,a^\dagger] + [a,G^\dagger] = 0 \tag{2.2}$$

$$[H,a^\dagger] + [a,H^\dagger] = F^\dagger F - GG^\dagger. \tag{2.3}$$

These conditions are of course strictly requirements to be satisfied by the initial choice of $F^{(0)}$, $G^{(0)}$ and $H^{(0)}$, vis-a-vis the Schrödinger operators $a^{(0)}$ and $a^{(0)\dagger}$.

A similar argument can be applied to find conditions on the coefficients L, M and N occurring in (1.10) in order that the equation admits a unitary solution; differentiating the relation $UU^\dagger = I$ we obtain the restrictions

$$L + M^\dagger = 0 \tag{2.4}$$

$$N + N^\dagger + LL^\dagger = 0. \tag{2.5}$$

At a formal level it appears that there is a one-one correspondence between triples (F,G,H) satisfying (2.2) and (2.3) and triples (L,M,N) satisfying (2.4) and

(2.5), given by

$$F = [M,a], \qquad G = [L,a] \tag{2.6}$$

$$H = Na + aN^{\dagger} + LaL^{\dagger} \tag{2.7}$$

and that the solutions of the corresponding equations (1.6) and (1.7), and (1.10) are related by the intertwining condition (1.9). In the examples to be considered below, explicit constructions will justify these formal arguments.

3. Reduced evolution and Feynman-Kac formula

It is well known that, under modest restrictions on the functions σ and m, if Y^x denotes the non-anticipating solution of the classical stochastic differential equation (1.8) with $Y_0^x = x$, $x \in \mathbb{R}$, then the formula

$$\mathcal{T}_t f(x) = \mathbb{E}[f(Y_t^x)]$$

defines a contraction semigroup $\mathcal{T}_t$ on the Banach space $C_0(\mathbb{R})$ of real valued continuous functions on $\mathbb{R}$ vanishing at infinity whose infinitesimal generator is the differential operator

$$\mathcal{L} = -\tfrac{1}{2}\sigma^2(x)\frac{\partial^2}{\partial x^2} + m(x)\frac{\partial}{\partial x}.$$

To find the quantum analog of this circle of ideas we must first construct the analogs of the conditional expectation maps given the time-t σ-fields, which we shall denote by $\mathbb{E}_t$. The existence of the $\mathbb{E}_t$ in the quantum theory is not automatic, since in general it is the exception rather than the rule for conditional expectations to exist in noncommutative probability, and provides a powerful incentive for an approach to quantum stochastic processes based on quantum stochastic differential equations of the type studied in this work.

We recall that, corresponding to the direct sum decomposition

$$L^2(\mathbb{R}_{\geq 0}) = L^2([0,t[) \oplus L^2([t,\infty[),$$

there is a natural tensor product decomposition of Fock space,

$$\Gamma(L^2(\mathbb{R}_{\geq 0})) = \Gamma(L^2([0,t[)) \otimes \Gamma(L^2([t,\infty[)),$$

in which the vacuum vector is a product vector,

$$\Omega(L^2(\mathbb{R}_{\geq 0})) = \Omega(L^2([0,t[)) \otimes \Omega(L^2([t,\infty[)).$$

For $T \in B(h_0 \otimes \Gamma(L^2(\mathbb{R}_{\geq 0})))$, we define the <u>time t conditional expectation</u> of T to be the unique operator $\mathbb{E}_t[T] \in B(h_0 \otimes \Gamma(L^2([0,t[)))$ such that, for arbitrary $\psi, \chi \in h_0 \otimes \Gamma(L^2([0,t[))$,

$$\langle \psi, \mathbb{E}_t[T]\chi \rangle = \langle \psi \otimes \Omega(L^2([t,\infty[)), T\chi \otimes \Omega(L^2([t,\infty[)) \rangle.$$

It is convenient to identify $\mathbb{E}_t[T]$ with the corresponding operator $\mathbb{E}_t[T]\otimes I$ in $B(h_0\otimes\Gamma(L^2(\mathbb{R}_{\geq 0})))$. Then the tower condition

$$\mathbb{E}_s\circ\mathbb{E}_t = \mathbb{E}_s, \qquad 0\leq s\leq t \tag{3.1}$$

holds; also if $S_1,S_2\in B(h_0\otimes\Gamma(L^2([0,t[))$ then (identifying these operators with $S_1\otimes I$, $S_2\otimes I$ also)

$$\mathbb{E}_t[S_1TS_2] = S_1\mathbb{E}_t[T]S_2. \tag{3.2}$$

Now suppose that $(a_t,a_t^\dagger: t\geq 0)$ satisfy (1.2), (1.6) and (1.7) and that $(U_t: t\geq 0)$ is a corresponding unitary solution of (1.10), whose coefficients are related to those of (1.6) and (1.7) by (2.6) and (2.7), such that

$$U_ta_0 = a_tU_t, \qquad U_ta_0^\dagger = a_t^\dagger U_t.$$

Define a family $\mathcal{J}_t: t\geq 0$ of linear maps from $B(h_0)$ to itself by

$$\mathcal{J}_t(X) = \mathbb{E}_0[U_tXU_t^{-1}].$$

Since both unitary conjugation and conditional expectation are completely positive and contractive (in the sense of the operator bound norm), $\mathcal{J}_t$ is a completely positive contraction. The following formal computation indicates that $(\mathcal{J}_t: t\geq 0)$ is a semigroup of such maps and exhibits the infinitesimal generator of this semigroup. We form the differential

$$\begin{aligned} d\mathcal{J}_t(X) &= d\mathbb{E}_0[U_tXU_t^{-1}] \\ &= \mathbb{E}_0[d(U_tXU_t^{-1})] = \mathbb{E}_0[(dU_t)XU_t^{-1} + U_tXdU_t^{-1} + dU_tXdU_t^{-1}] \\ &= \mathbb{E}_0[U_t\{(L_0dA + M_0dA^\dagger + N_0dt)X \\ &\quad + X(L_0^\dagger dA^\dagger + M_0^\dagger dA + N_0^\dagger dt) + L_0XL_0^\dagger dt\}U_t^{-1}] \end{aligned}$$

where we make use of (1.11). Using the tower condition (3.1) with $s = 0$ together with (3.2) and recalling that the differentials dA and $dA^\dagger$ point to the future and have zero expectations, we see that terms involving these vanish and we obtain

$$d\mathcal{J}_t(X) = \mathbb{E}_0[U_t\mathcal{L}(X)U_t^{-1}]dt = \mathcal{J}_t\mathcal{L}(X)dt$$

where $\mathcal{L}$ is the operator in $B(h_0)$,

$$\mathcal{L}(X) = N_0X + XN_0^\dagger + L_0XL_0^\dagger.$$

Since $\mathcal{L}$ is time independent, it follows formally that $(\mathcal{J}_t: t\geq 0)$ is a semigroup, of which $\mathcal{L}$ is the infinitesimal generator.

From (2.5) we may write $N_0 = -\frac{1}{2}L_0^\dagger L_0 + i\mathcal{H}_0$ where $\mathcal{H}_0$ is self-adjoint, hence $\mathcal{L}$ can be expressed as

$$\mathcal{L}(X) = -\tfrac{1}{2}\{L_0^\dagger L_0,X\} + i[\mathcal{H}_0,X] + L_0XL_0^\dagger$$

where $\{\ ,\ \}$ is the anticommutator,

$$\{S,T\} = ST + TS.$$

In [4] it is shown that the general form of the infinitesimal generator of a strongly continuous semigroup of completely positive maps is

$$\mathcal{L}(X) = -\tfrac{1}{2}\sum_j \{L_j^{\dagger}L_j, X\} + i[\mathcal{H}, X] + \sum_j L_j X L_j^{\dagger}.$$

The possibility of a stochastic dilation involving independent quantum Brownian motions for each index j is evident.

Another interesting semigroup is constructed simply by taking the time zero conditional expectation of U_t itself; using (1.11) and factorising $\mathbb{E}_0$ as $\mathbb{E}_0 \circ \mathbf{E}_t$ we see that $(\mathbb{E}_0[U_t]: t \geq 0)$ is a contraction semigroup of operators in h_0 with infinitesimal generator N_0,

$$e^{tN_0} = \mathbb{E}_0[U_t].$$

Perturbations of this semigroup can be constructed which constitute a noncommutative generalisation of the Feynman-Kac formula as follows.

Let $V_0 \in B(h_0)$ be such that the operators $V_t = U_t V_0 U_t^{-1}$ are mutually commutative (as will be so if V_0 is a function of q_0 alone, $V_0 = v_0(q_0)$, and the q_t constructed from the solution of (1.6) and (1.7) have this commutativity property), and consider the operators

$$S_t^{V_0} = \mathbb{E}_0\left[\exp\left\{-\int_0^t U_r V_0 U_r^{-1} dr\right\} U_t\right].$$

We again differentiate formally, obtaining via the fundamental theorem of calculus

$$dS_t^{V_0} = \mathbb{E}_0\left[\exp\left\{-\int_0^t U_r V_0 U_r^{-1} dr\right\}(-U_t V_0 U_t^{-1})U_t dt\right.$$

$$\left. + \exp\left\{-\int_0^t U_r V_0 U_r^{-1} dr\right\} dU_t\right].$$

Using (1.11) and the factorisation $\mathbb{E}_0 = \mathbf{E}_0 \circ \mathbb{E}_t$ we find that

$$dS_t^{V_0} = S_t^{V_0}(-V_0 + N_0)\, dt$$

that is, since $-V_0 + N_0$ is time-independent, $(S_t^{V_0}: t \geq 0)$ is a semigroup of which this is the infinitesimal generator. Thus

$$e^{t(N_0 - V_0)} = \mathbf{E}_0\left[\exp\left\{-\int_0^t U_r V_0 U_r^{-1} dr\right\} U_t\right].$$

In particular when $V = v(q)$ we obtain the Feynman-Kac formula

$$e^{t(N_0 - V_0)} = \mathbf{E}_0\left[\exp\left\{-\int_0^t v_0(q_r) dr\right\} U_t\right].$$

In §4 we shall show that some Feynman-Kac formulae known to physics are of this form.

4. Equations with constant noise coefficients

The consistency equation (2.2) is satisfied by taking the coefficients F and G of the noise terms in (1.6) to be scalar multiples of the identity,

$$F = \lambda I, \quad G = \mu I, \quad \lambda, \mu \in \mathbb{C};$$

(2.3) can then be satisfied by the choice

$$H = \tfrac{1}{2}(|\lambda|^2 - |\mu|^2)a.$$

With these choices (1.6) and (1.7) become

$$da = \lambda dA^{\dagger} + \mu dA + \tfrac{1}{2}(|\lambda|^2 - |\mu|^2)a\, dt \tag{4.1}$$

$$da^{\dagger} = \bar{\mu} dA^{\dagger} + \bar{\lambda} dA + \tfrac{1}{2}(|\lambda|^2 - |\mu|^2)a^{\dagger}\, dt. \tag{4.2}$$

Equations (4.1) and (4.2) may be transformed in two ways. A <u>gauge transformation</u>

$$A_t \to B_t = e^{-i\theta}A_t, \qquad A_t^{\dagger} \to B_t^{\dagger} = e^{i\theta}A_t^{\dagger} \tag{4.3}$$

where $\theta \in]-\pi,\pi]$ replaces the quantum Brownian motion $(A_t, A_t^{\dagger}: t \geq 0)$ by a family of operators $(B_t, B_t^{\dagger}: t \geq 0)$ satisfying identical algebraic relations and enjoying identical probabilistic properties in the Fock vacuum state, in other words another quantum Brownian motion. Secondly, a linear change of variable

$$a \to b = \alpha a + \beta a^{\dagger}, \qquad a^{\dagger} \to b^{\dagger} = \bar{\alpha} a^{\dagger} + \bar{\beta} a, \qquad \alpha, \beta \in \mathbb{C} \tag{4.3b}$$

is admissible provided the transformed variables b and $b^{\dagger}$ satisfy the basic commutation relation (1.1); the condition for this is that

$$|\alpha|^2 - |\beta|^2 = 1$$

and (4.3b) is then called a <u>linear canonical transformation</u>. Particular examples of linear canonical transformations are gauge transformations in the unknown

$$a \to b = e^{-i\phi}a, \qquad a^{\dagger} \to b^{\dagger} = e^{i\phi}a^{\dagger}, \qquad \phi \in]-\pi,\pi] \tag{4.4}$$

and <u>pseudo-rotations</u>,

$$\begin{pmatrix} a \\ a^{\dagger} \end{pmatrix} \to \begin{pmatrix} b \\ b^{\dagger} \end{pmatrix} = \begin{pmatrix} \cosh\chi & \sinh\chi \\ \sinh\chi & \cosh\chi \end{pmatrix} \begin{pmatrix} a \\ a^{\dagger} \end{pmatrix}, \qquad \chi \in \mathbb{R}. \tag{4.5}$$

By applying the gauge transformations (4.3) and (4.4) to the Brownian motion and the unknown, with the choices

$$\theta = \tfrac{1}{2}(\arg\lambda - \arg\mu), \qquad \phi = \tfrac{1}{2}(\arg\lambda + \arg\mu)$$

(4.1) and (4.2) are transformed to forms where the coefficients λ and μ are real and non-negative. The effect of transforming the variables with the pseudo-rotation (4.5) is then to replace the real coefficients (λ,μ) by (λ',μ'), where

$$\begin{pmatrix} \lambda' \\ \mu' \end{pmatrix} = \begin{pmatrix} \cosh\chi & \sinh\chi \\ \sinh\chi & \cosh\chi \end{pmatrix} \begin{pmatrix} \lambda \\ \mu \end{pmatrix}.$$

According to whether $\lambda = \mu$, $\lambda < \mu$ or $\lambda > \mu$, χ can then be chosen so that (λ',μ') is either (ρ,ρ), $(0,\rho)$ or $(\rho,0)$ where ρ is a non-negative parameter. Thus (4.1) and (4.2) reduce to one of three canonical forms

$$da = \rho(dA + dA^{\dagger}), \qquad da^{\dagger} = \rho(dA + dA^{\dagger}) \tag{4.6}$$

$$da = \rho dA - \tfrac{1}{2}\rho^2 a dt, \qquad da^{\dagger} = \rho dA^{\dagger} - \tfrac{1}{2}\rho^2 a^{\dagger} dt \tag{4.7}$$

$$da = \rho dA^{\dagger} + \tfrac{1}{2}\rho^2 a dt, \qquad da^{\dagger} = \rho dA + \tfrac{1}{2}\rho^2 a^{\dagger} dt. \tag{4.8}$$

The solution of (4.6) is clearly

$$a_t = a_0 + \rho(A_t + A_t^{\dagger}), \qquad a_t^{\dagger} = a_0^{\dagger} + \rho(A_t + A_t^{\dagger})$$

or equivalently

$$p_t = p_0, \qquad q_t = q_0 + 2^{\frac{1}{2}}\rho Q_t$$

where we write Q_t for the classical Brownian motion $A_t + A_t^{\dagger}$. The unitary operators

$$U_t = e^{-2^{\frac{1}{2}}\rho p_0 Q_t} = e^{i2^{\frac{1}{2}}\rho p_t Q_t}$$

intertwine the solutions at times t and 0 and satisfy

$$dU = (i2^{\frac{1}{2}}\rho p(dA + dA^{\dagger}) - \rho^2 p^2 dt)U, \qquad U_0 = I,$$

as is seen using Itô's formula. The corresponding Feynman-Kac formula is the classical one

$$e^{-t(\rho^2 p_0^2 + V(q_0))} = \mathbf{E}_0\left[\exp\left\{-\int_0^t V(q_0 + 2^{\frac{1}{2}}\rho Q_r)dr\right\} e^{i2^{\frac{1}{2}}\rho p_0 Q_t}\right].$$

Equation (4.7) is analogous to the stochastic differential equation defining the classical Ornstein-Uhlenbeck velocity process and has an analogous solution, namely

$$p_t = e^{-\frac{1}{2}\rho^2 t} p_0 + \int_0^t e^{-\frac{1}{2}\rho^2(t-r)}\, dP_r \tag{4.9}$$

$$q_t = e^{-\frac{1}{2}\rho^2 t} q_0 + \int_0^t e^{-\frac{1}{2}\rho^2(t-r)}\, dQ_r \tag{4.10}$$

where in addition to $Q_t = A_t + A_t^{\dagger}$, we introduce the canonically conjugate classical Brownian motion $P_t = i(A_t^{\dagger} - A_t)$. Note that the q_t commute for different times t. This is the so called <u>canonical Ornstein Uhlenbeck velocity process</u> of [2].

Following [2] we construct unitary operators U_t intertwining the solutions (4.9) and (4.10) with their initial values as follows. We first replace the Schrödinger realisation with $h_0 = L^2(\mathbb{R})$ by the equivalent "number operator representation", taking h_0 to be $\Gamma(\mathbb{C}) = \ell^2$ in which $a^{(0)}$ and $a^{(0)\dagger}$ act as

$$a^0(z_0,z_1,\ldots) = (z_1,\sqrt{2}z_2,\sqrt{3}z_3,\ldots)$$

$$a^{0\dagger}(z_0,z_1,\ldots) = (0,z_0,\sqrt{2}z_1,\ldots).$$

The tensor product $h_0 \otimes \Gamma(L^2(\mathbb{R}_{\geq 0}))$ is then itself a Fock space

$$h_0 \otimes \Gamma(L^2(\mathbb{R}_{\geq 0})) = \Gamma(C) \otimes \Gamma(L^2(\mathbb{R}_{\geq 0})) = \Gamma(C \oplus L^2(\mathbb{R}_{\geq 0})).$$

The operator in $\mathbb{C} \oplus L^2(\mathbb{R}_{\geq 0})$ $(z,f) \to (z',f')$, where

$$\begin{pmatrix} z' \\ f' \end{pmatrix} = \begin{pmatrix} e^{-\frac{1}{2}\rho^2 t} & B_t \\ C_t & I+D_t \end{pmatrix} \begin{pmatrix} z \\ f \end{pmatrix} \tag{4.11}$$

and

$$B_t f = \int_0^t e^{-\frac{1}{2}\rho^2(t-r)} f(r)\, dr$$

$$(C_t z)(r) = -\chi_{[0,t]}(r) e^{-\frac{1}{2}\rho^2 r}$$

$$(D_t f)(r) = \int \chi_{[0,t]}(r')\chi_{[r',t]}(r) e^{-\frac{1}{2}\rho^2(r-r')} f(r')\, dr',$$

is unitary [2]. Its second quantisation provides the required operator U_t, and satisfies the equation

$$dU = (\rho a dA^\dagger - \rho a^\dagger dA - \tfrac{1}{2}\rho^2 a^\dagger a dt)U.$$

Formally U is the "stochastic product integral"

$$U = \prod_0^t \exp\{\rho(a_0 dA^\dagger - a_0^\dagger dA)\}.$$

The corresponding Feynman-Kac formula

$$e^{-t\{\frac{1}{2}\rho^2 a_0^\dagger a_0 + V(q_0)\}} = \mathbb{E}_0\left[\exp\left\{-\int_0^t V\left(e^{-\frac{1}{2}\rho^2 r} q_0 + \int_0^r e^{-\frac{1}{2}\rho^2(r-r')} dQ_{r'}\right) dr\right\} \prod_0^t \exp\{\rho(a_0 dA^\dagger - a_0^\dagger dA)\}\right]$$

is essentially that known in the physics literature [1,6] as the "oscillator process" Feynman-Kac formula.

Equation (4.8) has solution analogous to that of (4.7), namely

$$p_t = e^{\frac{1}{2}\rho^2 t} p_0 - \int_0^t e^{\frac{1}{2}\rho^2(t-r)}\, dP_r$$

$$q_t = e^{\frac{1}{2}\rho^2 t} q_0 + \int_0^t e^{\frac{1}{2}\rho^2(t-r)}\, dQ_r.$$

Note that once again the q_t all commute. The unitary operators U_t intertwining (p_t,q_t) with (p_0,q_0) and satisfying

$$dU = (\rho a^{\dagger}dA^{\dagger} - \rho a dA - \tfrac{1}{2}\rho^2 aa^{\dagger}dt)U$$

are again given formally by a stochastic product integral

$$U = \prod_0^t \exp\{\rho(a_0^{\dagger}dA^{\dagger} - a_0 dA)\}.$$

In this case U_t can be defined rigorously as the unitary operator satisfying certain Euclidean covariance conditions which implements a non-unitary real-linear Bogolubov transformation analogous to (4.11). Details will be published elsewhere. The corresponding Feynman-Kac formula is

$$e^{-t\{\frac{1}{2}\rho^2 a_0 a_0^{\dagger}+V(q_0)\}} = \mathbf{E}_0\left[\exp\left\{-\int_0^t V\left(e^{\frac{1}{2}\rho^2 r}q_0 + \int_0^r e^{\frac{1}{2}\rho^2(r-r')}dQ_{r'}\right) dr\right.\right.$$
$$\left.\prod_0^t \exp\{\rho(a_0^{\dagger}dA^{\dagger} - a_0 dA)\}\right].$$

References

[1] Glimm, J. and Jaffe, A., Quantum physics - a functional integration point of view, Springer, New York (1981).

[2] Hudson, R.L., Ion, P.D.F. and Parthasarathy, K.R., Time orthogonal unitary dilations and noncommutative Feynman-Kae formulae, Commun. Math. Phys. 83, 261-80 (1982).

[3] Hudson, R.L., Karamdikar, R.L. and Parthasarathy, K.R., Towards a theory of noncommutative semimartingales adapted to Brownian motion and a quantum Itô's formula, these Proceedings.

[4] Lindblad, G., On the generators of quantum dynamical semigroups, Commun. Math. Phys. 48, 119-30 (1976).

[5] von Neumann, J., Die Eindeutigkeit der Schrödingerschen Operatoren, Math. Ann. 104, 571-8 (1937).

[6] Simon, B., Functional integration and quantum physics, Academic Press, New York (1979).

STOCHASTIC DIFFERENTIAL EQUATIONS

IN INFINITE DIMENSIONS

Kiyosi Ito

Department of Mathematics
Gakushuin University
Mejiro, Tokyo 171, Japan

1. Introduction

The main part of the construction of flows of diffeomorphisms determined by a stochastic differential equation :

(1.1) $dX_t = a(X_t)dt + b(X_t)dw_t$

is the following theorem which implies that for almost every sample, the solution of this equation is C^∞ in the initial data $X_0 = x$ under some smoothness assumptions(see P.Malliavin (1), K.D.Elworthy (2), F.Funaki(3), J.M.Bismut(4), and H.Kunita(5) for flows of diffeomorphisms and see also N. Ikeda and S. Watanabe (6) for a systematic treatment) :

Theorem. If $a(x)$, $b(x)$ and $f(x)$ are C^∞ functions whose support lies in the closed interval $[0,1]$, i.e. $a,b,f \in \mathcal{D}[0,1]$, then the equation (1.1) with the initial data

(1.2) $X_0 = f(x)$

has a unique solution $X_t = X_t(x)$ such that $X_t(\cdot) \in \mathcal{D}[0,1]$ for every t a.s. Also the process X_t is a sample continuous process with values in $\mathcal{D}[0,1]$, where the topology in $\mathcal{D}(0,1)$ is given by a sequence of norms :

(1.3) $\|f\|_n = \sup_x |f^{(n)}(x)| \qquad n = 0,1,2,\cdots$,

or equivalently

(1.3') $\|f\|_n^2 = \int_0^1 |f^{(n)}(x)|^2 dx, \quad n = 0,1,2,\cdots$.

In this paper we will prove this theorem from the view-point of stochastic differential equations in infinite dimensions. The equation (1.1) is regarded as a stochastic differential equation concerning a process $X_t = X_t(\cdot)$ with values in $L_2 = L_2(0,1)$, by writing (1.1) in the form

(1.4) $\quad dX_t = A(X_t)dt + B(X_t)dw_t, \quad X_0 = f$

where A and B are non-linear operators in L_2 defined by

(1.5) $\quad A(g)(x) = a(g(x)), \quad B(g)(x) = b(g(x)) \; (g \in L^2).$

To find a clue to the proof of differentiability of $X_t = X_t(x)$ in $x \in (0,1)$, we apply formal differentiation to (1.1) and obtain the following stochastic differential equation the derivative $Y_t(x) = X_t'(x)$ must satisfy :

(1.6)
$$dY_t(x) = a'(X_t(0) + \int_0^x Y_t(y)dy)Y_t(x)dt$$
$$+ b'(X_t(0) + \int_0^x Y_t(y)dy)Y_t(x)dw_t ,$$

which can be written in the form

(1.7)
$$dY_t = C_t(Y)Y_t dt + D_t(Y)Y_t dw_t ,$$
$$Y_0 = f'$$

where C_t and D_t are operator-valued processes adapted to the Wiener process w_t . Rewriting (1.1) in the form (1.4) is almost trivial, because (1.4) can be observed for each x separately. But rewriting (1.6) in (1.7) is important, because separate discussion in each x is impossible. The equation (1.7) is really a stochastic differential equation in infinite dimensions.

To prove the differentiability of $X_t(x)$ in x we first solve (1.7) and then check that

$$X_t(x) := X_t(0) + \int_0^x Y_t(y)dy, \quad x \in (0,1)$$

satisfies (1.4). The uniqueness of the solution of (1.4) implies that for almost every x we have

(1.8) $\quad X_t(x) = X_t(x) = X_t(0) + \int_0^x Y_t(y)dy ,$

which proves that $X_t(x)$ has an absolutely continuous (in x) version whose Radon-Nikodym derivative $Y_t(x)$ is square integrable in x. Repeating this argument we can complete the proof of our theorem. This is our rough idea whose details are given in the next section.

2. Proof of the theorem

Step 1. The equation (1.4) has a unique L_2-valued solution $X_t = X_t(\cdot)$ whose sample path is continuous (in t) with respect to the norm in L_2. To prove, we can use the Picard method as for the one-dimensional case, because A and B satisfy the Lipschitz condition:

$$\|A(g_1) - A(g_2)\| + \|B(g_1) - B(g_2)\| \leqq K\|g_1 - g_2\|$$

where the norm is the L_2-norm and K is a constant.

Step 2. The equation (1.7) can be solved by the Picard method as follows. We define a sequence of approximate solutions $Y_{n,t}$ as follows :

(2.1) $$Y_{0,t} = f'$$

$$Y_{n+1,t} = f' + \int_0^t Y_{n,s}(C_s(Y_{n,s})ds + D_s(Y_{n,s})dw_s)$$

We can find constants α and β such that

$$E(\|Y_{n+1,t}\|^2) = \alpha + \alpha\int_0^t E(\|Y_{n,s}\|^2)ds ,$$

and

$$E(\|Y_{1,t}\|^2) \leqq \alpha(1 + \beta t) \leqq \alpha e^{\beta t} .$$

Hence

(2.2) $$E(\|Y_{n,t}\|^2) \leqq \alpha e^{\beta t} \quad \text{for every } n.$$

Using this fact, observing that a' and b' are bounded and using the same technique as for one-dimensional case, we can prove that there exists a sample continuous process Y_t such that

(2.3) $$E(\|Y_{n,t} - Y_t\|^2) \to 0$$

Step 3. As we mentioned in Section 1,

$$X_t(x) = X_t(0) + \int_0^x Y_t(y)dy \quad \text{a.e. on } (0,1)$$

for every t. Hence the right hand side is an absolutely continuous version of $X_t(x)$. From now on we write this version by the same notation $X_t(x)$. Then

(2.4) $$Y_t(x) = X_t'(x) \quad \text{(Radon-Nykodym derivative)}$$

Step 4. Repeating the same procedure we can prove that $X_t^{(n)}(x)$ has an absolutely continuous version whose derivative is in L_2. However, there is one point we have to cope with. When we apply the formal differentian, we obtain a stochastic differential equation of the following type :

(2.5) $$dX_t^{(n)} = P_n(X_t^{(1)}, X_t^{(2)}, \cdots, X_t^{(n-1)})dt$$

$$+ Q_n(X_t^{(1)}, X_t^{(2)}, \cdots, X_t^{(n-1)})dw_t$$

where P_n and Q_n are polynomials with coefficients $a^{(i)}(X_t)$, and $b^{(i)}(X_t)$, $i = 0,1,2,\cdots,n$. To solve the equation for $X_t^{(n)}$ by the Picard method we have to check that

(2.6) $E(\|(X_t^{(n)})^p\|) < \infty$, $p = 1,2,\cdots$

by induction on n. Since the same method can apply for every n, we treat the case $n = 1$. In this case what we have to prove is that

(2.7) $E(\|Y_t^p\|) < \infty$, $p = 1,2,\cdots$

for the process Y_t mentioned above. Applying the stochastic chain rule to (2.1) we have

$$Y_{n+1,t}^p = (f')^p + \int_0^t Y_{n,t}^p (C_{p,s}ds + D_{p,s}dw_s)$$

where $C_{p,t}$ and $D_{p,t}$ are adapted to w_t and $E(C_{p,t}^2)$ and $E(D_{p,t}^2)$ are bounded. Hence we use the same technique as above to obtain

$$E(\| Y_{n+1,t}^p \|^2) \leqq \alpha_p e^{\beta_p t}$$

Since $\|Y_{n,t} - Y_t\| \to 0$, we can take a subsequence of $(Y_{n,t})_n$ which converges to Y_t almost everywhere on $(0,1) \times \Omega$. Hence we can use Fatou's lemma to conclude that

$$E(\|Y^p\|^2) \leqq \alpha_p e^{\beta_p t} < \infty .$$

References

(1) P. Malliavin, Stochastic calculus of variation and hypoelliptic operators. Proc. Intern. Symposium SDE Kyoto 1976, 195-263 Kinokuniya, Tokyo, 1978.

(2) K.D. Elworthy, Stochastic dynamical systems and flows. Stochastic Analysis, 79-95, Acad. Press New York, 1978.

(3) T. Funaki, Construction of a solution of random transport equation with boundry condition, J. Math. Soc. Japan 31 (1979), 719-744.

(4) J.M. Bismut, C.R. 290 (1980).

(5) H. Kunita, Proc. LMS Symp. on Stochastic Integrals, Durham, 1980.

(6) N. Ikeda - S. Watanabe, Stochastic Differential Equations and Diffusion Processes.

COMMUTING SEMIGROUPS OF ISOMETRIES AND KARHUNEN REPRESENTATION OF SECOND ORDER STATIONARY RANDOM FIELDS

by

G. Kallianpur
University of North Carolina at Chapel Hill

and

V. Mandrekar
University of North Carolina at Chapel Hill
and
Michigan State University

Keywords: Random fields, multiplicity, innovations, Karhunen representation.

This research was supported by AFOSR Grant No. 80-0080.

0. Introduction. In this paper we extend the work of [5] to continuous, stationary second order random fields (s.o.r.f.'s) depending on two continuous parameters. The "time domain" analysis of a s.o.r.f. is based on what appears to be a natural concept of a purely nondeterministic (PND) random field and yields the four-fold Wold decomposition of a s.o.r.f. obtained in Theorem 3.1. A new type of Karhunen representation in terms of stochastic integrals is obtained in Theorem 3.2 for a PND s.o.r.f.

These results are consequences of the work of Section 1 and 2 where a more general point of view is adopted. Our aim here is to obtain the appropriate generalization of the work of J.L.B. Cooper [1] to the case of two commuting continuous semigroups of isometries $\{S_u^{(1)}\}$, $\{S_v^{(2)}\}$ $(u, v \in \mathbb{R}_+)$ acting on a separable Hilbert space H. The basic condition imposed on the semigroups are (1.2) and (1.6) stated in Section 1. The three results beginning with Theorem 2.1 are concerned with a decomposition of H induced by the semigroups which satisfy (besides (1.1) and (1.2)) a condition of (2.1) stronger than (1.6). Theorem 2.3 gives the decomposition of H under (2.6). Theorems 2.1 and 2.3 are the key steps leading to the main result of Section 2 given in Theorem 2.4, viz., the four-fold Cooper decomposition of H

corresponding to semigroups satisfying conditions (1.1), (1.2) and (2.6). The latter decomposition is the direct generalization of Theorem 2.1 of [4], where a single continuous semigroup of isometries is considered.

An interesting new feature of the four-fold Cooper decomposition and also of the Karhunen representation for PND random fields is the extension of the Cramér-Hida theory of myltiplicity that emerges from this work. Associated with a continuous stationary s.o.r.f. (of two parameters) is a uniquely determined triplet of (possibly infinite) numbers $\{M_0, M_1, M_2\}$ which we call the multiplicities of the s.o.r.f. M_0 is the two-dimensional multiplicity and M_i is the i-directional multiplicity (i = 1, 2). Furthermore, the multiplicities are identified with the dimensions of certain subspaces of H. In this respect, the definition of M_0, M_1 and M_2 turn out to be the precise parallel of the definition of the multiplicities given in [5] for discrete s.o.r.f.'s.

Of the many open problems that remain to be investigated, the most important seem to be (i) the derivation of spectral criteria which ensure conditions (1.2), (1.6) and (2.1) and (ii) the relationship of the multiplicities with the spectral properties of the random field. Work on these questions is in progress.

1. A four-fold decomposition for commuting semigroups of isometries. Let $\{S_u^{(i)}\}$ $u \in \mathbb{R}_+$, i = 1, 2 be two strongly continuous semigroups of isometries on a separable Hilbert space H satisfying

$$S_u^{(1)}S_v^{(2)} = S_v^{(2)}S_u^{(1)} \qquad u, v \in \mathbb{R}_+, \; S_0^{(i)} = I. \tag{1.1}$$

Let $P^{(i)}(u)$ be the orthogonal projection onto $S_u^{(i)}(H)$ (i = 1, 2) and P(u, v) the orthogonal projection onto $S_u^{(1)}S_v^{(2)}(H)$. We also assume

$$P^{(1)}(u)P^{(2)}(v) = P(u, v) \text{ for all } (u, v) \in \mathbb{R}_+^2 . \tag{1.2}$$

Let $H_\infty^{(i)} = \bigcap_{u\geq 0} S_u^{(i)}(H)$, i = 1, 2. By (1.2) we get $H_\infty^{(1)} \cap H_\infty^{(2)} = H_\infty$ where

$H_\infty = \bigcap_{u,v\geq 0} S_u^{(1)} S_v^{(2)}(H)$ and

$$(1.3)\quad P^{(1)}(u)P_{H_\infty^{(2)}} = P_{H_\infty^{(2)}}P^{(1)}(u) \quad \text{and} \quad P^{(2)}(v)P_{H_\infty^{(1)}} = P_{H_\infty^{(1)}}P^{(2)}(v).$$

<u>Theorem 1.1</u>. Let $\{S_u^{(i)}\}$ $(u \in \mathbb{R}_+)$ be two strongly continuous semigroups of isometries satisfying (1.1) and (1.2). Then

$$H = H_0 \oplus H_1 \oplus H_2 \oplus H_\infty$$

where

(a) $H_0 = (H_\infty^{(1)})^\perp \cap (H_\infty^{(2)})^\perp$

(b) $H_1 = (H_\infty^{(1)})^\perp \cap H_\infty^{(2)}$

(c) $H_2 = H_\infty^{(1)} \cap (H_\infty^{(2)})^\perp$

(d) H_1, H_2 and H_∞ are invariant under $\{S_m^{(1)}\}$ $u \in \mathbb{R}_+$ and i = 1, 2.

<u>Proof:</u> We note that the four spaces in the above decomposition are clearly orthogonal. Since $P_{H_\infty^{(1)}}$ commutes with $P_{H_\infty^{(2)}}$ we get

$$I = (P_{H_\infty^{(1)}} + P_{(H_\infty^{(1)})^\perp})(P_{H_\infty^{(2)}} + P_{(H_\infty^{(2)})^\perp})$$

giving the decomposition. To prove (d) we observe that $S_u^{(1)}(H_\infty^{(1)}) = H_\infty^{(1)}$ ([4], Theorem 2.1) giving $S_u^{(1)}(H_\infty^{(1)})^\perp = (H_\infty^{(1)})^\perp$. By (1.1),

$$S_u^{(1)}(H_\infty^{(2)}) = \bigcap_{u\geq 0} S_v^{(2)} S_u^{(1)}(H) \subseteq \bigcap_{v\geq 0} S_v^{(2)}(H) = H_\infty^{(2)}.$$

Also $H_\infty^{(2)} = H_\infty^{(2)} \cap (H_\infty^{(1)})^\perp \oplus H_\infty$. Since H_∞^2 and H_∞ reduce $S_v^{(2)}$ we get $S_v^{(2)}(H_1) = H_1$. A similar argument shows that $S_u^{(1)}$, $S_v^{(2)}$ leave H_2 invariant. Clearly, $S_u^{(1)}S_v^{(2)}(H_\infty) = H_\infty$ completing the proof.

In general, we do not know whether $S_u^{(i)}$ $(i = 1, 2)$ $u \in \mathbb{R}_+$ leave H_0 invariant. However in applications to random fields they do. To verify this we start by defining a stationary random field.

A continuous second order random field (s.o.r.f.) X is a family of complex-valued random variables $\{X_{st}(\phi)\}$ where $(s, t) \in \mathbb{R}^2$, $\phi \in \Phi$, a Hausdorff space satisfying the first countability axiom and $E|X_{st}(\phi)|^2 < \infty$ for all s, t. The s.o.r.f. is called stationary if $EX_{st}(\phi) = m(\phi)$ (we take $m(\phi) \equiv 0$) and $EX_{st}(\phi)\overline{X_{u,v}(\psi)} = r(s - u, t - v; \phi, \psi)$. It will also be assumed that X is continuous, i.e.,

(i) if $\phi_n \to \phi$ then $E|X_{st}(\phi_n) - X_{st}(\phi)|^2 \to 0$ for each s, t, and

(ii) For each ϕ, $E|X_{st}(\phi) - X_{s't'}(\phi)|^2 \to 0$ as $(s, t) \to (s', t')$.

We need the following notation:

$L(X) = \overline{sp}\{X_{st}(\phi), (s, t) \in \mathbb{R}^2, \phi \in \Phi\}$,

$L(X; s, t) = \overline{sp}\ X_{uv}(\phi), u \le s, v \le t, \phi \in \Phi\}$,

$L^1(X; s) = \overline{sp}\{X_{uv}(\phi), u \le s, v \in \mathbb{R}, \phi \in \Phi\}$,

$L^2(X; t) = \overline{sp}\{X_{uv}(\phi), u \in \mathbb{R}, v \le t, \phi \in \Phi\}$,

$L^i(X; -\infty) = \bigcap_t L^i(X; t)$ $(i = 1, 2)$.

Let $\{U_s^1\}$ and $\{U_t^2\}$ be one-parameter groups of unitary operators on $L(X)$ such that $U_s^1 X_{uv}(\phi) = X_{u+s,v}(\phi)$ and $U_t^2 X_{uv}(\phi) = X_{u,v+t}(\phi)$ for all ϕ. Assume that for all $s,t \in \mathbb{R}_+$,

$$P_{L^1(X;\ s)} P_{L^2(X;\ t)} = P_{L(X;\ s,\ t)}. \tag{1.4}$$

Define $H = L^1(X; 0) \cap L^2(X; 0)$, $S_u^{(1)} = (U_u^1)^{-1}|_H$, $S_v^{(2)} = (U_v^2)^{-1}|_H$ for $u, v \in \mathbb{R}_+$. Then for $t < 0$

(1.5) $$S_u^{(1)} L^2(X;\ t) = L^2(X;\ t) \quad \text{and} \quad S_v^{(2)} L^1(X;\ t) = L^1(X;\ t).$$

Now $H_\infty^{(1)} = L^1(X;\ -\infty) \cap L^2(X;\ 0)$, $H_\infty^{(2)} = L^1(X;\ 0) \cap L^2(X;\ -\infty)$.

Thus $$(H_\infty^{(1)})^\perp = L^1(X;\ -\infty)^\perp \cap L^2(X;\ 0) \cap L^1(X;\ 0) \quad \text{and}$$

$$(H_\infty^{(2)})^\perp = L^2(X;\ -\infty)^\perp \cap L^1(X;\ 0) \cap L^2(X;\ 0).$$

We observe that by (1.5) and ([4] Theorem 2.1), the subspaces $L^1(X;\ -\infty)^\perp$, $L^2(X;\ -\infty)^\perp$ reduce $S_u^{(i)}$ $(i = 1, 2)$ $u \in \mathbb{R}_+$. Hence $S_u^{(i)}(H_\infty^{(1)})^\perp \subseteq (H_\infty^{(1)})^\perp$ and $S_v^{(i)}(H_\infty^{(2)})^\perp \subseteq (H_\infty^{(2)})^\perp$ for $i = 1, 2$, $u, v \in \mathbb{R}_+$, i.e.

$$S_u^{(i)}(H_0) = S_u^{(i)}[(H_\infty^{(1)})^\perp \cap (H_\infty^{(2)})^\perp] \subseteq (H_\infty^{(1)})^\perp \cap (H_\infty^{(2)})^\perp.$$

From now on we shall make the following assumption on $\{S_u^{(i)}\}$.

(1.6) $$S_u^{(i)}(H_0) \subseteq H_0 \quad \text{for } u \in \mathbb{R}_+ \text{ and } i = 1, 2.$$

Under the assumption (1.6), we have $\bigcap_{u\geq 0} S_u^{(i)}(H_0) \subseteq H_0$ for $i = 1, 2$. But $\bigcap_{u\geq 0} S_u^{(i)}(H_0) \subseteq H_\infty^{(i)}$ giving $\bigcap_{u\geq 0} S_u^{(i)}(H_0) = \{0\}$ for $i = 1, 2$.

In the next section we first study the Cooper decomposition of a Hilbert space H for which $H_\infty^{(i)} = \{0\}$ for $i = 1, 2$.

2. Four-fold Cooper decomposition for commuting isometries. Let $\{S_u^{(i)}\}$ $u \in \mathbb{R}_+$ $(i = 1, 2)$ be two strongly continuous semigroups of isometries satisfying (1.1), (1.2) and such that

(2.1) $$\text{(a)} \bigcap_{u\geq 0} S_u^{(1)}(H) = \{0\} \quad \text{and} \quad \text{(b)} \bigcap_{v\geq 0} S_v^{(2)}(H) = \{0\}.$$

For $i = 1, 2$ let

$$E^{(i)}[a, b) = P^{(i)}(a) - P^{(i)}(b) \quad \text{for } a < b.$$

Then, under (2.1)(a), $E^{(1)}$ extends to an orthogonal projection-valued spectral measure on the Borel subsets of $\mathbb{R}_+$ and $E^{(2)}$ extends similarly under (2.1)(b). By (1.2), the spectral measures $\{E^{(1)}(\Delta)\}$ and $\{E^{(2)}(\Delta')\}$ commute. Thus the family $E(\Delta \times \Delta') \overset{\text{def}}{=} E^{(1)}(\Delta)E^{(2)}(\Delta')$, Δ, $\Delta' \in \mathcal{B}(\mathbb{R}_+)$ generates a spectral measure on $\mathbb{R}_+^2$ by ([6], p. 19). In addition from $S_u^{(i)} E^{(i)}(\tilde{\Delta}) = E^{(i)}(\tilde{\Delta} + u)S_u^{(i)}$ $(i = 1, 2,\ \tilde{\Delta} \in \mathcal{B}(\mathbb{R}_+^2)$

it follows that

(2.2) $$S_u^{(1)}S_v^{(2)}E(\tilde{\Delta}) = E(\tilde{\Delta} + (u, v))S_u^{(1)}S_v^{(2)} \quad \text{for} \quad (u, v) \in \mathbb{R}_+^2 \text{ and}$$

$\tilde{\Delta} \in \mathcal{B}(\mathbb{R}_+^2)$.

We now proceed to get a Cooper Decomposicion. We need some concepts from the theory of multiplicity associated with a spectral measure. Let (X, A) be a measurable space and β a spectral measure on A with values in the class of orthogonal projections on a separable Hilbert space H. Then the spectral type ρ of an element $f \in H$ is defined to be the equivalence class of all finite measures on (X, A) equivalent (i.e., mutually absolutely continuous) with respect to $\rho_f(\Delta) = \|\beta(\Delta)f\|^2$.

An element f is said to be of maximal type if for all $g \in H$, ρ_g is absolutely continuous with respect to ρ_f $(\rho_g << \rho_f)$. A subspace M is called cyclic if $M = \overline{\text{sp}}\{\beta(\Delta)f, \Delta \in A\}$ for some $f \in H$. We denote M by H_f and note that H_f is isometric to $L_2(\rho_f)$. Following essentially the arguments in ([7]) we get the Hellinger-Hahn Theorem: Let $\{\beta(\Delta), \Delta \in \mathcal{B}(\mathbb{R}_+^2)\}$ be a spectral measure with its values in the (orthogonal) projections on H into H. Then

$$H = \sum_{i=1}^{M} \oplus H_{f_i}$$

with (i) $f_1 \in H$ of maximal type;

(ii) $M \leq \infty_0$ is uniquely determined (not depending on the choice of f_i's);

(iii) The spectral types of ρ_{f_i} (namely, ρ_i) are unique and satisfy $\rho_1 > \rho_2 > \ldots > \rho_M$. Here $\rho_i > \rho_j$ if $\rho_{f_j} << \rho_{f_i}$ and M is called the multiplicity of β.

We observe that if $\{\beta_j\}$ are spectral measures on (X, A) with values in Hilbert spaces K_j $(j = 1, 2)$ and J is a unitary operator from K_1 onto K_2 so that $J\beta_1(A)J^{-1} = \beta_2(A)$ $(A \in A)$ then β_1 and β_2 have the same spectral types. Let us write $\beta_1(\tilde{\Delta}) = E(\tilde{\Delta})$ and $\beta_2(\tilde{\Delta}) = E(\tilde{\Delta} + (u, v))P(u, v)$ for $\tilde{\Delta} \in \mathcal{B}(\mathbb{R}_+^2)$ and (u, v) fixed. Then (2.2) implies $J_{(u,v)}\beta_1(\tilde{\Delta})J^*_{(u,v)} = \beta_2(\tilde{\Delta})$ where $J_{u,v} = S_u^{(1)}S_v^{(2)}$ is the unitary operator on H onto $S_u^{(1)}S_v^{(2)}(H)$. As $E(A + (u, v)) \subseteq P(u, v)$ for $A = [a, b) \times (c, d]$ we get $E(\tilde{\Delta} + (u, v) \subseteq P(u, v)$ for all $\tilde{\Delta} \in \mathcal{B}(\mathbb{R}_+^2)$, giving $E(\tilde{\Delta} + (u, v))P(u, v) =$

$E(\tilde{\Delta} + (u, v))$. Since β_1 and β_2 have the same spectral types it follows that $\rho_f(\cdot + (u, v))$ is equivalent to $\rho_f(\cdot)$ for all $(u, v) \in \mathbb{R}^2_+$, i.e., ρ_f is quasi-invariant.

We now observe that a finite quasi-invariant measure σ on $\mathbb{R}^2_+$ is equivalent to μ_2, the restriction of Legesgue measure λ_2 on $\mathbb{R}^2$ to $\mathbb{R}^2_+$. This is seen as follows: For $A \in \mathcal{B}(\mathbb{R}^2_+)$ with $\mu_2(A) < \infty$, define the measure ν_1 by

$$\nu_1(A) = \int_{\mathbb{R}^2_+} \sigma(A + (u,v))\, d\mu_2 = \int_{\mathbb{R}^2_+}\int_{\mathbb{R}^2_+} 1_{(u,\infty)\times(v,\infty)}(x,y)\; 1_A((x,y)-(u,v))\; d\sigma\, d\mu_2$$

$$= \int_{\mathbb{R}^2_+}\int_{\mathbb{R}^2_+} 1_{(0,x]\times(0,y]}(u,v)\; 1_A((x,y) - (u,v))\; d\sigma\, d\mu_2 .$$

By the Fubini Theorem,

$$\nu_1(A) = \int_{\mathbb{R}^2_+}\int_0^x\int_0^y 1_A(x - u,\ y - v)\; d\mu_2\, d\sigma .$$

In the inner integral let $x - u = u'$ and $y - v = v'$. Then

$\nu_1(A) = \int_{\mathbb{R}^2_+} \mu_2(A \cap (0, x] \times (0, y])\, d\sigma = \nu_2(A)$, say. Note that $\nu_2(A) \le \mu_2(A)\sigma(\mathbb{R}^2_+)$ so that all integrals are finite. Also ν_1 and ν_2 being measures agreeing on the δ-ring $\{A;\ \mu_2(A) < \infty\}$, they agree on $\mathcal{B}(\mathbb{R}^2_+)$. By quasi-invariance of σ $\nu_1 \equiv \sigma$. Also $\nu_2(A) = 0$ implies $\mu_2(A \cap (0, x] \times (0, y]) = 0$ for σ - a.e. (x, y). By the quasi-variance of σ, we can find a sequence (x_n, y_n) in $\mathbb{R}^2_+$, $x_n \to \infty$, $y_n \to \infty$ such that $\mu_2(A \cap (0, x_n] \times (0, y_n]) = 0$ for every n. Hence $\mu_2(A) = \lim_n \mu_2(A\cap(0, x_n]\times(0,y_n])=0$ i.e., $\mu_2 << \nu_2 = \nu_1 \equiv \sigma$. But $\nu_2 << \mu_2$ giving the result.

Thus $\rho_f \equiv \mu_2$ for all f. We then say that E has Lebesgue spectral type. Let $\tilde{J}$ denote the unitary operator on $L_2(\rho_{f_i})$ onto $L_2(\mu_2)$ given by $\tilde{J}g = g\sqrt{d\rho_{f_i}/d\mu_2}$ for $g \in L_2(\rho_{f_i})$, $\tilde{\tilde{J}}$ the usual isomorphism of H_{f_i} onto $L^2(\rho_{f_i})$ and $J = \tilde{J}\tilde{\tilde{J}}$. Then J is a unitary operator on H onto $\sum_{i=1}^M \oplus L^2(\mathbb{R}^2_+, \mu_2)$. We note that $\sum_1^M \oplus L^2(\mathbb{R}^2_+, \mu_2) = L^2(\mathbb{R}^2_+, \mu_2; W)$ with W a Hilbert-space of dimension M and

$L^2(\mathbb{R}^2_+, \mu_2; W) = \{f;\ f\colon\ \mathbb{R}^2_+ \to W,$ measurable and $\|f\|_W \in L^2(\mathbb{R}^2_+, \mu)\}$ ([3], p. 52).

Theorem 2.1. Let $\{E(\tilde{\Delta}),\ \tilde{\Delta} \in \mathcal{B}(\mathbb{R}^2_+)\}$ be the spectral measure defined earlier and let J be as above. Then J is a unitary operator on H onto $L^2(\mathbb{R}^2_+, \mu_2; W)$ such that $J\,E(\tilde{\Delta})J^{-1}=$ multiplication by $1_{\tilde{\Delta}}(\cdot)$. In addition, E has uniform multiplicity M of Lebesgue type.

The first assertion follows from the Hellinger-Hahn Theorem. The second part can be proved exactly as in ([4], p. 324)].

Let $T_{(u,v)}$, $(u, v) \in \mathbb{R}^2_+$ be the translation to the right by (u, v) on $L^2(\mathbb{R}^2_+, \mu_2; W)$; namely,

$$T_{u,v}\, f(\cdot) = f(\cdot + u,\ \cdot + v).$$

Since $J\,E(\tilde{\Delta})x = 1_{\tilde{\Delta}}(\cdot)Jx$, we have with $S_{u,v} = S^{(1)}_u S^{(2)}_v$,

$$\begin{aligned} J\,S^*_{u,v}\,J^{-1}\,T_{u,v}\,J\,E(\tilde{\Delta})x &= J\,S^*_{u,v}\,J^{-1}\,1_{\tilde{\Delta}}(\cdot + (u,v))T_{u,v}(Jx) \\ &= J\,S^*_{u,v}\,J^{-1}\,J\,E(\tilde{\Delta} + (u,v))J^{-1}\,T_{u,v}(Jx) \\ &= J\,S^*_{u,v}\,E(\tilde{\Delta} + (u,v))J^{-1}\,T_{u,v}(Jx). \end{aligned}$$

By (2.2) this equals $J\,E(\tilde{\Delta})\,S^*_{u,v}\,J^{-1}\,T_{u,v}(Jx)$ which in turn is equal to $1_{\tilde{\Delta}}(\cdot)\cdot J\,S^*_{u,v}\,J^{-1}\,T_{u,v}(Jx)$, i.e., $J\,S^*_{u,v}\,J^{-1}\,T_{u,v}$ commutes with multiplication by $1_{\tilde{\Delta}}$. Using arguments similar to ([8], p. 217) we obtain that there exists B(W)-valued measurable function $K_{(u,v)}(\cdot)$ defined a.e. $[\mu_2]$ such that $J\,S^*_{u,v}\,J^{-1}\,T_{u,v}\,f(\cdot) = K_{u,v}(\cdot)\,f(\cdot + (u,v))$. Here B(W) denotes the class of bounded operators on W into W. Let $J\,S^*_{u,v}\,J^{-1} = \tilde{S}^*_{u,v}$. Then

$$\tilde{S}^*_{u_1,v_1}\,T_{u_1,v_1}\,\tilde{S}^*_{u_2,v_2}\,T_{u_2,v_2} = \tilde{S}^*_{(u_1+u_2,\ v_1+v_2)}\,T_{(u_1+u_2,\ v_1+v_2)}.$$

Hence for almost all triplets $\langle (s, t), (u_1, v_1), (u_2, v_2)\rangle$

$$K_{u_1,v_1}(s, t)\,K_{u_2,v_2}((u_1,v_1) + (s, t)) = K_{u_1+u_2,v_1+v_2}(s,t). \tag{2.3}$$

As in ([8], p. 217) we choose (s_0, t_0) so that (2.3) holds for all $((u_1,v_1),(u_2,v_2))$.

Now define

$$(Bf)(\cdot) = K_{(s_0,t_0)}(\cdot + (s_0, t_0))\, f(\cdot).$$

Then for almost all (u, v) with respect to $[\mu_2]$

$$B\, \tilde{S}^*_{u,v}\, B^{-1} f(\cdot) = f(\cdot + (u, v))$$

giving by continuity, equality for all $(u, v) \in \mathbb{R}^2_+$. Letting $J_1 = JB$ we have

$$(J_1\, S^*_{u,v}\, J_1^{-1})f(\cdot) = f(\cdot + (u, v)).$$

Hence $J_1\, S_{u,v}\, J_1^{-1} f(\cdot) = 1_{(u,\infty)\times(v,\infty)}(\cdot)\, f(\cdot - (u, v))$. Thus we have proved the following theorem.

Theorem 2.10. Let $\{S_t^{(i)}, t \in \mathbb{R}_+\}$ (i = 1, 2) be strongly continuous semigroups of isometries satisfying (1.1), (1.2) and (2.1). Then $H = \sum_{k=1}^M \oplus M_k$, where

(i) $M_k = \{\int_0^\infty\int_0^\infty f(u, v)\, d\xi_k(u, v),\ f \in L_2(\mathbb{R}^2_+, \mu_2)\}$.

(ii) $E(\tilde{\Delta})[\int_0^\infty\int_0^\infty f(u, v)\, d\xi_k(u, v)] = \iint_{\tilde{\Delta}} f(u, v)\, d\xi_k(u, v)$ for all $\tilde{\Delta} \in \mathcal{B}(\mathbb{R}^2_+)$.

(iii) $S_{s,t} \int_0^\infty\int_0^\infty f(u, v)\, d\xi_k(u, v) = \int_t^\infty\int_s^\infty f(u - s, v - t)\, d\xi_k(u, v)$.

(iv) $S^*_{s,t} \int_0^\infty\int_0^\infty f(u, v)\, d\xi_k(u, v) = \int_0^\infty\int_0^\infty f(u + s, v + t)\, d\xi_k(u, v)$.

Here the ξ_k's are mutually orthogonal, orthogonal set functions with $\|\xi_k(\Delta)\|^2 = \mu_2(\Delta)$, the Lebesgue measure on $\mathbb{R}^2_+$.

Since $\{S_t^{(i)}, t \in R_+\}$ (i = 1, 2) are strongly continuous semigroups of isometries there exist closed symmetric linear operators iH_1 and iH_2 as their respective infinitesimal generators [1]. Let H_1^* and H_2^* be the adjoints of H_1, H_2. Then H_1^* and H_2^* are well-defined since $\mathcal{D}(H_i)$ is dense in H and for $x \in \mathcal{D}_{H_i}$, $H_i^* x = H_i x$ (i = 1, 2). Furthermore they are closed. Let

$R_k^\perp = \{x \in \mathcal{D}_{H_k^*} : H_k^*\, x = -ix\}$ (k = 1, 2) be the deficiency subspaces of H_k (k = 1, 2).

Lemma 2.1. Let

$$x_k = 2\int_0^\infty\int_0^\infty e^{-(u+v)}\, d\xi_k(u, v) \quad , \quad k = 1, 2, \ldots, M.$$

Then $\{x_k\}$ is an orthonormal sequence contained in $R_1^\perp \cap R_2^\perp$.

Proof: The x_k's are obviously mutually orthogonal and $\| x_k \|^2 = 4\int_0^\infty\int_0^\infty e^{-2(u+v)} du dv = 1$.

By Theorem 2.2, using the arguments in ([4], p. 323) we have

$$S_t^{(1)*}\, x_k = 2\int_0^\infty\int_0^\infty e^{-(u+t)-v}\, d\xi_k(u, v) = e^{-t}\, x_k$$

so that

$$(t^{-1}[S_t^{(1)*} - I]x_k, y) = \frac{e^{-t}-1}{t}(x_k, y) \quad , \quad y \in H,\ t > 0.$$

It follows that $\underset{t\to 0}{\text{s-lim}}\ t^{-1}[S_t^{(1)*} - I]x_k$ exists, i.e., $x_k \in \mathcal{D}_{H_1^*}$ and

$$-iH_1^* x_k = \lim_{t\to 0} \frac{e^{-t}-1}{t} x_k = -x_k.$$

Hence $x_k \in R_1^\perp$. Similarly $x_k \in R_2^\perp$ and the lemma is proved.

Note that $\mathcal{M}_k = \overline{\text{sp}}\{E(\Delta)x_k,\ \Delta \in \mathcal{B}(\mathbb{R}_+^2)\}$ for each $k = 1, \ldots, M$. Lemma 2.1 immediately implies that $M \le \dim\,(R_1^\perp \cap R_2^\perp)$. Our aim is to prove equality.

Let us recall the definition of the operators H_1 and H_2. The element $\bar{x} \in \mathcal{D}_{H_j}$ if $\underset{h\to 0}{\text{s-lim}}[\frac{S_h^{(j)} - I}{h}]\bar{x}$ exists. The limit is denoted by $iH_j\bar{x}$, $(j = 1, 2)$. For our purposes we need to define a class $\mathcal{N}_k$ such that

(a) $\mathcal{N}_k \subset \mathcal{D}_{H_1} \cap \mathcal{M}_k \qquad (k = 1, \ldots, M)$ and

(b) $J(\mathcal{N}_k)$ is dense in $L^2(\mathbb{R}_+^2, \mu)$ where J is the unitary operator from $\mathcal{M}_k$ to $L^2(\mathbb{R}_+^2, \mu)$ which sends the element $\int_0^\infty\int_0^\infty h(u, v)\, d\xi_k(u, v)$ into $h \in L^2(\mathbb{R}_+^2, \mu)$.

Let $\tilde{C}$ be the class of all complex-valued functions $\tilde{\phi}$ on $\mathbb{R}_+^2$ such that $\tilde{\phi}(u, v) = \phi(u, v)$ for $(u, v) \in (0, \infty) \times (0, \infty)$ and $= 0$ elsewhere in $\mathbb{R}_+^2$, where $\phi \in C_0^\infty[(0, \infty) \times (0, \infty)]$. It is then easy to see that C is dense in $L^2(\mathbb{R}_+^2, \mu)$.

Now define

$$\mathcal{N}_k = \{\bar{x}_k : \bar{x}_k = \int_0^\infty\int_0^\infty \tilde{\phi}(u, v)\, d\xi_k(u, v) \quad , \quad \tilde{\phi} \in \tilde{C}\} .$$

Lemma 2.2. (i) $\mathcal{N}_k$ is a dense subset of $\mathcal{M}_k$,

(ii) $\mathcal{N}_k \subset \mathcal{D}_{H_1} \cap \mathcal{M}_k$ and

(iii) $J[H_1\bar{x}_k] = iD_1\tilde{\phi}$ where $D_1 = \frac{\partial}{\partial u}$.

Proof: (i) is immediate since $\tilde{C}$ is dense in $L^2(\mathbb{R}_+^2, \mu)$. To prove (ii) it is enough to show that if $\bar{x}_k \in \mathcal{N}_k$ then

$$s - \lim_{h \to 0} [\frac{S_h^{(1)} - I}{h}]\bar{x}_k \quad \text{exists.}$$

By the definition of $\tilde{C}$ it follows that

$$\int_0^\infty\int_0^\infty |\frac{\tilde{\phi}(u - h, v) - \tilde{\phi}(u, v)}{h} + D_1\tilde{\phi}(u, v)|^2 \, dudv \to 0 \quad \text{as}$$

$$h \to 0 \text{ and } \int_0^\infty\int_0^\infty |\frac{\tilde{\phi}(u - h, v)1_{[h,\infty)}(u) - \tilde{\phi}(u - h, v)}{h}|^2 \, dudv = 0$$

for h positive and small.

Since $D_1\tilde{\phi} \in L^2(\mathbb{R}_+^2, \mu)$, defining $\bar{\bar{x}}_k = - \int_0^\infty\int_0^\infty D_1\tilde{\phi}(u, v)\, d\xi_k(u, v)$ we have

$$||\frac{S_h^{(1)}\bar{x}_k - \bar{x}_k}{h} - \bar{\bar{x}}_k|| \to 0$$ as $h \to 0$ by Theorem 2.2(iii) and the triangle inequality. Hence $\bar{x}_k \in \mathcal{D}_{H_1}$ and $iH_1\bar{x}_k = \bar{\bar{x}}_k$. Thus $J[iH_1\bar{x}_k] = J[\bar{\bar{x}}_k] = -D_1\tilde{\phi}$ which proves (iii). □.

Denoting the inner product in $L^2(\mathbb{R}_+^2, \mu)$ by $<, >$ we obtain the following relations as a consequence of Lemma 2.2. Let

$y = \sum_{j=1}^M \int_0^\infty\int_0^\infty q_j(u, v)\, d\xi_j(u, v)$ be an arbitrary element of $\mathcal{H}$. Then

$$(H_1\bar{x}_k, y) = < iD_1\tilde{\phi}, q_k > .$$

In particular, choosing $y \in R_1^\perp \cap R_2^\perp$ we have

$$(H_1\bar{x}_k, y) = (\bar{x}_k, H_1^* y) = (\bar{x}_k, -iy) = < \tilde{\phi}, -iq_k > .$$

Hence $\quad < iD_1\tilde{\phi},\ q_k> = < \tilde{\phi},\ -iq_k>$

i.e., $\quad < \tilde{\phi},\ iD_1 q_k> = < \tilde{\phi},\ -iq_k>$,

where $D_1 q_k$ is the L^2-derivative of q_k which exists since $\underset{t\to 0}{s\text{-}\lim}\left[\frac{S_t^{(1)*}-I}{t}\right]y$ exists.

The above relation holds for every $k = 1,\ldots,M$ and for all $\tilde{\phi} \in \tilde{C}$ which is dense in $L^2(\mathbb{R}^2_+,\ \mu)$. It follows that $D_1 q_k = -q_k$.

Defining the distribution F_k by

$$F_k(\phi) = \int_0^\infty\int_0^\infty q_k(u,\ v)\ \phi(u,\ v)\ dudv \quad \text{for } \phi \in C_0^\infty[(0,\infty) \times (0,\infty)]$$

we have $D_1 F_k = -F_k$ where D_1 is the derivative in the distributional sense. We conclude from the hypoellipticity of the operator $D_1 + 1$ that q_k is a C^∞-function, in particular, continuously differentiable. ([2], Theorem 8, p. 313; Theorem 2, p. 302). Furthermore, q_k satisfies the equation

$$\frac{\partial q_k(u,\ v)}{\partial u} = -q_k(u,\ v) \quad \text{giving}$$

$$q_k(u,\ v) = c_k(v)\ e^{-u} + b_k(v) \quad , \quad (u,\ v \geq 0).$$

Since $\quad q_k \in L^2(\mathbb{R}^2_+,\ \mu)$, $\int_0^\infty |q_k(u,\ v)|^2\ du < \infty$ for a.e.v. This implies $b_k(v) = 0$ for a.e.v. and $q_k(u,\ v) = c_k(v)\ e^{-u}$ a.e.

Also since $y \in R_2^\perp$, repeating the above arguments (interchanging the roles of u and v) we have $\frac{\partial}{\partial v} q_k(u,\ v) = -q_k(u,\ v)$ from which it follows that

$$\frac{dc_k}{dv} = -c_k(v)\ . \quad \text{Thus } c_k(v) = a_k\ e^{-v} + d_k\ .$$

Now

$$\int_0^\infty\int_0^\infty |c_k(v)|^2\ e^{-2u}\ dudv = \int_0^\infty\int_0^\infty |q_k(u,v)|^2\ dudv < \infty$$

implies that $\int_0^\infty |c_k(v)|^2\ dv < \infty$. Hence we must have $d_k = 0$ and $q_k(u,\ v) = a_k\ e^{-u-v}$

where $\quad \sum_{k=1}^M |a_k|^2 = 4\sum_{k=1}^M \int_0^\infty\int_0^\infty |q_k(u,\ v)|^2\ du\ dv < \infty.$

We have shown that every element $y \in R_1^\perp \cap R_2^\perp$ is of the form

$$y = \sum_{k=1}^M a_k \int_0^\infty\int_0^\infty e^{-u-v}\, d\xi_k(u, v) = \sum_{k=1}^M \tfrac{1}{2} a_k x_k$$

where the x_k's are orthonormal elements with $x_k \in R_1^\perp \cap R_2^\perp$ (Lemma 2.1).

Hence $M = \dim (R_1^\perp \cap R_2^\perp)$. We have thus proved the following strengthening of Theorem 2.2.

<u>Theorem 2.3</u>. Let $\{S_t^{(i)}, t \in \mathbb{R}_+\}$ $(i = 1, 2)$ be continuous semigroups of isometries satisfying the conditions (1.1), (1.2) and (2.1). Then

(2.4) $$H = \sum_{k=1}^M \oplus M_k$$

where M_k is given by (i) of Theorem 2.2 and the multiplicity

(2.5) $$M = \dim (R_1^\perp \cap R_2^\perp). \qquad \square$$

Now let $\{S_u^{(i)}\}$ $(i = 1, 2;\ u \in \mathbb{R}_+)$ be two strongly continuous semigroups of isometries satisfying (1.1). (1.2), and (1.6). Then under (1.6), the semigroups $V_u^{(i)} = S_u^{(i)}|_{H_0}$ $(i = 1, 2;\ u \in \mathbb{R}_+)$ satisfy (2.1) with $H = H_0$. Then applying Theorem 2.3 to the semigroups $\{V_u^{(i)}\}$, since they are strongly continuous and satisfy (1.1) and (1.2), we find that

$$H_0 = \overline{\mathrm{sp}}\{E(\tilde{\Delta})x,\ x \in R_1^\perp \cap R_2^\perp\ \ \tilde{\Delta} \in B(\mathbb{R}_+^2)\}.$$

Note that $R_1^\perp \cap R_2^\perp \subseteq R_i^\perp \subseteq (H_\infty^{(i)})^\perp$ $(i = 1. 2)$ giving $R_1^\perp \cap R_2^\perp \subseteq H_0$. Thus the definition of $R_1^\perp \cap R_2^\perp$ corresponding to $\{V_u^{(i)}\}$ is the same as that corresponding to $\{S_u^{(i)}\}$.

Furthermore, $S_u^{(i)}|H_i$ $(i = 1, 2)$ satisfy (2.1)(a) and (2.1)(b) respectively. Hence using ([4], Theorem 2.1) we get

$$H_1 = \overline{\mathrm{sp}}\{E^{(1)}(\Delta)x,\ x \in R_1^\perp,\ \Delta \in B(\mathbb{R}_+)\} \cap H_\infty^{(2)}$$

and

$$H_2 = H_\infty^{(1)} \cap \overline{\mathrm{sp}}\{E^{(2)}(\Delta)x,\ x \in R_2^\perp,\ \Delta \in B(\mathbb{R}_+)\}.$$

Therefore, using Theorem 1.1 we have the following result.

Theorem 2.4. Let $\{S_u^{(i)}\}$ be two strongly continuous semigroups of isometries satisfying (1.1), (1.2) and (1.6). Then $H = H_0 \oplus H_1 \oplus H_2 \oplus H_\infty$, where

(i) $H_0 = \overline{sp}\{E(\tilde{\Delta})x,\ x \in R_1^\perp \cap R_2^\perp \text{ and } \tilde{\Delta} \in B(\mathbb{R}_+^2)\}$.

(ii) $H_1 = \overline{sp}\{E^{(1)}(\Delta)x,\ x \in R_1^\perp,\ \Delta \in B(\mathbb{R}_+)\} \cap H_\infty^{(2)}$.

(iii) $H_2 = \overline{sp}\{E^{(2)}(\Delta)x,\ x \in R_2^\perp,\ \Delta \in B(\mathbb{R}_+)\} \cap H_\infty^{(1)}$.

(iv) $S_u^{(i)}|H_\infty$ are unitary for i = 1, 2.

If we make the following assumption which implies (1.6),

(2.6) $$S_t^{(1)}H_\infty^{(2)} = H_\infty^{(2)} \quad\text{and}\quad S_t^{(2)}H_\infty^{(1)} = H_\infty^{(1)} ,$$

we have

$$\overline{sp}\{E^{(1)}(\Delta)x,\ x \in R_1^\perp,\ \Delta \in B(\mathbb{R}_+)\} \cap H_\infty^{(2)}$$

$$= \overline{sp}\{E^{(1)}(\Delta)P_{H_\infty^{(2)}}x,\ x \in R_1^\perp,\ \Delta \in B(R_+)\};$$

and $P_{H_\infty^{(2)}} P_{R_1^\perp} = P_{R_1^\perp} P_{H_\infty^{(2)}}$ since (2.6) implies $S_t^{(1)*}P_{H_\infty^{(2)}} = P_{H_\infty^{(2)}}S_t^{(1)*}$. This in turn gives

$$\overline{sp}\{E^{(1)}(\Delta)x,\ x \in R_1^\perp,\ \Delta \in B(R_+)\} \cap H_\infty^{(2)}$$

$$= \overline{sp}\{E^{(1)}(\Delta)x,\ x \in R_1^\perp \cap H_\infty^{(2)},\ \Delta \in B(R_+)\}.$$

A similar argument applies to H_2. We thus obtain the following result.

Theorem 2.5. Let $\{S_t^{(i)}\}$ (i = 1, 2) $t \in \mathbb{R}_+$ be two strongly continuous semigroups of isometries satisfying (1.1), (1.2) and (2.6). Then $H = H_0 \oplus H_1 \oplus H_2 \oplus H_\infty$ where

(a) $H_0 = \overline{sp}\{E(\tilde{\Delta})x,\ x \in R_1^\perp \cap R_2^\perp,\ \tilde{\Delta} \in B(\mathbb{R}_+^2)\}$.

(b) $H_1 = \overline{sp}\{E^{(1)}(\Delta)x,\ x \in R_1^\perp \cap H_\infty^2,\ \Delta \in B(\mathbb{R}_+)\}$.

(c) $H_2 = \overline{sp}\{E^{(2)}(\Delta)x,\ x \in R_2^\perp \cap H_\infty^1,\ \Delta \in B(\mathbb{R}_+)\}$.

(d) $S_t^{(i)}|H_\infty$ is unitary.

In view of Theorem 2.4 and ([4], Theorem 2.1) we get that the dim $(R_1^\perp \cap R_2^\perp)$ is the uniform multiplicity of two-dimensional Lebesgue type. In addition, $\dim(R_1^\perp \cap H_\infty^{(2)})$ and $\dim(R_2^\perp \cap H_\infty^{(1)})$ are the multiplicities of one-dimensional Lebesgue type of $E^{(1)}$ and $E^{(2)}$ respectively. Following our ideas in [5], we define the following.

Definition: The multiplicities of two commuting strongly continuous semigroups $\{S_u^{(i)}\}$ ($u \in \mathbb{R}_+$, $i = 1, 2$) satisfying (1.1), (1.2) and (2.6) are defined to be M_0, M_1 and M_2, the multiplicities of E, $E^{(1)}$ and $E^{(2)}$ respectively.

Theorem 2.5 shows that these multiplicities coincide with the two-dimensional, one-directional and two-directional multiplicities of the discrete isometries W_1 and W_2 given by the Cayley transforms of H_1 and H_2. Thus Theorem 2.5 generalizes ([4], Theorem 2.1). As already noted (2.6) is satisfied for the isometries associated with the s.o.r.f. for which (1.4) holds. In the general case, if in addition to (1.1), one has

$$S_u^{(i)} S_v^{(2)*} = S_v^{(2)*} S_u^{(1)} \qquad u, v \in \mathbb{R}_+$$

(i.e., if the semigroups are doubly commuting) then (2.6) is satisfied. Thus our result holds for strongly continuous, doubly commuting semigroups as for this case (1.2) is satisfied. In the next section we use the above decompositions to obtain Karhunen type representations for a continuous parameter, continuous s.o.r.f.

3. A Karhunen representation for stationary, PND s.o.r.f.'s. We shall first derive a four-fold Wold decomposition for a stationary s.o.r.f. As shown in Section 1, a stationary s.o.r.f. X satisfies (2.6) under the assumption (1.4). Hence we can apply Theorem 2.4 to $H = L(X;\, s_0,\, t_0)$ to obtain the following decomposition. Here, $(s_0, t_0) \in \mathbb{R}^2$ is arbitrary but fixed.

Theorem 3.1. Let $\{X_{s,t}\}$ $(s, t \in \mathbb{R}^2)$ be a (continuous) continuous parameter stationary s.o.r.f. satisfying (1.4). Then

$$L(X;\, s_0,t_0) = \sum_{k=1}^{M_0} \oplus M_k^0(s_0,t_0) \oplus \sum_{j=1}^{M_1} \oplus M_j^1(s_0) \oplus \sum_{k=1}^{M_2} \oplus M_j^2(t_0) \oplus L(X;\, -\infty) \tag{3.1}$$

where

(a) $M_k^0(s_0, t_0) = \{x;\ x = \int_{-\infty}^{t_0} \int_{-\infty}^{s_0} f(u, v)\, d\xi_k(u, v),\ f \in L_2(\lambda_2)\}$

where λ_2 is two dimensional Lebesgue measure and the $\xi_k(\tilde{\Delta})$ are mutually orthogonal, orthogonal set functions on $\mathbb{R}^2$ with $E\| \xi_k(\tilde{\Delta}) \|^2 = \lambda_2(\tilde{\Delta})$, $\tilde{\Delta} \in \mathcal{B}(\mathbb{R}^2)$;

(b) $M_j^{(i)}(s_0) = \{x;\ x = \int_{-\infty}^{s_0} f(u)\, d\xi_j^{(i)}(u),\ f \in L_2(\lambda_1)\}$, $(i = 1, 2)$, λ_1, the Lebesgue measure on $\mathbb{R}$ and $\{\xi_j^{(i)}(\Delta)\}_{j=1}^{M_i}$ are mutually orthogonal, orthogonal set functions with $E\| \xi_j^{(i)}(\Delta) \|^2 = \lambda_1(\Delta)$, $\Delta \in \mathcal{B}(\mathbb{R})$; (c) $L(X;-\infty) = L^1(X;-\infty) \cap L^2(X;-\infty)$.

<u>Proof</u>: In Theorem 2.4, choose

$H = L(X;\ s_0, t_0)$ and $S_t^{(i)} = U_t^{(i)^{-1}}|L(X;\ s_0, t_0)$, $t \in \mathbb{R}_+$ $(i = 1, 2)$.

Then $\{S_t^{(i)}\}$ are strongly continuous semigroups of isometries on H satisfying (1.1), (1.2) and (2.6). Hence, by Theorem 2.4, we have (3.1) satisfying (a), (b) and (c) with $M_0 = \dim (R_1^\perp \cap R_2^\perp)$, $M_j = \dim (R_j^\perp)$ $(i = 1, 2)$. By ([6], p. 38)

(3.2) $$R_1^\perp = [L^1(X;\ s_0) \ominus W_1 L^1(X;\ s_0)] \cap L^2(X;\ t_0)$$

where W_1 = Cayley transform of H_1. By Stone's Theorem $U_t^{(j)} = e^{itK_j}$ with K_j self-adjoint. Also by ([4], pp 331-332) $W_1 = V_1^{-1}|L^1(X;\ s_0)$ and $W_2 = V_2^{-1}|L^2(X;\ t_0)$ where V_j is the Cayley transform of K_j for j = 1, 2. As K_j commutes with $\{U_t^{(j)}\}$ its spectral measure commutes with $\{U_t^{(j)}\}$ for all $t \in \mathbb{R}$ and hence V_j^{-1} commutes with $\{U_t^{(j)}\}$. Thus for all $t \in \mathbb{R}$,

$$V_1^{-1}L^1(X;\ s_0 + s) = V_1^{-1}U_s^{(j)}L^1(X;\ s_0) = U_s^{(1)}V_1^{-1}L^1(X;\ s_0).$$

Also, $U_s^{(1)}L^2(X;\ t_0) = L^2(X;\ t_0)$. Furthermore, for all $t \in \mathbb{R}$, we have

$$U_t^{(2)}[L^1(X;\ s_0) \ominus W_1L^1(X;\ s_0)] = L^1(X;\ s_0) \ominus W_1L^1(X;\ s_0).$$

Hence $$[L^1(X;\ s + s_0) \ominus W_1L^1(X;\ s_0 + s)] \cap L^2(X;\ t_0 + t)$$

(3.3) $$= U_s^{(1)}[L^1(X;\ s_0) \ominus W_1L^1(X;\ s_0)] \cap U_t^{(2)}L^2(X;\ t_0)$$

$$= U_s^{(1)}U_t^{(2)}\ R_1^\perp.$$

This proves that dim $R_1^{\perp}$ is independent of (s_0, t_0). Similarly dim $(R_2^{\perp})$ is independent of (s_0, t_0). By a similar argument, we get the following analogue of (3.3),

$$[L^1(X; s_0+s) \ominus V_1^{-1}L^1(X; s_0+s)] \cap [L^2(X; t_0+t) \ominus V_2^{-1}L^2(X; t_0+t)]$$

$$= U_s^{(1)}U_t^{(2)}\{[L^1(X; s_0) \ominus V_1^{-1}L^1(X; s_0)] \cap [L^2(X; t_0) \ominus V_2^{-1}L^2(X; t_0)]\},$$

proving that dim $(R_1^{\perp} \cap R_2^{\perp})$ is independent of (s_0, t_0). □

Let us now define

$$N_0 = \sum_{k=1}^{M_0} \oplus \vee M^0(s_0, t_0), \; N_i = \sum_1^{M_1} \oplus \vee M_j^{(i)}(s_0, t_0) \quad (\text{for } i = 1, 2)$$

where $\vee$ denotes the "smallest subspace generated by" and is taken over all (s_0, t_0) in $\mathbb{R}^2$. Define also

$$\xi_{s,t}(\phi) = P_{N_0} X_{s,t}(\phi), \quad \zeta^i_{s,t}(\phi) = P_{N_i} X_{s,t}(\phi) \quad (i = 1, 2)$$

and $\eta_{s,t}(\phi) = P_{L(X; -\infty)} X_{s,t}$. Since N_0, N_1, N_2 and $L(X; -\infty)$ are invariant under $U_t^{(i)}$, $(i = 1, 2)$ for all $t \in \mathbb{R}$, we get that ξ, ζ^1, ζ^2 and η are stationary s.o.r.f.'s satisfying (1.1), (1.2) and (2.6). As in the discrete case, using ([5], Lemma 2.1) we obtain the following Lemmas .

Lemma 3.1 (a) (i) $L(\zeta^1) = N_1$; (ii) $L^1(\zeta^1; -\infty) = \{0\}$; (iii) $L^2(\zeta^1; -\infty) = L^2(\zeta^1; t)$ for all t, and (iv) $L(\zeta^1; -\infty) = \{0\}$.

(b) (i) $L(\zeta^2) = N_2$; (ii) $L^2(\zeta^2; -\infty) = \{0\}$; (iii) $L^1(\zeta^2; t) = L^1(\zeta^2; -\infty)$ for all t and $L(\zeta^2; -\infty) = \{0\}$.

(c) $L(\eta) = L^1(\eta; -\infty) \cap L^2(\eta; -\infty)$.

Lemma 3.2. (a) $L(\xi) = \sum_1^{M_0} \oplus M_k^0$ and $L^1(\xi; -\infty) \vee L^2(\xi; -\infty) = \{0\}$.

(b) $L(\zeta^i) = \sum_1^{M_i} \oplus M_j^i$ $(i = 1, 2)$. Here $M_k^0 = \bigvee_{(s,t)} M_k^0(s, t)$, $M_k^i = \bigvee_{s \in \mathbb{R}} M^i(s)$, $(i=1,2)$, $M_0 = \dim(R_1^{\perp} \cap R_2^{\perp})$, $M_1 = \dim(R_1^{\perp} \cap L^2(X; -\infty))$ and $M_2 = \dim(R_2^{\perp} \cap L^1(X; -\infty))$.

As in the discrete case we have the following

Definitions: A (continuous) parameter s.o.r.f. X is

(a) deterministic if $L(X; s, t) = L(X; -\infty)$ for some (hence for all $s, t \in \mathbb{R}^2$).

(b) nondeterministic if for some s, t, $L(X; s, t) \neq L(X; -\infty)$.

(c) purely nondeterministic if $L^1(X; -\infty) \cap L^2(X; -\infty) = \{0\}$.

(d) strongly purely nondeterministic if $L^1(X; -\infty) \vee L^2(X; -\infty) = \{0\}$.

(e) 1 - purely nondeterministic if $L^1(X; -\infty) = \{0\}$ and $L^2(X; -\infty) = L^2(X)$.

(f) 2 - purely nondeterministic if $L^2(X; -\infty) = \{0\}$ and $L^1(X; -\infty) = L^1(X)$.

The previous theorem shows that every (continuous) continuous parameter stationary s.o.r.f. can be decomposed into four parts: deterministic, 1-PND, 2-PND, and strongly PND.

The next theorem shows that every continuous stationary s.o.r.f. of two continuous parameters can be decomposed into four parts as follows.

Theorem 3.2 (Four-fold Wold Decomposition). Let X be a continuous stationary s.o.r.f. of two continuous parameters satisfying (1.4). Then for all $(s, t) \in \mathbb{R}^2$ and $\phi \in \Phi$,

$$X_{st}(\phi) = \xi_{st}(\phi) + \zeta^1_{st}(\phi) + \zeta^2_{st}(\phi) + \eta_{st}(\phi)$$

where (i) ξ is strongly PND, (ii) ζ^1 is 1-PND, (iii) ζ^2 is 2-PND, and (iv) η is deterministic.

Only the strongly PND stationary random fields have two-dimensional innovations i.e., $M^0_k \neq 0$ for some (hence for all) k. Also if a stationary s.o.r.f. has only two dimensional innovations then it is strongly PND. Thus the processes studied in [9] are strongly PND. Our work thus extends the work of [9].

Using methods similar to those for discrete parameter processes ([5]) we obtain the following generalized Karhunen (moving average) representation.

Theorem 3.3. Let X be a continuous stationary s.o.r.f. of two continuous parameters. Suppose further that X is PND. Then the following decomposition holds.

$$X_{st}(\phi) = \sum_{j=1}^{M_0} \int_{-\infty}^{s}\int_{-\infty}^{t} \alpha_0^j(s - u, t - v;\phi)\, dw_0^j(u, v)$$

$$+ \sum_{j=1}^{M_1} \sum_{k=1}^{M_1} C_t(j, k) \int_{-\infty}^{s} \alpha_1^j(s - u; \phi)\, dw_1^k(u)$$

$$+ \sum_{j=1}^{M_2} \sum_{k=1}^{M_2} D_s(j, k) \int_{-\infty}^{t} \alpha_2^j(t - v, \phi)\, dw_2^k(v).$$

(a) $\{w_0^j\}$ are mutually orthogonal processes of the kind already encountered in Theorem 2.3, viz., $E\, w_0^j(\tilde{\Delta}_1)\overline{w_0^\ell(\tilde{\Delta}_2)} = \delta_{j\ell}\, \lambda_2(\tilde{\Delta}_1 \cap \tilde{\Delta}_2)$ where $\tilde{\Delta}_1, \tilde{\Delta}_2 \in \mathcal{B}(\mathbb{R}^2)$;

$$E\, w_1^j(\Delta_1)\overline{w_1^k(\Delta_2)} = E\, w_2^j(\Delta_1)\overline{w_2^k(\Delta_2)}$$

$$= \delta_{jk}\, \lambda_1(\Delta_1 \cap \Delta_2) \quad \text{where} \quad \Delta_1, \Delta_2 \in \mathcal{B}(\mathbb{R}).$$

The families $\{w_0^j\}$, $\{w_1^j\}$ and $\{w_2^j\}$ are all mutually orthogonal.

Furthermore, $C_t = (C_t(j, k))$ and $D_s = (D_s(j, k))$

are groups of unitary matrices of orders M_1 and M_2 respectively;

(b) $M_0 = \dim (R_1^\perp \cap R_2^\perp)$ and

$$\sum_{j=1}^{M_0} \int_0^\infty\int_0^\infty |\alpha_0^j(u, v; \phi)|^2\, du dv < \infty ;$$

(c) $M_1 = \dim [R_1^\perp \cap L^2(X; -\infty)]$ and

$$\sum_{j=1}^{M_1} \int_0^\infty |\alpha_1^j(u; \phi)|^2\, du < \infty ;$$

(d) $M_2 = \dim [L^1(X; -\infty) \cap R_2]$ and

$$\sum_{j=1}^{M_2} \int_0^\infty |\alpha_2^j(v, \phi)|^2\, dv < \infty .$$

Remark: If $X_{s,t} = X_s$ where (X_s) is a continuous one parameter stationary process then it is easy to see that only the second term remains in the above decomposition and further, $C_t = I_{M_1}$ for all t, I_{M_1} being the $M_1 \times M_1$ identity matrix.

REFERENCES

1. Cooper, J.L.B. One parameter semigroups of isometric operators. Ann. of Math. 48, (1947) 827-842.

2. Friedman, Avner. Generalized functions and partial differential equations. Academic Press, New York.

3. Helson, H. Lectures on invariant subspaces. Academic Press, New York, 1963.

4. Kallianpur, G. and Mandrekar, V. Semigroups of isometries and the representation and multiplicity of weakly stationary stochastic processes. Arkiv för Mat. (1966) 319-335.

5. __________. Nondeterministic random fields and Wold and Halmos decompositions for commuting isometries. Tech. Report 2, Center for Stochastic Processes, University of North Carolina; November, 1981.

6. Nagy, Sz. B. Spectraldarstellung linearer transformationen des Hilbertschen Raumes. Ergebnisse der Mathematik und ihrer Grenzgebiete, Springer, 1942.

7. Plesner, A.I. Spectral theory of linear operators. Vol II, Unger, New York, 1969.

8. Reed, M. and Simon, B. Methods of Modern Mathematical Physics, III, Scattering Theory, Academic Press, New York, 1979.

9. Tjøstheim, D. Multiplicity theory of random fields using quantum mechanical methods. Prob. on Vector Spaces, Lecture Notes in Math #656, Springer-Verlag, 1978.

Robust filtering for systems with correlation between signal and observation

A contribution to the IFIP-ISI Conference at Bangalore, India, Jan. 1982

M. Kohlmann
Universität Bonn

1. The signal process is a Markov process $(x_t)_{t\in[0,\infty)}$ evolving on a σ- compact d - dimensional C^∞ - manifold, i.e. for $f \in C_0^\infty(M)$

$$f(x_t) - f(x_0) - \int A\, f(x_s)ds$$

is a martingale on the underlying filtered probability space (Ω, F, F_t, P), where A is the extended generator of (x_t) in the sence of [J1]

$$A = X_0 + \frac{1}{2}\sum^m X_i^2 .$$

Here X_0 and X_i, $i = 1, \ldots, m$ are C^∞ - vectorfields.

The signal (x_t) is to be estimated from noisy observations of this,

$$dy_t^j = h_j(x_t)dt + dv_t^j \quad , \quad h_j \in C^2(M)$$

$$y_0^j = 0$$

$j = 1, \ldots, k$.

Formally, the problem takes the following form when using the perhaps better known notation of stochastic differential equations:

$$dx_t = X_0(x_t)dt + \sum_{i=1}^m X_i(x_t) \circ dw_t^i \quad , \quad x_0 = x$$

$$dy_t = h(x_t)dt + dv_t \quad , \quad y_0 = 0 .$$

There are (at least) two well known closed forms for the filter

$$\pi_t(f) = E[f(x_t) \mid Y_t] ,$$

where $Y_t = \sigma(y_s : s \le t)$. On the one hand it is given as a space integral in the Kallianpur - Striebel formula, on the other hand it can be written down in the form of a stochastic differential equation, which is known as Zakai's equation. When deriving these equations it turns out to be more convenient to consider the whole problem under a different measure P_0 for which (y_t) is a Brownian motion independent of (w_t) , and instead of $\pi_t(f)$ we give the formulas for an unnormalised version of π_t ,

$$\sigma_t(f) = E^0[\zeta \; f(x_t) \mid Y_t] ,$$

where E^0 is the expectation with respect to P_0 , and

$$\zeta^{-1} = \frac{dP_0}{dP} = \exp\left(-{}_0^\infty\!\!\int h(x_u)dv_u - \frac{1}{2}\,{}_0^\infty\!\!\int h^2(x_u)du\right) .$$

The original $\pi_t(f)$ can be computed from $\sigma_t(f)$ by

$$\pi_t(f) = {}^{\sigma_t(f)}/_{\sigma_t(1)} .$$

For simplicity, let's first assume that (x_t) and (y_t) are both one dimensional, and that (w_t) and (v_t) are independent. The Kallianpur - Striebel formula takes the following form

$$\tilde\sigma_t(f) = \int_M E^0_{x,0}[f(x_t) \cdot \zeta] \; \pi(dx)$$

where (M,π) is the sample path probability space. The Zakai equation takes the following form

$$d\sigma_t(f) = \sigma_t(\tilde A f)dt + \sigma_t(h \cdot f) \circ dy_t$$

where $\tilde A = A - \frac{1}{2}h^2$.

For problems of practical design and approximations Clark [Ć1] requires a more special form of the filter:
The solutions should be robust: it is desirable to find a function

$$\tilde\sigma_t(f, y)$$

defined for <u>each</u> $y \in C\left([0, \infty), \mathbb{R}^k\right)$, such that $\sigma_t(f, y)$ is

(i) a version of $\sigma_t(f)$

and (ii) continuous in y.

Furthermore, of course, the filter should be computable in a recursive way.

The pioneering work towards such robust solutions to the filter problem was done by Davis [D1, D2, D3, D4]. The most general case under correlation between the noises in signal and observation Davis can treat in the framework of his approach is strictly limited to the case of a one dimensional observation. I shall show that this generalizes to higher dimensions under senseful conditions. This work was carried out in [EK1] with slightly different techniques.

2. Just to give a rough idea how to compute $\sigma_t(f,y)$ in the uncorrelated case we start out with the Zakai equation

$$\begin{aligned} d\sigma_t(f) &= \sigma_t(\tilde{A}f)dt + \sigma_t(hf) \circ dy_t \\ \sigma_0 &= M \,. \end{aligned} \qquad (*)$$

Davis has solved the problem by considering both Zakai's equations <u>and</u> the Kallianpur - Striebel formula. In this formula he seperates out a multiplicative functional which turns out to be a product of a Gauge transformation and a Feynman - Kac transformation. For this functional he computes the generator of the semigroup associated with the multiplicative functional and so finds the desired result.

I want to give some more direct derivation. If the drift term in the above Zakai equation were absent, we would find a solution in the form

$$\sigma_t(f, y) = \langle e^{y_t h} f, \pi \rangle \,.$$

In the case with drift term the Doss - Sussman - technique of solving stochastic differential equations gives us the solution of $(*)$ in the form

$$\sigma_t(f, y) = \langle T_{Ot}^{y}(e^{y_t h}) , \pi \rangle$$

where T_{Ot}^{y} is a semigroup with generator

$$A_t^y = e^{y_t h} \tilde{A} e^{-y_t h}$$

I don't want to go into the details of Doss - Sussman's techniques. The form of the generator A_t^y can more easily be motivated if we assume for a moment that the equation (*) can be written in density form ($\tilde{A}^*$ adjoint of $\tilde{A}$) :

$$dq_t = \langle \tilde{A}^* f , q_t \rangle dt + \langle hf , q_t \rangle \circ dy_t$$

Transform this by

$$\tilde{q}_t = \exp(-q_t h(x_t))qt$$

to find a pathwise version

$$d\tilde{q}_t = \exp(-y_t h(x_t)) \left[\tilde{A}^*(e^{y_t h(x_t)} \tilde{q}_t) \right] dt$$

Here we find the (adjoint) of the generator we are looking for. So there is the problem of determining a semigroup which belongs to the generator A_t^y .

One can motivate from different points of view that this generator stems from a multiplicative functional, so that our next aim is to determine this multiplicative functional α_t^s , such that

$$\alpha_t^s f(x_t) - \alpha_s^s f(x_s) - \int_s^t \alpha_u^s A_u^y f ds = m_t^{y,f}$$

is a P_o - martingale.
Putting again

$$g(x_s) = e^{y_s h(x_s)} f(x_s)$$

we find that

$$\alpha_t^s e^{y_t h(x_t)} f(x_t) - \alpha_s^s e^{y_s h(x_s)} f(x_s) - {}_s\int^t \alpha_u^s e^{y_u h(x_u)} \tilde{A} f(x_u)\,du$$

should be a P_0 - martingale. As by definition

$$f(x_t) - f(x_s) - {}_s\int^t A\, f(x_u)\,du$$

is a P - martingale, we should compare ζ ,

$$\zeta^{-1} = \frac{dP_0}{dP}$$

and

$$\alpha_1^0 e^{y_1 h(x_1)} ,$$

or more explicitly

$$\alpha_t^s e^{y_t h(x_t)} = \exp\left({}_s\int^t h(x_u)\,dy_u - \tfrac{1}{2}{}_s\int^t h^2(x_u)\,du\right)$$

$$= e^{y_t h(x_t)} \exp\left(-{}_s\int^t y_u\,dh(x_u) - \tfrac{1}{2}{}_s\int^t h^2(x_u)\,du\right)$$

by integration by parts. So the multiplicative functional turns out to be

$$\alpha_t^s(y) = \exp\left(-{}_s\int^t y_u\,dh(x_u) - \tfrac{1}{2}{}_s\int^t h^2(x_u)\,du\right) .$$

The associated two parameter semigroup is given by

$$T_{s,t}^y f(x) = E_{x,s}^0\,[f(x_t)\,\alpha_t^s] ,$$

and so the robust solution to the Zakai equation is given by

$$\sigma_t(f,y) = \langle e^{y_t h} f,\ \pi_t^y \rangle$$

where

$$\pi_t^y = U_{t,0}^y \pi$$

satisfies formally the Fokker - Planck equation

$$\frac{d}{dt}\pi_t^y = (A_t^y)\ \pi_t^y$$

$$\pi_0^y = \pi \ ,$$

the solutions of which have been studied by Pardoux [P1].

So far the uncorrelated case. The effect of the uncorrelatedness is most explicitly seen in the definition of the semigroup $T_{s,t}^y$: As (x_t) is not influenced by observations the above definition makes sense when we regard $y \in C([0,\infty), \mathbb{R}^k)$ just as parameters as the dependence of y in $T_{s,t}^y$ appears only in $\alpha_t^s(y)$.

3. Things become quite more involved when we consider the correlated case. We now have the following system

$$dx_t = X_0(x_t)dt + \sum X_i(x_t) \circ dw_t^i \ , \ x_0 = x$$

$$dy_t = h(x_t)dt + dv_t \ , \ y_0 = 0 \in \mathbb{R}^k \ ,$$

where for simplicity we assume $k = 2$. The correlation is assumed to be of the form

$$\langle w^i , v^j \rangle_t = a_{ij} \cdot t \ , \ a_{ij} \in \mathbb{R} \ , \ 1 \le i \le m \ , \ j = 1,2 \ .$$

Some algebraic manipulations allow us to make the influence of y explicit in the signal equation after some (Girsanov) measure transformation:

<u>Theorem</u>: Let

$$\zeta^{-1} = \exp\left(\int_0^\infty \sum h^i(x_u)dy_u^i - \frac{1}{2}\int_0^\infty (h^i(x_u))^2 du\right)$$

and put

$$\frac{dP_0}{dP} = \zeta \ .$$

There are C^∞ - vectorfields Y_j , $1 \le j \le m$, and a standard m - dimensional P_0 - Brownian motion $b_t = (b_t^1, \ldots ,b_t^m)$ which is independent of y_t^1 and y_t^2 , such that

$$dx_t = Y_0(x_t)dt + Z_1(x_t)\circ dy_t^1 + Z_2(x_t)\circ dy_t^2 + \sum_{j=1}^{m} Y_j(x_t)\circ db_t^j$$

where $Z_j = \sum_i a_{ij}X_i$.

Thus we cannot proceed as in the uncorrelated case. But in certain cases Kunita's decomposition [K1,K2] of solutions of stochastic differential equations helps us out of this difficulty. We make the assumption that Z_1 and Z_2 commute (for more general conditions, see [K2]). Then a solution of

$$dx_t = Y_0(x_t)dt + Z_1(x_t)\circ dy_t^1 + Z_2(x_t)\circ dy_t^2 + \sum Y_j(x_t)\circ db_t^j$$

is given by

$$x_t(x_0) = G(y^1(t)\ ,\ y^2(t)\ ,\ \eta_t)$$

where $G(t_1,t_2,x)$ is the integral manifold to the solution of

$$d\zeta_t = Z_1\circ dy_t^1 + Z_2\circ dy_t^2$$

which exists by the Frobenius theorem, and η_t is a solution of

$$d\eta_t = {}^*Y_0(\eta_t)dt + \sum {}^*Y_j(\eta_t)\ \ db_t^j$$

where ${}^*Y_j = \emptyset_y(t)^{-1}_*Y_j$, and $\emptyset_y(t)$ is the diffeomorphism on M inducted by

$$\emptyset_y(t) = G(y^1(t)\ ,\ y^2(t)\ ,\ x)$$

One can now show that the solutions of η_t depend continuously on $y\in C([0,\infty),\mathbb{R}^k)$, and so we can proceed as in the uncorrelated case after - roughly speaking - replacing (x_t) by $(\emptyset_y(t)\circ\eta_t)$. Zakai's equation for this case turns out to be

$$d\sigma_t(f) = \sigma_t(\tilde{A}f)dt + \sigma_t(D_1f)\circ dy_t^1 + \sigma_t(D_2f)\circ dy_t^2$$

where

$$D_i = Z_i + h_i$$

$$\tilde{A} = A - \frac{1}{2}(D_1^2 + D_2^2)$$

$$= Y_0 + \frac{1}{2}\sum Y_j^2 - \frac{1}{2}(D_1 h_1 + D_2 h_2) .$$

The next step should be to make some transformation which turns this equation into a pathwise solvable equation. Under the condition that $Z_i h_j = 0$ for $i,j = 1,2$ this operator is given by

$$B_t^y = B_{y^1(t),y^2(t)}$$

which formally is a solution of

$$dB = (Z_1 + h_1)B dt_1 + (Z_2 + h_2)B dt_2 .$$

Note that in the uncorrelated case

$$B_t^y = \exp(y_t h) .$$

B_t^y turns out to be the product of some operator $C_y(t) = C_{y^1(t),y^2(t)}$ and $\emptyset_y(t)$

$$B_t^y = C_{y(t)}\emptyset_y(t) .$$

Then, just as in the uncorrelated case, we find a robust solution by means of a semigroup which has to be constructed, to the operator

$$B_t^y\left[*Y_0 + \frac{1}{2}\sum *Y_j^2 - \frac{1}{2}(D_1 h_1 + D_2 h_2)\right](B_t^y)^{-1}$$

or more simply by only considering $C_{y(t)}$, to the operator

$$A_t^y = C_{y(t)}\left[*Y_0 + \frac{1}{2}\sum(*Y_j)^2 - \frac{1}{2}\emptyset_y^*(t)(D_1 h_1 + D_2 h_2)\right]C_{y(t)}^{-1} .$$

Again we loook for a multiplicative functional corresponding to a semigroup with generator A_t^y, i.e. we look for $\alpha_t^s(y)$, such that

$$\alpha_t^s f(\eta_t) - \alpha_s^s f(\eta_s) - \int \alpha_u^s A_u^y f(\eta_u) du$$

is a P_0 - martingale. α_t^s is found by comparing the P_0 - martingale

$$\alpha_t^s C_{y(t)} f(\eta_t) - \alpha_s^s C_{y(s)} f(\eta_s) - {}_s^t\int \alpha_u^s A_u^y (C_{y(u)} f(\eta_u)) du$$

with the P_0 - martingale

$$f(\eta_t) - f(\eta_s) - {}_s\int^t (*Y_0 + \tfrac{1}{2}\sum *Y_j^2) f(\eta_u)du .$$

and the P - martingale

$$f(x_t) - f(x_s) - \int_s^t Af(x_s)ds .$$

So, again we have to compare φ with $\alpha_t^s \, C_{y(t)}$, where x_t^s then turns out to be

$$\alpha_t^s = \exp[- \sum_{i=1}^{2} {}_s\int^t *Y_0 g_u^i(\eta_u)du + \sum_j {}_s\int^t *Y_j g_u^i(\eta_u) \circ db_u^j + \frac{1}{2} {}_s\int^t \emptyset_y^*(u) D_j h_i(\eta_u)du,$$

where $g_u^1(\eta_u) = \int_0^{y^1(u)} G_{sy^2(u)} h^1(\eta_u)ds$

and $G_u^2(\eta_u)$ is defined analogously.

To solve the problem completely now, let

$$T_{s,t}^y f(x) = E_{x,s}^0 [f(\eta_t)\alpha_t^s(y)]$$

so that analogously to what we said in the beginning

$$\sigma_t(f,y) = \langle T_{0t} B_t^y \, f(\eta_t) \, , \, \pi \rangle$$

$$= \langle B_t^y f(\eta_t) \, , \, \pi_t^y \rangle$$

where again π_t^y satisfies the Fokker - Planck equation

$$\frac{d}{dt} M_t^y = (A_t^y)^* \pi_t^y \, , \; \pi_0^y = \pi .$$

Michael Kohlmann
Universität Bonn
Institut für Angewandte Mathematik
Abtlg.Wahrscheinlichkeitstheorie und
mathematische Statistik
Wegelerstr.6-10, D-5300 Bonn,FRGermany

[C1] Clark, J.M.C. The Design of Robust Approximations to the Stochastic Differential Equations of Nonlinear Filtering, in "Communication Systems and Random Process Theory" ed. J.K. Skwirzynski, NATC ASI series Sijthoff and Noordhoff. Alphen aan den Rijn (1978).

[D1] Davis, M.H.A. A Pathwise Solution of the Equations of Nonlinear Filtering, preprint presented at the 12th European Meeting of Statisticians, Varna Bulgaria (1979).

[D2] Davis, M.H.A. On a Multiplicative Functional Transformation Arising in Nonlinear Filtering Theory, submitted to Zeits. für Wahrs. (1980).

[D3] Davis, M.H.A. Pathwise Nonlinear Filtering - The Correlated Noise Case, Preprint presented at the Séminaire de Probabilités, Rouen, June 1980.

[D4] Davis, M.H.A. Pathwise Nonlinear Filtering, preprint presented at the NATO ASI, Les Arcs, France (1980).

[EK1] Elliott, R.J., Kohlmann, M. Robust Filtering for Correlated Multidimensional Observations, Math.Z. 178, 559-578 (1981)

[K1] Kunita, H. On the representation of solutions of stochastic differential equations, Séminaire de Probabilités XIV ed. J. Azema, M. Yor, LN in Mathematics 748, Springer Verlag, Berlin-Heidelberg-New York (1980).

[K2] Kunita, H. On the decomposition of solutions of stochastic differential equations. London Mathematical Society Symposium on Stochastic Integrals, Durham, July 1980.

[K3] Kunita, H. Cauchy problems for stochastic partial differential equations arizing in non-linear filtering theory. To appear in Systems & Control Letters.

[K4] Kunita, H. Densities of a measure valued process governed by a stochastic partial differential equation. To appear in Systems & Control Letters.

[P1] Pardoux, E. Backward and forward stochastic partial differential equations associated with nonlinear filtering problems. Proc. IEEE Conference on Decision and Control. Ft. Lauderdale, Florida, December 1979.

Ito formula for generalized Brownian functionals

Izumi KUBO

Department of Mathematics, Nagoya University

§1. Introduction

Probabilists often use the notation

$$\ell_t(a) = \int_0^t \delta(B(s) - a)ds \tag{1. 1}$$

for the representation of the local time of a Brownian motion $B(t)$. But the integrand is usually understood as a formal expression. Here we are going to give a definition of $F(B(t))$ as a generalized Brownian functional for any slowly increasing generalized function F; that is, F belongs to the Schwartz space $\mathscr{S}^*(R)$. Further define a stochastic integral by using creation operators ∂_t^* as

$$\int_s^t F(B(r))\, dB(r) \equiv \int_s^t dr\ \partial_r^* F(B(r)). \tag{1. 2}$$

We will show Ito's formula:

$$F(B(t)) - F(B(s)) = \int_s^t F'(B(r))dB(r) + \frac{1}{2}\int_s^t F''(B(r))\, dr. \tag{1. 3}$$

The definition (1. 2) is consistent with the usual one for a suitable function F. H. Tanaka and M. Fukushima [4] have used Ito formula to define the last term of (1. 3) for a suitable F. In our setting, the last term can be defined for a general F without the use of Ito's formula.

§2. Generalized Brownian functionals

Here we refer to results in I. Kubo - S. Takenaka [2], which are reformulations of T. Hida's work [1]. In our treatment, the space of testing Brownian functionals (we have called them testing random variables) is closed in multiplication and also in differentiations $\partial_t = \partial/\partial x(t)$. This fact assures a similarity to the theory of usual generalized functions.

Let T be a complete separable metric space with a σ-finite Borel measure ν without atoms. For example, we may consider cases of $T = R$,

$R\times\{1, 2, \cdots, d\}$, R^d, P^d, S^d, etc. with the natural Riemannian volumes. We suppose the existence of a Gel'fand triplet

$$E \subset L^2(T, \nu) \subset E^*$$

topologized by a countable system of consistent inner products $(\ ,\ )_p$; $p \in Z$, which have the following properties: There exists a positive number ρ less than 1 such that

$$(2.1) \qquad \rho\| \xi \|_{p+1} \geq \| \xi \|_p \quad \text{for any} \quad \xi \in E,\ p \in Z$$

(generally, we can choose such inner products). Let E_p be the completion of E with respect to the inner product $(\ ,\ )_p$. Then E_{-p} is the dual space of E_p, $p \geq 0$; that is, for $\zeta \in E_0$, $(\xi, \zeta)_0$ gives a continuous linear functional of $\xi \in E_p$ with norm $\| \zeta \|_{-p}$. For $\xi \in E_1$, we can define the evaluating map $\delta_t : \xi \to \xi(t)$ such that δ_t belongs to E_{-1} and the mapping $t \to \delta_t$ from T to E_{-1} is continuous. Finally, we assume

$$(2.2) \qquad \| \delta \|^2 \equiv \int_T \| \delta_t \|_{-1}^2 \, d\nu(t) < \infty.$$

We can easily see that the spaces of the above examples admit such Gelfand triplets. In this article, we denote by $<\ ,\ >$ the canonical bilinear forms between any dual pairs. Then by Bochner-Minlos' theorem, we have a probability measure μ on E^* such that

$$(2.3) \qquad \int_{E^*} \exp[i <x, \xi>] \, d\mu(x) = \exp[- \tfrac{1}{2}\| \xi \|_0^2].$$

Since the measure μ is quasi-invariant under the shift $x \to x + \xi$ for ξ in E, we can define the following transformation S:

$$(2.4) \qquad (S\varphi)(\xi) \equiv \int_{E^*} \varphi(x+\xi) \, d\mu(x)$$

$$= \int_{E^*} \varphi(x) \exp[<x, \xi> - \tfrac{1}{2}\| \xi \|_0^2] \, d\mu(x)$$

for $\varphi \in L^2(E^*,\mu)$. Then the image space $F^{(0)} \equiv S(L^2(E^*,\mu))$ is a Hilbert space with the reproducing kernel $\exp[<\xi, \eta>]$, $\xi, \eta \in E$ and S is an isomorphism from $L^2(E^*, \mu)$ to $F^{(0)}$. We can introduce inner products $(\ ,\ )_{(p)} = (\ ,\ )_{F^{(p)}}$ for the linear set $\overset{o}{F} \equiv \{ \varphi =$

$\sum c_j \exp[<\xi, \eta_j>]$; $c_j \in R$, $\eta_j \in E\}$ such that

(2. 5) $$(\exp[<\xi,\eta>], \exp[<\xi,\zeta>])_{F^{(p)}} \equiv \exp[(\eta,\zeta)_p].$$

Let $F^{(p)}$ be the completion of $\overset{\circ}{F}$ with respect to the inner product $(\ ,\ )_{(p)}$, $p \in Z$. Then each element of $F^{(p)}$ is a continuous functional on E and the natural inclusions

$$F^{(p+1)} \subset F^{(p)}, \ p \in Z,$$

hold. Moreover $F^{(-p)}$ is the dual space of $F^{(p)}$ in the same sense as in the above. Put $F \equiv \bigcap_p F^{(p)}$ and $F^* \equiv \bigcup_p F^{(p)}$ and topologize them as the projective limit and the inductive limit, respectively. Then we have a new Gelfand triplet $F \subset F^{(0)} \subset F^*$. We can prove that each element U of F is an analytic functional in ξ in the sense of Fréchet derivative. Furthermore, the functional derivative

$$\frac{\delta}{\delta\xi(t_1)} \cdots \frac{\delta}{\delta\xi(t_n)} U(\xi)$$

belongs to F for each fixed $\underline{t} = (t_1,\cdots,t_n) \in T^n$ and it belongs to $E^{\hat{\otimes} n}$ (the n-fold symmetric tensor product of E) for fixed $\xi \in E$.

Put $H^{(p)} = S^{-1}F^{(p)}$ and induce an inner product on $H^{(p)}$ from $F^{(p)}$. Let H be the projective limit of $H^{(p)}$ as $p \to \infty$. Then we have the inclusions

$$H \subset \cdots \subset H^{(p+1)} \subset H^{(p)} \subset \cdots \subset H^{(0)} = L^2(E^*, \mu), \ p \geq 0.$$

Let $H^{(-p)}$ be the dual of $H^{(p)}$ and let H^* be the inductive limit of $H^{(p)}$ as $p \to -\infty$. Then we have one more Gelfand triplet $H \subset H^{(0)} = L^2(E^*, \mu) \subset H^*$. Since the restriction of S to $H^{(p)}$ gives an isomorphism from $H^{(p)}$ to $F^{(p)}$ for $p \geq 0$, we can extend S to H^* in such a way that its restriction to $F^{(p)}$ gives an isomorphism from $H^{(p)}$ to $F^{(p)}$ for any $p \in Z$. Thus we have the diagram

(2. 6)
$$\begin{array}{ccccc} H & \subset & H^{(0)} = L^2(E^*,\mu) & \subset & H^* \\ \downarrow S & & \downarrow S & & \downarrow S \\ F & \subset & F^{(0)} & \subset & F^* . \end{array}$$

We call an element of H^* *a generalized random variable*.

We can show that the multiplication $(\varphi,\psi) \to \varphi\cdot\psi$ is continuous on

H. Let us define the derivative ∂_t by

(2. 7) $$\partial_t \varphi \equiv S^{-1} \frac{\delta}{\delta \xi(t)} S\varphi, \quad t \in T.$$

Then ∂_t is a continuous derivation on H. Its dual ∂_t^* acts continuously on H^* and satisfies

(2. 8) $$\partial_t^* \psi = S^{-1}(\xi(t) \cdot (S\psi)(\xi)) \qquad \text{for } \psi \in H^*.$$

For ζ in $L^2(T, \nu) = E_0$, take a sequence $\{\zeta_n\} \subset E$ with $\| \zeta_n - \zeta \|_0 \to 0$ as $n \to \infty$ and put

(2. 9) $$I(\zeta)(x) \equiv \underset{n \to \infty}{\text{l.i.m.}} \langle x, \zeta_n \rangle .$$

Then $\zeta \to I(\zeta)$ is an isometry from $E_0 = L^2(T, \nu)$ into $H^{(0)} = L^2(E^*, \mu)$, moreover $I(\zeta)$ is a Gaussian random variable with mean zero and variance $\| \zeta \|_0^2$. We can easily see that for $\xi \in E$

(2. 10) $$\begin{aligned} I(\zeta)(x + \xi) &= I(\zeta)(x) + \langle \xi, \zeta \rangle \quad \text{in } H^{(0)}, \\ S(I(\zeta))(\xi) &= \langle \xi, \zeta \rangle = (\xi, \zeta)_0. \end{aligned}$$

Let us define a Gaussian random measure $\{W(A)\}$ by

(2. 11) $$W(A) \equiv I(\chi_A) \qquad \text{for } \nu(A) < \infty.$$

Then the multiple Wiener integrals can be defined as usual;

(2. 12) $$I_n(f_n) \equiv \int \cdots \int_{T^n} f_n \, dW(t_1) \cdots dW(t_n)$$

for $f_n \in L^2(T^n, \nu^n) = E_0^{\otimes n}$. Let us denote by $\hat{L}^2(T^n, \nu^n)$ the Hilbert space of symmetric L^2-functions. Obviously, it is identified with the n-fold symmetric tensor product space $E_0^{\hat{\otimes} n}$.

Theorem 2. 1. *(i) For* $f_n \in E_0^{\hat{\otimes} n}$*, it holds that*

$$\begin{aligned} I_n(f_n) &= \int \cdots \int_{T^n} d\nu(t_1) \cdots d\nu(t_n) f_n(t_1, \cdots, t_n) \partial_{t_1}^* \cdots \partial_{t_n}^* 1, \\ S(I_n(f_n))(\xi) &= \langle f_n, \xi^{\otimes n} \rangle . \end{aligned}$$

(ii) Any φ *in* $H^{(0)} = L^2(E^*, \mu)$ *can be represented by the orthogonal sum*

$$\varphi = \sum_{n=0}^{\infty} I_n(f_n) \quad \text{with} \quad \| \varphi \|_{H^{(0)}}^2 = \sum_{n=0}^{\infty} n! \| f_n \|_{E_0^{\hat{\otimes} n}}^2,$$

where f_n *is a symmetric kernel in* $E_0^{\hat{\otimes} n}$ *which is given by*

$$f_n(t_1,\cdots,t_n) = \frac{1}{n!}\frac{\delta}{\delta\xi(t_1)}\cdots\frac{\delta}{\delta\xi(t_n)}(S\varphi)(0).$$

Now we suppose that

(2. 13) $\quad T = R \times \{1,2,\cdots,d\}$

and ν is the ordinary Lebesgue measure on T. Then for $\xi \in E$ (resp. for $\zeta \in E^*$), we define a vector valued function $\underline{\xi}$ (resp. generalized function $\underline{\zeta}$) on R by

$$\underline{\xi}(t) \equiv (\xi(t,1),\cdots,\xi(t,d)) \quad (\text{resp. } \underline{\zeta}(\cdot) \equiv (\zeta(\cdot,1),\cdots,\zeta(\cdot,d))),$$

and we have

$$\langle\xi,\ \zeta\rangle = \sum_{j=1}^{d}\langle\xi(\cdot,j),\zeta(\cdot,j)\rangle \equiv \langle\underline{\xi},\ \underline{\zeta}\rangle .$$

A d-dimensional Brownian motion $B(t) = (B_1(t),\cdots, B_d(t))$ can be defined by

(2. 14) $$B_j(t) \equiv \begin{cases} I(\chi_{[0,\ t]\times\{j\}}) & \text{if } t \geq 0, \\ -I(\chi_{[t,\ 0)\times\{j\}}) & \text{if } t < 0, \end{cases} \qquad j=1,2,\cdots,d.$$

Let $\mathcal{B}_t$ be the σ-field generated by $\{B(s);\ s < t\}$.

Theorem 2. 2. *Assume that* $\varphi_t(x)$ *is a* (t, x)*-measurable,* $\mathcal{B}_t$*-adapted function in* $H^{(0)}$ *for each* t *with* $\int\|\varphi_t\|^2_{H^{(0)}}dt < \infty$. *Then we have that*

$$\int\varphi_t\, dB_j(t) = \int dt\ \partial^*_{\{t,j\}}\varphi_t \qquad \text{in } H^*,$$

equivalently that

$$S(\int\varphi_t\, dB_j(t))(\xi) = \int dt\,\xi(t,j)(S\varphi_t)(\xi).$$

§3. Ito formula

Now we define a generalized random variable $F(I(\zeta_1),\cdots,I(\zeta_n))$ for an n-dimensional slowly increasing generalized function $F \in \mathcal{S}^*(R^n)$. and for linearly independent functions $\underline{\zeta} = (\zeta_1,\cdots,\zeta_n)$ in E_0. For a positive definite $n\times n$-matrix A, denote by $P_A(\underline{u})$ the Gaussian density function with mean zero and covariance matrix A;

(3. 1) $$P_A(\underline{u}) = (2\pi)^{-n/2}(\det A)^{-1/2}\exp[-\tfrac{1}{2}(\underline{u}A^{-1},\ \underline{u})].$$

Then

(3. 2) $$F_A(\underline{\underline{u}}) \equiv F * P_A(\underline{\underline{u}})$$

is a rapidly decreasing function in $\mathcal{S}(R^n)$ and converges to F in the space $\mathcal{S}^*(R^n)$ as $A \downarrow 0$. For $\underline{\underline{\zeta}} = (\zeta_1, \cdots, \zeta_n)$, we denote as

$$I(\underline{\underline{\zeta}}) \equiv (I(\zeta_1), \cdots, I(\zeta_n)) \quad \text{and} \quad \langle\xi, \underline{\underline{\zeta}}\rangle \equiv (\langle\xi,\zeta_1\rangle, \cdots, \langle\xi,\zeta_n\rangle).$$

Then by (2. 10), we have

(3. 3) $$S(F_A(I(\underline{\underline{\zeta}})))(\xi) = \int_{E^*} F_A(I(\underline{\underline{\zeta}}) + \langle\xi, \underline{\underline{\zeta}}\rangle) \, d\mu = \int_{R^n} F_A(\underline{\underline{u}} + \langle\xi, \underline{\underline{\zeta}}\rangle) P_\Gamma(\underline{\underline{u}}) \, d\underline{\underline{u}} = F_{A+\Gamma}(\langle\xi, \underline{\underline{\zeta}}\rangle),$$

where Γ is the $n \times n$-matrix whose entries are $\langle\zeta_i, \zeta_j\rangle = (\zeta_i, \zeta_j)_0$, $1 \le i,j \le n$. On the other hand, we can check that $\{\| F_{A+\Gamma}(\langle\xi,\underline{\underline{\zeta}}\rangle)\|_{(p)}$; $A > 0\}$ is bounded for $p < -1$, if Γ is not degenerate. Hence the convergence $F_{A+\Gamma}(\langle\xi, \underline{\underline{\zeta}}\rangle) \to F_\Gamma(\langle\xi, \underline{\underline{\zeta}}\rangle)$ as $A \downarrow 0$ for each fixed $\xi \in E$ implies its convergence in F^*, because $F \subset F^{(0)} \subset F^*$ is a Gelfand triplet. Thus we can define

(3. 4) $$F(I(\underline{\underline{\zeta}})) \equiv S^{-1} F_\Gamma(\langle\xi, \underline{\underline{\zeta}}\rangle)$$

as an element of H^*, if $\zeta_1, \cdots, \zeta_n$ are linearly independent.

Theorem 3. 1. *Let* $\underline{\underline{\zeta}} = (\zeta_1, \cdots, \zeta_n)$ *be linearly independent and let* Γ *be the* $n \times n$*-matrix* $(\langle\zeta_i, \zeta_j\rangle)_{i,j=1}^n$. *We have the following:*

(i) If F_k *converges to* F *in* $\mathcal{S}^*(R^n)$ *as* $k \to \infty$, *then* $F_k(I(\underline{\underline{\zeta}}))$ *converges to* $F(I(\underline{\underline{\zeta}}))$ *in* H^* *as* $k \to \infty$ and

(ii) $$S(F(I(\underline{\underline{\zeta}})))(\xi) = F_\Gamma(\langle\xi, \underline{\underline{\zeta}}\rangle).$$

Theorem 3. 2. *We assume that* $T = R \times \{1, \cdots, d\}$ *and that* $B(t) = (B_1(t), \cdots, B_d(t))$ *is the d-dimensional Brownian motion defined by* (2. 14). *Then for* F *in* $\mathcal{S}^*(R^d)$ *and* $t > s > 0$, *we have*

(i) $$F(B(t)) - F(B(s)) = \sum_j \int_s^t dr \; \partial^*_{(r,j)} \frac{\partial}{\partial u_j} F(B(r)) + \frac{1}{2} \int_s^t \Delta F(B(r)) \, dr;$$

(ii) additionally, if $\frac{\partial}{\partial u_j} F$, $1 \le j \le d$, *are in* $L^2(P_{tI}(\underline{\underline{u}}) d\underline{\underline{u}})$, *then*

$$F(B(t)) - F(B(s)) = \sum_j \int_s^t \frac{\partial}{\partial u_j} F(B(r)) \, dB_j(r) + \frac{1}{2} \int_s^t \Delta F(B(r)) \, dr.$$

Proof. Noting that $P_{tI}(\underline{\underline{u}}) = (2\pi t)^{-d/2}\exp[-\frac{1}{2t}(\underline{\underline{u}}, \underline{\underline{u}})]$ is the heat kernel, we have the relation

$$\frac{d}{dt} P_{tI}\left(\int_0^t \underline{\underline{\xi}}(r)dr - \underline{\underline{u}}\right) = \sum_j \xi(t,j)\left(\frac{\partial}{\partial u_j} P_{tI}\right)\left(\int_0^t \underline{\underline{\xi}}(r)dr - \underline{\underline{u}}\right)$$

$$+ \frac{1}{2} \Delta P_{tI}\left(\int_0^t \underline{\underline{\xi}}(r)\, dr - \underline{\underline{u}}\right).$$

By Theorem 3.1 (ii), we have that

$$S(F(B(t)))(\xi) - S(F(B(s)))(\xi) = \int_s^t \frac{d}{dr} F*P_{rI}\left(\int_0^r \xi(v)dv\right) dr$$

$$= \sum_j \int_s^t \xi(t,j) S\left(\frac{\partial}{\partial u_j} F(B(r))\right)dr + \frac{1}{2}\int_s^t S(\Delta F(B(r)))dr.$$

By (2.8), we have the first assertion. The second assertion follows from the fact that L^2-norms of $\partial/\partial u_j F(B(r))$ are bounded for $r \in [s, t]$.

§4. Remarks

Remark 4.1. Take $F(u) = |u - a|$, $u \in R$, then we have

(4.1) $$\ell_t(a)-\ell_s(a) = |B(t)-a|-|B(s)-a|-\int_s^t \operatorname{sign}(B(r)-a)dB(r)$$

$$= \int_s^t \delta(B(r) - a)\, dr.$$

The first equality has been obtained by H. Tanaka. M. Fukushima [4] has defined the integral $\int_s^t \delta(B(r) - a)\, dr$ by the second equality of (4.1). More generally, he has defined $\int_s^t F''(B(r))dr$ by using Ito formula ;

(4.2) $$\int_s^t F''(B(r))dr \equiv 2\, F(B(t)) - 2\, F(B(s)) - 2\int_s^t F'(B(r))dB(r),$$

if F' belongs to $L^2_{loc}(R)$. T. Yamada [5] has treated generalized functions such as Cauchy's principal value, Hadamard's finite part, v.p.$\frac{1}{x_+}$, etc., in connection with local times. In our setting, we defined $F(B(r))$ and $\int F(B(r))dr$ as elements of H^* for any slowly increasing generalized function F and we showed that the formula (4.2) is valid as a theorem.

The generalized random variable $\delta(I(\zeta) - a)$ has interesting properties. In the following , we will note some of them.

Remark 4.2. Let $\{\zeta_j\}_{j=1}^n$ be linearly independent functions in E_p and let ψ be in $H^{(p)}$ for a $p \in Z$. Then for F in $\mathcal{S}^*(R^n)$, we have that $F(I(\underline{\zeta}))\psi$ belongs to H^*. In particular, if $p=0$ and if the equality

$$(4.\ 3) \qquad (S\psi)(\xi+\alpha_1\zeta_1+\cdots+\alpha_n\zeta_n) = (S\psi)(\xi) \quad \text{for any } \xi,\ \alpha_1,\cdots,\alpha_n,$$

holds, then ψ is a random variable independent of $\{I(\zeta_j);\ j=1,\cdots,n\}$. An extended form of the result is as follows: If (4. 3) holds for a $p \geq 0$, then

$$(4.\ 4) \qquad S\colon F(I(\underline{\zeta}))\psi \to F_\Gamma(\langle\xi,\ \underline{\underline{\zeta}}\rangle)(S\psi)(\xi).$$

We omit the proof of the first assertion. Suppose that (4. 3) holds. Let $\{\eta_j\}_{j=1}^\infty$ be a complete orthonormal system of $E_0 = L^2(T,\nu)$ such that $\{\eta_j\}_{j=1}^n$ is spanned by $\{\zeta_j\}_{j=1}^n$. Then we know that $\{I(\eta_j);\ 1 \leq j < \infty\}$ is a family of independent Gaussian random variables with mean zero and variance one and that $\psi \in H^{(0)} = L^2(E^*,\ \mu)$ can be represented by an orthogonal sum;

$$\psi = \sum_{\underline{\underline{k}}\geq 0} c_{\underline{\underline{k}}} H_{\underline{\underline{k}}}(I(\eta_{\underline{\underline{k}}})) \quad \text{with} \quad (S\psi)(\xi) = \sum_{\underline{\underline{k}}\geq 0} c_{\underline{\underline{k}}} \ \langle\xi,\ \eta_{\underline{\underline{k}}}\rangle^{\underline{\underline{k}}},$$

where we denote by $H_k(u)$ the Hermite polynomials defined by

$$\sum_{k=0}^{\infty} \frac{1}{k!} z^k H_k(u) = \exp[zu - \tfrac{1}{2}z^2]$$

and we use the notation of multi-indices $\underline{\underline{k}} = (k_1,\cdots,k_n,\cdots)$, $c_{\underline{\underline{k}}} = c_{k_1,k_2,\cdots}$, $H_{\underline{\underline{k}}}(\underline{\underline{u}}) = H_{k_1}(u_1)\cdots H_{k_n}(u_n)\cdots$, $\underline{\underline{u}}^{\underline{\underline{k}}} = u_1^{k_1}\cdots u_n^{k_n}\cdots$, etc.

By (4.3), we see that $c_{\underline{\underline{k}}} = 0$ if $k_1+\cdots+k_n \geq 1$; that is, ψ is written only by $\{I(\eta_j);\ j \geq n+1\}$. Therefore ψ is independent of $\{I(\eta_j)\}_{j=1}^n$, equivalently, of $\{I(\zeta_j)\}_{j=1}^n$. Then (4. 4) is seen by

$$\begin{aligned} S(F(I(\underline{\zeta}))\psi)(\xi) &= \int_{E^*} F(I(\underline{\zeta}) + \langle\xi,\ \underline{\underline{\zeta}}\rangle)\ \psi(x+\xi)d\mu(x) \\ &= \int_{E^*} F(I(\underline{\zeta}) + \langle\xi,\ \underline{\underline{\zeta}}\rangle)\ d\mu\cdot\int_{E^*} \psi(x+\xi)\ d\mu \\ &= F_\Gamma(\langle\xi,\ \underline{\underline{\zeta}}\rangle)\cdot(S\psi)(\xi). \end{aligned}$$

We can prove the general case, by approximation.

Remark 4.3. L. Streit and T. Hida [3] have used the generalized Brownian functional $\delta(B(t) - a)$ for a description of Feynman path integral in the connection with the formula

$$(4.5) \qquad E[\varphi|B(t) = a] = \frac{<\varphi, \delta(B(t) - a)>}{<1, \delta(B(t) - a)>} \qquad \text{for} \quad \varphi \in H.$$

The result can be extended as follows. Let $\{\zeta_j\}_{j=1}^n$ be linearly independent functions in E_0 and let Γ be the $n\times n$-matrix with entries $<\zeta_i, \zeta_j>$, $1 \le i,j \le n$. Then for $\varphi \in H$, we have that

$$(4.6) \qquad E[\varphi|I(\zeta_1) = a_1, \cdots, I(\zeta_n) = a_n] = \frac{<\varphi, \delta(I(\underline{\underline{\zeta}}) - \underline{\underline{a}})>}{<1, \delta(I(\underline{\underline{\zeta}}) - \underline{\underline{a}})>}$$

for the n-dimensional delta function δ and that

$$(4.7) \qquad <1, \delta(I(\underline{\underline{\zeta}}) - \underline{\underline{a}})> = P_\Gamma(\underline{\underline{a}}).$$

Proof. The equality (4. 7) follows from (3. 2), because generally the equality

$$(4.8) \qquad <1, \psi> = (S\psi)(0)$$

holds for $\psi \in H^*$. We will show (4. 6). Let A be a regular matrix with the property $A^*\Gamma A = I$, where I is the $n\times n$-identity matrix. Put $\underline{\underline{\eta}} \equiv \underline{\underline{\zeta}}A$ and $\underline{\underline{b}} \equiv \underline{\underline{a}}A$. Then we have the equalities

$$(4.9) \qquad S(\delta(I(\underline{\underline{\zeta}}) - \underline{\underline{a}}))(\xi) = P_\Gamma(<\xi, \underline{\underline{\zeta}}> - \underline{\underline{a}}) = P_I(<\xi, \underline{\underline{\eta}}> - \underline{\underline{b}})\det A.$$

By the definition of Hermite polynomials in Remark 4. 2, we have

$$P_I(<\xi, \underline{\underline{\eta}}>-\underline{\underline{b}}) = \sum_{\underline{\underline{k}}} \frac{1}{\underline{\underline{k}}!}<\xi, \underline{\underline{\eta}}>^{\underline{\underline{k}}} H_{\underline{\underline{k}}}(\underline{\underline{b}})\exp[-\tfrac{1}{2}\underline{\underline{b}}^2]$$

with $\underline{\underline{k}}! \equiv k_1!\cdots k_n!$ and $\underline{\underline{b}}^2 \equiv b_1^2 + \cdots + b_n^2$. Therefore, we have

$$F(\underline{\underline{b}}) \equiv \frac{<\varphi, \delta(I(\underline{\underline{\zeta}}) - \underline{\underline{a}})>}{<1, \delta(I(\underline{\underline{\zeta}}) - \underline{\underline{a}})>} = \sum_{\underline{\underline{k}}} \frac{1}{\underline{\underline{k}}!} H_{\underline{\underline{k}}}(\underline{\underline{b}})<S\varphi(\xi), <\xi, \underline{\underline{\eta}}>^{\underline{\underline{k}}}>$$

$$= \sum_{\underline{\underline{k}}} \frac{1}{\underline{\underline{k}}!} H_{\underline{\underline{k}}}(\underline{\underline{b}})U^{(|\underline{\underline{k}}|)}(\xi; \underline{\underline{\eta}}^{\otimes\underline{\underline{k}}})$$

with $|\underline{\underline{k}}| \equiv k_1+\cdots+k_n$ and $\eta_{\underline{\underline{k}}}^{\otimes\underline{\underline{k}}} \equiv \eta_1^{\otimes k_1}\otimes\cdots\otimes\eta_n^{\otimes k_n}$. We can show that the series converges in $L^2(P_I(\underline{\underline{b}})d\underline{\underline{b}})$ and also uniformly in each bounded subset of R^n, if $\varphi \in H$. Since the Hilbert space of all $\{I(\zeta_j)\}_{j=1}^n$-measurable L^2-functions is spanned by $\{H_{k_1}(I(\eta_1))\cdots H_{k_n}(I(\eta_n));\ 0 \le$

$k_1,\cdots,k_n < \infty\}$ and since

$$<H_{\underline{\underline{\ell}}}(I(\underline{\underline{\eta}})),\varphi> = \sum_{\underline{\underline{k}}} \frac{1}{\underline{\underline{k}}!}<<\xi\ \underline{\underline{\eta}}>^{\underline{\underline{k}}},\ (S\varphi)(\xi)>\int_{R^n} H_{\underline{\underline{k}}}(\underline{\underline{u}})H_{\underline{\underline{\ell}}}(\underline{\underline{u}})P_I(\underline{\underline{u}})d\underline{\underline{u}},$$

$$= <H_{\underline{\underline{\ell}}}(I(\underline{\underline{\eta}})),\ F(I(\underline{\underline{\eta}}))>,$$

we have (4. 6).

Remark 4. 4. The meaning of the formula (4. 4) can be more precisely stated for the case that $\{\zeta_j\}_{j=1}^n$ is included in E. For φ in H, there exists a continuous mapping $\varphi(x|\underline{\underline{a}})$ from R^n into H, such that $\{\varphi(x|\underline{\underline{a}})\ ;\ \underline{\underline{a}} \in R^n\}$ is independent of $\{I(\zeta_j) = <x,\ \zeta_j>;\ 1 \le j \le n\}$ and that

$$(4.\ 10)\qquad \begin{cases} \delta(<x,\ \underline{\underline{\zeta}}> - \underline{\underline{a}})\cdot\varphi(x) = \delta(<x,\ \underline{\underline{\zeta}}> - \underline{\underline{a}})\cdot\varphi(x|\underline{\underline{a}}) & \text{in } H^*, \\ \varphi(x) = \varphi(x|<x,\ \underline{\underline{\zeta}}>) & \end{cases}$$

holds.

Let A, $\underline{\underline{b}}$ and $\underline{\underline{\eta}}$ be the $n\times n$-matrix, the vector and the vector valued function as in Remark 4. 3. Then $\delta(<x,\ \underline{\underline{\zeta}}>-\underline{\underline{a}}) = \delta(<x,\ \underline{\underline{\eta}}>-\underline{\underline{b}})\det A$ holds as seen already. Put $U(\xi) = (S\varphi)(\xi)$. Since $U(\xi)$ is analytic in the sense of Fréchet derivative, for $\xi^\perp \equiv \xi-\sum_{j=1}^n<\xi,\ \eta_j>\eta_j$ we have

$$(4.\ 11)\qquad U(\xi) = U(\xi^\perp+\sum_{j=1}^n<\xi,\ \eta_j>\eta_j)$$

$$= \sum_{\underline{\underline{k}}} \frac{1}{\underline{\underline{k}}!}<\xi,\ \underline{\underline{\eta}}>^{\underline{\underline{k}}}\ U^{(|\underline{\underline{k}}|)}(\xi^\perp;\ \underline{\underline{\eta}}^{\otimes\underline{\underline{k}}}).$$

Put $\varphi_{\underline{\underline{k}}} \equiv S^{-1}U^{(|\underline{\underline{k}}|)}(\xi^\perp;\ \underline{\underline{\eta}}^{\otimes\underline{\underline{k}}})$. Then we can estimate the norm of $\varphi_{\underline{\underline{k}}}$ in $H^{(p)}$ as follows ;

$$\|\varphi_{\underline{\underline{k}}}(x)\|_{H^{(p)}} \le c(\underline{\underline{k}}!)^{1/2}\rho_1^{|\underline{\underline{k}}|}\|\varphi\|_{H^{(p+q)}}$$

with constants $c = c(p,q,\|\eta\|_p)$ and $\rho_1 = \rho_1(p,q,\|\eta\|_p) < 1$ depending only on p,q and $\|\eta\|_p$ for sufficiently large q (applying Theorem 6. 2 in [2]). Therefore

$$\psi(x|\underline{\underline{u}}) \equiv \sum_{\underline{\underline{k}}} \frac{1}{\underline{\underline{k}}!}\underline{\underline{u}}^{\underline{\underline{k}}}\ \varphi_{\underline{\underline{k}}}(x)$$

converges in H for each $\underline{\underline{u}}$. By the definition of $\varphi_{\underline{\underline{k}}}(x)$,

$$(S\varphi_{\underline{\underline{k}}})(\xi+\alpha_1\eta_1+\cdots+\alpha_n\eta_n) = (S\varphi_{\underline{\underline{k}}})(\xi)$$

holds. Observing the proof of Remark 4. 2, we can assert that the random variables $\{\varphi_{\underline{k}}(x);\ \underline{k}\}$ are independent of $\{<x, \eta_j>;\ 1 \le j \le n\}$. Thus $\psi(x|\underline{u})$ is independent of $\{<x, \zeta_j>;\ 1 \le j \le n\}$. Since

$$S(\delta(<x, \underline{\eta}> - \underline{b})\ H_{\underline{k}}(<x,\underline{\eta}>))(\xi) = (\delta_{\underline{b}}(\cdot)H_{\underline{k}}(\cdot))*P_I(<\xi, \underline{\eta}>)$$

$$= H_{\underline{k}}(\underline{b})P_I(<\xi, \underline{\eta}> - \underline{b}) = H_{\underline{k}}(\underline{b})S(\delta(<x,\underline{\eta}> - \underline{b}))(\xi),$$

it follows from Remark 4. 2 and (4. 11) that

$$S(\delta(<x, \underline{\eta}> - \underline{b})\varphi)(\xi) = \sum_{\underline{k}} H_{\underline{k}}(\underline{b})\cdot S(\delta(<x, \underline{\eta}>-\underline{b}))(\xi)(S\varphi_{\underline{k}})(\xi)$$

$$= S(\delta(<x, \underline{\eta}> - \underline{b})\cdot S(\psi(x|\underline{b})) = S(\delta(<x, \underline{\eta}> - \underline{b})\cdot\psi(x|\underline{b})).$$

Therefore, the function $\varphi(x|\underline{a}) \equiv \psi(x|\underline{a}A)$ is the desired one.

REFERENCES

[1] Hida, T.; Analysis of Brownian functionals. Carleton Math. Lect. Notes no. 13, second ed. (1978)

[2] Kubo, I & Takenaka, S.; Calculus on Gaussian white noise I, II and III. Proc. Japan Acad., 56A, (1980), 376-380, 441-416 and ibid. 57A, (1981), 433-437.

[3] Streit, L.& Hida, T.; Generalized Brownian functionals and the Feynman integral. Preprint.

[4] Fukushima, M.; A decomposition of additive functionals of finite energy. Nagoya Math. J. 74 (1979), 137-168.

[5] Yamada, T.; On some representations concerning stochastic integrals. Preprint.

[6] Yor, M.; Sur la transforme de Hilbert des temps locaux browniens, et une extension de la formule d'Ito. Preprint.

Donsker's Delta Function as a Generalized Brownian Functional and its Application

Hui-Hsiung Kuo*

Department of Mathematics, Louisiana State University
Baton Rouge, Louisiana 70803, USA

§1. Introduction.

Let $C[0,1]$ denote the Banach space of real-valued continuous functions ω on $[0,1]$ such that $\omega(0) = 0$. Let ν denote the Wiener measure on $C[0,1]$. Then the coordinate evaluation $B(t,\omega) = \omega(t)$ is a Brownian motion starting at the origin. Donsker's delta function $\delta_{t,x}$, $0 < t < 1$ and $x \in R$, is defined formally by

$$\delta_{t,x}(\omega) = \frac{1}{2\pi}\int_{-\infty}^{\infty} e^{iy(\omega(t)-x)}\,dy, \qquad \omega \in C[0,1] \ . \tag{1}$$

Obviously, $\delta_{t,x}$ does not exist in the ordinary sense as a Wiener functional on the probability space $(C[0,1],\nu)$. Nevertheless, it can be used to solve certain partial differential equations. For instance, for V bounded below, the function

$$u(t,x) = \int_{C[0,1]} \delta_{t,x}(\omega)\,\exp\Big[-\int_0^t V(\omega(s))ds\Big]d\nu(\omega) \tag{2}$$

is a solution of the following partial differential equation (see [1,2] or [9, p.51]):

$$\begin{aligned} &\frac{\partial u}{\partial t} = \frac{1}{2}\frac{\partial^2 u}{\partial x^2} - V(x)u \\ &u(t,x) \longrightarrow 0 \quad \text{as} \quad x \longrightarrow \pm\infty \\ &u(t,x) \longrightarrow \delta(x) \quad \text{as} \quad t \longrightarrow 0 \ . \end{aligned} \tag{3}$$

---

* Research supported by NSF grant MCS-8100728.

The purpose of this paper is to show that $\delta_{t,x}$ is a generalized Brownian functional in the sense of Hida's theory [3,4,5]. In fact, we will find a representation for $\delta_{t,x}$ from which the equation (3) follows easily. This representation is motivated by Example 1 in [10] and provides more information on what $\delta_{t,x}$ actually does than the formal proof given in [9, pp. 51-52].

§2. Generalized Brownian functionals.

In this section we describe briefly Hida's theory of generalized Brownian functionals [3,4,5]. Let $\mathcal{S}$ be the Schwartz space of rapidly decreasing real-valued functions on R. The dual space $\mathcal{S}^*$ is the space of tempered distributions. We have $\mathcal{S} \subset L^2(R) \subset \mathcal{S}^*$ and there is a unique probability measure μ on $\mathcal{S}^*$ such that

$$\int_{\mathcal{S}^*} \exp[i\langle x, \xi\rangle] d\mu(x) = \exp[-|\xi|^2/2] \equiv C(\xi), \qquad \xi \in \mathcal{S},$$

where $|\cdot|$ denotes the $L^2(R)$-norm. The probability space $(\mathcal{S}^*, \mu)$ is a realization of Brownian white noise $\dot{B}$ so that we will use either x or $\dot{B}$ to denote the element of $\mathcal{S}^*$.

The Hilbert space $L^2(\mathcal{S}^*)$ of Brownian functionals has the following Wiener-Ito decomposition:

$$L^2(\mathcal{S}^*) = \sum_{n=0}^{\infty} \oplus K_n ,$$

where K_n consists of the n-homogeneous chaos. Define a transform $\mathcal{T}$ on $L^2(\mathcal{S}^*)$ by

$$(\mathcal{T}\phi)(\xi) = \int_{\mathcal{S}^*} e^{i\langle x, \xi\rangle} \phi(x) d\mu(x), \qquad \xi \in \mathcal{S}.$$

If $\phi \in K_n$, then there exists a unique function F in $\hat{L}^2(R^n)$ (symmetric $L^2(R^n)$-functions) such that

$$(\mathcal{T}\phi)(\xi) = i^n C(\xi) \int_{R^n} F(t_1,\dots,t_n)\xi(t_1)\dots\xi(t_n)dt_1\dots dt_n .$$

The map $\phi \rightarrow F$ from K_n into $\hat{L}^2(R^n)$ is unitary up to a constant, i.e.,

$$\|\phi\| = \sqrt{n!}\, |F|.$$

Let $H^k(R^n)$ be the Sobolev space of order k of functions defined on R^n. Let $\hat{H}^k(R^n) = H^k(R^n) \cap \hat{L}^2(R^n)$. The dual space of $\hat{H}^k(R^n)$ is $\hat{H}^{-k}(R^n)$ and we have the triple $\hat{H}^k(R^n) \subset \hat{L}^2(R^n) \subset \hat{H}^{-k}(R^n)$ for $k > 0$. Define $K_n^{(n)}$ and $K_n^{(-n)}$ as follows:

$$K_n^{(n)} = \mathcal{J}^{-1}\{i^n C(\xi) \int_{R^n} F(t_1,\ldots,t_n)\xi(t_1)\ldots\xi(t_n)dt_1\ldots dt_n;\ F \in \hat{H}^{\frac{n+1}{2}}(R^n)\},$$

$$K_n^{(-n)} = \mathcal{J}^{-1}\{i^n C(\xi) \int_{R^n} F(t_1,\ldots,t_n)\xi(t_1)\ldots\xi(t_n)dt_1\ldots dt_n;\ F \in \hat{H}^{-\frac{n+1}{2}}(R^n)\}.$$

Endow the norms on $K^{(n)}$ and $K_n^{(-n)}$ so that we have the diagram:

$$\text{(4)} \qquad \begin{array}{ccccc} K_n^{(n)} & \subset & K_n & \subset & K_n^{(-n)} \\ \updownarrow & & \updownarrow & & \updownarrow \\ \sqrt{n!}\,\hat{H}^{\frac{n+1}{2}}(R^n) & \subset & \sqrt{n!}\,\hat{L}^2(R^n) & \subset & \sqrt{n!}\,\hat{H}^{-\frac{n+1}{2}}(R^n) \end{array}$$

where the vertical maps are unitary equivalence under the correspondence ϕ and F. Define

$$(L^2)^+ = \sum_{n=0}^{\infty} \oplus K_n^{(n)}$$

and

$$(L^2)^- = \sum_{n=0}^{\infty} \oplus K_n^{(-n)}.$$

$(L^2)^+$ and $(L^2)^-$ are the spaces of test functionals and generalized Brownian functionals, respectively. Moreover, we have the continuous inclusions $(L^2)^+ \subset L^2(\mathcal{S}^*) \subset (L^2)^-$.

§3. One-dimensional example.

The representation for $\delta_{t,x}$ is motivated by the one-dimensional version of Example 1 in [10], i.e.

$$\text{(5)} \qquad \int_{-\infty}^{\infty} e^{iyx}dy = \sqrt{2\pi} \sum_{k=0}^{\infty} (-1)^k (k!2^{2k})^{-1} H_{2k}\left(\frac{x}{\sqrt{2}}\right),$$

where $H_n(x) = (-1)^n e^{x^2} \dfrac{d^n}{dx^n} e^{-x^2}$ is the Hermite polynomial of degree n.

The representation (5) can be derived formally as follows. Consider the generating function of $H_n(x)$,

$$e^{-t^2+2tx} = \sum_{n=0}^{\infty} \frac{t^n}{n!} H_n(x).$$

Let $t = iy/\sqrt{2}$ and replace x by $x/\sqrt{2}$. Then

$$e^{iyx} = e^{-y^2/2} \sum_{n=0}^{\infty} i^n y^n (n!\ 2^{n/2})^{-1} H_n(\tfrac{x}{\sqrt{2}}). \tag{6}$$

By integrating Equation (6) formally, we get the representation (5). It is easy to check that the series in (5) does not converge in $L^2(\lambda)$, $d\lambda(x) = \frac{1}{\sqrt{2\pi}} e^{-x^2/2}dx$. However, it is convergent in the distribution sense as shown below.

In [7], Ito introduces the Hilbert space $\mathcal{S}_p$, $p \in R$, as the completion of $\mathcal{S}$ with respect to the norm

$$\|f\|_p = \{\sum_{n=0}^{\infty} (n + \tfrac{1}{2})^{2p} (\int_{-\infty}^{\infty} f(x)e_n(x)dx)^2\}^{1/2},$$

where $e_n(x) = (n!2^n\sqrt{2\pi})^{-1/2} H_n(x/\sqrt{2})e^{-x^2/4}$. Obviously, $\mathcal{S}_p^* = \mathcal{S}_{-p}$, $\mathcal{S}^* = \bigcup_p \mathcal{S}_p^*$ and we have the following continuous inclusions:

$$\mathcal{S}_p \subset L^2(R) \subset \mathcal{S}_p^*, \quad p > 0.$$

For $f \in \mathcal{S}_p$, define $\tau(f)(x) = f(x)(2\pi)^{1/4} e^{x^2/4}$. Let $Q_p = \{\tau(f);\ f \in \mathcal{S}_p\}$ be given the norm

$$|\tau(f)|_p = \|f\|_p.$$

Then we have the following continuous inclusions:

$$Q_p \subset L^2(\lambda) \subset Q_p^* = Q_{-p}, \quad p > 0.$$

It is easy to check that the sequence $\{H_n(x/\sqrt{2});\ n=0,1,2,\ldots\}$ is orthogonal in Q_p^* and

$$|H_n((\cdot)/\sqrt{2})|_{-p} = (n!2^n)^{1/2}(n + \tfrac{1}{2})^{-p}, \quad p > 0.$$

Therefore, the square of $|\cdot|_{-p}$-norm of the series in (5) is given by

$$\sum_{k=0}^{\infty} (k!2^{2k})^{-2}(2k)!2^{2k}(2k+\tfrac{1}{2})^{-2p}$$
$$\sim \sum_{k=1}^{\infty} (\pi k)^{-1/2}(2k+\tfrac{1}{2})^{-2p}.$$

Since the last series is convergent when $p > \frac{1}{4}$, we have proved the following

Theorem 1. $\int_{-\infty}^{\infty} e^{iyx}dy \in \mathcal{G}_p^*$ for all $p > \frac{1}{4}$, i.e. the series in the representation (5) converges in $\mathcal{G}_p^*$ when $p > \frac{1}{4}$.

§4. Donsker's delta function .

For $t > 0$, let $\theta(t)$ denote the characteristic function of $[0,t]$ and $\rho(t) = t^{-1/2}\theta(t)$. Note that in the probability space $(\mathcal{J}^*, \mu)$, $B(t,\dot{B}) = \langle\dot{B}, \theta(t)\rangle$ is a Brownian motion. Therefore, we can rewrite $\delta_{t,x}$ in Equation (1) as

$$\delta_{t,x}(\dot{B}) = \frac{1}{2\pi}\int_{-\infty}^{\infty} e^{iy(\langle\dot{B},\theta(t)\rangle - x)}dy. \tag{7}$$

We will prove that $\delta_{t,x}$ is a generalized Brownian functional i.e. $\delta_{t,x} \in (L^2)^-$.

From Equation (6), we have

$$e^{iy(v-z)} = \{e^{-y^2/2}\sum_{n=0}^{\infty} i^n y^n (n!2^{n/2})^{-1}H_n(\tfrac{v}{\sqrt{2}})\}e^{-iyz}. \tag{8}$$

Note that

$$\int_{-\infty}^{\infty} e^{-iyz}y^n e^{-y^2/2}dy = \sqrt{2\pi}\,(\tfrac{-i}{\sqrt{2}})^n H_n(\tfrac{z}{\sqrt{2}})e^{-z^2/2}.$$

Hence, after integrating Equation (8), we get

$$\int_{-\infty}^{\infty} e^{iy(v-z)}dy = \sqrt{2\pi}\,e^{-z^2/2}\sum_{n=0}^{\infty}(n!2^n)^{-1}H_n(\tfrac{v}{\sqrt{2}})\,H_n(\tfrac{z}{\sqrt{2}}). \tag{9}$$

Let $v = \langle\dot{B},\rho(t)\rangle$, $z = x/\sqrt{t}$ and replace y by $y/\sqrt{t}$ in Equation (9). We then obtain formally

(10) $$\mathcal{E}_{t,x}(\dot{B}) = \frac{1}{\sqrt{2\pi t}}\, e^{-x^2/2t} \sum_{n=0}^{\infty} \frac{1}{n!2^n} H_n\left(\frac{x}{\sqrt{2t}}\right) H_n\left(\frac{\langle \dot{B}, \rho(t)\rangle}{\sqrt{2}}\right).$$

Lemma 1. Let $f \in L^2(R)$ and $\|f\| = 1$. Then $H_n\left(\frac{\langle \cdot, f\rangle}{\sqrt{2}}\right) \in K_n^{(-n)}$ and

$$\left\|H_n\left(\frac{\langle \cdot, f\rangle}{\sqrt{2}}\right)\right\|^2_{K_n^{(-n)}} = n!2^n \int_{R^n} (1+|s|^2)^{-\frac{n+1}{2}} |\hat{f}(s_1)\ldots\hat{f}(s_n)|^2 ds_1\ldots ds_2,$$

where $\hat{f}$ is the Fourier transform of f.

Proof. $H_n\left(\frac{\langle \cdot, f\rangle}{\sqrt{2}}\right)$ is represented by (see, e.g. [5, p. 139])

$$F_n(t_1,\ldots,t_n) = (\sqrt{2})^n f(t_1)\ldots f(t_n).$$

Hence,

$$\hat{F}_n(s_1,\ldots,s_n) = (\sqrt{2})^n\, \hat{f}(s_1)\ldots\hat{f}(s_n).$$

The Sobolev $\hat{H}^{-\frac{n+1}{2}}(R^n)$-norm of F_n is given by (see e.g. [12, p. 155])

$$\|F_n\|^2_{\hat{H}^{-\frac{n+1}{2}}(R^n)} = \int_{R^n} (1+|s|^2)^{-\frac{n+1}{2}} |\hat{F}_n(s)|^2 ds.$$

The lemma then follows from Diagram (4).

Lemma 2. We have for $n \geq 2$,

$$\left\|H_n\left(\frac{\langle \cdot, \rho(t)\rangle}{\sqrt{2}}\right)\right\|^2_{K_n^{(-n)}} \leq n!2^{n+1}\left(\frac{t}{2\pi}\right)^n \sigma_n,$$

where σ_n is the surface area of the unit sphere $\{s \in R^n;\ |s| = 1\}$.

Proof. By a direct computation, we obtain

$$(\rho(t))^\wedge(s) = \sqrt{\frac{2}{\pi t}}\, e^{-\frac{ist}{2}}\, \frac{1}{s} \sin \frac{st}{2}.$$

Therefore, for all $(s_1,\ldots,s_n) \in R^n$,

(11) $$|(\rho(t))^\wedge(s_1)\ldots(\rho(t))^\wedge(s_n)|^2 \leq \left(\frac{t}{2\pi}\right)^n.$$

Moreover, it is easy to check that for $n \geq 2$,

(12) $$\int_{R^n} (1+|s|^2)^{-\frac{n+1}{2}} ds \leq 2\,\sigma_n.$$

The lemma follows easily from (11), (12) and Lemma 1.

Theorem 2. Donsker's delta function

$$\delta_{t,x}(\dot{B}) = \frac{1}{2\pi} \int_{-\infty}^{\infty} e^{iy(\langle\dot{B},\,\theta(t)\rangle - x)} dy$$

belongs to $(L^2)^-$, i.e., the series

$$\delta_{t,x}(\dot{B}) = \frac{1}{\sqrt{2\pi t}} e^{-x^2/2t} \sum_{n=0}^{\infty} \frac{1}{n!2^n} H_n\left(\frac{x}{\sqrt{2t}}\right) H_n\left(\frac{\langle\dot{B},\rho(t)\rangle}{\sqrt{2}}\right).$$

converges in $(L^2)^-$. Further, the convergence is uniform in $x \in R$.

Proof. By Lemma 2 and Equation (10), we have

$$\left\| \sum_{n=2}^{\infty} \frac{1}{n!2^n} H_n\left(\frac{x}{\sqrt{2t}}\right) H_n\left(\frac{\langle\cdot,\rho(t)\rangle}{\sqrt{2}}\right)\right\|^2_{(L^2)^-}$$

$$\leq \sum_{n=2}^{\infty} \frac{1}{n!2^{2n-1}} H_n^2\left(\frac{x}{\sqrt{2t}}\right)\left(\frac{t}{\pi}\right)^n \sigma_n.$$

Now, from [6, Formula (21·3·3)] or [11, Formula (8·91·10)], we have

$$\sup_{\substack{t>0\\ x\in R}} \left|(\sqrt{\pi}\, n!2^n)^{-1/2} e^{-x^2/4t} H_n\left(\frac{x}{\sqrt{2t}}\right)\right| = 0(n^{-1/12}).$$

Therefore, we have for all $t > 0$, $x \in R$,

$$\left\| \frac{1}{\sqrt{2\pi t}} e^{-x^2/2t} \sum_{n=2}^{\infty} \frac{1}{n!2^n} H_n\left(\frac{x}{\sqrt{2t}}\right) H_n\left(\frac{\langle\cdot,\rho(t)\rangle}{\sqrt{2}}\right)\right\|^2_{(L^2)^-}$$

$$\leq \frac{\beta}{t} e^{-x^2/2t} \sum_{n=2}^{\infty} n^{-1/6}\left(\frac{t}{2\pi}\right)^n \sigma_n,$$

where β is a constant independent of t and x. Note that $\sigma_n = (\Gamma(n/2))^{-1}\, 2\pi^{n/2}$ (see, e.g. [8, p. 1427]). Therefore, the last series is convergent and this proves the theorem.

§5. An application.

In this section we give a simple application of $\delta_{t,x}$ in solving partial differential equations, i.e. we will prove that

$$u(t,x) = \left(\delta_{t,x},\ \exp\left[-\int_0^t V(\langle\cdot,\theta(s)\rangle)ds\right]\right) \tag{13}$$

solves Equation (3). Here $(\cdot,\cdot)$ denotes the pairing of $(L^2)^-$ and $(L^2)^+$. We assume that V is a function such that $\exp[-\int_0^t V(\langle\cdot,\theta(s)\rangle)ds]$ and $V(\langle\cdot,\theta(t)\rangle)\exp[-\int_0^t V(\langle\cdot,\theta(s)\rangle)ds]$ are in $(L^2)^+$. Note that we have replaced the formal expression in Equation (2) by $u(t,x)$ as defined in (13) in terms of white noise.

Lemma 3. Let ϕ be a test functional. Then

$$\int_{-\infty}^{\infty} f(x)(\delta_{t,x},\phi)dx = (f(\langle\cdot,\theta(t)\rangle),\phi).$$

Proof. Just apply the Fourier inverse formula.

Lemma 4. $V(x)u(t,x) = \left(V(\langle\cdot,\theta(t)\rangle)\delta_{t,x},\ \exp\left[-\int_0^t V(\langle\cdot,\theta(s)\rangle)ds\right]\right)$

Proof. Apply Lemma 3 with $f(x) = V(x)H_n(x/\sqrt{2t})$ and $\phi(\dot{B}) = \exp[-\int_0^t V(\langle\dot{B},\theta(s)\rangle)ds]$. Then

$$\int_{-\infty}^{\infty} V(x)H_n(x/\sqrt{2t})(\delta_{t,x},\phi)dx = (V(\langle\cdot,\theta(t)\rangle)H_n(\langle\cdot,\rho(t)\rangle/\sqrt{2}),\phi).$$

i.e.

$$\int_{-\infty}^{\infty} V(y)u(t,y)H_n(y/\sqrt{2t})dy = (V(\langle\cdot,\theta(t)\rangle)H_n(\langle\cdot,\rho(t)\rangle/\sqrt{2}),\phi).$$

Therefore, by the representation of $\delta_{t,x}$,

$$\left(V(\langle\cdot,\theta(t)\rangle)\delta_{t,x},\ \exp\left[-\int_0^t V(\langle\cdot,\theta(s)\rangle)ds\right]\right) \tag{14}$$

$$= \frac{1}{\sqrt{2\pi t}}e^{-x^2/2t}\sum_{n=0}^{\infty}\frac{1}{n!2^n}H_n(x/\sqrt{2t})\int_{-\infty}^{\infty} V(y)u(t,y)H_n(y/\sqrt{2t})dy.$$

Now, observe that

$$\xi_n(x) = (n!2^n\sqrt{2\pi t})^{-1/2}\, e^{-x^2/4t} H_n(x/\sqrt{2t}), \quad n = 0,1,2,\ldots$$

is an orthonormal basis of $L^2(\mathbb{R})$. Hence the $L^2(\mathbb{R})$-expansion of $V(x)u(t,x)e^{x^2/4t}$ with respect to $\{\xi_n\}$ is

$$V(x)u(t,x)e^{x^2/4t}$$

$$= \sum_{n=0}^{\infty} \frac{1}{n!2^n\sqrt{2\pi t}}\, e^{-x^2/4t} H_n(x/\sqrt{2t}) \int_{-\infty}^{\infty} V(y)u(t,y)H_n(y/\sqrt{2t})dy.$$

This shows that the right hand side of Equation (14) is $V(x)u(t,x)$ and the lemma is proved.

Lemma 5.

$$\left(\frac{d}{dt} H_n(\langle\cdot,\rho(t)\rangle/\sqrt{2}),\ \exp[-\int_0^t V(\cdot,\theta(s)\rangle)ds]\right)$$

$$= -\frac{n}{2t}\left(H_n(\langle\cdot,\rho(t)\rangle/\sqrt{2}),\ \exp[-\int_0^\infty V(\langle\cdot,\theta(s)\rangle)ds]\right).$$

Proof. Note that

$$H_n(\langle\dot{B},\rho(t)\rangle/\sqrt{2}) = H_n(B(t)/\sqrt{2}t) .$$

Hence, by Ito's lemma, we have

$$\frac{d}{dt} H_n(\langle\dot{B},\rho(t)\rangle/\sqrt{2})$$

$$= H_n'(\langle\dot{B},\rho(t)\rangle/\sqrt{2})\left(\frac{\dot{B}(t)}{\sqrt{2t}} - \frac{\langle\dot{B},\theta(t)\rangle}{2t\sqrt{2t}}\right) + \frac{1}{4t} H_n''(\langle\dot{B},\rho(t)\rangle/\sqrt{2}).$$

By the identity $H''(x) - 2xH_n'(x) + 2n\, H_n(x) = 0$, we have

(15)
$$\frac{d}{dt} H_n(\langle\dot{B},\rho(t)\rangle/\sqrt{2})$$

$$= H_n'(\langle\dot{B},\rho(t)\rangle/\sqrt{2})\, \frac{\dot{B}(t)}{\sqrt{2t}} - \frac{n}{2t} H_n(\langle\dot{B},\rho(t)\rangle/\sqrt{2}).$$

On the other hand, we can first write $\dot{B}(t)$ as $\lim_{a\downarrow 0} a^{-1}(B(t+a) - B(t))$ and then take the conditional expectation with respect to the σ-field generated by $\{\langle\cdot,\theta(s)\rangle;\ s \le t\}$ to conclude that

(16) $$\left(H_n'(<\cdot,\rho(t)>/\sqrt{2})\dot{B}(t),\ \exp\left[-\int_0^t V(<\cdot,\theta(s)>)ds\right]\right) = 0.$$

The lemma follows easily from (15) and (16).

Theorem 3. The function

$$u(t,x) = \left(\delta_{t,x},\ \exp\left[-\int_0^t V(<\cdot,\theta(s)>)ds\right]\right)$$

is a solution of the partial differential equation

$$\frac{\partial u}{\partial t} = \frac{1}{2}\frac{\partial^2 u}{\partial x^2} - V(x)u$$

and satisfies the boundary conditions:

$$u(t,x) \to 0 \quad \text{as} \quad x \to \pm\infty$$

$$u(t,x) \to \delta(x) \quad \text{as} \quad t \to 0.$$

Proof. By using the representation of $\delta_{t,x}$ in Theorem 2 we can check easily

$$\frac{\partial}{\partial t}\delta_{t,x} = -\frac{1}{2t}\delta_{t,x} + \frac{x^2}{2t^2}\delta_{t,x}$$

$$-\frac{x}{2t\sqrt{2t}}\frac{1}{\sqrt{2\pi t}}e^{-x^2/2t}\sum_{n=0}^{\infty}\frac{1}{n!2^n}H_n'\left(\frac{x}{\sqrt{2t}}\right)H_n\left(\frac{<\dot{B},\rho(t)>}{\sqrt{2}}\right)$$

$$+\frac{1}{\sqrt{2\pi t}}e^{-x^2/2t}\sum_{n=0}^{\infty}\frac{1}{n!2^n}H_n\left(\frac{x}{\sqrt{2t}}\right)\left\{\frac{d}{dt}H_n\left(\frac{<\dot{B},\rho(t)>}{\sqrt{2}}\right)\right\}$$

and

$$\frac{\partial^2}{\partial x^2}\delta_{t,x} = \left(\frac{x^2}{t^2} - \frac{1}{t}\right)\delta_{t,x}$$

$$-\frac{x}{t\sqrt{2t}}\frac{1}{\sqrt{2\pi t}}e^{-x^2/2t}\sum_{n=0}^{\infty}\frac{1}{n!2^n}H_n'\left(\frac{x}{\sqrt{2t}}\right)H_n\left(\frac{<\dot{B},\rho(t)>}{\sqrt{2}}\right)$$

$$-\frac{1}{t\sqrt{2\pi t}}e^{-x^2/2t}\sum_{n=0}^{\infty}\frac{n}{n!2^n}H_n\left(\frac{x}{\sqrt{2t}}\right)H_n\left(\frac{<\dot{B},\rho(t)>}{\sqrt{2}}\right).$$

Therefore, by Lemma 5, we have

$$\left(\frac{\partial}{\partial t}\delta_{t,x},\ \exp\left[-\int_0^t V(\langle\cdot,\theta(s)\rangle)ds\right)\right.$$

$$=\frac{1}{2}\left(\frac{\partial^2}{\partial x^2}\delta_{t,x},\ \exp\left[-\int_0^t V(\langle\cdot,\theta(s)\rangle)ds\right]\right),$$

i.e.

$$\left(\frac{\partial}{\partial t}\delta_{t,x},\ \exp\left[-\int_0^t V(\langle\cdot,\theta(s)\rangle)ds\right]\right)=\frac{1}{2}\frac{\partial^2 u}{\partial x^2}. \tag{17}$$

Finally, note that

$$\frac{\partial u}{\partial t}=\left(\frac{\partial}{\partial t}\delta_{t,x},\ \exp\left[-\int_0^t V(\langle\cdot,\theta(s)\rangle)ds\right]\right)$$

$$-\left(V(\langle\cdot,\theta(t)\rangle)\,\delta_{t,x},\ \exp\left[-\int_0^t V(\langle\cdot,\theta(s)\rangle)ds\right]\right).$$

Hence, by (17) and Lemma 4,

$$\frac{\partial u}{\partial t}=\frac{1}{2}\frac{\partial^2 u}{\partial x^2}-V(x)u.$$

The boundary conditions follow easily from the representation of $\delta_{t,x}$ in Theorem 2.

References

1. Donsker, M. D., On function space integrals, in "Analysis in Function Space" edited by W. T. Martin and I. E. Segal (1963), 17-30, MIT Press.

2. Donsker, M. D., and Lions, J. L., Volterra variational equations, boundary value problems and function space integrals, Acta Math. 108 (1962), 147-228.

3. Hida, T., Analysis of Brownian functionals, Carleton Math. Lecture Notes, No. 13 (1975), Carleton University, Ottawa.

4. Hida, T., Generalized multiple Wiener integrals, Proc. Japan Acad., 54, ser. A (1978), 55-58.

5. Hida, T., Brownian motion, Application of Math., vol. 11 (1980), Springer-Verlag.

6. Hille, E. and Phillips, R. S., Functional analysis and semi-groups, Amer. Math. Soc. Colloq. Publ. vol. XXXI (1957)

7. Ito, K., Stochastic analysis in infinite dimensions, Proc. International conference on stochastic analysis, Evanston, Academic Press (1978), 187-197.

8. Iyanaga, S. and Kawada, Y., Encyclopedic dictionary of Math., editors, English transl. (1977), MIT Press.

9. Kuo, H. -H., Gaussian measures in Banach spaces, Lecture Notes in Math. Vol. 463 (1975), Springer-Verlag.

10. Kuo, H. -H., On Fourier transform of generalized Brownian functionals, to appear in J. Multivariate Analysis.

11. Szego, G., Orthogonal polynomials, Amer. Math. Soc. Colloq. Publ. Vol. XXIII (1939).

12. Yosida, K., Functional Analysis, 3rd. ed. (1971), Springer-Verlag.

Note. During the conference we learned from Professor T. Hida that he had also obtained recently the representation for $\delta_{t,x}$. We would like to thank Professors K. Ito and S. Watanabe for discussions on Donsker's delta function during the conference.

THE VARIATIONAL PRINCIPLE FOR STATIONARY GAUSSIAN MARKOV FIELDS

S.KUSUOKA
University of Tokyo, Japan

1. Introduction.

To begin with, let us explain our notation. Let μ_m, $m = 0,1,2,\ldots$, denote the Gaussian measure on $S'(\mathbb{R}^d)$ such that

$$\int_{S'} \exp\ (i\ {}_{S}\langle\phi,w\rangle_{S'})\ \mu_m(dw) = \exp(-\frac{1}{2}\int_{\mathbb{R}^d} |(1-\Delta)^{-m/2}\phi(x)|^2\,dx)$$

for any $\phi \in S(\mathbb{R}^d)$. Let $P_D(f;\mu_m)$ denote $\frac{1}{|D|}\log\int_{S'} \exp(\int_D f(T_x w)\,dx)\,\mu_m(dw)$ for any bounded domain D and any Borel function $f : S'(\mathbb{R}^d) \to \mathbb{R}$, where $|D|$ denotes the volume of D and T_x, $x \in \mathbb{R}^d$, denotes the shift operator in $S'(\mathbb{R}^d)$ given by $T_x w(\cdot) = w(\cdot+x)$, $w \in S'(\mathbb{R}^d)$. Then we see that $-\infty < P_D(f;\mu_m) \le \infty$. Now let $\overline{P}(f;\mu_m) = \overline{\lim_{n\to\infty}}\, P_{D_n}(f;\mu_m)$ and $\underline{P}(f;\mu_m) = \underline{\lim_{n\to\infty}}\, P_{D_n}(f;\mu_m)$ for any Borel function $f : S'(\mathbb{R}^d) \to \mathbb{R}$, where D_n denotes $(-n,n)^d$, $n = 1,2,\ldots$. Let P denote the set of all stationary probability measures on $S'(\mathbb{R}^d)$.

Then we may expect that there exists a lower semi-continuous function $H(\cdot;\mu_m) : P \to [0,\infty]$, and the variational principle holds:

$$\overline{P}(f;\mu_m) = \underline{P}(f;\mu_m) = \sup\{\int_{S'} f(w)\,R(dw) - H(R;\mu_m)\ ;\ R \in P\}$$

for a certain class of Borel functions $f : S'(\mathbb{R}^d) \to \mathbb{R}$. Our main end is to find the appropriate definition of $H(\cdot;\mu_m)$ and to study what kind of Borel functions satisfy the above variational principle.

In their paper [3] and [4], Guerra, Rosen and Simon studied the the variational principle for μ_1, the free Boson field measure. They gave the definition of the entropy with respect to μ_1, which corresponds to $-H(\cdot;\mu_1)$ in this paper, and they showed the variational principle in the case that $d = 2$ and $f(\phi) = \int_{(0,1)^2} :p(\phi):(x)\,dx$. However, they defined the entropy only on a certain subclass of P and did not show the upper semi-continuity of the entropy. We shall define $H(\cdot;\mu_m)$

in the different manner from theirs and show its semi-continuity.

Let us explain our strategy briefly. First we define $H(\cdot;\mu_0):P \to [0,\infty]$ and show the variational principle for μ_0, a Gaussian white noise. Since a Gaussian white noise is a random measure independent at each point, we can use the same method as used in statistical mechanics. Next we define $H(\cdot;\mu_m) : P \to [0,\infty]$, $m=1,2,\ldots$, by $H(R;\mu_m) = H((1-\Delta)^{m/2}R;\mu_0)$ for each $R \in P$, and we show the variational principle for μ_m. We also show that $-H(\cdot;\mu_1)$ coincides with the entropy introduced by Guerra, Rosen and Simon [3] .

The author wishes to express his gratitude to Prof. S.R.S.Varadhan for useful conversation during his stay in Japan.

2. The variational principle for a Gaussian white noise.

Let F_D denote the sub-σ-field of the Borel field over $S'(\mathbb{R}^d)$ generated by continuous functions $\{ {}_S\langle\phi,\cdot\rangle_{S'} ;\ \phi \in S(\mathbb{R}^d)$ and the support of ϕ is contained in $D \}$ for any domain D in $\mathbb{R}^d$.

Definition 2.1. For any $R \in P$ and any bounded domain D in $\mathbb{R}^d$, we define $H_D(R;\mu_0)$ by

$$H_D(R;\mu_0) = \begin{cases} \frac{1}{|D|}\int_{S'} \log\left(\frac{dR|F_D}{d\mu_0|F_D}\right) dR, & \text{if } R|_{F_D} \text{ is absolutely continuous} \\ \text{relative to } \mu_0|_{F_D} \text{ and } \int_{S'} \left|\log\left(\frac{dR|F_D}{d\mu_0|F_D}\right)\right| dR < \infty, & \\ \infty, & \text{otherwise.} \end{cases}$$

By using the same argument as the proof of Theorem VI 6 in Guerra, Rosen and Simon [3], we get the following

Proposition 2.1. $\{ H_{D_{2^n}}(R;\mu_0) ;\ n=1,2,\ldots\}$ is an increasing sequence for any $R \in P$.

Definition 2.2. We define $H(\cdot;\mu_0) : P \to [0,\infty]$ by

$$H(R;\mu_0) = \lim_{n\to\infty} H_{D_{2^n}}(R;\mu_0) \quad \text{for any } R \in P.$$

Theorem 2.1. $H(\cdot;\mu_0) : P \to [0,\infty]$ is lower semi-continuous and affine. Moreover $\{ R \in P :\ H(R;\mu_0) \le K \}$ is compact in P for any $K \ge 0$.

Proof. The proof of the affineness of $H(\cdot;\mu_0)$ goes similarly to the proof of Lemma VI.13 in [3]. It is easy to see that $H_D(\cdot;\mu_0):P\to[0,\infty]$ is lower semi-continuous and $\{R\in P;\ H_D(R;\mu_0)\le K\}$ is compact for any bounded domain D and $K\ge 0$. Then our asertion follows from Proposition 2.1 easily.

For any $t,s\in\mathbb{R}$ and $1\le p<\infty$, let $W_p^{t,s}$ denote a Banach space with a norm $\|\ \|_{W_p^{t,s}}$ given by

$$W_p^{t,s} = \{u\in S'(\mathbb{R}^d)\ ;\ (1+|x|^2)^{s/2}(1-\Delta)^{t/2}u\in L^p(\mathbb{R}^d)\},\ \text{and}$$

$$\|u\|_{W_p^{t,s}} = \|(1+|x|^2)^{s/2}(1-\Delta)^{t/2}u\|_{L^p(\mathbb{R}^d)}\ .$$

Then we get the following.

<u>Theorem 2.2</u>. Let $f: S'(\mathbb{R}^d)\to\mathbb{R}$ be a bounded Borel function, and suppose that $f|_{W_p^{t,s}}: W_p^{t,s}\to\mathbb{R}$ is continuous for some $t<-\frac{d}{2}$, $s<-d$ and $2\le p<\infty$. Then

(2.1) $\overline{P}(f;\mu_0) = \underline{P}(f;\mu_0) = \sup\{\int_{S'} f\,dR - H(R;\mu_0)\ ;\ R\in P\}$.

In particular, any bounded continuous function f defined in $S'(\mathbb{R}^d)$ satisfies (2.1).

To give a proof of Theorem 2.2, we introduce the following

<u>Definition 2.3</u>. We say that a Borel function f defined in $S'(\mathbb{R}^d)$ belongs to a class A_{μ_0}, if f satisfies the following three conditions.

(1) $\int_{S'} |f|\,dR<\infty$ for any $R\in P$ with $H(R;\mu_0)<\infty$.

(2) $\overline{P}(f;\mu_0) = \underline{P}(f;\mu_0) = \sup\{\int_{S'} f\,dR - H(R;\mu_0)\ ;\ R\in P\}$.

(3) If $R_n\to R$, $n\to\infty$, in P and $\sup_n H(R_n;\mu_0)<\infty$, then

$$\int_{S'} f\,dR_n \to \int_{S'} f\,dR\ .$$

Then we obtain the following two propositions.

<u>Proposition 2.2</u>. Suppose that $f: S'(\mathbb{R}^d)\to\mathbb{R}$ is a bounded F_D-measurable function for some bounded domain D. Then $f\in A_{\mu_0}$.

<u>Proposition 2.3</u>. Suppose that D_n's, $n=1,2,\ldots$, are bounded domains and g_n's are F_{D_n}-measurable non-negative functions. Suppose moreover

that f and f_n's are bounded Borel functions defined in $S'(\mathbb{R}^d)$ such that $|f(w) - f_n(w)| \le \sum_{k=n}^{\infty} g_k(w)$ for any $w \in S'(\mathbb{R}^d)$. If $f_n \in A_{\mu_0}$, $n=1, 2,\dots$, and if $\overline{P}(q\cdot \sum_{k=n}^{\infty} g_k ; \mu_0) \to 0$ as $n \to \infty$ for any $q > 1$, then $f \in A_{\mu_0}$.

Now we give a sketch of the proof of Theorem 2.2. Let $\rho \in C_0^{\infty}(\mathbb{R}^d)$ such that $\rho(x) \ge 0$, $x \in \mathbb{R}^d$, $\int_{\mathbb{R}^d} \rho(x)\,dx = 1$ and $\operatorname{supp} \rho \subset (-\frac{1}{2}, \frac{1}{2})^d$. Let $\rho_n(x) = \int_{(-n,n)^d} \rho(x-y)\,dy$, $n=0,1,2,\dots$, for any $x \in \mathbb{R}^d$. Then $\rho_n \in C_0^{\infty}(\mathbb{R}^d)$ and $\rho_n(x) = 1$, $x \in (-n+\frac{1}{2}, n-\frac{1}{2})^d$.

First suppose that $f : S'(\mathbb{R}^d) \to \mathbb{R}$ is a bounded Borel function such that $f|_{W_p^{t,s}} : W_p^{t,s} \to \mathbb{R}$ is Lipschitz continuous for some $t < -\frac{d}{2}$, $s < -d$ and $2 \le p < \infty$, i.e. there exists a constant C such that

$$|f(w_1) - f(w_2)| \le C\, \|w_1 - w_2\|_{W_p^{t,s}} \quad \text{for any } w_1, w_2 \in W_p^{t,s}.$$

Let g_n be a Borel function defined in $S'(\mathbb{R}^d)$ given by

$$g_n(w) = \begin{cases} \|(\rho_n - \rho_{n-1})w\|_{W_p^{t,s}}, & \text{if } \rho_n w \in W_p^{t,s}, \\ \infty, & \text{otherwise,} \end{cases}$$

and let $f_n(w) = f(\rho_n w)$, $n=1,2,\dots$ and $w \in S'(\mathbb{R}^d)$. Then it is easy to see that $|f(w) - f_n(w)| \le C \sum_{k=n}^{\infty} g_k(w)$ for any $w \in S'(\mathbb{R}^d)$. From Proposition 2.2 we see that $f_n \in A_{\mu_0}$, $n=1,2,\dots$. On the other hand we can show that $\overline{P}(q\cdot \sum_{k=0}^{\infty} g_k ; \mu_0) < \infty$ and $\overline{P}(q\cdot \sum_{k=n}^{\infty} g_k ; \mu_0) \to 0$ as $n \to \infty$ for any $q > 1$. Thus we have $f \in A_{\mu_0}$ by Proposition 2.3, and futhermore we get

$$(2.2)\quad \sup\{ \int_{S'} \|w\|_{W_p^{t,s}} R(dw) - H(R;\mu_0)\ ;\ R \in P \text{ and } H(R;\mu_0) < \infty \}$$
$$\le \overline{P}(\|\cdot\|_{W_p^{t,s}} ; \mu_0) < \infty \quad \text{for any } t < -\frac{d}{2},\ s < -d \text{ and } 2 \le p < \infty.$$

Let t' and s' be numbers such that $t < t' < -\frac{d}{2}$ and $s < s' < -d$. Then $W_p^{t',s'} \subset W_p^{t,s}$ and the inclusion is a compact map (cf. [5]). Thus any bounded continuous function on $W_p^{t,s}$ can be approximated by bounded

Lipschitz continuous functions on $W_p^{t,s}$ uniformly on any bounded set in $W_p^{t',s'}$. From this fact we can show that any bounded continuous function on $W_p^{t,s}$ belongs to A_{μ_0}, $t < -\frac{d}{2}$, $s < -d$ and $2 \le p < \infty$, by using (2.2). This implies our assertion.

Remark 2.1. Theorem 2.2 implies that $R(W_p^{t,s}) = 1$, if $H(R;\mu_0) < \infty$, for any $t < -\frac{d}{2}$, $s < -d$ and $2 \le p < \infty$.

Theorem 2.3. For any $R \in P$, $H(R;\mu_0) = \sup\{ \int_{S'} f\,dR - \overline{P}(f;\mu_0)$; f is a bounded continuous function defined in $S'(\mathbb{R}^d) \}$.

The proof of Theorem 2.3 goes similarly to the proof of Ruelle [6] 3.12 Theorem.

Let $g : \mathbb{R}^d \to \mathbb{R}$ be a tempered increasing smooth function such that $g(-\xi) = -g(\xi)$ for any $\xi \in \mathbb{R}^d$. Let $S_g : S'(\mathbb{R}^d) \to S'(\mathbb{R}^d)$ be a bijective bicontinuous map given by $S_g w = \overline{F}[\exp(i\ g(\xi))\cdot F[w](\xi)]$ for each $w \in S'(\mathbb{R}^d)$, where F and $\overline{F}$ denote the Fourier transform and the inverse Fourier transform respectively. Then we get the following

Corollary to Theorem 2.3. $H(S_g R;\mu_0) = H(R;\mu_0)$ for any $R \in P$.

Proof. Note that $S_g\mu_0 = \mu_0$. Then we see that $\overline{P}(f(S_g\cdot);\mu_0) = \overline{P}(f;\mu_0)$ for any bounded Borel function $f : S'(\mathbb{R}^d) \to \mathbb{R}$. Therefore our assertion follows from Theorem 2.3 immediately.

3. The variational principle for μ_m, $m = 1,2,\ldots$.

Definition 3.1. We define $H(\cdot;\mu_m) : P \to [0,\infty]$, $m = 1,2,\ldots$, by

$$H(R;\mu_m) = H((1-\Delta)^{m/2}R;\mu_0) \quad \text{for any } R \in P.$$

Then the following is an immediate consequence of Theorem 2.2 and Theorem 2.3.

Theorem 3.1. (1) $\overline{P}(f;\mu_m) = \underline{P}(f;\mu_m) = \sup\{ \int_{S'} f\,dR - H(R;\mu_m);\ R \in P \}$ for any bounded continuous function $f : S'(\mathbb{R}^d) \to \mathbb{R}$.

(2) $H(R;\mu_m) = \sup\{ \int_{S'} f\,dR - \overline{P}(f;\mu_m)$; $f : S'(\mathbb{R}^d) \to \mathbb{R}$ is bounded and continous $\}$ for any $R \in P$.

The following shows that we can give another definition for $H(\cdot;\mu_m)$.

Theorem 3.2. Suppose that R is an element of P .

(1) $H(R;\mu_m) < \infty$, if and only if $R|_{F_D}$ is absolutely continuous relative to $\mu_m|_{F_D}$ and $\int_{S'} |\log(\frac{dR|_{F_D}}{d\mu_m|_{F_D}})|\, dR < \infty$ for any bounded domain D, and

$$\overline{\lim_{n\to\infty}} \frac{1}{|D_n|} \int_{S'} \log(\frac{dR|_{F_{D_n}}}{d\mu_m|_{F_{D_n}}})\, dR < \infty .$$

(2) If $H(R;\mu_m) < \infty$, then

$$H(R;\mu_m) = \overline{\lim_{n\to\infty}} \frac{1}{|D_n|} \int_{S'} \log(\frac{dR|_{F_{D_n}}}{d\mu_m|_{F_{D_n}}})\, dR$$

$$= \underline{\lim_{n\to\infty}} \frac{1}{|D_n|} \int_{S'} \log(\frac{dR|_{F_{D_n}}}{d\mu_m|_{F_{D_n}}})\, dR .$$

Remark 3.1. Theorem 3.2 shows that $-H(\cdot;\mu_1)$ coincides with the entropy with respect to μ_1 introduced by Guerra, Rosen and Simon [3].

Proof. We prove our assertion, only when $m=1$. Let f be a bounded continuous $F_{D_{n/2}}$-measurable function defined in $S'(\mathbb{R}^d)$. Let ℓ be a positive number and $G_k = (-k(n+\ell), k(n+\ell))^d$, $k=1,2,\ldots$. Then by the Hölder inequality and the stationarity of μ_1 , we have

$$P_{G_k}(f;\mu_1) = \frac{1}{|G_k|} \log \int_{S'} \exp(\int_{G_k} f(T_x w)\, dx)\ \mu_1(dw)$$

$$\le \frac{1}{|G_k|} \frac{1}{|G|} \int_G dx \log \int_{S'} \exp(\sum_{\alpha\in\{-k,\ldots,k-1\}^d} |G|\, f(T_{(n+\ell)\alpha+x} w))\ \mu_1(dw)$$

$$= \frac{1}{|G_k|} \log \int_{S'} \exp(|G| \sum_{\alpha\in\{-k,\ldots,k-1\}^d} f(T_{(n+\ell)\alpha} w))\ \mu_1(dw) ,$$

where G denotes $(0,n+\ell)^d$. Then by virtue of the Checkerboard Estimate in [3] Theorem III.12, there exists an absolute constant $p_\ell > 1$ such that $p_\ell \to 1$ as $\ell \to \infty$ and

$$p_\ell \cdot P_{G_k}(f;\mu_1) \le \frac{1}{|G_k|} \sum_{\alpha\in\{-k,\ldots,k-1\}^d} \log \int_{S'} \exp(p_\ell |G| f(T_{(n+\ell)\alpha} w)\, \mu_1(dw)$$

$$= \frac{1}{(n+\ell)^d} \log \int_{S'} \exp(p_\ell (n+\ell)^d f(w))\ \mu_1(dw) .$$

Thus letting $k \to \infty$, we get

$$p_\ell \cdot \overline{P}(f;\mu_1) \le \frac{1}{(n+\ell)^d} \log \int_{S'} \exp(p_\ell (n+\ell)^d f(w))\, \mu_1(dw) .$$

Replacing f by $(p_\ell (n+\ell)^d)^{-1} f$ and adapting Theorem 3.1, we obtain

(3.1) $$\int_{S'} f\, dR \le p_\ell (n+\ell)^d H(R;\mu_1) + \log \int_{S'} \exp(f(w))\, \mu_1(dw)$$

for any bounded continuous $F_{D_{n/2}}$-measurable function f and $R \in P$.

Let $S_n(R) = \sup\{ \int_{S'} f\, dR - \log \int_{S'} \exp(f(w))\, \mu_1(dw)$; f is a bounded continuous F_{D_n}-measurable function $\}$ for any $R \in P$. Then we have from (3.1)

(3.2) $$\frac{S_n(R)}{|D_n|} \le \frac{p_\ell (2n+\ell)^d}{(2n)^d} H(R;\mu_1) \quad \text{for any } R \in P .$$

Therefore letting $n \to \infty$ first and letting $\ell \to \infty$ later, we get

(3.3) $$\overline{\lim_{n\to\infty}} \frac{S_n(R)}{|D_n|} \le H(R;\mu_1) \quad \text{for any } R \in P .$$

On the other hand, it is easy to see that

$|D_n| \{ \int_{S'} f\, dR - P_{D_n}(f;\mu_1) \} \le S_{n+k}(R)$ for any bounded continuous F_{D_k}-measurable function f. Thus letting $n \to \infty$, we get

$\int_{S'} f\, dR - \overline{P}(f;\mu_1) \le \underline{\lim}_{n\to\infty} \frac{S_n(R)}{|D_n|}$. However, from 3.1 we can show that

$H(R;\mu_1) = \sup\{ \int_{S'} f\, dR - \overline{P}(f;\mu_1)$; $f : S'(\mathbb{R}^d) \to \mathbb{R}$ is a bounded continuous F_D-measurable function for some bounded domain D $\}$. Thus we get

(3.4) $$H(R;\mu_1) \le \underline{\lim}_{n\to\infty} \frac{S_n(R)}{|D_n|} \quad \text{for any } R \in P .$$

Note that $S_n(R)$ is increasing in n, and that

$$S_n(R) = \begin{cases} \int_{S'} \log\left(\frac{dR|_{F_{D_n}}}{d\mu_1|_{F_{D_n}}}\right) dR , & \text{if } R|_{F_{D_n}} \text{ is absolutely continuous} \\ & \text{relative to } \mu_1|_{F_{D_n}} \text{ and } \int_{S'} \left|\log\left(\frac{dR|_{F_{D_n}}}{d\mu_1|_{F_{D_n}}}\right)\right| dR < \infty , \\ \infty, & \text{otherwise.} \end{cases}$$

Then this shows our assertion.

Theorem 3.3. Suppose that $f : S'(\mathbb{R}^d) \to \mathbb{R}$ is a F_D-measurable function for some bounded domain D, and that $\int_{S'} \exp(q\, f(w))\, \mu_m(dw) < \infty$ for any $q > 1$. Let $F_f : P \to (-\infty, \infty]$ be given by

$$F_f(R) = \begin{cases} -\int_{S'} f\, dR + H(R;\mu_m), & \text{if } \int_{S'} \max\{ f, 0 \}\, dR < \infty, \\ \infty, & \text{otherwisc.} \end{cases}$$

Then $F_f : P \to (-\infty, \infty]$ is lower semi-continuous and affine, and the set $\{ R \in P ;\, F_f(R) \le K \}$ is compact in P for any $K \in \mathbb{R}$. Furthermore,

$$\overline{P}(f;\mu_m) = \underline{P}(f;\mu_m) = \sup\{ -F_f(R) ;\, R \in P \}.$$

The proof of Theorem 3.3 is done by using the Checkerboard Estimate and a lemma like Proposition 2.3.

Example. Let $d = 2$ and $m = 1$, and let $f : S'(\mathbb{R}^d) \to \mathbb{R}$ be given by $f(\phi) = -\int_{(0,1)^d} :p(\Phi):(x)\, dx$, where p is a polynomial $p(X) = \sum_{k=0}^{2r} a_k X^k$ with $a_{2r} > 0$. Then it is well known that f satisfies the assumption of Theorem 3.3. Therefore we can easily see that

$$\lim_{n\to\infty} \frac{1}{|D_n|} \log \int_{S'} \exp\left(\int_{D_n} - :p(\phi):(x)\, dx \right) \mu_1(d\phi)$$

$$= \overline{P}(f;\mu_1) = \sup\{ -F_f(R) ;\, R \in P \}.$$

This is the variational principle given by Guerra, Rosen and Simon [3] and [4].

Remark 3.2. It is shown in Fröhlich and Simon [2] that in the situation above, $-F_f(\cdot) - \overline{P}(f;\mu_1) : P \to [-\infty, 0]$ can be regarded as an entropy relative to a certain Euclidean field for some special polynomials p.

References.

[1] Donsker M.D., and Varadhan S.R.S., Asymptotic Evaluation of Certain Markov Process Expectations for large Time — III, Comm. Pure Appl. Math., 29(1976), 389-461.

[2] Frölich J., and Simon B., Pure states for general $P(\phi)_2$ theories; Construction, regularity and variational equality, Ann. of Math. 105 (1977), 493-526.

[3] Guerra F., Rosen L., and Simon B., The $P(\phi)_2$ Euclidean quantum field theory as classical statistical mechanics, Ann. of Math. 101(1975), 111-259.

[4]——, Boundary conditions for the $P(\phi)_2$ Euclidean field theory, Ann. Inst. H. Poincaré – Section A 25(1976), 231-334.

[5] Kusuoka S., The support property of a Gaussian white noise and its applications, to appear in J. Fac. Sci. Univ. Tokyo Sect. I.

[6] Ruelle D., Thermodynamic Formalism, Addison-Wesley Publishing Company Inc., Massachusetts, 1978.

PATHWISE DIFFERENTIABILITY WITH RESPECT TO A PARAMETER OF SOLUTIONS OF STOCHASTIC DIFFERENTIAL EQUATIONS

Michel METIVIER

Ecole Polytechnique - 91128 Palaiseau - France

Abstract :

We consider a stochastic differential equation

$$X^u(t) = V^u(t) + \int_0^t \sigma(u,s,X^u_{s-})dS_s + \int_0^t f(u,s,X^u_{s-},x)\ q(ds,dx)$$

where S *is a semimartingale and* q *a random measure and where the "coefficients" depend on a parameter* u . *We prove under suitable differentiability-conditions that the solution* $X^u(t,\omega)$ *can be choosen for each* u *in such a way that the mapping* $u \sim X^u(t,\omega)$ *is continuously differentiable for every* (t,ω) .

1. INTRODUCTION

The goal of this paper is to prove that under sufficient differentiability conditions on the coefficients, stochastic differential equations of the type

$$(1.1) \qquad X^u(t) = V^u(t) + \int_0^t \sigma(u,s,X^u_{s-})dS_s + \int_0^t f(u,s,X^u_{s-},x)\ q(ds,dx)$$

where S is a semimartingale, q a random measure with zero dual predictable projection and u a parameter taking its values in a bounded closed subset G of $\mathbb{R}^d$, admit for each u a solution which can be determined in such a way that P.a.s. the functions $u \sim X^u(t,\omega)$ are for every t continuously differentiable.

This is a concept of differentiability different from the one considered by Gikhmann (see [4] and [5]), who studied the differentiability of the mapping $u \sim X^u_t(.)$ as a mapping from G into $L^p(\Omega)$ for some p and in the framework of Ito-equations. Recently Bichteler took the same point of view and considered equations of the type (1.1) with q = u and S and X^u possibly infinite dimensional. J. Jacod in [6] considered differentiability "in probability".

Pathwise differentiability was considered first by Y.M. Blagovečenskii and M.I. Freidlin ([3]) and more recently by P. Malliavin and M. Bismut for the solutions of Ito-Stratonovitch equation as functions of the initial conditions (see [2] and [9]). In [8] H. Kunita proved pathwise differentiability with respect to the initial conditions for the solutions of an equation driven by a continuous martingale. In [12] P.A. Meyer proved the same result for equations driven by a semimartingale (equations of Doléans-Dade-Protter type).

We consider here equations of type (1.1) with coefficients depending on a parameter u. A typical particular case is given by the Ito-Skorokhod equation :

$$(1.2)\qquad X^u(t) = V^u(t) + \int_0^t \sigma(u,s,X^u_{s^-},.)dw_s + \int_0^t b(u,s,X^u_{s^-},.)ds + \int_0^t f(u,s,X^u_{s^-},.,x)\, q(ds,dx)$$

where w is a brownian motion and q a Poisson measure with levy-measure $\alpha(dx)$.

In section 2 we recall a few facts on the type of equations which are studied here. In section 3 we give sufficient conditions for the continuity of solutions with respect to u and in section 4 we deal with differentiability.

2. THE EQUATION UNDER CONSIDERATION

2.1 - Inequalities for stochastic integrals

We assume that the random measure q in (1.1) is of the form $\mu(\omega;ds;du) - \nu(\omega;ds;du)$ where $\mu(\omega;]0,t],du)$ is for each ω and t a borelian measure in an open subset $\mathbb{E}$ of $\mathbb{R}^m - \{0\}$ such that, for some $\alpha > 0$

$\int \frac{|x|^\alpha}{1+|x|^\alpha} |\mu|(\omega;]0,t],du) < \infty$ ($|\mu|$ denotes the variation of μ and α does not depend on ω and t) and where ν is the dual predictable projection of μ).

$\mathbb{H}$ denotes a separable Hilbert space. We have shown in [9] (see also J. Jacod [6]) the existence of an increasing positive adapted process b and of a process $\{\overset{o}{q}(\omega,s,.) : (\omega,s) \in \Omega \times \mathbb{R}^+\}$ the values of which are measures on $\mathbb{E} \times \mathbb{E}$ such that :

i) For each $\mathbb{H}$-valued function h on $\mathbb{E}$ such that $\langle h(x),h(y)\rangle_{\mathbb{H}}$ is $\overset{o}{q}(\omega,s,ds \otimes dy)$ integrable, the integral $\int \langle h(x),h(y)\rangle_{\mathbb{H}}\, \overset{o}{q}(\omega,s,dx\otimes dy)$ defines a positive optional process ;

ii) if Y is an $\mathbb{H}$-valued $\mathcal{P}\otimes\mathcal{B}_{\mathbb{E}}$ measurable(*) function on $\mathbb{R}^+\times\Omega\times\mathbb{E}$ and if we denote by $\lambda_s(Y)$ the $\mathbb{H}$-valued positive random variable

$$\lambda_s(Y) := \int \langle Y(s,.,x),\ Y(s,.,y)\rangle_{\mathbb{H}}\ \overset{o}{q}(.,s,dx\otimes dy)$$

(set to be equal to $+\infty$ when the integral does not exist) and

iii) the following inequality holds for every stopping time τ

(*) $\mathcal{P}$ is the σ-algebra of predictable subsets of $\mathbb{R}^+\times\Omega$ and $\mathcal{B}_{\mathbb{E}}$ of Borel subsets of $\mathbb{E}$.

$$(2.1)\qquad E\Big(\sup_{t<\tau}\Big\|\int_{]0,t]\times\mathbb{E}} Y(s,.,x)q(.,ds,dx)\Big\|^2\Big) \le 4E\Big(\int_{[0,\tau[}\lambda_s(Y)db_s\Big)$$

where $\left(\int_{]0,t]\times\mathbb{E}} Y(s,.,x)q(.,ds,dx)\right)_{t\geq 0}$ is the stochastic integral process of Y with respect to q which is defined as soon as the process $\left(\int_{]0,t]}\lambda_s(Y)db(s)\right)_{t\geq 0}$ is finite.

If S is a $\mathbb{K}$-valued ($\mathbb{K}$: separable Hilbert space) right continuous semimartingale we know that there exist two positive increasing adapted processes a and $\tilde{a}$ such that for every $\mathcal{L}(\mathbb{K};\mathbb{H})$-valued locally bounded predictable process $\{f(s,\omega);(s,\omega)\in\mathbb{R}^+\times\Omega\}$ and every stopping time τ :

$$(2.2)\qquad E\Big(\sup_{t<\tau}\Big\|\int_{]0,t]} f(s,.)dS_s\Big\|^2\Big) \le E\Big(\tilde{a}_{\tau-}\cdot\int_{[0,\tau[}\|f(s)\|^2da(s)\Big)$$

To simplify the writing we shall call Z_t the process $Z_t := (S_t,q(.,]0,t],dx))$ which takes its values in $(\mathcal{L}(\mathbb{K};\mathbb{H})\times\mathcal{M}^\alpha)$ where $\mathcal{M}^\alpha$ is the space of borelian measures ν on $\mathbb{E}$ such that
$\int_{\mathbb{E}}\frac{|x|^\alpha}{1+|x|^\alpha}|\nu|(du)<\infty$.

Setting $A_t := b(t)+a(t)$ $\tilde{A}_t := 8+2\tilde{a}_t$ $\Phi := (f,Y)$

$$(2.3)\qquad \int_{]0,t]}\Phi(s)dZ_s := \int_{]0,t]} f(s,.)dS_s + \int_{]0,t]\times\mathbb{E}} Y(s,.,x)q(.,ds,dx)$$

and

$$(2.4)\qquad \lambda_s(\Phi) := \|f(s,.)\|^2 + \lambda_s(Y)$$

the following inequality holds for every stopping time

$$(2.5)\qquad E\Big(\sup_{t<\tau}\Big\|\int_{]0,t]}\Phi(s)dZ_s\Big\|^2\Big) \le E\Big(\tilde{A}_{\tau-}\cdot\int_{]0,\tau]}\lambda_s(\Phi)dA_s\Big)$$

Extending a classical argument on martingales (see [13]) it is also easy to see that for every $p\geq 2$ exists an increasing positive adapted process $(\tilde{A}^p_t)_{t\geq 0}$ such that for every stopping

$$(2.6)\qquad E\Big(\sup_{t<\tau}\Big\|\int_{]0,t]}\Phi(s)dZ_s\Big\|^p\Big) \le E\Big(\tilde{A}^p_{\tau-}\cdot\int_{[0,\tau[}\big(\lambda_s(\Phi)\big)^{p/2}dA_s\Big)$$

We recall that in the case of equation (1.2), if $\Phi := (f_1,f_2,Y)$ and if we set, with the above notations,

$$\int_{]0,t]} \Phi_s dZ_s := \int_{]0,t]} f_1(s,.)dw_s + \int_{]0,t]} f_2(s,.)ds + \int_{]0,t]\times \mathbb{E}} Y(s,.,x)q(ds,dx) \tag{2.7}$$

one has $A_t = 2t$ $\tilde{A}_t = 8+2t$ and

$$\lambda_s(\Phi) := \|f_1(s,.)\|^2 + \|f_2(s,.)\|^2 + \int_{\mathbb{E}} |Y(s,.,x)|^2 \alpha(dx) \tag{2.8}$$

2.2 - Hypothesis on equation (1.1)

The space of parameters u is an open bounded subset G of $\mathbb{R}^d$.

In equation (1.1) σ is a mapping from $(G \times \mathbb{R}^+ \times \Omega \times \mathbb{H})$ into $\mathcal{L}(\mathbb{K};\mathbb{H})$ which is continuous on $\mathbb{H}$ and such that for every $h \in \mathbb{H}$ and $u \in G$ the process $\{\sigma(u,s,\omega,h) : (s,\omega) \in \mathbb{R}^+ \times \Omega\}$ is predictable. f is a mapping of $(G \times \mathbb{R}^+ \times \Omega \times \mathbb{H},\mathbb{E})$ into $\mathbb{H}$ which if continuous on $\mathbb{H}$ and such that for every $u \in G$, $h \in \mathbb{H}$ the mapping $(s,\omega,x) \leadsto f(u,s,\omega,h,x)$ is $\mathcal{P}\otimes\mathcal{B}_{\mathbb{E}}$ measurable.

In the sequel *we shall call* g *the couple* (σ,f) and, according to the notations of (2.1), the equation (1.1) will be written in the *abbreviate form* :

$$X^u(t) = V^u(t) + \int_0^t g(u,s,X^u_{s^-})dZ_s \tag{2.9}$$

Here V^u is for each $u \in G$ a given $\mathbb{H}$-valued adapted cad-lag process.

3. CONTINUITY OF THE SOLUTIONS WITH RESPECT TO u.

3.1 - Hypothesis

L is an increasing positive adapted process and p is a positive real number with $p \geq d + \varepsilon$ for some $\varepsilon > 0$.

If ξ is a cad-lag $\mathbb{H}$-valued adapted process we write $g(u,\xi)$ for the process $(s,\omega) \leadsto g(u,s,\omega,\xi_{s^-}(\omega))$ and $\lambda_s \circ g(u,\xi)$ for the positive functional of this process defined by formula (2.4).

With these notations we formulate the following hypothesis :

(H_1) $\sup_{s\leq t} \|V^u_s - V^v_s\| \leq L_t \|u-v\|$ for all t, u and $v \in G$ and $\sup_{u\in G}\sup_{s<t} \|V^u_s\| < \infty$

(H_2) (Lipschitz hypothesis)

$$\forall t \in \mathbb{R}^+ \int_{]0,t]} [\lambda_s \circ (g(u,\xi)-g(u,\xi'))]^{p/2} dA_s \leq \int_{]0,t]} \sup_{r\leq s} \|\xi_r - \xi'_r\|^p dL_s$$

for every couple (ξ,ξ') of $\mathbb{H}$-valued adapted cad-lag processes, P.a.s.

(H₃) $$\int_{]0,t]} [\lambda_s o g(u,\xi)]^{p/2} dA_s \leq \int_{]0,t]} (1 + \sup_{r\leq s} \|\xi_r\|^p) dL_s$$

for every $u \in G$ every $\mathbb{H}$-valued adapted cad-lag ξ, P.a.s.

(H_4) There exists a positive increasing (possibly constant) function Ψ on $\mathbb{R}^+$, for every stopping time τ the following inequality holds for every $\mathbb{H}$-valued cad-lag adapted ξ every u and v in G :

$$E\left(\sup_{t<\tau}\left[\lambda_t o[g(u,\xi)-g(v,\xi)]\right]^{p/2}\right) \leq \|u-v\|^{d+\varepsilon}\Psi\left(E(\sup_{t<\tau}\|\xi_t\|^p)\right) .$$

Example : Assume for example, that in equation (1.1) q is a Poisson measure with Levy measure α and for some $h_0 \in \mathbb{H}$ and all $T > 0$:

$$\sup_{u\in G,t<T} \|\sigma(u,t,h_0)\|^2 + \int_{\mathbb{E}} \|f(u,t,h_0,x)\|^2 \alpha(dx) < \infty .$$

Then hypothesis (H_2) and (H_3) are implied by the following global Lipschitz hypothesis : for every h and $h' \in \mathbb{H}$, $u \in G$:

$$\|\sigma(u,t,h)-\sigma(u,t,h')\|^2 + \int_{\mathbb{E}} \|f(u,t,h,x)-f(u,t,h',x)\|^2 \alpha(dx) \leq L_t \|h-h'\|^2$$

where L is an increasing adapted process.

3.2 - Theorem

1°) Under the above hypothesis (H_1) to (H_4), the equation (2.7) has for each u a unique strong solution X^u on $\mathbb{R}^+$ and the random function $(t,\omega,u) \sim X_t^u(\omega)$ can be determined in such a way that $u \sim X_t^u(\omega)$ is continuous on G for every t and ω while the mapping $t \sim X_t^{(.)}(\omega)$ is for each ω cad-lag from $\mathbb{R}^+$ into the set $C_b^{\mathbb{H}}(G)$ of bounded continuous $\mathbb{H}$-valued functions on G endowed with the uniform topology.

2°) There exists an increasing sequence (σ_n) of stopping times and constants $K(\Psi,n,p,Z)$ such that :

a) $\lim_n P\{\sigma_n < T\} = 0$ *for every* $T > 0$

b) $E\left(\sup_{t<\sigma_n} \|X^u(t)-X^v(t)\|^p\right) \leq K(\Psi,n,p,Z) \|u-v\|^p$.

Proof.

Note that existence and uniqueness of the strong solution of (1.1) for each u is guaranteed by (H_1) to (H_3) (cf. [10]).

The stopping times σ_n are defined as follows :

$$\sigma_n := \inf\{t : \widetilde{A}_t^p \vee L_t \vee \sup_{\substack{u\in G\\ s\leq t}} \|V_s^u\|^p \vee A_t > n\}$$

Next we have the following lemmas

3.3 - Lemma 1

$$E\left(\sup_{t<\sigma_n} \|X_t^u\|^p\right) \leq 2^p(n+n^2) \sum_{j=0}^{2^p n^2} (2^p n^2)^j$$

Proof of Lemma 1

We remark that $A^p_{\sigma_n^-} \leq n, L_{\sigma_n^-} \leq n, \sup_{t<\sigma_n} \sup_u \|V_t^u\|^p \leq n$.

We then apply inequality (2.6) to the second member of (2.7) and get

$$E\left(\sup_{t<\sigma_n} \|X_t^u\|^p\right) \leq 2^{(p-1)}\, n + 2^{(p-1)}\, E\left(\widetilde{A}^p_{\sigma_n^-} \int_{]0,\sigma_n[} [\lambda_s o g(u,X^u)]^{p/2}\, dA_s\right)$$

and property (H_3) gives for every stopping time $\tau \leq \sigma_n$

$$E\left(\sup_{t<\tau} \|X_t^u\|^p\right) \leq 2^{(p-1)}(n+n^2) + 2^{(p-1)}\, n\, E\left(\int_{]0,\tau[} (\sup_{s<t} \|X_s^u\|^p)\, dL_t\right).$$

Applying the "Gronwall stochastic lemma" as in [11] section 7.1 we get the inequality of the lemma.

3.4 - Lemma 2

There exist constants $K(\Psi,n,p,A,\widetilde{A}^p)$ such that

$\forall\, u,v$ $$E\left(\sup_{t<\sigma_n} \|X_t^u - X_t^v\|^p\right) \leq K(\Psi,n,p,A,\widetilde{A}^p)\, \|u-v\|^p$$

Proof of Lemma 2

Applying again inequality (2.6) to the stochastic integrals $\int_{]0,t]} (g_s(u,X^u_{s-}) - g_s(v,X^u_{s-}))dZ_s$ and $\int_{]0,t]} [g_s(v,X^u_{s-}) - g_s(v,X^v_{s-})]dZ_s$

and using properties (H_1), (H_2) and (H_4) we can write for every stopping time $\tau \leq \sigma_n$:

$$E\Big(\sup_{s<\tau}\|X^u(s)-X^v(s)\|^p\Big) \leq 3^{p-1}n^p\|u-v\|^p + 3^{(p-1)}n\Psi\Big(E\Big(\sup_{s<\tau}\|X^u_s\|^p\Big)\Big)$$

$$+ 3^{(p-1)}n\, E\Big(\int_{]0,\tau[}(\sup_{t<s}\|X^u(t)-X^v(t)\|^p)dL_s\Big) .$$

Applying as above the same "Gronwall-inequality" we obtain the lemma.

Theorem 3.2 is now a direct consequence of the following lemma with is a straightforward extension of a lemma as stated by Neveu in [13] (see also P. Priouret [14] chap. 3, lemme 13).

3.5 - Lemma 3

Let $\{Y(t,\omega,u) : t \in \mathbb{R}^+, \omega \in \Omega, u \quad G\}$ *an* $\mathbb{H}$*-valued random function such that for every* $u : t \rightsquigarrow Y(t,\omega,u)$ *is a.s. cad-lag and such that for every* t *:*

$$E\Big(\sup_{s<t}\|Y_{s,u} - Y_{s,v}\|^p\Big) \leq a_{t,p}\|u-v\|^{d+\varepsilon} .$$

Then there exists a mapping $Y^* : (t,\omega,u) \rightsquigarrow Y^*(t,\omega,u) \in \mathbb{H}$ *such that*

a) $u \rightsquigarrow Y^*(t,\omega,u)$ *is continuous*

b) $\forall u \in G$, $Y(t,u,.) = Y^*(t,u,.)$ *for all* t *a.s.*

c) $t \rightsquigarrow Y^*(t,.,\omega)$ *is for* P*-almost all* ω *a cad-lag mapping from* $\mathbb{R}^+$ *into* $C_b^{\mathbb{H}}(G)$ *endowed with the uniform topology.*

Proof.

We omit the proof which is pretty similar to the one given in [14].
This finishes the proof of theorem 3.2. ∎

4. PATHWISE DIFFERENTIABILITY

4.1 - Hypothesis

We consider the same equation (1.1) or in abbreviated notation : (2.9).

For a couple $g := (\sigma,f)$ of "coefficients as in (1.1) we write to simplify :

$$\|g(u,s,\omega,h,.)\|_\Lambda := \Big[\|\sigma(u,s,\omega,h)\|^2_{\mathcal{L}(\mathbb{K};\mathbb{H})} + \int_{\mathbb{E}\times\mathbb{E}} \langle f(u,s,\omega,h,x),f(u,s,\omega,h,y)\rangle_{\mathbb{H}}\, \mathring{q}(\omega,s,dx\otimes dy)\Big]^{\frac{1}{2}} .$$

We set $v_t^* := \sup_{u \in G} \sup_{s<t} \|D_u V_s^u\| + \|V_s^u\| + \|D_{u^2}^2 V_s^u\|$ were $D_u \Phi$ denotes the first order derivative and $D_{u^2}^2 \Phi$ the second order derivative with respect to u of a function Φ of u .

In the hypothesis below C is a constant.

[D_1] For all t and ω the derivatives $D_u V^u(t,\omega)$ and $D_{u^2}^2 V^u(t,\omega)$ exist and $v_t^* < \infty$

[D_2] The derivatives $D_u g(u,s,h,x)$ $D_{u^2}^2 g(u,s,h,x)$ $D_{u,h}^2 g(u,s,h,x)$ and $D_x g(u,s,h,x)$ exist and

$$\sup_{u,s,h} (\|D_u g(s,u,h)\|_\Lambda + \|D_{u^2}^2 g(s,u,h)\|_\Lambda + \|D_{uh}^2 g(s,u,h)\|_\Lambda + \|D_h g(s,u,h)\|_\Lambda) \leq C$$

[D_3] For all h,h',u and v :

$$\|D_h g(s,u,h) - D_h g(s,v,h')\|_\Lambda \leq C(\|h-h'\| + \|u-v\|) .$$

4.2 - Theorem

Under the above hypothesis [D_1] *to* [D_3] *equation* (1.1)*(or* (2.9)*) has a unique (up to indistinguability) solution* X^u *on* $\mathbb{R}^+$ *and there exists a version* $(\omega,t,u) \sim X_t^u(\omega)$ *of this random function such that for* P*-almost all* ω *:*

a) $u \sim X_t^u(\omega)$ *is continuously differentiable for every* t

b) $t \sim X_t^{(.)}(\omega)$ *and* $t \sim D_u X_t^{(.)}(\omega)$ *are cad-lag for the uniform norm on* $C_b(G;\mathbb{H})$ *and* $C_b(G;\mathcal{L}(G;\mathbb{H}))$ *respectively.*

c) *For every* u *the stochastic process* $(D_u X_t^u)_{t\geq 0}$ *is a strong solution of the following stochastic equation (where* X^u *is the process solution of* 2.7 *as in theorem* 3.2*) :*

$$(4.1) \qquad Y^u(t) = D_u V_t^u + \int_{]0,t]} \left(D_u g(s,u,X_{s^-}^u) + D_h g(s,u,X_{s^-}^u) \circ Y_s^u \right) dZ_s \quad .$$

Proof.

The proof is in several steps corresponding to lemmas 4 and 5 and section 4.5 bellow.

4.3 - Lemma 4

Under hypothesis [D_1], [D_2], [D_3], *equations* (2.9) *and* (4.1) *satisfy the conditions* (H_1) *to* (H_4) *of section* 3.1 *for every* $p \geq 2$ *on any interval* $]0,\sigma_n]$ *as defined in theorem* 1.

Proof.

Let us first consider equation (2.7). (H_1) is trivially implied by [D_1]. [D_2] implies also the Lipschitz property (H_2) and conditions (H_3) and (H_4), which is here expressed in the much stronger form $\|g(s,u,x)-g(s,v,x)\|_\Lambda \leq C\,\|u-v\|$.

We turn now to equation (4.1). The only condition (H_i) which is not immediately implied by the hypothesis of the lemma is condition (H_4). We write

$$\|D_u g(s,v,X^v_{t-}) - D_u g(s,u,X^u_{t-}) + D_h g(s,v,X^v_{t-}) \circ \xi_{t-} - D_h g(s,u,X^u_{t-}) \circ \xi_{t-}\|^p$$

$$\begin{aligned}
&\leq 4^{p-1}\{\|D_u g(s,v,X^v_{t-}) - D_u g(s,u,X^v_{t-})\|^p_\Lambda\} + \\
&\quad + 4^{p-1}\{\|D_u g(s,u,X^v_{t-}) - D_u g(s,u,X^u_{t-})\|^p_\Lambda\} \\
&\quad + 4^{p-1}\{\|[D_h g(s,v,X^v_{t-}) - D_h g(s,u,X^v_{t-})] \circ \xi_{t-}\|^p_\Lambda\} \\
&\quad + 4^{p-1}\{\|[D_h g(s,u,X^v_{t-}) - D_h g(s,u,X^u_{t-})] \circ \xi_{t-}\|^p_\Lambda\} \\
&\leq 4^{p-1}\, c^p(\|u-v\|^p + \|X^v_{t-} - X^u_{t-}\|^p + \\
&\quad + 4^{p-1}\, c^p\|u-v\|^p\|\xi_{t-}\|^p + 4^{p-1}\, c^p\|(X^v_{t-} - X^u_{t-}) \circ \xi_{t-}\|^p \quad .
\end{aligned}$$

One knows from lemma 2 that there exists an increasing sequence (σ_n) of stopping times and constants C_n such that

$$E\Big(\sup_{s<\sigma_n}\|Y^u(s)-Y^v(s)\|^{2p}\Big) \leq C_n\|u-v\|^{2p} .$$

If we write for every stopping time

$$E\Big(\sup_{t<\tau\wedge\sigma_n}\|(X^v_t-X^u_t) \circ \xi_{t-}\|^p\Big) \leq$$

$$\leq \Big[E\Big(\sup_{t<\tau\wedge\sigma_n}\|X^v_t-X^u_t\|^{2p}\Big)\Big]^{\frac{1}{2}}\Big[E\Big(\sup_{t<\tau\wedge\sigma_n}\|\xi_t\|^{\frac{2p}{2p-1}}\Big)\Big]^{\frac{2p-1}{2}}$$

$$\leq C_n^{\frac{1}{2}}\|u-v\|^p\, E\Big(\sup_{t<\tau\wedge\sigma_n}\|\xi_t\|^\alpha\Big)^{p/\alpha}$$

with $\alpha = \frac{2p}{2p-1}$

Therefore

$$E\Big(\sup_{s<\tau\wedge\sigma_n}\|g(s,u,\xi_{s-})-g(s,v,\xi_{s-})\|^p_\Lambda\Big) \leq 4^{(p-1)}c^p\|u-v\|^p\Big[1+C_n+E\Big(\sup_{t<\tau\wedge\sigma_n}\|\xi_{t-}\|^p\Big)\Big]$$
$$+ C_n^{\frac{1}{2}}\Big[E\Big(\sup_{t<\tau\wedge\sigma_n}\|\xi_{t-}\|^\alpha\Big)\Big]^{p/\alpha} .$$

If we remark that $E\left(\sup_{t<\tau\wedge\sigma_n} \|\xi_{t^-}\|^p\right) \geq \left[E\left(\sup_{t<\tau\wedge\sigma_n} \|\xi_{t^-}\|^\alpha\right)\right]^{p/\alpha}$

we see that property (H) holds with

$$\Psi(\rho) = 1 + C_n + (1 + C_n^{\frac{1}{2}})\rho$$

4.4 - Lemma 2

If we define

$$\Phi_t(e,u,\lambda) = \frac{1}{\lambda}[X_t^{u+\lambda e} - X_t^u - \lambda Y_t^u \circ e]$$

there exists an increasing sequence (τ_n) *of stopping times such that* $\lim_n P\{\tau_u < T\} = 0$ *and a sequence* C_n *of constants such that*

$$E\left\{\sup_{t<\tau_n} \|\Phi_t(e,.,\lambda)\|^2_{L^2(G)}\right\} \leq C_n\,\lambda^2$$

Proof.

For each u the process $(\Phi_t(e,u,\lambda))_{t\leq T}$ is solution of

$$\Phi_t(e,u,\lambda) = \frac{1}{\lambda}(V_t^{u+\lambda e} - V_t^u - \lambda D_e V_t^u) + \tag{4.2}$$

$$+ \int_{]0,t]} \frac{1}{\lambda}\Big[g(s,u+\lambda e,X_{s^-}^{u+\lambda e}) - g(s,u,X_{s^-}^u) -$$

$$\lambda D_e g(s,u,X_{s^-}^u) - \lambda D_h g(s,u,X_{s^-}^u) \circ Y_s^u \circ e\Big] dS_s$$

We may write for $h,h' \in \mathbb{H}$ and $\eta \in \mathcal{L}(\mathbb{H};\mathbb{H})$

$$g(s,u+\lambda e,h') - g(s,u,h) - \lambda D_e g(s,u,h) - \lambda D_h g(s,u,h) \circ \eta \circ e = \tag{4.3}$$

$$= \lambda D_e g(s,u,h') + D_h g(s,u,h) \circ (h'-h) - \lambda D_e g(s,u,h) - \lambda D_h g(s,u,h) \circ \eta \circ e +$$

$$+ h(s,u,h,h',\eta,\lambda,e)$$

$$= D_h g(s,u,h) \circ (h'-h-\lambda\eta \circ e) + \widetilde{\mathbb{H}}(s,u,h,h',\eta,\lambda)$$

with

$$\|\mathbb{H}(s,u,h,h',\eta,\lambda)\|_\Lambda \leq |\lambda| K(\|h-h'\| + |\lambda|) \tag{4.4}$$

for some constant K

The equation (4.2) can therefore be written

(4.5) $$\Phi_t(e,u,\lambda) = H_t(u,\lambda,e) + \int_{]0,t]} D_h g(s,u,X^u_{s^-}) \circ \Phi_{s^-}(e,u,\lambda)dZ_s$$

where the process $(H(u,\lambda,e)$ satisfies

(4.6) $$\|H_t(u,\lambda,e)\|_{\mathbb{H}} \leq |\lambda|\ v^k_t + \left\|\int_{]0,t]} \frac{1}{\lambda}\ \widetilde{\mathbb{H}}(s,u,X^{u+\lambda e}_{s^-}, X^u_{s^-}, Y^u_{s^-} \circ e)dZ_s\right\| .$$

Using (4.5) we obtain from (4.6) for every stopping time σ :

$$E\left(\sup_{t<\sigma} \|H_t(u,\lambda,e)\|^2\right) \leq 2\ \lambda^2\ v^*_{\sigma^-} + E\left(\widetilde{A}_{\tau^-} \cdot \int_{]0,\tau[} [\lambda^2 + C^2 \|X^{u+\lambda e}_{s^-} - X^u_s\|^2]dA_s\right)$$

Using then theorem we see that there exists a sequence (σ_n) of stopping times and a sequence of constants (K_n) such that

(4.7) $$\sup_{s<\sigma_n} (\widetilde{A}_s \vee A_s) \leq n \quad \text{and}$$

(4.8) $$E(\sup_{t<\sigma_n} \|H_t(u,\lambda,e)\|^2) \leq K_n\ \lambda^2$$ (use a standard stopping procedure for processes $v^*, \widetilde{A}$ and A).

This implies

(4.9) $$E\left(\sup_{t<\sigma_n} \int_G \|H_t(u,\lambda,e)\|^2 du\right) \leq \int_G K_n\ \lambda^2\ du \leq \widetilde{K}_n\ \lambda^2$$

We next consider the $L^2(G)$-valued process $(\Phi_t(e,.,\lambda))_{t\leq T}$

Since $D_h g$ is bounded by some constant C , inequality (4.6) shows that the $L^2(G)$-valued process Φ_t satisfies an inequality of the following type for every stopping time $\tau \leq \sigma_n$

$$E\left\{\sup_{t<\tau} \|\Phi_t(e,.,\lambda)\|_{L^2(G)}\right\} \leq 2\ \widetilde{K}_n\ \lambda^2 + 2\ E\left(\widetilde{A}_{\tau^-} \int_{[0,\tau[} C^2 \sup_{s<t} \|\Phi_s(e,.,\lambda)\|^2_{L^2(G)} dA_t\right)$$

$$\leq 2\ \widetilde{K}_n\ \lambda^2 + 2n\ C^2 \int_{[0,\tau[} \sup_{s<t} \|\Phi_s(e,.,\lambda)\|_{L^2(G)} dA_t$$

The already used "Gronwall inequality" of [11] shows immediately the existence of a constant C_n as in the lemma.

4.5 - End of the proof of the theorem

We make use of the following easily proved property : let $f \in L^2_{\mathbb{H}}(\overline{G})$ let $f \in L^2(\mathbb{G}\,;\mathbb{H}) \cap C(G\,;\mathbb{H})$ and $\overline{f} \in L^2(G;\mathcal{L}(\mathbb{H}\,;\mathbb{H}) \cap C(G;\mathcal{L}(\mathbb{H}\,;\mathbb{H})$ such that for all $e \in \mathbb{R}^d$, all $u \in \mathbb{R}^d$ and some decreasing sequence $\lambda_k \downarrow 0$:

$$\lim_{k\to\infty} f(u+\lambda_k e) - f(u) - \lambda_k \overline{f}(u) \circ e_{\,L^2(G;\mathbb{H})} = 0 \quad .$$

Then $\overline{f}$ is the derivative of f in the sense of distributions and therefore in the ordinary sense in every point $u \in G$. Let us consider for each ω and n a P-negligeable set Ω_n and a sequence λ_k such that $\lambda_k \downarrow 0$ and

$$\lim_{k\to\infty} \sup_{t<\tau_n(\omega)} \|\Phi_t(e,.,\omega,\lambda_k)\|_{L^2(G)} = 0 \quad \text{for every } \omega \notin \Omega_n \quad .$$

The above property shows that for every $\omega \notin \Omega_n$ and $t < \tau_n(\omega)$, $Y^u_t(\omega)$ is the derivative of $u \rightsquigarrow X^u_t(\omega)$ at point u. Therefore $Y^u_t(\omega)$ is the derivative of $u \rightsquigarrow X^u_t(\omega)$ for all $t < \tau_n(\omega)$ and $\omega \notin (\bigcup_n \Omega_n)$.

This proves the theorem. ∎

BIBLIOGRAPHY

1 BICHTELER, S. : *Stochastic integrations with stationary independant increments.* to appear in Z. Wahr. verw. Geb.

2 BISMUT, M. : *A generalized formula of Ito and some other properties of stochastic flows.* Z. Wahr. verw. Geb. 55, 331-350 (1981).

3 BLAGOVEČENSKII, Y.M., FREIDLIN, M.I. : *Some properties of diffusion processes depending on a parameter.* DAN, 138 (1961) Sov. Math. 2, 633-636.

4 GIKHMAN, I.I. : *On the theory of differential equations of random processes.* Uhr. Mat. Zb. 2, 4, 37-63 (1950).

5 GIKHMAN, I.I., SKOROKHOD, A.V. : *Stochastic differential equations.* Springer Verlag, 1972.

6 JACOD, J. : *Calcul stochastique et problèmes de martingales.* Lecture Notes in Math. 714, Springer-Verlag, New York, 1979.

7 JACOD, J. : *Equations différentielles stochastiques : continuité et dérivabilité en probabilité.* Preprint.

8 KUNITA, H. : *On the decomposition of solutions of stochastic differential equations.* Proc. of the L.M.S. Symposium on Stochastic Different. Equations, Durham, Juillet 1980, Lecture Notes in Math. Springer-Verlag, 1981.

9 MALLIAVIN, P. : *Stochastic calculus of variations and Hypoelliptic operators.* Proc. of the Intern. Symposium on Stochastic Different. Equations of Kyoto, 195-263 (1976). Tokyo, Kinokuniya and New York, Wiley, 1978.

10 METIVIER, M. : *Stability theorems for stochastic Integral equations driven by random measures and semimartingales.* J. Integral Equations, 3, 109-135 (1981).

11 METIVIER, M., PELLAUMAIL, J. : *Stochastic Integration.* Acad. Press, New York,1980.

12 MEYER, P.A. : *Flot d'une équation différentielle stochastique.* Séminaire de Probabilité XV. Lecture Notes in Math. 850, Springer-Verlag, 1981.

13 NEVEU, J. : *Intégrales stochastiques et applications.* Cours de 3e cycle. Université de Paris VI, 1971-1972.

14 PRIOURET, P. : *Processus de diffusion et équations différentielles stochastiques.* Ecole d'Eté de Probabilités de St-Flour. Lecture Notes in Math. 390, Springer-Verlag, 1974.

QUELQUES RESULTATS ANALYTIQUES SUR LE SEMI-GROUPE D'ORNSTEIN-UHLENBECK EN DIMENSION INFINIE

par P. A. Meyer, Université Louis-Pasteur, Strasbourg

Le semi-groupe d'Ornstein-Uhlenbeck sur l'espace du mouvement brownien, et le << calcul différentiel et intégral >> qui lui est associé, ont été récemment utilisés par Malliavin pour sa démonstration probabiliste du théorème d'hypoellipticité de Hörmander. La démonstration la plus classique du théorème analogue, dans le cas elliptique, repose sur la théorie des intégrales singulières. On peut donc se demander si en fait, la démonstration de Malliavin ne repose pas sur des estimations d'intégrales singulières sur l'espace de Wiener lui même. Je ne suis pas arrivé à présenter la démonstration de Malliavin sous cette forme, mais il est tout de même vrai qu'il existe, sur l'espace de Wiener, un théorème qui correspond, en dimension finie, au fait que les transformations de Riesz sont des opérateurs bornés sur les $\mathcal{L}^p$. Nous allons de même interpréter l'inégalité de Sobolev logarithmique de Gross comme une inégalité concernant les potentiels de Riesz en dimension infinie, et en indiquer une généralisation (établie dans un article commun avec D. Bakry).

La première partie de ce rapport n'est qu'une présentation commentée de ces résultats, établis dans $[4]_a$ et $[4]_b$. La dernière partie, consacrée aux gradients itérés, est nouvelle, et les démonstrations y sont complètes (le début étant supposé connu).

Les résultats présentés n'ont à peu près rien à voir avec la structure spéciale du mouvement brownien, et s'étendent à toutes les mesures gaussiennes sur les e.l.c. (voir la remarque finale). En revanche, les démonstrations utilisent cette structure particulière, et il serait amusant de regarder s'il existe des démonstrations plus << intrinsèques >>. De même, mon ignorance de la théorie des mesures gaussiennes m'empêche de rendre justice aux auteurs qui ont étudié des questions analogues sur des espaces gaussiens généraux. On peut estimer que tous les résultats dans $\mathcal{L}^2$ ont été établis par Feissner, Gross, Hida, Kuo, Nelson*... et que les résultats $\mathcal{L}^p$ sont probablement nouveaux. Il y a quelque rapport , toutefois, avec les travaux de Shikegawa, motivés eux aussi par les idées de Malliavin.

*Voir Yuh-Jia LEE. Fundamental solutions for differential equations associated with the number operator. Trans. Amer. Math. Soc. 268, 1981, p. 467, et la bibliographie de cet article.

1. INTEGRALES SINGULIERES CLASSIQUES DANS $\mathbb{R}^d$

Rappelons d'abord quelques résultats tout à fait classiques sur les multiplicateurs de Fourier, dont les démonstrations figurent dans le livre de Stein [6]. L'analogie va nous guider tout au long de ce travail, et nous allons la souligner en conservant les mêmes notations, que voici

NOTATION	OPERATEUR SUR LES FONCTIONS SUR $E=\mathbb{R}^d$	MULTIPLICATEUR DE FOURIER
D_k	Dérivée partielle	iu_k
L	Laplacien	$-\|u\|^2$
P_t	Semi-groupe brownien e^{tL} (normalisation des analystes).	$e^{-t\|u\|^2}$
Q_t	Semi-groupe de Cauchy (noyau de Poisson du demi-espace).	$e^{-t\|u\|}$
C	Générateur de Cauchy $(-\sqrt{-L})$	$-\|u\|$
R	Potentiel de (P_t), potentiel newtonien	$1/\|u\|^2$
V	Potentiel de Cauchy	$1/\|u\|$
R^α	Potentiel de Riesz (noté d'habitude $I^{2\alpha}$)	$c_\alpha\|u\|^{-2\alpha}$ $(0<\alpha<d/2)$

Le mouvement brownien des probabilistes correspond au multiplicateur $e^{-t|u|^2/2}$: son usage compliquerait ici les formules. Signalons aussi que les potentiels de Riesz ont une interprétation probabiliste dans le domaine $0<\alpha\leqq 1$. Voici les résultats classiques :

TRANSFORMATIONS DE RIESZ : Les multiplicateurs $iu_k/|u|$ définissent des opérateurs bornés sur $\mathcal{L}^p(\mathbb{R}^d)$ pour $1<p<\infty$. Voir Stein, [6], chap. III.

Ces opérateurs seront notés $\mathcal{R}_k$. Pour d=1, $\mathcal{R}$ est la transformation de Hilbert.

POTENTIELS DE RIESZ : R^α définit un opérateur borné de $\mathcal{L}^p$ dans $\mathcal{L}^q$ pour $1<p<\infty$, $0<\alpha<d/2p$, $1/q= 1/p - 2\alpha/d$. Voir Stein [6], p. 119.

Si l'on tient compte du premier théorème, le second est étroitement lié aux théorèmes de Sobolev classiques (Stein, p. 125).

Transformons l'énoncé du premier théorème, d'une manière qui s'étendra à des situations plus générales. Soit f une fonction qui appartient à l'espace de Schwartz $\underline{\underline{S}}$; alors la transformée de Riesz $\mathcal{R}_k Cf$ est $-D_k f$, et le théorème nous dit que $\|D_k f\|_p \leqq c_p \|Cf\|_p$ [1] . Posons d'autre part

$$\Gamma(f,g) = \textstyle\sum_k D_k f D_k g$$

1. La notation $\| \ \|_p$ désigne la norme L^p, la notation c_p une quantité dépendant de p seulement, dont la valeur exacte importe peu.

Nous avons alors

(1) $$\|\sqrt{\Gamma(f,f)}\|_p \leqq c_p \|Cf\|_p$$

Mais d'autre part $Cf=\Sigma_k R_k D_k f$, de sorte que la relation (1) peut être remplacée par une <u>équivalence</u> des normes $\mathcal{L}^p$. Le point important est ici la possibilité d'oublier la structure différentiable, les dérivées partielles, etc : $\Gamma(f,g)$ peut être défini à partir du semi-groupe (P_t) seul, par la formule $\Gamma(f,g)=L(fg)-gLf-fLg$.

2. SEMI-GROUPES SYMETRIQUES

Soit maintenant un bon espace mesurable E, muni d'une mesure σ-finie μ, et d'un semi-groupe (P_t) de noyaux markoviens ($P_t 1=1$), symétrique par rapport à μ :

$$< P_t f,g >_\mu = < f,P_t g >_\mu \quad \text{(f,g mesurables bornées)}$$

Il est bien connu qu'alors P_t induit une contraction sur tout espace $\mathcal{L}^p(\mu)$: nous supposerons que le semi-groupe est fortement continu sur chacun de ces espaces ($p<\infty$). En tant qu'opérateur borné autoadjoint sur $\mathcal{L}^2$, on sait que P_t admet une représentation spectrale du type suivant (avec une famille spectrale E_λ indépendante de t)

$$P_t = \int_0^\infty e^{-t\lambda} dE_\lambda \ .$$

Soit $\phi(\lambda)$ une fonction sur $[0,\infty[$. Pour souligner l'analogie avec la section précédente, nous dirons que l'opérateur auto-adjoint (peut être non borné) $\int_0^\infty \phi(\lambda)dE_\lambda$ correspond au <u>multiplicateur spectral</u> ϕ . Nous pouvons alors transporter la liste précédente (avec disparition des opérateurs de dérivées partielles)

NOTATION	OPERATEUR	MULTIPLICATEUR SPECTRAL $\phi(\lambda)$
P_t	Semi-groupe	$e^{-t\lambda}$
L	Générateur (<< laplacien >>)	$-\lambda$
Q_t	Semi-groupe de Cauchy	$e^{-t\sqrt{\lambda}}$
C	Générateur de Cauchy ($-\sqrt{-L}$)	$-\sqrt{\lambda}$
R	Potentiel	λ^{-1}
V	Potentiel de Cauchy ($R^{1/2}$)	$\lambda^{-1/2}$
R^α	Potentiel de Riesz	$\lambda^{-\alpha}$

Pour les trois dernières fonctions, on convient que $\phi(0)$ vaut 0, non $+\infty$.

Le problème consistant à trouver des conditions sur un multiplicateur, assurant que l'opérateur correspondant est borné sur les $\mathcal{L}^p$ ($1<p<\infty$) a été étudié par Stein [7], au moyen de méthodes de Littlewood-Paley (reposant en partie sur des inégalités de martingales). Stein démontre ainsi que la réponse est positive pour le multiplicateur $\phi(\lambda)=e^{iu}$ (potentiel de Riesz d'ordre imaginaire pur).

Si le domaine de L contient une algèbre suffisamment riche, on peut aussi définir l'opérateur bilinéaire $\Gamma(f,g)=L(fg)-gLf-fLg$, et l'on montre que $\Gamma(f,f)$ est une fonction positive. Il est donc raisonnable de poser, par analogie avec le cas classique, le problème suivant :

PROBLEME DES << TRANSFORMEES DE RIESZ >> : Les normes $\|\sqrt{\Gamma(f,f)}\|_p$ et $\|Cf\|_p$ sont elles équivalentes, pour $1<p<\infty$?

(Pour p=2, les normes sont égales à un facteur 2 près).

On a d'autre part un très vague problème :
PROBLEME DES << POTENTIELS DE RIESZ >> : R^α a t'il des propriétés régularisantes (en un sens à préciser) pour α grand ?

Le premier problème a donné lieu à des réponses positives : Stein a étudié dans [7] les laplaciens sur les groupes de Lie compacts. Ses méthodes de Littlewood-Paley s'appliquent à tous les semi-groupes de convolution symétriques sur $\mathbb{R}^d$ ($[5]_a$ et $[5]_b$) mais seulement pour $p\geqq 2$.

3. LE SEMI-GROUPE D'ORNSTEIN-UHLENBECK

A partir de maintenant, E désigne l'espace de toutes les fonctions continues w de $[0,\infty[$ dans $\mathbb{R}$, telles que $w(0)=0$, muni de la topologie de la convergence compacte. La mesure μ de la section 2 sera la mesure de Wiener sur E. Nous allons définir un semi-groupe sur E, le <u>semi-groupe d'Ornstein-Uhlenbeck</u>, qui est symétrique par rapport à μ. Le procédé le plus rapide consiste à parachuter la formule de Mehler

$$P_t f(w) = \int_E f(we^{-t/2}+u\sqrt{1-e^{-t}}\,)\mu(du) \tag{1}$$

qui définit évidemment un noyau markovien. Reste à vérifier la propriété de semi-groupe et la symétrie, en faisant agir P_t sur des fonctions assez simples. Sans entrer dans les détails, esquissons quelques points dont nous nous servirons.

Soit E' l'ensemble de toutes les applications α de $\mathbb{R}_+$ dans $\mathbb{R}$, à support compact et à variation bornée, continues à droite, telles que $\alpha(0)=0$. E et E' sont mis en dualité par la forme bilinéaire

$$\{w,\alpha\} = -\int_0^\infty w(s)\,d\alpha(s) = \int_0^\infty \alpha(s)\,dw(s) \quad \text{(intégrale stochastique triviale)}$$

On pose

$$q(\alpha) = \int_0^\infty |\alpha(s)|^2 ds\ ,\quad e_\alpha(w)=e^{i\{w,\alpha\}},\quad \varepsilon_\alpha(w) = e_\alpha(w)e^{-q(\alpha)/2}\ . \tag{2}$$

La transformée de Fourier de μ est $\hat{\mu}(\alpha)= e^{-q(\alpha)/2}$. Les fonctions $\{\cdot,\alpha\}$ sont dites <u>linéaires</u> , l'algèbre qu'elles engendrent est celle des <u>polynômes</u> sur E . Quant aux combinaisons linéaires des fonctions e_α (ou ε_α), elles constituent l'algèbre des <u>polynômes trigonométriques</u> sur E. Ces deux algèbres sont denses dans tous les $\mathcal{L}^p$ (p fini).

P_t agit très simplement sur les polynômes trigonométriques :

(3) $$P_t \varepsilon_\alpha = \varepsilon_{\alpha e^{-t/2}}$$

formule d'où l'on tire très simplement la propriété de semi-groupe et la symétrie. Sur les polynôles, l'action de P_t se décrit ainsi : soit $\alpha_1,\ldots,\alpha_n$ un système orthonormal fini dans E' (par rapport à la forme quadratique q) et soit $H(x_1,\ldots,x_n)$ un polynôme d'Hermite de degré k sur $\mathbb{R}^n$. Soit h(w) le polynôme $H(\{w,\alpha_1\},\ldots,\{w,\alpha_n\})$ sur E. Alors

(4) $$P_t h = e^{-kt/2} h$$

L'algèbre des polynômes est donc stable par (P_t) et par son générateur L : cela permet d'introduire l'opérateur bilinéaire Γ, substitut du gradient en dimension infinie.

Du point de vue de la décomposition spectrale, il est très facile de décrire P_t : soit J_k la projection orthogonale, dans $\mathcal{L}^2(\mu)$, sur le k-ième chaos de Wiener ($J_0 f$ est l'intégrale $\mu(f)$). Alors nous avons

(5) $$P_t f = \Sigma_k \, e^{-kt/2} J_k$$

Donc les multiplicateurs spectraux $\phi(\lambda)$ de la section 2 sont ici des <u>suites</u> $\phi(k)$ (multiplicateurs d'Hermite), et le trou entre 0 et la première valeur propre 1/2 simplifie grandement la théorie des potentiels de Riesz : $(k/2)^{-\alpha}$ pour $k>0$ (0 pour k=0) est une suite bornée pour tout α complexe de partie réelle positive.

Tout cela a un sens en fait pour toute mesure gaussienne sur tout espace vectoriel << raisonnable >>, mais l'emploi de l'intégrale stochastique sur l'espace du mouvement brownien va jouer un rôle essentiel. Tout d'abord, elle nous permet de remplacer l'espace $\mathcal{L}^p$ (ou l'espace $\mathcal{L}^p_0$ des éléments de $\mathcal{L}^p$ d'intégrale nulle) par l'espace H^p ou H^p_0 , avec une norme équivalente pour $1<p<\infty$. On a alors le résultat suivant , très utile techniquement (et qu'il faudra améliorer dans la dernière section).

LEMME . Soit R l'opérateur potentiel (multiplicateur d'Hermite 2/k pour $k>0$, <u>0 pour k=0</u>. Alors R/2 est une contraction de H^p pour $1\leq p<\infty$.

Soit T l'opérateur associé à la suite $\phi(k)=\sqrt{1-1/k}$ pour $k>0$ ($\phi(0)=0$). Alors T est borné sur H^p pour $1<p<\infty$, donc sur $\mathcal{L}^p$ pour $1<p<\infty$.

(Il suffit de développer $\sqrt{1-x}$ en série de Taylor).

4. INEGALITES DE SOBOLEV LOGARITHMIQUES

La célèbre inégalité de Sobolev logarithmique de Gross (équivalente au théorème d'hypercontractivité de Nelson) s'énonce de la manière suivante. Soit f un élément de $\mathcal{D}_2(L)$, le domaine de L dans $\mathcal{L}^2(\mu)$. Alors f appartient aussi à l'espace d'Orlicz $\mathcal{L}^2\log\mathcal{L}$, et l'on a

(6) $$\mu(|f|^2\log|f|) \leqq \|f\|_2^2\log\|f\|_2 - 2\langle f,Lf\rangle_\mu$$

Cette inégalité est remarquablement précise, et nous allons perdre un peu d'information en l'interprétant de la manière suivante : supposons que $\mu(f)=0$, et posons $-Cf=g$ de sorte que $f=Vg$ ($V=R^{1/2}$, potentiel de Cauchy). Le dernier terme à droite est $2\langle g,g\rangle = 2\|g\|_2^2$. D'autre part, V est donné par un multiplicateur d'Hermite borné, donc il est continu de $\mathcal{L}^2$ dans $\mathcal{L}^2$, et le premier terme à droite est négatif pour $\|g\|_2$ petit. Nous déduisons donc de (6) que

$V=R^{1/2}$ est borné de $\mathcal{L}^2$ dans $\mathcal{L}^2\log\mathcal{L}$.

[Rappelons une fois pour toutes que le multiplicateur d'Hermite est pris nul en 0 : Vf est donc le potentiel de $f-\mu(f)$ pour le semi-groupe de Cauchy. Pour l'opérateur potentiel de Cauchy lui même, cela revient à travailler sur $\mathcal{L}_0^2$. De même pour tous les R^α].

Les beaux résultats de Feissner [3] étendant l'inégalité de Gross peuvent aussi être interprétés - de manière moins évidente - comme des énoncés concernant V : V est borné de $\mathcal{L}^2\log^n\mathcal{L}$ dans $\mathcal{L}^2\log^{n+1}\mathcal{L}$ pour n entier (positif ou négatif). Autrement dit, nous tenons là une propriété de régularité de $R^{1/2}$, et de tous les $R^{k/2}$, $k\in\mathbb{N}$, et comme R^z a un sens pour z dans un demi-plan, l'idée naturelle est d'utiliser (comme Feissner lui même) l'interpolation complexe. D'autre part, le théorème de Stein rappelé à la fin de la section 2 est du même type, pour z imaginaire pur. Le premier travail consiste donc à étendre le théorème de Stein aux espaces d'Orlicz (les inégalités BDG en théorie des martingales le permettent), et la seconde partie du travail est l'interpolation proprement dite. On obtient

THEOREME 1. L'opérateur potentiel de Riesz R^z pour $z=\alpha+i\beta$ ($\alpha\geqq 0$) est borné de l'espace d'Orlicz $\mathcal{L}^p\log^r\mathcal{L}$ dans $\mathcal{L}^p\log^{r+p\alpha}\mathcal{L}$ pour $1<p<\infty$, r réel.

5. TRANSFORMATIONS DE RIESZ EN DIMENSION INFINIE

Soit $\alpha\in E'$. Nous désignons par D_α l'opérateur non borné qui associe à f la dérivée dans la direction de la fonction continue $\bar{\alpha}(t)=\int_0^t\alpha(s)ds$

$$D_\alpha f(w) = \lim_{s\to 0}\frac{1}{s}(f(w+s\bar{\alpha})-f(w))$$

la limite étant prise en un sens convenable (au sens $\mathcal{L}^p$ par exemple). Pour les polynômes, les quotients différentiels convergent partout, et dans tous les $\mathcal{L}^p$ (p fini), et la dérivée est un polynôme de degré inférieur (par exemple, $D_\alpha\{.,\beta\}$ est la constante $q(\alpha,\beta)$, la forme bilinéaire associée à la forme quadratique q). Les D_α ne commutent pas avec P_t, mais on a la formule fondamentale

(7) $$P_tD_\alpha = e^{t/2}D_\alpha P_t \quad , \quad LD_\alpha = D_\alpha L + \frac{1}{2}D_\alpha$$

et d'autre part on a

(8) $$\Gamma(f,f) = \Sigma_n (D_{\alpha_n} f)^2$$

pour toute base orthonormale (α_n) de $L^2(\mathbb{R}_+,\mathbb{R}^d)$ formée d'éléments de E'. Le théorème suivant correspond alors exactement au résultat classique de la section 1 sur les transformées de Riesz :

THEOREME 2. On a une équivalence de normes dans $\mathcal{L}^p$, $1<p<\infty$

(9) $$c_p \|Cf\|_p \leq \|\sqrt{\Gamma(f,f)}\|_p \leq c'_p \|Cf\|_p .$$

En fait, cette inégalité est établie pour de << bonnes >> fonctions, par exemple les polynômes, ou les polynômes trigonométriques, et s'étend par densité aux domaines appropriés.

La démonstration de ce théorème est très compliquée, et repose sur des inégalités de Littlewood-Paley-Stein, alourdies par le fait que P_t et D_α ne commutent pas (heureusement, le commutateur est simple). Je l'ai vérifiée plusieurs fois, sans y trouver d'erreur, et j'ai été rassuré de trouver une démonstration complètement différente de Muckenhoupt en dimension 1 (Hermite conjugate expansions, TAMS 139, 1969, p. 243-260).

6. CALCULS D'ORDRE SUPERIEUR

Nous commençons par quelques notations.

a) Nous fixons une base orthonormale (α_n) comme ci-dessus. Etant donné un multiindice $m=(n_1,\dots,n_k)\in\mathbb{N}^k$, nous désignons par D_m l'opérateur $D_{\alpha_{n_k}}\dots D_{\alpha_{n_1}}$, et nous posons pour tout polynôme f

(10) $$\Gamma_k(f,f) = \Sigma_{m\in\mathbb{N}^k} (D_m f)^2 \quad \text{(k-ième gradient itéré)}$$

Ainsi $\Gamma(f,f)=\Gamma_1(f,f)$. On conviendra que $\Gamma_0(f,f)=f^2$.

Nous verrons plus loin que ces fonctions ne dépendent pas de la base utilisée.

b) Soit J_k l'opérateur de projection orthogonale sur le k-ième chaos de Wiener (J_k correspond au multiplicateur d'Hermite $\phi(i)=1$ si $i=k$, 0 si $i\neq k$). J_k est borné de $\mathcal{L}^2$ dans $\mathcal{L}^2$, donc de $\mathcal{L}^2$ dans $\mathcal{L}^p$ pour tout p fini (car tous les $\mathcal{L}^p$ induisent la même topologie sur le k-ième chaos), donc de $\mathcal{L}^p$ dans $\mathcal{L}^p$ pour $2\leq p<\infty$, d'où par transposition pour $1<p\leq 2$ aussi.

Nous dirons que f est d'ordre $>n$ si $J_k f=0$ pour $k\leq n$.

c) Nous définirons l'espace de Sobolev W_k^p comme le complété de l'espace des polynômes pour la norme

(11) $$\|f\|_{p,k} = \Sigma_{i\leq k} \|C^i f\|_p \quad (C^0 f=f).$$

Comme C=VL, et V est borné de $\mathcal{L}^p$ dans $\mathcal{L}^p$, la norme analogue

(12) $$\|f\|'_{p,2k} = \Sigma_{i\leq k} \|L^i f\|_p$$

est équivalente à $\|f\|_{p,2k}$.

d) Nous dirons qu'une fonction f est une <u>fonction-test</u> si elle appartient à $W_{p,k}$ pour tout k et tout p fini. On notera la différence avec le cas classique, où les inégalités de Sobolev permettent de remplacer $\cap_{p,k} W_{p,k}$ par $\cap_k W_{2,k}$. Ce dernier espace ne sera pas une algèbre en général : prenons par exemple le cas de la droite, munie de sa mesure gaussienne standard μ . On peut alors montrer que f appartient à $\cap_k W_{2,k}$ si et seulement si $f=e^{x^2/4}g$, où g appartient à l'espace $\underline{S}$ usuel sur $\mathbb{R}$. Alors la fonction $e^{x^2/8}$ appartient à $\cap_k W_{2,k}$, mais non son carré.

L'un de nos buts ci-dessous consiste à montrer que l'espace des fonctions-test est une <u>algèbre</u>, contenant l'algèbre des polynômes.

Nous commençons par énoncer un théorème, mais nous ne le démontrerons pas complètement tout de suite, car la démonstration nous écarterait du sujet. Nous en démontrerons 1) le premier cas non trivial, 2) une forme affaiblie qui suffira à étudier les fonctions-test. La démonstration complète exige un lemme, qui sera rejeté en appendice.

THEOREME 3. On a pour tout k et tout p fini, pour tout polynôme f

(13) $$\|\sqrt{\Gamma_k(f,f)}\|_p \leq c_{p,k}\|f\|_{p,k}$$

<u>Forme affaiblie</u> : remplacer le second membre par $c_{p,k}\|f\|'_{p,2k}$.

DEMONSTRATION. Nous considérons un système de fonctions de Rademacher $r_m(t)$ ($t\in[0,1]$) où m parcourt $\mathbb{N}^k$. Nous posons $f_m=D_m f$, et nous appliquons le théorème 2 au polynôme

$$g_t = \Sigma_{m\in I}\, r_m(t) f_m \qquad (\text{ I partie finie de } \mathbb{N}^k) .$$

soit

$$\|(\Sigma_n (D_{\alpha_n} g_t)^2)^{1/2}\|_p^p \leq c\|Cg_t\|_p^p \quad (\|Lg_t\|_p \text{ pour la forme affaiblie }).$$

Nous intégrons en t. Du côté gauche, désignons par G l'application $f\mapsto (D_{\alpha_n} f)_{n\in\mathbb{N}}$ des polynômes dans les suites de polynômes ; alors l'expression s'écrit $E[\int \| \Sigma_{m\in I}\, r_m(t)Gf_m\|^p_{\ell^2}\, dt]$. Appliquant l'inégalité de Khintchine dans l'espace de Hilbert ℓ^2, ceci est équivalent à $\|(\Sigma_{m\in I} \|Gf_m\|^2_{\ell^2})^{1/2}\|_p^p$, qui pour $I\uparrow\mathbb{N}^k$ tend vers $\|\sqrt{\Gamma_{k+1}(f,f)}\|_p^p$.

Du côté droit, nous avons $E[\int|\Sigma_{m\in I}\, r_m(t)Cf_m|^p dt]$ (L au lieu de C pour la forme affaiblie, ici et dans la suite), qui d'après l'inégalité de Khintchine est équivalent à $\|(\Sigma_{m\in I} (Cf_m)^2)^{1/2}\|_p^p$. Si au lieu de $CD_m f$ nous avions ici $D_m Cf$, nous trouverions lorsque $I\uparrow\mathbb{N}^k$ $\|\sqrt{\Gamma_k(Cf,Cf)}\|_p^p$, et un raisonnement immédiat par récurrence nous permettrait d'achever la démonstration. Mais, plus généralement, il nous suffirait pour achever, de savoir que

$$CD_m f = D_m Cf + D_m Kf$$

où K est un opérateur qui transforme les polynômes en polynômes, et tel que $\|Kf\|_{p,k} \leqq c\|Cf\|_{p,k}$. Nous traiterons ce problème dans l'appendice. Pour l'instant, nous nous bornons à deux situations :

a) Forme affaiblie . La relation (7) nous donne aussitôt

(14) $$LD_m f = D_m Lf + \frac{k}{2} D_m f$$

d'où la conclusion.

b) Estimation de Γ_2 . Nous remarquons d'abord que, si f est une constante, $CD_\alpha f = D_\alpha Cf = 0$. Il nous suffit donc de regarder le cas où f est d'ordre $\geqq 1$. Nous partons de la formule (7), pour faire un calcul formel :

$$P_s D_\alpha f = D_\alpha P_s f + D_\alpha (e^{s/2}-1) P_s f$$

Nous avons $Q_t f = \int \mu_t(ds) P_s f$, où (μ_t) est le semi-groupe stable d'ordre 1/2 sur $\mathbb{R}_+$. Donc en intégrant par rapport à $\mu_t(ds)$

$$Q_t D_\alpha f = D_\alpha Q_t f + D_\alpha H_t f \qquad H_t = \int \mu_t(ds)(e^{s/2}-1) P_s$$

Du point de vue des multiplicateurs d'Hermite, P_s est associé à la suite $\phi_s(k) = e^{-sk/2}$ $(k \geqq 1)$, $(e^{s/2}-1)P_s$ à $e^{-s(k-1)/2} - e^{-sk/2}$, et H_t (comme $\int \mu_t(ds) e^{-ps} = e^{-t\sqrt{p}}$) à la suite $e^{-t\sqrt{(k-1)/2}} - e^{-t\sqrt{k/2}}$ $(k \geqq 1$; 0 pour k=0). Dérivons maintenant pour t=0 :

$$CD_\alpha f = D_\alpha Cf + D_\alpha Kf \quad , \text{ K correspondant à la suite } \sqrt{k/2} - \sqrt{(k-1)/2}$$

ainsi $Kf = (T-I)Cf$, T étant l'opérateur de multiplicateur $\sqrt{1-1/k}$ mentionné dans les dernières lignes de la section 3. Il transforme les polynômes en polynômes (comme tous les opérateurs donnés par des multiplicateurs d'Hermite), et nous avons vu à la fin de la section 3 que T est borné sur les L^p, d'où le résultat désiré.

Toutefois, il reste à justifier le calcul ci-dessus. Pour cela, nous nous plaçons dans $\mathcal{L}^2$: comme f est supposée d'ordre $\geqq 1$, $\|P_s f\|_2 \leqq e^{-s/2}\|f\|_2$, ce qui justifie l'intégration par rapport à $\mu_t(ds)$. Après cela, comme f est un polynôme, on n'a plus que des sommes finies, et la dérivation en t se justifie de manière évidente.

REMARQUES. 1) En fait, on peut aboutir à des équivalences de normes : la norme $\Sigma_{i \leq k} \|C^i f\|_p$ est équivalente à la norme $\Sigma_{i \leq k} \|\sqrt{\Gamma_k(f,f)}\|_p$. Tout au moins, cela est vrai pour k=0,1,2 (j'ai eu la paresse de regarder au delà). Voici l'esquisse de la démonstration pour k=2. Si l'on sait majorer la norme dans $\mathcal{L}^p$ de $\sqrt{\Gamma_k(f,f)}$ pour k=0,1,2, où f est un polynôme, on sait majorer les normes dans $\mathcal{L}^p$ de f (trivial) et Cf (th.2). Reste

C^2f . La démonstration du th.3, où toutes les étapes sont des équivalences, nous permet de majorer la norme de $(\Sigma_n(CD_{\alpha_n}f)^2\ )^{1/2}$, alors que c'est $(\Sigma_n\ D_{\alpha_n}Cf)^2)^{1/2} = \sqrt{\Gamma(Cf,Cf)}$ qu'il nous faudrait. Nous écrivons alors

$$D_\alpha P_s f = P_s D_\alpha f + (e^{-s/2}-1)P_s D_\alpha f \quad , \text{ etc.}$$

en imitant la démonstration précédente, pour aboutir à

$$D_\alpha Cf \ = CD_\alpha f - UD_\alpha f \ = SCD_\alpha f$$

où U est l'opérateur de multiplicateur $(\sqrt{(k+1)/2} - \sqrt{k/2})$, et S est l'opérateur de multiplicateur $\sqrt{1+1/k}$, borné dans $\mathcal{L}^p$ pour la même raison que T. On sait alors que $S\otimes I$ est un opérateur borné de $\mathcal{L}^p\otimes\ell^2=\mathcal{L}^p(\ell^2)$ dans lui même (Stein[6] p. 115, 7.12). Notre résultat était une majoration en norme de la suite $(CD_{\alpha_n}f)_n$ dans $\mathcal{L}^p(\ell^2)$, en appliquant S nous savons majorer la norme de la suite $(SCD_{\alpha_n}f)_n = (D_{\alpha_n}Cf)$, et nous avons le résultat cherché.

REMARQUES. 2) La forme affaiblie du théorème nous suffit à voir que $\Gamma_k(f,f)$ est <u>fini</u> pour tout polynôme, ce qui nous permet de définir $\Gamma_k(f,g)$ par polarisation. Le théorème suivant va entraîner qu'en fait $\Gamma_k(f,f)$ est un polynôme (et ne dépend pas de la base utilisée).

THEOREME 4. Soit f un polynôme. Nous avons

$$\Gamma_{k+1}(f,f) = L\Gamma_k(f,f)-2\Gamma_k(f,Lf)-k\Gamma_k(f,f) \tag{15}$$

DEMONSTRATION. Par définition de Γ, nous avons

$$\begin{aligned} L((D_mf)^2 &= 2D_mf\ LD_mf + \Gamma(D_mf,D_mf) \\ &= 2D_mf\ D_mLf + k(D_mf)^2 + \Gamma(D_mf,D_mf) \quad (14) \end{aligned}$$

Sommons sur un ensemble fini $I\subset\mathbb{N}^k$, et passons à la limite. $\Sigma_{m\in I}(D_mf)^2$ tend en croissant vers $\Gamma_k(f,f)$, qui appartient à $\mathcal{L}^p$ pour tout p d'après le théorème précédent (la forme affaiblie suffit), donc la convergence a en fait lieu dans $\mathcal{L}^p$. Comme L est un opérateur fermé, il nous suffit de montrer que le côté droit aussi converge dans $\mathcal{L}^p$. Or $k\Sigma(D_mf)^2$ converge dans $\mathcal{L}^p$ vers $k\Gamma_k(f,f)$, $\Sigma_{m\in I}\ D_mf\ D_mLf$ converge vers $\Gamma_k(f,Lf)$ (polariser pour se ramener à la convergence monotone). Enfin, $\Sigma_I\ \Gamma(D_mf,D_mf) = \Sigma_{m\in I,n}\ (D_{\alpha_n}D_mf)^2$ tend en croissant vers $\Gamma_{k+1}(f,f)\in\mathcal{L}^p$.

[Note : le cas trivial p=1, correspondant aux normes $\|\ \|_{2,k}$, nous aurait suffi].

Avec cela, nous pouvons prouver que les fonctions-test forment une algèbre, propriété qui était énoncée dans [4] comme une conjecture. Nous montrons un peu mieux (Il y aurait lieu d'étudier aussi les indices impairs, mais cela semble difficile - peut être une méthode d'interpolation marcherait elle ? Il faudrait aussi établir une inégalité du type Hölder, avec des exposants différents).

THEOREME 5. Soient f,g deux éléments de $W_{2p,2k}$. Alors leur produit fg appartient à $W_{p,2k}$.

DEMONSTRATION. Cela peut être réduit à un problème sur des polynômes : montrer que si $\|f\|_{2p,2k} \leqq 1$, $\|g\|_{2p,2k} \leqq 1$, on a $\|fg\|_{p,2k} \leqq c_{p,k}$. On se ramène au cas où f=g, et on raisonne par récurrence, avec l'hypothèse

$$\text{si } \|f\|_{2p,2k} \leqq 1 \text{ , alors pour tout } i \leqq k \quad \|\Gamma_i(f,f)\|_{p,2k-2i} \leqq c_{p,k,i}$$

qui est triviale pour k=0 (pour i=0, elle signifie que $f^2 \in W_{p,2k}$, la conclusion du théorème). Montrons qu'elle passe bien du rang k au rang k+1 . Supposons $\|f\|_{2p,2k+2} \leqq 1$. Les nouvelles inégalités à établir sont

$$\|\Gamma_{k+1}(f,f)\|_{p,0} \leqq c_{p,k+1,0}$$

qui est exactement le théorème 3, et aussi

$$\|L\Gamma_i(f,f)\|_{p,k-i} \leqq c_{p,k+1,i}$$

qui résulte de l'hypothèse de récurrence et du th.4 : $L\Gamma_i(f,f) = 2\Gamma_i(f,Lf) + i\Gamma_i(f,f) + \Gamma_{i+1}(f,f)$.

7. REMARQUE FINALE

Soit μ une mesure gaussienne sur un << bon >> e.l.c. E. Il existe alors une suite de formes linéaires continues u_n qui engendre la tribu borélienne de E. Par le procédé d'orthonormalisation usuel, nous pouvons supposer que cette suite est orthonormale pour la forme quadratique q associée à μ (nous supposerons pour simplifier que le support de μ est E tout entier, et que E est de dimension infinie). Soit alors u l'application $(u_n)_n$ de E dans $\mathbb{R}^{\mathbb{N}}$; elle est mesurable, l'image de μ est la mesure gaussienne standard sur $\mathbb{R}^{\mathbb{N}}$, que nous désignerons par $\overline{\mu}$. Nous noterons $\overline{P}_t$, $\overline{\mathcal{L}}^p$, etc, tous les éléments de la théorie relatifs à $\overline{\mu}$. L'application qui à une fonction f sur $\mathbb{R}^{\mathbb{N}}$ associe $f\circ u$ sur E définit un isomorphisme des $\overline{\mathcal{L}}^p$ sur les $\mathcal{L}^p$, qui transforme les polynômes en polynômes, transforme $\overline{P}_t f$ en $P_t(f\circ u)$ sur E, etc. On en déduit que tous les résultats établis pour la mesure brownienne passent à la mesure gaussienne standard $\overline{\mu}$, et de là à toutes les mesures μ << raisonnables >>.

REFERENCES

[1] T.HIDA. Brownian motion. Springer, 1980.

[2] L. GROSS. Logarithmic Sobolev inequalities. Amer. J. Math. 97, 1976, p. 1061-1083.

[3] G.F. FEISSNER. Hypercontractive semigroups and Sobolev's inequality. Trans. Amer. M. Soc. 210, 1975, p. 51-62.

$[4]_a$, $[4]_b$ P.A. MEYER. Note sur le processus d'Ornstein-Uhlenbeck. Inégalités de Sobolev logarithmiques (avec D. BAKRY). Sém. Prob. XVI, Lecture Notes in M. 1982, Springer.

$[5]_a$, $[5]_b$. P.A. MEYER. Démonstration probabiliste de certaines inégalités de Littlewood-Paley. Sém. Prob. X, p. 125-183. Lecture Notes in M. 511, Springer 1976, et (corrigé) : Retour sur la théorie de Littlewood-Paley, Sém. Prob. XV, Lecture Notes 850, Springer 1981.

[6] E.M. STEIN. Singular integrals and differentiability properties of functions. Princeton Math. Series n° 30, 1970.

[7] E.M. STEIN. Topics in harmonic analysis related to the Littlewood-Paley theory. Princeton Ann. Math. Studies 63, 1970.

APPENDICE

Nous allons achever ici la démonstration du théorème 3. Elle va nous entraîner assez loin du texte principal.

Rappelons qu'il s'agit d'évaluer un commutateur du type

$$CD_m f = D_m Cf + D_m K_i f$$

où D_m est un opérateur de dérivation d'ordre i. En fait, si f est un polynôme appartenant à la somme des chaos de Wiener d'ordre 0,1,...i-1, on a $CD_m f = D_m Cf = 0$. Donc il suffit de traiter le cas où f est d'ordre $\geqq i$. Reprenant alors le raisonnement du texte (estimation de Γ_2, après la formule (14)), et tenant compte du fait que $D_m P_s = e^{is/2} P_s D_m$, nous trouvons que $K_i = (T_i - I)C$, où T_i est associé au multiplicateur

$$\phi_i(k) = 0 \text{ pour } k \leqq i \ , \quad \phi_i(k) = \sqrt{1 - i/k} \text{ pour } k > i$$

[Comme dans le texte principal, on doit justifier le calcul formel en raisonnant dans $\mathcal{L}^2$: si f est d'ordre $\geqq i$, $\|P_s f\|_2$ est majorée par une exponentielle $ce^{-is/2}$, ce qui justifie l'intégration par rapport à $\mu_t(ds)$, et la dérivation en t parce que f est un polynôme].

<u>Tout revient donc à vérifier que</u> T_i <u>est borné dans</u> $\mathcal{L}^p$.

Désignons par Θ_i l'espace des fonctions d'ordre $\geqq i$, noyau du projecteur $\Sigma_{k<i} J_k$ (donc fermé dans $\mathcal{L}^p$), image du projecteur $\Pi_i = \Sigma_{k \geqq i} J_k$. Nous allons établir :

LEMME. Pour tout p et tout i, il existe une norme $\| \ \|_{p,i}$ sur Θ_i , équivalente sur Θ_i à la norme $\| \ \|_p$, et pour laquelle l'opérateur $iR/2$ sur Θ_i est une contraction.

Nous aurons alors l'amusant résultat suivant, qui contient comme cas particulier ($h(x) = \sqrt{1 - ix}$) la propriété que nous cherchons :

THEOREME 5. Soit $h(x) = \Sigma a_n x^n$ une série de Taylor de rayon de convergence ρ, et soit $i > 1/\rho$. L'opérateur associé à la suite

$$\phi(k) = 0 \text{ pour } k < i \ , \quad \phi(k) = h(1/k) \text{ pour } k \geqq i$$

est borné dans $\mathcal{L}^p$, $1 < p < \infty$.

DEMONSTRATION. On a $\| R/2 \|_{p,i} \leqq 1/i < \rho$, donc l'opérateur $U=h(R/2)$ est bien défini et borné sur Θ_i , pour la norme $\| \ \|_{p,i}$ ou la norme équivalente $\| \ \|_p$. Quant à l'opérateur cherché, c'est le composé $U\Pi_i$. Bien entendu , la condition sur les i premiers $\phi(k)$ est inessentielle .

DEMONSTRATION DU LEMME. Nous allons nous placer dans le cas i=2. Il n'y a pas de modification importante aux ordres supérieurs.

Soit f une fonction d'ordre $\geqq 2$. Comme f est d'ordre $\geqq 1$, son espérance est nulle , et f admet une représentation

$$f = \int_0^\infty u_s dB_s$$

où (u_s) est prévisible. Pour le moment, faisons simplement des calculs formels. Comme f est d'ordre $\geqq 2$, u_s a lui même une espérance nulle, donc s'écrit $\int_0^s u_{sr} dB_r$, et l'on a

$$f = \int_0^\infty dB_s \int_0^s u_{sr} dB_r \quad , \quad (\text{ on convient que } u_{sr}=0 \text{ pour } r \geqq s)$$

$$P_t f = e^{-t/2} \int_0^\infty dB_s \; P_t \int_0^s u_{sr} dB_r = e^{-t} \int_0^\infty dB_s \int_0^s P_t u_{sr} dB_r$$

(cf. $[4]_a$, formule (20)). <u>Nous prendrons</u>

(16) $$\| f \|_p = \| (\iint u_{sr}^2 dr ds)^{1/2} \|_p$$

de sorte que, (P_t) étant un noyau markovien symétrique ($[4]_a$, (18))

$$\| P_t f \|_p = e^{-t} \| (\int (P_t u_{rs})^2 dr ds)^{1/2} \|_p \leqq e^{-t} \| f \|_p$$

d'où l'on tire que $\| Rf \|_p \leqq \| f \|_p$, et $\| R/2 \|_p \leqq 1/2$.

Le point essentiel est maintenant de voir que <u>la norme $\| f \|_p$ est équivalente à</u> $\| f \|_p$. En voici le principe. Nous écrivons d'abord les inégalités de Burkholder, qui nous disent que la norme $\| f \|_p$ est équivalente à $\| (\int_0^\infty u_s^2 ds)^{1/2} \|_p$. Or ceci peut être interprété comme une norme dans un espace $\mathcal{L}^p(H)$, où H est l'espace de Hilbert $\mathcal{L}^2(\mathbb{R}_+, ds)$: celle de la variable aléatoire

$$U(w) = (s \mapsto u_s(w)) \in H \text{ p.s.}$$

Introduisons la martingale hilbertienne $U_r = E[U | \mathcal{F}_r]$, et son processus croissant scalaire $\langle U,U \rangle$; formellement, comme $u_s = \int_0^\infty u_{sr} dB_r$

$$U_r = (s \mapsto \int_0^r u_{sr} dB_r)$$

$$d\langle U,U \rangle_r = (\int_0^\infty u_{sr}^2 \, ds) dr$$

et le résultat cherché découle de l'équivalence de norme $\| U \|_p \sim \| \sqrt{\langle U,U \rangle_\infty} \|_p$ (inégalités de Burkholder hilbertiennes). Il faut donc seulement justifier les calculs formels ci-dessus, pour des f constituant un ensemble dense dans Θ_2 : existence de << bons >> u_{sr} mesurables par rapport au couple, appartenance de U à H, calcul de U_r et de $\langle U,U \rangle_r$.

On sait que les fonctions $g(w) = \exp(\{\alpha,w\} - \frac{1}{2}q(\alpha))$, $\alpha \in E'$ (cf. la section 3) forment un ensemble total dans tout $\mathcal{L}^p$ (on pourrait utiliser les polynômes trigonométriques, qui en sont la version complexe). Donc nous pouvons tester la validité des calculs avec des fonctions f de la forme $g-J_0g-J_1g$, pour lesquels on a le calcul explicite suivant, en posant $g_t = E[g|\mathcal{F}_t]$: on sait bien que

$$\begin{aligned} g_t &= 1+\int_0^t \alpha_s g_s dB_s \\ &= 1 + \int_0^t \alpha_s dB_s + \int_0^t \alpha_s(g_s-1)dB_s \\ &= 1 + \int_0^t \alpha_s dB_s + \int_0^t dB_s \int_0^s \alpha_s\alpha_r g_r dB_r \end{aligned}$$

d'où

$$f = \int_0^\infty \alpha_s(g_s-1)dB_s \ , \ u_s = \alpha_s(g_s-1) \ , \ u_{sr} = \alpha_s\alpha_r g_r I_{\{r<s\}}$$

sans qu'aucun problème de mesurabilité se pose. Ensuite

$$U = (\ s \mapsto \alpha_s(g_s-1)\ )\ (\ \in H, \text{ car } \int_0^\infty \alpha_s^2 ds < \infty \text{ et } g^* < \infty \text{ p.s. })$$

$$U_r = (\ s \mapsto \alpha_s(g_{s\wedge r}-1))$$

Soit (e_n) une base orthonormale de H, et U_r^n la martingale réelle $\langle e_n, U_r\rangle_H$. On a pour $r<r'$ $U_{r'}^n - U_r^n = \int_r^{r'} \alpha_s e_n(s)(g_s-g_r)ds + \int_{r'}^\infty (g_{r'}-g_r)\alpha_s e_n(s)ds$, d'où sans peine $dU_r^n = p_r^n dg_r$, avec $p_r^n = \int_r^\infty \alpha_s e_n(s)ds$, et $d\langle U^n,U^n\rangle_r = (p_r^n)^2 d\langle g,g\rangle_r = (p_r^n)^2\alpha_r^2 g_r^2 dr$. Sommons sur n : $\Sigma_n(p_r^n)^2 = \int_r^\infty \alpha_s^2 ds$, donc $\langle U,U\rangle_\infty = \int_0^\infty \alpha_r^2 g_r^2 dr \int_r^\infty \alpha_s^2 ds$ <u>est bien égal</u> à $\int_0^\infty u_{sr}^2 dsdr$. En fait, cela n'est pas tout à fait suffisant, car il faut étendre ce résultat aux combinaisons linéaires de fonctions f du type précédent, ce qui revient à calculer $\langle U,U'\rangle_\infty$ pour les martingales associées à deux fonctions f et f'. Nous laisserons cela au lecteur.

Terminons en esquissant la récurrence, sur le passage de l'ordre 2 à l'ordre 3 : une fonction f d'ordre ≥ 3 s'écrira de même

$$f = \int_0^\infty u_t dB_t = \int_{t>s} u_{ts} dB_t dB_s = \int_{t>s>r} u_{tsr} dB_t dB_s dB_r$$

et nous prendrons naturellement

$$[\![f]\!]_p = \|(\int u_{tsr}^2 dtdsdr)^{1/2}\|_p$$

Pour montrer l'équivalence de cette norme avec celle de $\mathcal{L}^p$, on utilise l'équivalence déjà établie

$$\|f\|_p \sim \|(\int u_{ts}^2 dtds)^{1/2}\|_p$$

et on interprète cela comme la norme de U dans $\mathcal{L}^p(H)$, H étant cette fois $\mathcal{L}^2(\mathbb{R}_+^2,\ dtds)$ et U la fonction $u_{..}(w)$. Puis on applique à nouveau les inégalités de Burkholder hilbertiennes.

ON A WAVE EQUATION ASSOCIATED WITH PREDICTION ERRORS FOR A STATIONARY GAUSSIAN PROCESS

Yasunori Okabe

Department of Mathematics
University of Tokyo
Hongo, Tokyo, 113 Japan

§1. Introduction

Let $\mathbf{X} = (X(t); t \in \mathbb{R})$ be a real stationary mean continuous Gaussian process with expectation zero. The purpose in this paper is to derive a wave equation for the prediction error for the problem of prediction given bounded interval for $\mathbf{X}$. For that purpose we restrict in this paper to the case $\mathbf{X}$ is a stationary solution of $[\alpha,\beta,\gamma]$-Langevin equation introduced in [4]. We follow the notation and terminology in [4].

Let us give a triple $[\alpha,\beta,\gamma]$ satisfying the conditions:

(1.1) $\alpha > 0$, $\beta \in \mathbb{R}$ and γ is a bounded signed measure on $(-\infty,0)$.

Definition 1.1. We say that $\mathbf{X}$ is a stationary solution of $[\alpha,\beta,\gamma]$-Langevin equation if (i) $\mathbf{X}$ has continuous paths

(ii) there exists a one-dimensional Brownian motion $(B(t); t \in \mathbb{R})$ such that $\sigma(X(s); s \in (-\infty,t]) = \sigma(B(s_1)-B(s_2); s_1,s_2 \in (-\infty,t])$ for any $t \in \mathbb{R}$

(iii) with probability one, $(X(t); t \in \mathbb{R})$ and $(B(t); t \in \mathbb{R})$ satisfy

(1.2) $X(t)-X(s) = -\int_s^t (\beta X(u) + \int_{(-\infty,0)} X(u+\tau)\gamma(d\tau))du + \alpha(B(t)-B(s))$

for any $s,t \in \mathbb{R}, s < t$.

We call a stochastic differential equation (1.2) (or its differential form) $[\alpha,\beta,\gamma]$-Langevin equation. We note that γ in (1.2) is different up to sign from γ in the original definition of $[\alpha,\beta,\gamma]$-Langevin equation in [4]. In the sequel we treat the case $\mathbf{X}$ is a stationary solution of $[\alpha,\beta,\gamma]$-Langevin equation for some triple $[\alpha,\beta,\gamma]$. We note that the triple $[\alpha,\beta,\gamma]$ is uniquely determined ([4]).

In order to state main theorem, we shall prepare some notation.

For any $a,b \in \mathbf{R}, a < b$, we define σ-fields $\mathbf{F}(a,b)$ and $\mathbf{F}(a)$ by

(1.3) $\mathbf{F}(a,b) = \sigma(X(s); s \in [a,b])$ and $\mathbf{F}(a) = \sigma(X(a))$

and then, for $b > a > 0$, two prediction errors $D(a,b)$ and $D_M(a,b)$ by

(1.4) $D(a,b) = \|X(b)-E(X(b)|\mathbf{F}(-a,a))\|^2$

(1.5) $D_M(a,b) = \|E(X(b)|\mathbf{F}(-a,a))-E(X(b)|\mathbf{F}(a))\|^2.$

We note that $D_M = 0$ if and only if $\mathbf{X}$ has a simple Markovian property and so D_M is a prediction error indicating the gap from Markovian property of $\mathbf{X}$. Then we shall prove in §7 the following

Theorem 7.2. We suppose that γ in (1.1) has a continuous density $\gamma(\cdot)$ with $\int_{-\infty}^{0}(1+\sqrt{|s|})|\gamma(s)|ds < \infty$. Then $D-D_M$ satisfies the following wave equation:

$$\left(\frac{\partial^2}{\partial b^2} - \frac{\partial^2}{\partial a^2}\right)(D(a,b) - D_M(a,b)) = 0 \quad \text{for} \quad 0 < a < b < \infty.$$

We state the content of this paper. In §2 we shall prepare a general theory for a stationary solution for $[\alpha,\beta,\gamma]$-Langevin equation, modifying the results in [4]. By taking the same procedure as in [3], we shall in §3 construct innovation processes associated with bounded interval. In §4 we shall obtain some representation theorems for predictors given bounded intervals as Wiener integrals with respect to innovation processes. The representation kernels in the above Wiener integrals are called forward and backward prediction kernels. We shall in §5 derive an integro-differential equation of Riccati type for the forward prediction kernel. By using this equation we shall in §6 obtain some relation between prediction kernels and investigate their regularity. After the above preparation we shall in §7 prove main Theorem 7.2 in this paper.

§2. General theory for stationary solution for $[\alpha,\beta,\gamma]$-Langevin equation

Let $\mathbf{X}$ be a stationary solution for $[\alpha,\beta,\gamma]$-Langevin equation with triple $[\alpha,\beta,\gamma]$ satisfying (1.1). It then follows from (ii) in Definition (1.1) that $\mathbf{X}$ is purely non-deterministic and so $\mathbf{X}$ has a spectral density Δ of Hardy class. We denote by h the outer function of Δ:

(2.1) $$h(\zeta) = \exp\left(\frac{1}{2\pi i}\int_{\mathbf{R}}\frac{1+\lambda\zeta}{\lambda-\zeta}\,\frac{\log\Delta(\lambda)}{1+\lambda^2}d\lambda\right) \qquad (\zeta \in \mathbf{C}^+)$$

and by E the Fourie transform of h. Then, similarly as in Theorem 3.1 in [4] we see

Proposition 2.1.

(2.2) $$X(t) = \frac{1}{\sqrt{2\pi}}\int_{-\infty}^{t} E(t-s)dB(s) \qquad (t \in \mathbb{R})$$

(2.3) $$h(\zeta) = \frac{\alpha}{\sqrt{2\pi}} \frac{1}{\beta+\hat{\gamma}(\zeta)-i\zeta} \qquad (\zeta \in \mathbb{C}^+)$$

We find from Proposition 2.1 that $\mathbf{X}$ is a unique stationary solution of $[\alpha,\beta,\gamma]$-Langevin equation. This is a canonical representation for $\mathbf{X}$. As a backward canonical representation for $\mathbf{X}$, we find from (2.3)([3]) that

Proposition 2.2. (i) There exists a one-dimensional Brownian motion $(B_-(t);t \in \mathbb{R})$ such that for any $t \in \mathbb{R}$

(2.4) $$\sigma(X(s);s \in [t,\infty)) = \sigma(B_-(s_1) - B_-(s_2);s_1,s_2 \in [t,\infty)),$$

(2.5) $$X(t) = \frac{1}{\sqrt{2\pi}}\int_{t}^{\infty} E(s-t)dB_-(s).$$

(ii) $\mathbf{X}$ satisfies the following stochastic differential equation:

(2.6) $$X(s)-X(t) = -\int_{s}^{t} (\beta X(u)+\int_{(-\infty,0)} X(u-\tau)\gamma(d\tau))du+\alpha(B_-(t)-B_-(s))$$

for any $s,t \in \mathbb{R}, s < t$.

By modifying the proof in Proposition 3.1 in [4] we see

Proposition 2.3. (i) Reh is bounded and integrable in $\mathbb{R}$.

(ii) $E(|t|) = 2\int_{\mathbb{R}} e^{-it\xi}\mathrm{Reh}(\xi)d\xi \quad (t \in \mathbb{R})$.

(iii) E is bounded, continuous on $[0,\infty)$ and vanishes at infinity.

Similarly as in Proposition 3.2 in [4] we have

Proposition 2.4.

(i) $E(t) = \sqrt{2\pi}\alpha-\int_{0}^{t}(\beta E(s)+\int_{[-s,0)} E(s+\tau)\gamma(d\tau))ds \qquad$ for any $t \in (0,\infty)$.

(ii) $E(0+) = \sqrt{2\pi}\alpha$.

(iii) $(D^+E)(t) = -\beta E(t)-\int_{[-t,0)} E(t+\tau)\gamma(d\tau)$,

where $(D^+E)(t)$ denotes the right differential coefficient at t of E.

(iv) $(D^+E)(0+) = -\beta E(0+) = -\sqrt{2\pi}\alpha\cdot\beta$.

Furthermore, denoting by R the covariance function of $\mathbf{X}$, we find similarly as in Proposition 3.4 in [4] that

Proposition 2.5.

(i) $R(t) = R(0)-\int_0^t(\beta R(s)+\int_{-\infty}^0 R(s+\tau)\gamma(d\tau))ds$ for any $t \in (0,\infty)$.

(ii) $R'(t) = -\beta R(t)-\int_{-\infty}^0 R(t+\tau)\gamma(d\tau)$ for any $t \in (0,\infty)$.

(iii) $R'(0+) = -\frac{\alpha^2}{2}$

§3. Innovation processes ν_a^+ and ν_a^- $(a \in \mathbf{R})$

For any $a \in \mathbf{R}$ we define a reference family $(\mathbf{F}_a^+(t);t \in [0,\infty))$ by

(3.1) $\mathbf{F}_a^+(t) = \mathbf{F}(a)$ for $t=0$, $\mathbf{F}(a,a+t)$ for $t \in (0,\infty)$.

Proposition 3.1. There exists a one-dimensional Brownian motion $\nu_a^+ = (\nu_a^+(t);t \in [0,\infty))$ such that (i) $\nu_a^+(0) = 0$,

(ii) $\nu_a^+ \perp\!\!\!\perp X(a)$,

(iii) $\mathbf{F}_a^+(t) = \sigma(X(a))\vee\sigma(\nu_a^+(s);s \in [0,t])$ for any $t \in [0,\infty)$,

(iv) $X(t+a)-X(a) = -\int_0^t(\beta X(s+a)+\int_{-\infty}^0 E(X(s+a+\tau)\,|\,\mathbf{F}_a^+(s))\gamma(d\tau))ds+\alpha\nu_a^+(t)$

for any $t \in [0,\infty)$.

Proof. We define three stochastic processes $(Z(t);t \in \mathbf{R})$, $(W(t);t \in [0,\infty))$ and $(\Phi(t);t \in [0,\infty))$ by

(3.2) $Z(t) = \alpha^{-1}(X(t+a)-E(X(t+a)\,|\,\mathbf{F}(a)))$,

(3.3) $W(t) = B(t+a)-B(a)$,

(3.4) $\Phi(t) = -(\beta Z(t)+\int_{-\infty}^0 Z(t+\tau)\gamma(d\tau))$.

It then follows from Definition 1.1 that

(3.5) $Z(t) = \int_0^t \Phi(s)ds+W(t)$ for any $t \in [0,\infty)$,

(3.6) $(W(t);t \in [0,\infty))$ is a one-dimensional Brownian motion $(W(0)=0)$,

(3.7) $\Phi(t) = \Phi(t,\omega)$ is (t,ω)-measurable such that $\int_0^t E(|\Phi(s)|^2)ds < \infty$ for any $t \in (0,\infty)$,

(3.8) $\sigma(\Phi(s),W(s);s\ [0,t]) \perp\!\!\!\perp \sigma(W(u)-W(v);u,v \in [t,\infty))$ for any $t \in (0,\infty)$.

Therefore it follows from [1] and [2] that the process ν_a^+ defined by

(3.9) $\nu_a^+(t) = Z(t)-\int_0^t E(\Phi(s)\,|\,\mathcal{F}(s))ds$

is a one-dimensional Brownian motion satisfying the following condition

(3.10) $\mathcal{F}(s) \sigma(Z(s); s \in [0,t]) = \sigma(\nu_a^+(s); s \in [0,t])$ for any $t \in [0,\infty)$.

Then we find from (3.1),(3.2),(3.4),(3.5),(3.9) and (3.10) that $\boldsymbol{\nu}_a^+$ is a desired process. (Q.E.D)

Similarly, defining a reference family $(\mathbb{F}_a^-(t); t \in [0,\infty))$ by

(3.11) $\mathbb{F}_a^-(t) = \mathbb{F}(a)$ for $t=0$, $\mathbb{F}(a-t,a)$ for $t \in (0,\infty)$,

we find from Proposition 2.2 that

Proposition 3.2. There exists a one-dimensional Brownian motion $\boldsymbol{\nu}_a^- = (\nu_a^-(t); t \in [0,\infty))$ such that (i) $\nu_a^-(0) = 0$,

(ii) $\boldsymbol{\nu}_a^- \perp\!\!\!\perp X(a)$,

(iii) $\mathbb{F}_a^-(t) = \sigma(X(a)) \vee \sigma(\nu_a^-(s); s \in [0,t])$ for any $t \in [0,\infty)$,

(iv) $X(a-t)-X(a) = -\int_0^t (\beta X(a-s)+\int_{-\infty}^0 E(X(a-s-\tau)|\mathbb{F}_a^-(s))\gamma(d\tau))ds+\alpha\nu_a^-(t)$

for any $t \in [0,\infty)$.

§4. Prediction formula

We define a stochastic process $(Y_-(t); t \in \mathbb{R})$ by

(4.1) $$Y_-(t) = \int_{(-\infty,0)} X(t+\tau)\gamma(d\tau).$$

It then follows from (1.2) and Proposition 3.1 (iv) that

Lemma 4.1. For any $a \in \mathbb{R}$ and $t \in (0,\infty)$

$$\nu_a^+(t) = -\alpha^{-1}\int_0^t (Y_-(s+a)-E(Y_-(s+a)|\mathbb{F}_a^+(s)))ds+B(t+a)-B(a).$$

We define a function $P(t,s)\ (0 \leq s \leq t < \infty)$ by

(4.2) $$P(t,s) = -\alpha^{-1}E(X(t)(Y_-(s)-E(Y_-(s)|\mathbb{F}_0^+(s))))+\sqrt{2\pi}^{-1}\Xi(t-s).$$

Then we see from (2.2),(4.1) and Lemma 4.1 that

Lemma 4.2. For any $a \in \mathbb{R}$ and $0 < s < t < \infty$,

$$P(t,s) = \frac{\partial}{\partial s} E(X(a+t)\nu_a^+(s)).$$

We denote by $\Xi(t)$ the normarized covariance function of $\mathbf{X}$:

(4.3) $$\Xi(t) = R(t)R(0)^{-1}.$$

By virtue of Proposition 3.1 (i)(ii)(iii), we can show ([3])

Theorem 4.1. For any $a \in \mathbb{R}$ and $t \in (0,\infty)$,

$$X(a+t) = \Xi(t)X(a)+\int_0^t P(t,s)d\nu_a^+(s).$$

In the same way, we define a stochastic process $(Y_+(t);t\in\mathbf{R})$ by

(4.4) $$Y_+(t) = \int_{(-\infty,0)} X(t-\tau)\gamma(d\tau).$$

Then we see from (2.5) and Proposition 3.2 (iv) that

Lemma 4.3. For any $a\in\mathbf{R}$ and $t\in(0,\infty)$,

$$\nu_a^-(t) = -\alpha^{-1}\int_0^t (Y_+(a-s)-E(Y_+(a-s)\,|\,\mathbf{F}_a^-(s)))ds+B_-(a)-B_-(a-t).$$

Noting that $\mathbf{X}$ is one-dimensional stationary process, we can show by (4.2) and Lemma 4.3 that

Lemma 4.4. For any $a\in\mathbf{R}$ and $0 < s < t < \infty$,

$$P(t,s) = \frac{\partial}{\partial s} E(X(a-t)\nu_a^-(s))$$

In the same way as in Theorem 4.1 we can show by Proposition 3.2 (i)(ii)(iii) that

Theorem 4.2. For any $t\in\mathbf{R}$ and $t\in(0,\infty)$,

$$X(a-t) = \Xi(t)X(a)+\int_0^t P(t,s)d\nu_a^-(s).$$

Therefore, it follows from Propositions 3.1 (i)(ii)(iii), 3.2 (i)(ii)(iii), Theorems 4.1 and 4.2 that

Theorem 4.3. (prediction formula (1)) For any $a\in\mathbf{R}$ and $0<s<t<\infty$,

(i) $$E(X(a+t)\,|\,\mathbf{F}_a^+(s)) = \Xi(t)X(a)+\int_0^s P(t,u)d\nu_a^+(u),$$

(ii) $$E(X(a-t)\,|\,\mathbf{F}_a^-(s)) = \Xi(t)X(a)+\int_0^s P(t,u)d\nu_a^-(u).$$

Next we define a function $Q(t,s)\,(0\ s,t)$ by

(4.5) $$Q(t,s) = -\alpha^{-1}E(X(-t)(Y_-(s)-E(Y_-(s)\,|\,\mathbf{F}_0^+(s)).$$

Then we see from (2.4) and Lemma 4.3 that

Lemma 4.5. For any $a\in\mathbf{R}$ and $0 < s,\ t < \infty$,

$$Q(t,s) = \frac{\partial}{\partial s} E(X(a+t)\nu_a^-(s)).$$

Furthermore we can see from Definition 1.1 (ii), Lemma 4.1 and (4.5) that

Lemma 4.6. For any $a\in\mathbf{R}$ and $0 < s,\ t < \infty$,

$$Q(t,s) = \frac{\partial}{\partial s} E(X(a-t)\nu_a^+(s)).$$

Therefore, similarly as in Theorems 4.1 and 4.2, we can obtain

Theorem 4.4. (prediction formula (2)) For any $a \in \mathbb{R}$ and $0<s, t<\infty$,

(i) $$E(X(a+t)|\mathbf{F}_a^-(s)) = \Xi(t)X(a)+\int_0^s Q(t,u)d\nu_a^-(u),$$

(ii) $$E(X(a-t)|\mathbf{F}_a^+(s)) = \Xi(t)X(a)+\int_0^s Q(t,u)d\nu_a^+(u).$$

Taking account of Theorems 4.3 and 4.4, we call P(resp. Q) forward (resp. backward) prediction kernel.

§5. Integro-differential equation of Riccati type for kernel P

By Proposition 2,3, (4.1),(4.2),(4.5), Theorems 4.3(i) and 4.4(i),

Lemma 5.1. (i) P and Q are bounded continuous.

(ii) $$\sup_{t\in(0,\infty)} \int_0^t P(t,u)^2 du, \quad \sup_{t\in(0,\infty)} \int_0^\infty Q(t,u)^2 du \leqslant R(0).$$

Theorem 5.5. The kernel P satisfies the following equation:

(5.1) $$\frac{\partial}{\partial t} P(t,s) = -\beta P(t,s)-\int_{[s-t,0)} P(t+\tau,s)\gamma(d\tau)+$$
$$+\alpha^{-1}\int_s^\infty \Big(\int_{(-\infty,s-t-v]} P(s-t-\tau,v)\gamma(d\tau)\Big)\Big(\int_{(-\infty,-v)} P(-\tau',v)$$
$$\gamma(d\tau')\Big)dv \quad (0 \leqslant s < t),$$

(5.2) $$P(s,s) = \alpha.$$

Proof. We define $\tilde{P}(t,s) = P(t,s)-\sqrt{2\pi}^{-1}E(t-s)$. Then it follows from Dedinition 1.1 (ii),(iii), (4.1) and (4.2) that

(5.3) $$\tilde{P}(t,s) = -\beta\int_s^t \tilde{P}(u,s)du+\alpha^{-1}\int_s^t E(Y_-(u)(Y_-(s)-E(Y_-(s)|\mathbf{F}_0^+(s)))du.$$

Fix any $u \in (s,t)$. Then we see from (4.1) and (4.2) that

(5.4) $$E(Y_-(u)(Y_-(s)-E(Y_-(s)|\mathbf{F}_0^+(s)))$$
$$= \int_{(-\infty,-u]} E(X(u+\tau)(Y_-(s)-E(Y_-(s)|\mathbf{F}_0^+(s)))\gamma(d\tau)-\alpha^{-1}\int_{[s-u,0)}$$
$$\tilde{P}(u+\tau,s)\gamma(d\tau).$$

Furthermore, it follows from Proposition 3.2 (ii),(4.1), Theorems 4.2, 4.3 (ii) and Lemma 5.1 (ii) that for any $\tau \in (-\infty,-u)$

$$(5.5)\qquad E(X(u+\tau)(Y_-(s)-E(Y_-(s)|\mathbf{F}_0^+(s))))$$

$$= \int_{(-\infty,-s]} \left(\int_s^{(s-u-\tau)\wedge(-\tau')} P(s-u-\tau,v)P(-\tau',v)dv\right)\gamma(d\tau')$$

$$= \int_s^{s-u-\tau} P(s-u-\tau,v)\left(\int_{(-\infty,-v]} P(-\tau',v)\gamma(d\tau')\right)dv.$$

Therefore, it follows from (5.3),(5.4) and (5.5) that

$$(5.6)\qquad \tilde{P}(t,s) = -\beta\int_s^t \tilde{P}(u,s)du-\int_s^t \left(\int_{[s-u,0)}\tilde{P}(u+\tau,s)\gamma(d\tau)\right)du+$$

$$+\alpha^{-1}\int_s^t \left(\int_{(-\infty,-u]}\gamma(d\tau)\left(\int_s^{s-u-\tau}P(s-u-\tau,v)\right.\right.$$

$$\left.\left.\left(\int_{(-\infty,-v]}P(-\tau',v)\gamma(d\tau')dv\right)\right)\right)du$$

Thus, we find from Proposition 2.4 (i) and (5.6) that

$$(5.7)\qquad P(t,s) = \alpha-\beta\int_s^t P(u,s)du-\int_s^t \left(\int_{[s-u,0)}P(u+\tau,s)\gamma(d\tau)\right)du+$$

$$+\alpha^{-1}\int_s^t \left(\int_{(-\infty,-u]}\gamma(d\tau)\left(\int_s^{s-u-\tau}P(s-u-\tau,v)\right.\right.$$

$$\left.\left.\left(\int_{(-\infty,-v]}P(-\tau',v)\gamma(d\tau')\right)dv\right)\right)du.$$

Consequently we can differentiate (5.7) with respect to t to obtain Theorem 5.1. (Q.E.D)

§6. Relation between prediction kernels P and Q.

In this section we shall derive some relation between prediction kernels P and Q.

Lemma 6.1. For any $s, t \in \mathbb{R}$, $0 < s < t$,

$$P(t,s) = -\alpha^{-1}\int_{-\infty}^{-s}\left(\int_s^{-\tau}P(-\tau,u)Q(t-s,u)du\right)\gamma(d\tau)+\sqrt{2\pi}^{-1}E(t-s).$$

Proof. By (4.1) and (4.2),

$$(6.1)\quad P(t,s) = -\alpha^{-1}\int_{-\infty}^{-s}E(X(t)(X(s+\tau)-E(X(s+\tau)|\mathbf{F}_0^+(s))\gamma(d\tau)+\sqrt{2\pi}^{-1}E(t-s).$$

Therefore, noting Proposition 3.2, we find from Theorems 4.2, 4.3 (ii) and 4.4 (i) that Lemma 6.1 is proved. (Q.E.D)

Lemma 6.2. For any $s, t \in \mathbb{R}$, $0 < s < t$,

$$Q(t,s) = -\alpha^{-1}\int_s^{s+t} P(s+t,u)\left(\int_{-\infty}^{-u} P(-\tau,u)\gamma(d\tau)\right)du.$$

Proof. By (4.1) and (4.5),

(6.2) $$Q(t,s) = -\alpha^{-1}\int_{-\infty}^{-s} E((X(-t)-E(X(-t)|\mathbf{F}_{\bullet}^{+}(s)))(X(s+\tau)$$

$$-E(X(s+\tau)|\mathbf{F}_0^{+}(s))))\gamma(d\tau).$$

Therefore, we see from Theorems 4.2 and 4.3 that

$$Q(t,s) = -\alpha^{-1}\int_{-\infty}^{-s}\left(\int_s^{(-\tau)\wedge(s+t)} P(s+t,u)P(-\tau,u)\gamma(d\tau)\right)$$

$$= -\alpha^{-1}\int_s^{s+t} P(s+t,u)\left(\int_{-}^{-u} P(-\tau,u)\gamma(d\tau)\right)du. \qquad \text{(Q.E.D}$$

We define a function δ on $(0,\infty)$ by

(6.3) $$\delta(t) = \alpha^{-1}\int_{(-\infty,0)} P(-\tau,t)\gamma(d\tau).$$

Then we see from Lemma 5.1 that

Lemma 6.3. (i) δ is bounded.

(ii) $\lim_{t\to\infty} \delta(t) = 0.$

(iii) $\delta \in L^2(0,\infty).$

By using δ in (6.3) we can rewrite Theorem 5.1, Lemmas 6.1 and 6.2 as follows.

Lemma 6.4.

(i) $$\frac{\partial}{\partial t} P(t,s) = -\beta P(t,s) - \int_{[s-t,0)} P(t+\tau,s)\gamma(d\tau) +$$

$$+\int_s^{\infty}\left(\int_{(-\infty,s-t-v)} P(s-t-\tau,v)\gamma(d\tau)\right)\delta(v)dv.$$

(ii) $$Q(t,s) = -\int_s^{s+t} P(s+t,u)\delta(u)du.$$

(iii) $$P(t,s)-\sqrt{2\pi}^{-1}E(t-s) = -\int_s^{\infty}\delta(u)Q(t-s,u)du$$

In particular we see from Lemma 5.1, 6.3 (iii) and 6.4 (i) that

Lemma 6.5. $P^{(1,0)}(t,s) = \frac{\partial}{\partial t}P(t,s)$ is bounded in $\{(t,s) \in \mathbf{R};\ 0 \leqslant s < t\}$.

Lemma 6.6. If γ in (1.1) satisfies the following conditions:

(6.4) $$\gamma(\{t\}) = 0 \quad \text{for any} \quad t \in (-\infty,0),$$

(6.5) $$\int_{-\infty}^{0}\sqrt{|s|}\,\|\gamma\|(ds) < \infty,$$

then

(i) δ is bounded and continuous,

(ii) δ is integrable,

(iii) $P \in C^1$ and first derivatives of P are bounded,

(iv) $\frac{\partial}{\partial t}P(t,s)+\frac{\partial}{\partial s}P(t,s) = -\delta(s)\int_s^t P(t,u)\delta(u)du.$

Proof. (i) and (ii) follows from (6.3) and (6.4), noting Lemma 5.1. By Proposition 2.4, Lemma 6.5 and (i)(ii) in Lemma 6.6, we can differentiate both sides in Lemma 6.4 (ii)(iii) with respect to t and s and add them to get (iv). Furthermore we see from Lemmas 5.1, 6.4(i) and 6.6 (i) that $P^{(1,0)}(t,s)$ is bounded and continuous and so we find from Lemma 6.6 (iv) that $P^{(0,1)}(t,s) = \frac{\partial}{\partial s}P(t,s)$ is so. (Q.E.D)

Similarly, by Lemmas 5.1, 6.5 and 6.6 (i), we can differentiate both sides in Lemma 6.4 (i) to obtain

Lemma 6.7. If γ in (1.1) satisfies condition (6.4), then

(i) $Q \in C^1$ and first derivatives of Q are bounded,

(ii) $\frac{\partial}{\partial t}Q(t,s)-\frac{\partial}{\partial s}Q(t,s) = -P(t+s,s)\delta(s).$

Finally we shall show

Lemma 6.8. We suppose that there exists a continuous function γ such that

(6.6) $$\gamma(ds) = \gamma(s)ds$$

(6.7) $$\int_{-\infty}^{0}(1+\sqrt{|s|})|\gamma(s)|ds) < \infty.$$

Then, $\delta \in C^1$ and $P,\ Q \in C^2$.

Proof. By (6.3) and Lemma 6.4 (iii),

(6.8) $$\alpha\delta(s) = \sqrt{2\pi}^{-1}\int_s^\infty E(t-s)\gamma(-t)dt+\int_s^\infty\gamma(-t)\left(\int_s^\infty\delta(u)Q(t-s,u)du\right)dt.$$

Therefore, by Proposition 2.4, Lemmas 6.5, 6.6 (ii)(iii) and 6.7 (i), we can differentiate both sides in (6.8) to find that $\delta \in C^1$. Furthermore, by Theorem 5.1, Lemma 6.6 (i)(ii)(iii) and the fact $\delta \in C^1$, we can differentiate both sides in Lemmas 6.4 (i) and 6.6 (iv) find that

$P \in C^2$. Consequently it follows from Lemma 6.4 (i) that $Q \in C^2$.

(Q.E.D)

§7. Prediction error and its associated wave equation

By Theorems 4.1, 4.2 and 4.3, we have the following representation for prediction error.

Theorem 7.1. For any $a,b \in \mathbf{R}$, $a < b$ and $t \in (0,\infty)$,

$$\|X(b+t)-E(X(b+t)|\mathbf{F}(a,b)\|^2 = \|X(a-t)-E(X(a-t)|\mathbf{F}(a,b)\|^2 =$$

$$= \int_{b-a}^{b-a+t} P(b-a+t,s)^2 ds.$$

In particular we find from Theorems 4.1 (i) and 7.1 that

Lemma 7.1. (i) $D(a,b) = \int_{2a}^{a+b} P(a+b,u)^2 du$,

(ii) $D_M(a,b) = \int_0^{2a} Q(b-a,u)^2 du$.

Now we are in a position to prove

Theorem 7.2. We suppose that γ in (1.1) has a continuous density $\gamma(\cdot)$ with (6.7). Then $D - D_M$ satisfies the following wave equation:

$$\left(\frac{\partial^2}{\partial b^2} - \frac{\partial^2}{\partial a^2}\right) (D(a,b)-D_M(a,b)) = 0. \quad \text{for} \quad 0 < a < b < \infty.$$

Proof. We find from Lemmas 6.8 and 7.1 that D and D_M are C^2-functions. Differentiating both sides in Lemma 7.1 (i), we have

$$\text{(7.1)} \qquad \frac{\partial}{\partial b} D(a,b) = \alpha^2+2\int_{2a}^{a+b} P(a+b,u)P^{(1,0)}(a+b,u)du.$$

Furthermore, differentiating (7.1) with respect to a and b, we find

$$\text{(7.2)} \qquad \frac{\partial^2}{\partial a \partial b} D(a,b) = \frac{\partial^2}{\partial b^2} D(a,b)-4P(a+b,2a)P^{(1,0)}(a+b,2a).$$

On the other hand, noting (7.1) and differentiating both sides in Lemma 7.1 (i) with respect to a twice, we have

$$\text{(7.3)} \qquad \frac{\partial^2}{\partial a^2} D(a,b) = \frac{\partial^2}{\partial a \partial b} D(a,b)-4P(a+b,2a)(P^{(1,0)}(a+b,2a)+$$

$$+2P^{(0,1)}(a+b,2a)).$$

Therefore it follows from (7.2) and (7.3) that

$$\text{(7.4)} \quad \left(\frac{\partial^2}{\partial a^2}-\frac{\partial^2}{\partial b^2}\right)D(a,b) = -8P(a+b,2a)(P^{(1,0)}(a+b,2a)+P^{(0,1)}(a+b,2a)).$$

Next, differentiating both sides in Lemma 7.1 (ii) with respect to a and b, respectively, we find

$$\frac{\partial}{\partial a} D_M(a,b) = 2Q(b-a,2a)^2 - \frac{\partial}{\partial b} D_M(a,b). \tag{7.5}$$

Furthermore, differentiating (7.5) with respect to a and b, respectively, we see from Lemmas 6.4 (ii) and 6.7 (ii) that

$$\left(\frac{\partial^2}{\partial a^2} - \frac{\partial^2}{\partial b^2}\right) D_M(a,b) = 2\left(\frac{\partial}{\partial a} - \frac{\partial}{\partial b}\right)(Q(b-a,2a)^2) = \tag{7.6}$$

$$= 8Q(b-a,2a)(Q^{(0,1)}(b-a,2a) - Q^{(1,0)}(b-a,2a))$$

$$= -8P(a+b,2a)\delta(2a)\int_{2a}^{a+b} P(a+b,u)\delta(u)du.$$

Thus we find from Lemma 6.6 (iv), (7.4) and (7.6) that Theorem 7.2 is proved. (Q.E.D)

Reference

[1] T. Kailath, A note on least squares estimator by the innovation method, SIAM. J. Control 10(1972) 477-486.

[2] G. Kallianpur, M. Fujisaki and H. Kunita, Stochastic differential equations for the non-linear filtering problem, Osaka J. Math. 9(1972) 19-40.

[3] Y. Okabe, Innovation processes associated stationary Gaussian processes with application to the problem of prediction, Nagoya Math. J. 70(1978) 81-104.

[4] Y. Okabe, On a stochastic differential equation for a stationary Gaussian process with T-positivity and the fluctuation-dissipation theorem, J. Fac. Sci. Univ. Tokyo, Sect. IA 28(1981) 169-213.

[5] Y. Okabe, On a stochastic differential equation for a stationary Gaussian process with finite multiple Markovian property and the fluctuation-dissipation theorem, J. Fac. Sci. Univ. Tokyo, Sect. IA 28(1981) 793-804.

A STOCHASTIC DYSON SERIES EXPANSION

K.R. Parthasarathy and K.B. Sinha
Indian Statistical Institute
Delhi Centre

1. Introduction Suppose $A_1,A_2,\ldots,A_k$; $B_1,B_2,\ldots,B_k$ and V are selfadjoint operators on a separable Hilbert space $\mathcal{H}$. Consider the formal expressions

$$H_o = \frac{1}{2}\sum_j A_j^2$$
$$H_1 = \frac{1}{2}\sum_j (A_j+B_j)^2 + V \tag{1.1}$$

We may consider H_1 as a perturbation of H_o. The operators $\{B_j\}$ may be said to introduce a 'gauge perturbation' and the operator V a 'potential perturbation'. The case when $A_j = \frac{1}{i}\frac{\partial}{\partial x_j}$ and the operators B_j and V are multiplications by scalar or vector valued functions occurs frequently in quantum mechanics.

The aim of the present note is to present some formulae for the semigroups e^{-tH_o} and e^{-tH_1} when A_i, B_i, V are bounded and indicate a possible generalization for a special case of unbounded operators. The formulae will be in terms of expectations of some random operator valued evolutions. The random operator valued evolution corresponding to the the case of H_1 can be expressed as an infinite series involving the evolution corresponding to H_o and certain repeated stochastic integrals. This turns out to be a 'stochastic Dyson series'.

2. The case of bounded operators We have the well known formula

$$\frac{1}{\sqrt{2\pi}} \int e^{itx} \cdot e^{-x^2/2}\, dx = e^{-t^2/2} .$$

Replace t by $\sqrt{t}\,A$ where A is a selfadjoint operator. Then the spectral theorem yields

$$\frac{1}{\sqrt{2\pi}} \int e^{i\sqrt{t}\, x\, A}\, e^{-x^2/2}\, dx = e^{-\frac{t}{2}A^2} , \quad t > 0 ,$$

where l.h.s. is a strong Bochner integral. We can express the same equation in terms of a standard brownian motion process $w(t)$:

$$E\, e^{i\, w(t)A} = e^{-\frac{t}{2}A^2}, \quad t > 0 .$$

Put

$$U(s,t) = U(s,t,w,A) = e^{i(w(t)-w(s))A} . \tag{2.1}$$

If A is moreover bounded we can express this in terms of Ito differentials [1]:

$$\begin{aligned} dU &= U[iA\, dw - \tfrac{1}{2} A^2\, dt] \\ U(s,s) &= 1, \quad t > s \end{aligned} \tag{2.2}$$

Thus (2.1) is a solution of (2.2). Further (2.1) satisfies the following:

(i) $U(s,t)\, U(t,u) = U(s,u)$ for all $s < t < u$.

(ii) $E\, U(s,t) = \exp[-\frac{1}{2}(t-s)A^2]$.

In other words $U(s,t)$ is an evolution for each fixed brownian path and its expectation is given by (ii) above. We imitate this idea in the case of several bounded operators $A_1, A_2, \ldots, A_k$ and consider the sothcastic differential equation in k independent standard brownian motion processes $w_j(t)$, $j = 1,2,\ldots,k$; $t > 0$.

$$\begin{aligned} dU &= U[i \sum_j A_j\, dw_j - \tfrac{1}{2} \sum A_j^2\, dt] \\ U(s,s) &= 1, \quad t > s, \\ U &= U(s,t) = U(s,t,\underline{w},A_1,A_2,\ldots,A_k) \end{aligned} \tag{2.3}$$

where $\underline{w}(t) = (w_1(t), w_2(t), \ldots, w_j(t))$. A fairly routine application of Ito's theory of stochastic integrals [1] for separable Hilbert space valued nonanticipating functionals of $\underline{w}$ yields the following result:

Theorem 2.1 Let $A_1, A_2, \ldots, A_k$ be bounded selfadjoint operators on $\mathcal{H}$. Then there exists a family of unitary operators $\{U = U(s,t) = U(s,t,\underline{w},A_1,A_2,\ldots,A_k),\ t > s\}$ satisfying the following:

(i) for each fixed $s < t$, U is strongly measurable in the increments of the brownian path $\underline{w}$ during the period $[s,t]$;

(ii) for each fixed $\underline{w}$, U is strongly continuous in s,t;

(iii) for each fixed $\underline{w}$, and $s < t < u$,

$$U(s,u) = U(s,t)\, U(t,u)$$

(iv) U satisfies the strong stochastic differential equation (2.3) (for each fixed vector in $\mathcal{H}$);

(v) $E\, U(s,t) = \exp[-\frac{1}{2}(t-s) \sum_j A_j^2]$.

Proof The reader may refer to [2].

Let now $B_1, B_2, \dots, B_k$, V be bounded selfadjoint operators. Consider the stochastic differential equation:

$$d\Gamma = \Gamma dJ, \quad \Gamma = \Gamma(s,t); \; \Gamma(s,s) = 1 \; ; \tag{2.4}$$

$$dJ = i \sum_{j=1}^{k} UB_j U^{-1} dw_j - \frac{1}{2} U \sum_j B_j^2 U^{-1} dt + U(\frac{1}{2} \sum_j [B_j, A_j] + V) U^{-1} dt \tag{2.5}$$

where U is given by Theorem 2.1. A routine Picard method together with the standard theory of stochastic integration and repeated application of Ito's formula show that there exists a unique solution $\Gamma = \Gamma(s,t) = \Gamma(s,t,\underline{w},A_1,A_2,\dots,A_k;B_1,\dots,B_k;V)$ satisfying the following:

Theorem 2.2 There exists a family $\{\Gamma = \Gamma(s,t) = \Gamma(s,t,\underline{w};\, A_1,\dots,A_k;B_1,\dots,B_k;V), t>s\}$ of bounded operators satisfying the following:

(i) for each fixed $s < t$, Γ is strongly measurable in the increments of the brownian path $\underline{w}$ during the period $[s,t]$;

(ii) for each $\underline{w}, \Gamma$ is strongly continuous in s,t;

(iii) if $\tilde{U}(s,t) = \Gamma(s,t)\, U(s,t)$, then

$\tilde{U}(s,u) = \tilde{U}(s,t)\, \tilde{U}(t,u)$ for all $s < t < u$;

(iv) $d\tilde{U} = \tilde{U}\{i\Sigma(A_j+B_j)dw_j - \frac{1}{2}\Sigma(A_j+B_j)^2 dt + V\, dt\}$;

$\tilde{U}(s,s) = 1$

(v) $E\, \tilde{U}(s,t) = \exp[-(t-s)\{\frac{1}{2}(A_j+B_j)^2 + V\}]$

(vi) $\tilde{U}(s,t) = \sum_{n=0}^{\infty} D_n(s,t)\, U(s,t),$

$D_0(s,t) = 1,$

$D_n(s,t) = \int_s^t D_{n-1}(s,\tau)\, dJ(\tau), \; n = 1,2, \dots ,$

where the infinite series converges in the strong mean square sense.

Remark The expansion of the 'random evolution' $\tilde{U}(s,t)$ in terms of $D_n U$ is the stochastic Dyson series we have referred to in the title of the article. Indeed, if $B_j = 0$ for all j, we obtain the usual Dyson series with respect to the evolution $U(s,t)$ for the perturbation arising from V.

3. An example where A_j's are unbounded but B_j and V are bounded.

Let $\mathcal{H} = L_2(\mathbb{R}^k, \mathbb{C}^m)$ be the Hilbert space of all $\mathbb{C}^m$-valued square integrable maps with respect to the Lebesgue measure on $\mathbb{R}^k$. Let $A_j = i^{-1}\frac{\partial}{\partial x_j}$ be the standard selfadjoint differential operator on $\mathcal{H}$. Suppose $B_j(\underline{x})$, $j = 1,2,\ldots,k$ and $V(\underline{x})$ are d x d Hermitian matrix valued borel functions such that

$$\operatorname*{ess.sup}_{\underline{x}} \max\{||V(\underline{x})|| \ , \ ||B_j(\underline{x})|| \ \ ||\frac{\partial B_i}{\partial x_j}(\underline{x})||;\ 1 \le i,j \le k\} < \infty.$$

Let $B_1,B_2,\ldots,B_k$, V be multiplication operators by the corresponding matrix valued functions. Then

$$U(s,t,\underline{w}) = e^{i\sum_{j=1}^{k}(w_j(t)-w_j(s))A_j}$$

is well defined as a unitary operator valued evolution satisfying Theorem 2.1, where (2.3) is fulfilled on the domain of the Laplace operator.

In view of the imprimitivity conditions satisfied by translation on multiplication operators, (2.5) can be written as a stochastic differential equation in matrix valued functions:

$$dJ = i\sum_{j=1}^{k} B_j(\underline{x}+\underline{w}(t)-\underline{w}(s))dw_j(t) - \frac{1}{2}(\sum_{j=1}^{k} B_j^2(\underline{x}+\underline{w}(t)-\underline{w}(s))dt$$

$$+ \{V(\underline{x}+\underline{w}(t)-\underline{w}(s)) + \frac{i}{2}\sum_{j=1}^{k}\frac{\partial B_j}{\partial x_j}(\underline{x}+\underline{w}(t)-\underline{w}(s))\}dt. \qquad (3.1)$$

Thus J and therefore Γ are defined as m x m matrix valued multiplication operators and and Theorem 2.2 holds. When B_j are 0 and V is scalar valued, then Theorem 2.2 becomes the Feyman-Kac formula. In view of this, the expression $\Gamma(s,t)$ may be called the Feynman-Kac cocycle. The general result in this context is given in the next theorem when $k = 3$.

<u>Theorem 3.1</u> : Let B_1,B_2,B_3 and V be such that $B_j \in L^4(\mathbb{R}^3) + L^\infty(\mathbb{R}^3)$ for j=1,2,3; $\operatorname{div} \underline{B} \in L^2(\mathbb{R}^3) + L^\infty(\mathbb{R}^3)$ and $V \in L^\infty(\mathbb{R}^3)$. Then there exists a family $\{\Gamma(t,s) \equiv \Gamma(t,s;\underline{w}, B_j,V)\}$ of unitaries in $\mathcal{H}$ satisfying:

(i) for $s < t$, $\Gamma(t,s)$ is strongly $\mathcal{B}(s,t)$-measurable,

(ii) for each $\underline{w}$, $\Gamma(t,s)$ is strongly continuous in s and t,

(iii) $$\Gamma(t,s,\underline{w}) = \exp[i\int_s^t \{\underline{B}(\cdot+\underline{w}(\tau)-\underline{w}(s))\cdot d\underline{w}(\tau) - \frac{1}{2}\operatorname{div}\underline{B}(\cdot+\underline{w}(\tau)-\underline{w}(s))d\tau\} + \int_s^t V(\cdot+\underline{w}(\tau)-\underline{w}(s))d\tau]$$

(iv) $\tilde{U}(t,s) \equiv U(t,s)\,\Gamma(t,s)$ is an evolution satisfying
$$E\,\tilde{U}(t,s) = \exp[-(t-s)\{\frac{1}{2}\sum_{j=1}^{3}(-i\partial_j + B_j)^2 + V\}] .$$

Proof We first assume that B_j and V are C_o^∞ functions and hence define bounded operators in $\mathcal{H}$ so that (2.4) and (3.1) can be solved by Dyson series which coincides with the exponential series for (iii).

Next consider sequences $B_j^{(n)}$, $V^{(n)}$ in C_o^∞ such that they converge to given B_j and V in the assumed L^p-topologies. Setting $H^{(n)} \equiv \frac{1}{2}\sum_{j=1}^{3}(-i\partial_j+B_j^{(n)})^2 + V^{(n)}$, one notes that $H^{(n)}$ converges to H in the strong resolvent sense [3, page 284]. This implies that the semigroup $e^{-tH^{(n)}}$ converges to e^{-tH} strongly [3, page 286]. On the other hand, by choosing a subsequence if necessary, we can assume that $B_j^{(n)}$, div $\underline{B}^{(n)}$ and $V^{(n)}$ converge pointwise and hence $\Gamma^{(n)}(t,s;\underline{w})$ converges strongly to $\Gamma(t,s;\underline{w})$ for a.a.$\underline{w}$. Now an application of dominated convergence theorem to the $\mathcal{H}$-valued Bochner integrals $E\,\tilde{U}^{(n)}(t,s)$ gives the desired result.

The restriction on V of Theorem 3.1 can be relaxed further to the case when $V \in L^2(\mathbb{R}^3) + L^\infty(\mathbb{R}^3)$. However in this case, the approximating sequence $E\,\tilde{U}^{(n)}(t,s)$ converges only weakly. For details on this point and some applications of the formula (iii) in the spectral theory of the operator H, the reader is referred to [4].

We end with a few final remarks. A natural question is: Is the kind of evolutions, described in the above theorems, the only one possible? More specifically, let U(t,s;w) be a unitary family for $t \geq s$ satisfying:

(a) $U(s,s;w) = I$; $U(u,t)U(t,s) = U(u,s)$ $u \geq t \geq s$,

(b) $U(t,s;w)$ is $\mathcal{B}(s,t]$-measurable

(c) $U(t,s;w)$ is strongly continuous in t and s.

(d) $U(t+h, s+h;w) = U(t,s;\theta_h w)$ where θ_h is a measure preserving transformation on w satisfying (i) $\theta_{h_1}\theta_{h_2} = \theta_{h_1+h_2}$, (ii) $\theta_h^{-1}\{\mathcal{B}(s,t]\} = \mathcal{B}(s+h,t+h]$ for all $h > 0$, $s < t$. Then one wants to know the most general structure of such a family of evolutions.

As a simpler subcase, if one assumes instead of (c) that U(t,s) is norm continuous, then one can easily see that E U(t,s) is a norm continuous contractive semigroup in t and hence has a bounded dissipative operator A for its generator viz. Re $A \geq 0$. Then one can completely describe such a unitary evolution by a pair of selfadjoint bounded operators B and C such that U satisfies the S.D.E. (in strong sense)

$$dU(t,s;w) = [i\,C\,dw + (iB - \tfrac{1}{2}C^2)dt]\,U(t,s;w),$$

$$U(s,s) = I).$$

For obvious domain problems, a similar result for the case when only strong continuity is assumed in (c), is hard to obtain. However if one assumes instead that the strongly continuous contractive semigroup EU(t,s) is a selfadjoint semigroup, then one can obtain the following S.D.E.:

$$d\cdot e^{-\alpha A}\, U(t,s,w) = (i\, e^{-\alpha A}\, C\, dw - \frac{1}{2} e^{-\alpha A}\, A\, dt)\, U(t,s),$$

with $U(s,s) = I$, α strictly positive and C a densely defined symmetric operator such that $C^*C = A \geq 0$.

If one drops the homogeneity assumption (d), then EU(t,s) will not be a semigroup and will generally satisfy strong time-inhomogeneous differential equation. An S.D.E. of the above type can again be established but we have not yet studied the details of such a case.

References

[1] H.P. McKean, Stochastic Integrals, Academic Press, New York, 1969.

[2] K.R.Parthasarathy and K.B.Sinha, A random Trotter-Kato product formula, Statistics and Probability: Essaysin Honour of C.R.Rao (G.Kallianpur et al ed.), North Holland, 553-565, 1982.

[3] M. Reed and B.Simon, Methods of Modern Mathematical Physics Vol. I, Academic Press, 1972.

[4] B. Simon, Functional Integration and Quantum Physics, Academic Press, 1979.

ON POISSON MULTIPLE STOCHASTIC INTEGRALS AND ASSOCIATED EQUILIBRIUM MARKOV PROCESSES

D. Surgailis

Institute of Mathematics and Cybernetics
Vilnius, Lithuanian SSR

0. Introduction. Let $q(dx)$ be the centered Poisson random measure (r.m.) in $X \subseteq R^d$ with variance $\mu(dx)$, defined on a probability space $(\Omega, \underline{\underline{F}}, P)$, and let $q^{(n)}(f) = \int_{X^n} f(x_1,\dots,x_n)q(dx_1)\dots q(dx_n)$, $f \in L^2(X^n) = L^2(X^n, \mu^n)$ denote (Poisson) multiple stochastic integral (m.s.i.) with respect to $q(dx)$. We discuss the following questions associated with such integrals:

(1) generalized Wick product $:q_1 \dots q_n:$ of given random variables (r.v.) $q_1,\dots,q_n$, in particular of linear variables $q_j = q^{(1)}(f_j)$, $f_j \in L^2(X)$, $j=1,\dots,n$, and their relationship to local functionals of linear generalized random fields (Sect.2-3);

(2) equilibrium Markov processes which values at each time are point measures in X and the transition semigroup $P(T_t)$, $t \geq 0$ acts in $L^2(\Omega) = L^2(\Omega;P)$ according to

$$P(T_t)q^{(n)}(f_1 \otimes \dots \otimes f_n) = q^{(n)}(T_t f_1 \otimes \dots \otimes T_t f_n) . \qquad (1)$$

Here, T_t, $t \geq 0$ is a given (sub-Markov) semigroup in $L^2(X)$ (Sect.4). The semigroup $P(T_t)$ can be regarded as the Poisson analog of the Ornstein-Uhlenbeck (O-U) semigroup.

Poisson m.s.i. were introduced by K.Ito [6] and studied later e.g. in [5, 7, 15, 20]. The semigroup $P(T_t)$ was studied by the author in [20].

<u>1. Poisson m.s.i.: the basic properties</u>. Let $X \subseteq \mathbb{R}^d$ be an open set, $\underline{\underline{B}}(X)$ be its Borel subsets and $\underline{\underline{B}}_c(X)$ its relatively compact subsets. Let be given a Poisson random measure $p = p(A)$, $A \in \underline{\underline{B}}_c(X)$ with mean μ such that $\mu(A) < \infty$ $\forall A \in \underline{\underline{B}}_c(X)$ and $\mu(\{x\}) = 0$ $\forall x \in X$. Denote $q = p - \mu$ the centered Poisson r.m., and $q^{(n)}(f)$, $f \in L^2(X^n)$, $n \geqslant 1$ the (Poisson) m.s.i. with respect to q. We note the following basic properties of such integrals:

$$q^{(n)}(f) = q^{(n)}(\mathrm{sym}\, f) \in L^2(\Omega) , \tag{2}$$

$$E[\, q^{(n)}(f) \,] = 0 , \tag{3}$$

$$E\left[q^{(n)}(f)\, \overline{q^{(m)}(g)} \right] = \delta_{mn}\, n!\, (\mathrm{sym} f, g)_n , \tag{4}$$

$f \in L^2(X^n)$, $g \in L^2(X^m)$, $m,n \geqslant 1$, where δ_{mn} is Kronecker's δ $(\cdot,\cdot)_n$ is the scalar product in $L^2(X^n)$ and sym denotes the symmetrization.

Set $L^2(X^0) = \mathbb{C}$, $q^{(0)}(f) = f$, $f \in \mathbb{C}$, $\underline{\underline{F}} = \sigma(q(A) \colon A \in \underline{\underline{B}}_c(X))$. It is known [6] that Poisson m.s.i. constitute a complete orthogonal system in $L^2(\Omega) = L^2(\Omega, \underline{\underline{F}}, P)$. This means that any r.v. $\xi \in L^2(\Omega)$ can be expanded uniquely in series of m.s.i. which converge in $L^2(\Omega)$:

$$\xi = \sum_{n=0}^{\infty} q^{(n)}(f_n)/n! , \tag{5}$$

$(f_0, f_1, \dots) \equiv f \in \exp(L^2(X))$ (= the Fock space).

Denote $q(f) = q^{(1)}(f) = \int_X f(x) q(dx)$ the linear integral. The relation $\exp\{q(f)\} \in L^2(\Omega)$ ($f \in L^2(X)$) is equivalent to [20]

$$\int_{\{\mathrm{Re}\, f(x) > 1\}} \exp\{2 \mathrm{Re} f(x)\}\, d\mu < \infty \tag{6}$$

If $f \in L^2(X)$ and (6) holds, then

$$E[\exp\{q(f)\}] = \exp\left\{ \int_X (e^f - 1 - f)\, d\mu \right\} \tag{7}$$

and

$$\exp\{q(f)\}/E[\exp\{q(f)\}] = \sum_{n=0}^{\infty} q^{(n)}((\otimes(e^{f}-1))^{n})/n! \quad . \tag{8}$$

2. Generalized Wick products. In contrast with Gaussian m.s.i., the Poisson integrals of the form $q^{(n)}(f_1\otimes\cdots\otimes f_n)$ are not polynomials (or any other functions) of linear r.v. $q(f_1), \ldots, q(f_n)$ unless $f_1,\cdots,f_n$ are indicator functions. Below we introduce some polynomial forms of r.v. $q(f_1),\ldots,q(f_n)$ which we call generalized Wick products (g.W.p.) , and investigate their relationship with Poisson m.s.i. The notion of g.W.p. is not dependent of any particular assumption on the distribution of a given system of r.v. and might be of interest itself.

Let be given a finite system of r.v. $(q) = (q_1,\ldots,q_n)$. We assume that all moments of r.v. $q_1,\ldots,q_n$ are finite but no other conditions on their distribution are assumed. Set

$$:x_1\ldots x_n: = P_{(q)}(x_1,\ldots,x_n)$$

$$= \partial^{n}(\exp\{\textstyle\sum a_j x_j\}/E[\exp\{\textstyle\sum a_j q_j\}])/\partial a_1\ldots\partial a_n\Big|_{a_1=\ldots=a_n=0} \tag{9}$$

$P_{(q)}(x_1,\ldots,x_n)$ is polynomials in $x_1,\ldots,x_n$. In particular, $:x_1: = x_1 - E\,q_1$, $:x_1x_2: = x_1x_2 - x_1Eq_2 - x_2Eq_1 + 2Eq_1Eq_2 - Eq_1q_2$ etc. We call $:q_1\ldots q_n:$ the generalized Wick product (g.W.p.) of r.v. $q_1,\ldots,q_n$. If $q_1 = \ldots = q_n = q$, the polynomials $P_n(x) = :x^n: = P_{(q)}(x,\ldots,x)$ are defined by the generating function

$$\sum_{n=0}^{\infty} z^n P_n(x)/n! = e^{zx}/\varphi(z) \quad , \tag{10}$$

where $\varphi(z) = E[\exp\{zq\}]$, $z\in\mathbb{C}$. Polynomials with the generating function (10) are known as Appell's polynomials and were studied e.g. in [3, 17] . A characteristic feature of Appell's polynomials is the differentiation rule: $P_n'(x) = nP_{n-1}(x)$. Special cases of such polynomials are (a) Hermite polynomials (q is standart Gaussian r.v.), (b) Bernoulli polynomials (q is uniformly distributed in $[0, 1]$), (c) Euler polynomials (q is Bernoulli r.v. with $P(q=1) = P(q=-1) = 1/2$). Among Appell's polynomials, only Hermite ones are orthogonal [17]. A probabilistic formula for coefficients of polynomials (9) is given in

<u>Proposition 1</u>.

$$:x_1\ldots x_n: \;=\; \sum_U x^U \sum_{\{V\}} (-1)^r\, C(q^{V_1})\ldots C(q^{V_r}) \quad , \tag{11}$$

$$x_1\ldots x_n \;=\; \sum_U :x^U: \sum_{\{V\}} C(q^{V_1})\ldots C(q^{V_r}) = \sum_U :x^U: \langle q^{U^c} \rangle \quad , \tag{12}$$

where the sum $\sum_U$ is taken over all subsets $U \subseteq \{1,\ldots,n\}$ including $U = \emptyset$, $x^U = \prod_{i\in U} x_i$, the sum $\sum_{\{V\}}$ is taken over all partitions $\{V\} = \{V_1,\ldots,V_r\}$, $r \geqslant 1$ of $U^c = \{1,\ldots,n\}\setminus U$, $\langle q^U \rangle = E[\prod_{i\in U} q_i]$ and $C(q^V) = C(q_i : i \in V)$ is the semiinvariant of r.v. q_i , $i \in V$.

Proof. According to the definition (9), $:x_1\ldots x_n: \;=\; :x_1\ldots x_{n-1}: x_n - \partial^n (f_1 f_2)/\partial a_1\ldots\partial a_n \big|_{a_1=\ldots=a_n=0}$, where

$$f_1 = \exp\{\sum_{j=1}^{n-1} a_j x_j\} / E[\exp\{\sum_{j=1}^{n-1} a_j q_j\}]$$

$$f_2 = \partial \log E[\exp\{\sum_{j=1}^{n} a_j q_j\}] / \partial a_n \big|_{a_n=0} .$$

This implies easily the recursive relation

$$:x_1\ldots x_n: \;=\; :x_1\ldots x_{n-1}: x_n - \sum C(q^V)\, :x^{V^c}: \quad , \tag{13}$$

where the sum is taken over all $V \subseteq \{1,\ldots,n\}$ such that $n \in V$, $V^c = \{1,\ldots,n\}\setminus V$. The same recursive relation is satisfied by the polynomials defined by the right hand side of (11). (12) can be proved analogously. ☒

Below we describe a simple combinatoric rule saying how products of g.W.p. can be expressed as sums of g.W.p., which is analogical to the well-known diagram formalism for Gaussian r.v. [1, 11].

Let be given a collection of mutually disjoint finite sets $W_1, \ldots, W_k$; $W = W_1 \cup \ldots \cup W_k$. Following [11] , we call the diagram a partition $\{V\} = \{V_1,\ldots,V_r\}$ $(r \geqslant 1)$ of W by (non-empty) sets $V_1,\ldots,V_r$. Elements V_i of this partition such that $|V_i| = 1$ we call the free elements while all other elements V_i , $|V_i| \geqslant 2$ will be called edges (of the diagram $\{V\}$). A subset $U \subseteq W$ is called flat if it is contained in some W_j, $j = 1,\ldots,k$.

Let be given a collection $(q) = (q_i,\ i \in W)$ of random variables. To any diagram $\{V\}$ there corresponds the r.v.

$$I_{\{V\}} = :q^{\widetilde{W}}: \prod_V C(q^V) \quad , \tag{14}$$

where $\widetilde{W} \subseteq W$ is the set of all free elements of $\{V\}$ and the product is taken over all edges V of $\{V\}$ (We set $:q^{\emptyset}: = 1$ and $\prod_V \ldots = 1$ if the diagram contains no edges).

Proposition 2.

$$:q^{W_1}: \ \ldots \ :q^{W_k}: \ = \sum I_{\{V\}} \quad , \tag{15}$$

where the sum is taken over all diagrams without flat edges.

Proof. We use the following variant of the Leonov-Širyaev formula ([10], eq.):

$$\langle q^W \rangle = \sum_{U \subseteq W} \langle q^{U_1^c} \rangle \ldots \langle q^{U_k^c} \rangle \sum_{\{V\}} C(q^{V_1}) \ldots C(q^{V_r}) \tag{16}$$

where $U_i = W_i \cap U$, $U_i^c = W_i \setminus U_i$, $i=1,\ldots,k$ and the second sum is taken over all partitions $\{V\} = \{V_1,\ldots,V_r\}\, (r \geqslant 1)$ of U such that none of V_i is flat.

The proof of (15) is by induction in $|W|$. By (12),

$$x^W = \sum_{U_1\subseteq W_1} \cdots \sum_{U_k\subseteq W_k} :x^{U_1}: \ \ldots \ :x^{U_k}: \langle q^{U_1^c}\rangle \ldots \langle q^{U_k^c}\rangle$$

$$= \sum_{U\subseteq W} :x^U: \ \langle q^{U^c}\rangle \ .$$

Hence

$$:x^{W_1}: \ \ldots \ :x^{W_k}: \ = \sum_{U\subseteq W} :x^U: \langle q^{U^c}\rangle - \sum{}^{*} :x^{U_1}: \ldots :x^{U_k}: \langle q^{U_1^c}\rangle \ldots \langle q^{U_k^c}\rangle ,$$

where the sum $\sum^*$ is taken over all subsets $U_1\subseteq W_1,\ldots, U_k\subseteq W_k$ except the case when $U_1 = W_1,\ldots, U_k = W_k$ simultaneously. As $\sum|U_k| < \sum|W_k| = |W|$, by induction we have

$$:x^{W_1}: \ \ldots \ :x^{W_k}: \ = \sum_{U\subseteq W} :x^U: \ \langle q^{U^c}\rangle \ -$$

$$- \sum_{U\subseteq W} \ \sum_{U\subseteq\widetilde{U}\subset W,\widetilde{U}\neq W} \ \sum_{\{V\}} :x^U: C(q^{\widetilde{V}_1})\ldots C(q^{\widetilde{V}_r}) \ \langle q^{\widetilde{U}_1^c}\rangle \ldots \langle q^{\widetilde{U}_k^c}\rangle$$

where $\widetilde{U}_i = \widetilde{U}\cap W_i$, $\widetilde{U}_i^c = W_i\setminus\widetilde{U}_i$ and the sum $\sum_{\{V\}}$ is taken over all partitions $\{\widetilde{V}_1,\ldots,\widetilde{V}_r\}$ of $\widetilde{U}\setminus U$ such that none of $\widetilde{V}_i$ is flat. By (16), this proves (15). ⊠

If the system $(q_i,\ i\in W)$ is Gaussian, then $C(q^V) = 0$ for $|V|>2$ and the sum (15) is taken over all diagrams $\{V_1,\ldots,V_r\}$ such that either $|V_i| = 1$ (i.e. V_i is free) or $|V_i| = 2$ (and V_i is not flat).

The <u>support</u> of a diagram $\{V\} = \{V_1,\ldots,V_r\}$ is the smallest set $M\subseteq\{1,\ldots,k\}$ such that all edges of $\{V\}$ belong to $\bigcup_{i\in M} W_i$. A diagram without free elements is said <u>undecomposable</u> if it cannot be written as a union of two diagrams with disjoint supports. (Given two diagrams $\{V_i, i=1,\ldots,r\}$ and $\{V'_j, j=1,\ldots,r\}$, their union is the diagram $\{V_i\cap V'_j, i=1,\ldots,r, j=1,\ldots,r\}$).

__Proposition 3.__ Assume in addition that $E[q_i] = 0$, $i \in W$. Then

(a) $E[:q^U:] = 0$, $\emptyset \neq U \subseteq W$,

(b) $E[:q^{W_1}: \ldots :q^{W_k}:] = \sum C(q^{V_1}) \ldots C(q^{V_r})$,

(c) $C(:q^{W_1}:,\ldots,:q^{W_k}:) = \sum C(q^{V_1}) \ldots C(q^{V_r})$,

where the sum in (b) is taken over all diagrams $\{V\} = \{V_1,\ldots,V_r\}$ without free elements and flat edges, and in (c) over all such undecomposable diagrams, respectively.

We omit the proof of this proposition. For the corresponding result in case of Gaussian system (q) , see [11], Prop.1.1.

__3. Local functionals of generalized random fields.__ Denote $S = S(R^d)$ the Schwartz space of rapidly decreasing C^∞-functions $f: \mathbb{R}^d \to \mathbb{C}$. A (generalized 2nd order) random field (r.f.) is a linear continuous mapping $\xi : S \to L^2(\Omega)$. With every open set $U \subseteq \mathbb{R}^d$ we relate the σ-algebra $\underline{\underline{F}}_U^\xi$, generated by r.v. $\xi(f)$, supp $f \subset U$. Set $\underline{\underline{F}}^\xi = \underline{\underline{F}}_{\mathbb{R}^d}^\xi$.

R.f. η is said __subordinated__ to a (stationary) r.f. ξ if $\underline{\underline{F}}^\eta \subseteq \underline{\underline{F}}^\xi$ and η is stationary connected with ξ (see [1] for details). R.f. η is said __local__ with respect to a given r.f. ξ if η is subordinated to ξ and $\underline{\underline{F}}_U^\eta \subseteq \underline{\underline{F}}_U^\xi$ for any open set $U \subset \mathbb{R}^d$. A closely related notion is that of an __additive local functional__ (a.l.f.) $A = A(U)$, $U \in \underline{\underline{B}}_c(\mathbb{R}^d)$ [2] . Roughly, an a.l.f. is obtained from a local r.f. η by integration: $A(U) = \eta(1_U)$ provided the latter is discretizable [1] . The most important class of local fields of a given Gaussian stationary r.f. ξ with the spectral representation $\xi(f) = \int_{\mathbb{R}^d} \hat{f}(x)\, Z(dx)$, $f \in S$ is given by its Wick powers:

$$:\xi^n:(f) = \int_{(\mathbb{R}^d)^n} \hat{f}(x_1 + \dots + x_n)\, Z(dx_1)\dots Z(dx_n)\ , \ n \geq 1. \quad (17)$$

Recently, Dobrušin and Kelbert [2, 8] had given a complete description of a.l.f. of stationary Gaussian r.f. , under some assumptions on the spectral measure $F(dx) = E[\,|Z(dx)|^2\,]$.

Motivated by the discussion in Simon [16], §V.1 we have suggested the following generalization of Wick powers which yields local fields.

<u>Definition 1</u> [19]. Let ξ be a stationary r.f. in $\mathbb{R}^d$. Assume that there exists a sequence $(\delta_k)_{k=1}^{\infty} \subset S$ convergent to Dirac's δ in S' (= the dual of S) and a sequence of polynomials $P^{(k)}(z) = \sum_{j \leq n} a_j^{(k)} z^j$, $k = 1,2,\dots$ with coefficients $a_j^{(k)}$ depending on ξ and δ_k, such that $a_n^{(k)} = 1$ and either $a_j^{(k)} = 0$ or $|a_j^{(k)}| \to \infty\ (k \to \infty)$, $j = 0,1,\dots,n-1$, and for any $f \in S$ there exists the limit in probability

$$\lim_{k \to \infty} \int_{\mathbb{R}^d} P^{(k)}(\xi(\delta_k(x - \cdot)))\, f(x)dx\ , \quad (18)$$

which is a (generalized) r.f. in $\mathbb{R}^d$. We call this r.f. the n-th <u>renormalized power</u> (r.p.) of r.f. ξ.

In particular, the n-th Wick power (17) corresponds to $P^{(k)}(x) = H_n(x/D_k)D_k^n$, where $D_k^2 = E[\xi^2(\delta_k)]$, and H_n is Hermite polynomial (the limit (18) is discussed in [16], Th. V.3).

Consider now linear r.f. ξ in $\mathbb{R}^d$:

$$\xi(f) = \int_{\mathbb{R}^\nu} (Bf)(x)\, q(dx)\ , \quad f \in S\ , \quad (19)$$

where q is the centered Poisson r.m. in $\mathbb{R}^\nu$ ($\nu \geq 1$) with variance dx, and $B: S \to L^2(\mathbb{R}^\nu) = L^2(\mathbb{R}^\nu; dx)$ is continuous linear operator. Among linear r.f., several classes are of particular interest (Markov fields [9, 18], self-similar fields [19]). In order to clarify the connection between (19), Def.1 and Sect. 1-2 , let us introduce the so-called Q-integral.

Denote $\underline{\underline{V}}_n$ the collection of all partitions of the set $\{1,\dots,n\}$ and let $\Lambda_n(\mathbb{R}^\nu)$ denote the linear space of all measurable functions $f: (\mathbb{R}^\nu)^n \to \mathbb{C}$ such that for any $\{V\} = \{V_1,\dots,V_r\} \in \underline{\underline{V}}_n$, $f_{\{V\}} \in L^2((\mathbb{R}^\nu)^r)$, where

$$f_{\{V\}}(x_1,\dots,x_r) = f(y_1,\dots,y_n)$$

and $y_i = x_j$, $i \in V_j$, $i = 1,\dots,r$. For any $f \in \Lambda_n(\mathbb{R}^\nu)$ set

$$Q_n(f) = \sum_{\{V\}\in \underline{\underline{V}}_n} q^{(r)}(f_{\{V\}}) , \qquad (20)$$

where $q^{(r)}(\cdot)$ is m.s.i. with respect to the Poisson r.m. q . We call (20) the <u>Q-integral</u> of f .

<u>Proposition 4</u> [19]. Let $f_i \in L^p(\mathbb{R}^\nu)$ $\forall\, p \in [2, 2n]$, $i = 1,\dots,n$, $q_i = q(f_i)$, $(q) = (q_1,\dots,q_n)$, $f = f_1 \otimes \dots \otimes f_n$. Then $f \in \Lambda_n(\mathbb{R}^\nu)$ and

$$Q_n(f) = :q_1 \dots q_n: .$$

Assume that r.f. ξ (19) is stationary , and set $P^{(k)}(q_k) = :(q_k)^n:$, where $q_k = \xi(\delta_k)$. Under some conditions on B and $(\delta_k)_{k=1}^{\infty}$ it can be shown that the limit (18) exists, is a local field with respect to ξ and can be expressed as Q-integral. In the case of self-similar field ξ (19), the details can be found in [19]. Unfortunately, this approach to the construction of local subordinate fields seems to be not applicable in the case of linear generalized Markov fields ξ (the kernel of the operator B in such case is not square integrable at the origin and the limiting Q-integral is not defined).

4. Markov equilibrium processes associated with Poisson m.s.i.

Let $X \subseteq R^d$, μ, q, $q^{(n)}(\cdot)$ be the same as in Sect. 1, and let A be a contraction in $L^2(X) = L^2(X,\mu)$. There exists a unique contraction $P(A)$ in $L^2(\Omega)$ such that

$$P(A)\, q^{(n)}(f_1 \otimes \ldots \otimes f_n) = q^{(n)}(Af_1 \otimes \ldots \otimes Af_n) \qquad (21)$$

for any $n \geq 0$, $f_1, \ldots, f_n \in L^2(X)$ ([16], § I.4).

Let us introduce the following terminology. Let $(K, \underline{\underline{K}})$ be a measurable space with a σ-finite measure χ, and let B be a continuous linear operator in $L^2(K) = L^2(K,\chi)$. We say that B is positivity preserving and write $B \rhd 0$ if $f \geq 0$, $f \in L^2(K)$ implies $Bf \geq 0$ (χ-a.e.). We call an operator $B \rhd 0$ sub-Markov if $Bf \leq 1$ for any $f \leq 1$, $f \in L^2(K)$, and Markov if $Bf_n \nearrow 1$ (χ-a.e.) for some sequence $f_n \nearrow 1$, $f_n \in L^2(K)$. Finally, we say that B is doubly sub-Markov (resp. doubly Markov) if both operators B and B^* (= the adjoint of B in $L^2(K)$) are sub-Markov (resp. Markov).

Theorem 1 [20]. Let X, μ, q, $q^{(n)}(\cdot)$ be as above, and let A be a contraction in $L^2(X)$. Then $P(A) \rhd 0$ iff A is doubly sub-Markov; in the latter case $P(A)$ is also doubly Markov.

In the Gaussian case (when q is Gaussian r.m. with variance μ) $P(A) \rhd 0$ for any contraction A ([16], Th.I.12). A probabilistic proof of the sufficiency part of Th.1 consists in construction of a discrete time Markov process for which $P(A)$ is the transition operator. Below we describe an analogous continuous time Markov process given a (continuous time) doubly sub-Markov semigroup T_t, $t \geq 0$ in $L^2(X)$, although such construction involves some additional technical assumptions on T_t. In particular, we assume that there exists a σ-finite positive measure μ^* on X such that for any

$t > 0$ and for any bounded continuous function $f: X \to C$,

$$\int_X (f - T_t f)\, d\mu \quad = \quad \int_X \int_0^t T_{t-s} f \, ds d\mu^* . \tag{22}$$

Typically, $\mu^*(dx) = -A^* 1(x) \mu(dx)$, where A^* is the generator of the adjoint semigroup T_t^* .

Let p be the Poisson r.m. in X with mean μ , i.e. $p = q + \mu$, and let be given another Poisson r.m. $\tilde{p}$ in $\tilde{X} = X \times (0,\infty)$ with mean $\tilde{\mu}(dx,ds) = \mu^*(dx)ds$, which is independent of p . Write

$$p = \sum_{j \geq 1} \delta_{y_j} , \tag{23}$$

$$\tilde{p} = \sum_{k \geq 1} \delta_{(\tilde{y}_k, \tau_k)} , \tag{24}$$

Assume that every point y_j , $\tilde{y}_k \in X$ undertakes independent evolution $y_j(t)$, $0 \leq t < \xi_j$, $\tilde{y}_k(t)$, $0 \leq t < \tilde{\xi}_k$ in X according to the semigroup T_t , where ξ_j , $\tilde{\xi}_k$ are terminal times. Set

$$p_t(f) = \int_X f(x) p_t(dx) = \sum_{t < \xi_j} f(y_j(t)) + \sum_{\tau_k \leq t < \tau_k + \tilde{\xi}_k} f(\tilde{y}_k(t - \tau_k)) . \tag{25}$$

It is easy to observe that p_t , $t \geq 0$ is a stationary Markov process which values at each time are point measures in X . The second sum in (25) comes from immigration after $t = 0$ of new identical independent particles; the immigration intensity at $(x,t) \in \tilde{X}$ is independent of the past of the process $(p_s, s \leq t)$ and is equal to $\tilde{\mu}(dx,ds)$. Independent evolutions of infinite particle systems, with immigration and death, not necessarily in equilibrium, and limit theorems for them were studied by a number of authors (see e.g. [12]).

Let $(\Omega, \underline{\underline{F}}, P)$ be the basic probability space on which the process p_t (25) is defined. Denote $p = p_0$, $\underline{\underline{F}} = \sigma(p_0) \subseteq \underline{\underline{F}}$, and let

$P(T_t)$ be the contraction semigroup in $L^2(\underline{\underline{F}}) = L^2(\Omega, \underline{\underline{F}}, P)$ given by (1). Any $\underline{\underline{F}}$-measurable function $F:\Omega \to \mathbb{C}$ can be identified with some measurable function $M_0(X) \to \mathbb{C}$, where $M_0(X)$ is the set of all point measures in X which are finite on compact subsets of X, with the σ-algebra generated by cylinder sets. Let $F \in L^2(\underline{\underline{F}})$.
We claim that

$$P(T_t)F = E\left[F(p_t) | \underline{\underline{F}} \right] . \tag{26}$$

It suffices to verify (26) for $F = \exp\{-p(f)\}$, where $f \geqslant 0$ is bounded and continuous. According to (7),(8) and (1),

$$P(T_t)F = \sum_{n=0}^{\infty} q^{(n)}((\otimes T_t(e^{-f}-1))^n) \exp\{ \int_X (e^{-f}-1)d\mu\}/n! =$$

$$= \exp\left\{p(\log(T_t(e^{-f}-1)+1)) + \int_X ((e^{-f}-1)-T_t(e^{-f}-1))d\mu\right\} . \tag{27}$$

On the other hand, by (23)-(25) and (7),

$$E\left[F(p_t)|\underline{\underline{F}}\right] = E\left[\exp\{-\sum_{t<\xi_j} f(y_j(t))\}| \underline{\underline{F}}\right]$$

$$E\left[\exp\{-\sum_{\tau_k \leq t < \tau_k+\tilde{\xi}_k} f(\tilde{y}_k(t-\tau_k))\}\right] =$$

$$= \prod_j (T_t(e^{-f}-1)(y_j) + 1) \cdot E\left[\prod_{\tau_k \leq t} (T_{t-\tau_k}(e^{-f}-1)(\tilde{y}_k) + 1)\right] =$$

$$= \exp\left\{p(\log(T_t(e^{-f}-1) + 1)) + \int_0^t \int_X \tilde{\mu}(dx,ds)T_{t-s}(e^{-f}-1)\right\} .$$

By (22) and (27), this yields (26).

The characteristic functional of the process $q_t = p_t - \mu$, $t \geqslant 0$ is equal to

$$E\left[\exp\left\{ i \sum_{j=1}^{n} q_{t_j}(f_j)\right\}\right] = \exp\left\{ \sum_{j=1}^{n} \int_X ((e^{if_j} -1-if_j)d\mu + \right.$$

$$\left. + \sum_{1 \leq k < j \leq n} \int_X (e^{if_k} -1)T_{\Delta t_k} e^{if_{k+1}} \ldots T_{\Delta t_{j-2}} e^{if_{j-1}} T_{\Delta t_{j-1}}(e^{if_j} -1)d\mu\right\} . \tag{28}$$

Here $0 \leq t_1 < \ldots < t_n$, $n \geq 1$, $\Delta t_k = t_{k+1} - t_k$, $f_1, \ldots, f_k \in L^2(X)$ are real functions. Note that all finite dimensional distributions of q_t are infinitely divisible. The process q_t (or p_t) is <u>reversable</u> iff the semigroup T_t is self adjoint in $L^2(X)$.

Denote $q_{t,k}$, $t \geq 0$ the corresponding process with μ replaced by $k\mu$, $k = 1,2,\ldots$, and set $\overline{q_{t,k}} = q_{t,k}/\sqrt{k}$. It follows from (28) that finite dimensional distributions of $\overline{q_{t,k}}$ converge as $k \to \infty$ to the corresponding distributions of Gaussin O-U process $\bar{q}_t$ with mean zero and covariance $E[\bar{q}_0(f)\bar{q}_t(g)] = \int_X fT_t g \, d\mu$, $f,g \in L^2(X)$. The corresponding semigroup $\bar{P}(T_t)$ acts on (Gaussian) m.s.i. similarly as $P(T_t)$.

Let us consider some examples.

Let $X = \{1\}$, $\mu(X) = \mu$, $T_t = e^{-ct}$, $c > 0$. In such a case $p_t = q_t + \mu$ is stationary birth and death process on $\mathbb{Z}_+$ with invariant mean μ Poisson measure and the transition rates $\lambda_i^+ = \lambda_{i,i+1} = c\mu$, $\lambda_i^- = \lambda_{i,i-1} = ci$, $i \in \mathbb{Z}_+$, $\lambda_{ij} = dP(t,i,j)/dt|_{t=0}$.

Another example: $X = \mathbb{R}_+$, $\mu(dx) = dx$, $T_t = e^{-t/2}$. Introduce the centered Poisson process $q(x) = q(0,x)$, $x \geq 0$ and $(\underline{\underline{F}}_x)_{x \geq 0}$ the natural right continuous filtration associated with $q(x)$. Any zero mean r.v. $\xi \in L^2(\underline{\underline{F}}_\infty)$ can be represented as stochastic integral: $\xi = \int_0^\infty f(x)\, dq(x)$, where f is <u>predictable</u> with respect to $(\underline{\underline{F}}_x)$ and $E\left[\int_0^\infty |f(x)|^2 \, dx\right] < \infty$ [13]. Denote $L^2(\underline{\underline{F}}.)$ the class of all such f's. It is easy to observe that $P(T_t)$ maps $L^2(\underline{\underline{F}}.)$ onto itself and that for any $f \in L^2(\underline{\underline{F}}.)$,

$$P(T_t) \int_0^\infty f(x)\, dq(x) = \int_0^\infty P(T_t) f(x)\, dq(x) \quad e^{-t/2}. \tag{29}$$

A similar relation, with $q(x)$ replaced by the Brownian motion, is satisfied by the O-U process studied by Meyer [14]. The evolution

q_t is extremely simple in this example: every particle stays at its initial position for exponentially distributed lifetime, independently of others, while new identical particles immigrate the space-time $\mathbb{R}_+ \times (0, \infty)$ according to the Poisson law with mean $dxdt/2$.

We end the paper with a negative result about the <u>hypercontractivity</u> of the semigroup $P(T_t)$ which is in contrast with the so-called Bernoulli approximation of the O-U semigroup [4] .

<u>Proposition 5</u>. For any $1 \leq a < a' < \infty$, $t > 0$ and $C > 0$ there exists $F : \Omega \to \mathbb{R}_+$ such that $\infty > E[(P(T_t)F)^{a'}] > C\, E[F^a]$.

Proof. There exists (measurable) subsets $A, B \subset X$ such that $0 < \mu(A) < \infty$, $0 < \mu(B) < \infty$ and $0 < D \equiv \int_B (T_t 1_A)^{a'} d\mu$. Set $F = F(b) = \exp\{p(b\, 1_A)\}$, where $b > 0$ is a parameter. By (7),(8)

$$\log C\, E[F(b)^a] = \log C + (e^{ab} - 1)\mu(A) ,$$

$$\log E[(P(T_t)F(b))^{a'}] = \int_X ((T_t(1_A(e^b - 1) + 1)^{a'} - 1)\, d\mu +$$

$$+ a'(e^b - 1)(\mu(A) - \int_X T_t 1_A\, d\mu)$$

$$\geqslant D\, e^{a'b} - \mu(B)$$

as $\int_X T_t 1_A\, d\mu \leq \mu(A)$ (this follows from the fact that T_t is doubly sub-Markov). Now let $b \to +\infty$. ☒

References

1. Dobrušin, R.L., Gaussian and their subordinated self-similar random generalized fields. Ann. Probab. 7 (1979), 1-28.

2. Dobrušin, R.L., Kelbert, M.Ja., Local additive functionals of Gaussian generalized fields (Russian). Uspehi Matem. Nauk, 34 (1979), 223-224.

3. Geronimus, J., On a class of Appell polynomials. Comm. Soc. Math. Kharkoff, Ser. 4, 8 (1934), 13-23.

4. Gross, L., Logarithmic Sobolev inequalities. Amer. J. Math., 97 (1975), 1061-1083.

5. Hida, T., Stationary stochastic processes. Princeton, N.J.: Princeton Univ. Press 1970.

6. Ito, K., Spectral type of shift transformations of differential process with stationary increments. Trans. Amer. Math. Soc. 81 (1956), 253-263.

7. Kabanov, Ju.M., On extended stochastic integrals (Russian). Teor. Verojatn. i Primenen. 20 (1975), 725-737.

8. Kelbert, M.Ja., The structure of local additive functionals of Gaussian generalized fields. Abstracts 3rd Vilnius Conf. Probab. Math. Statist., Vilnius, 1981.

9. Kusuoka, S., Markov fields and local operators. J. Fac. Sci., Univ. Tokyo, Ser.A, 26 (1979), 199-212.

10. Leonov, V.P., Širyaev, A.N., Sur le calcul des semi-invariants (en russe). Teor. Verojatn. i Primenen. 4 (1959), 342-355.

11. Malyšev, V.A., Cluster expansions in lattice models of statistical physics and quantum field theory (Russian). Uspehi Matem. Nauk 35 (1980), 3-53.

12. McDonald, J.N., Weiss, N.A., A system of Markov processes with random lifetimes. Z. Wahrscheinlichkeitstheorie verw. Gebiete 56 (1981), 287-315.

13. Meyer, P.A., Un cours sur les intégrales stochastiques. Semin. Probab. X . Lecture Notes Math. 511 . Springer 1976.

14. Meyer, P.A., Note sur le processus d'Ornstein - Uhlenbeck (to appear in Semin. Probab. XVI).

15. Ogura, H., Orthogonal functionals of the Poisson process. IEEE Trans. Inform. Theory IT-18 (1972), 473-480.

16. Simon, B., The $P(\varphi)_2$ Euclidean (quantum) field theory. Princeton, N.J.: Princeton Univ. Press 1974.

17. Shohat, J., The relation of the classical orthogonal polynomials to the polynomials of Appell. Amer. J. Math. 58 (1936), 453-464.

18. Surgailis, D., On the Markov property of a class of linear infinitely divisible fields. Z. Wahrscheinlichkeitstheorie verw. Gebiete 49 (1979), 293-311.

19. Surgailis, D., On infinitely divisible self-similar random fields. Ibid. 58 (1981), 453-477 .

20. Surgailis, D., On Poisson multiple stochastic integrals and associated Markov semigroups. J. Probab. Theory Math.Statist. (to appear)

INVITATION TO WHITE NOISE CALCULUS

Shigeo Takenaka
Nagoya University, Nagoya 464 Japan

In recent years, starting from some early work of P. Lévy, Professor T. Hida has developed a theory of generalized Brownian functionals or, as we prefer to call it, *white noise calculus* ([2],[7]). Hida's main idea is to treat the derivative of the Brownian motion $\{\dot{B}(t)\}$ as a complete orthonormal system (c.o.n.s.) in the Schwartz space S^* and use it for the analysis of nonlinear functionals of white noise.

In this paper, I present a one-dimensional version of a reformulation of Hida's theory due to I. Kubo and myself [5]. We hope that it gives a simple description of the white noise - or causal-calculus.

1. Definitions and Formulas. In this section we present some definitions and formulae. Let us begin by fixing the definition of the Hermite polynomial H_n;

$$(1)\quad H_n(x) = (-1)^n \exp(x^2/2) \frac{d^n}{dx^n} \exp(-x^2/2) .$$

Based upon this definition H_n is a polynomial of order n and the highest coefficient is 1, that is $H_n(x) = x^n + \dots$. Consider the space

$$(2)\quad L_2 = L^2(R, \frac{1}{\sqrt{2\pi}} \exp(-x^2/2)\, dx = d\mu(x)),$$

then $\{h_n = \frac{1}{\sqrt{n!}} H_n\}$ is a c.o.n.s. in L_2. After this, we denote the integration with respect to $d\mu(x)$ by E^x.

The generating function of the Hermite polynomials is

$$(3)\quad M(t,x) \equiv \sum_{n=0}^{\infty} H_n(x)\frac{t^n}{n!} = \exp(tx-t^2/2) .$$

Using this generating function we can get easily the following formulas:

$$(4)\quad x\cdot H_n(x) = H_{n+1}(x) + n\cdot H_{n-1}(x) ,$$

$$(5)\quad H_n'(x) = n\cdot H_{n-1}(x).$$

The additive formula of the Hermite polynomial is obtained from the following formula of generating function:

$$(6)\quad M(t,\sqrt{a}\xi + \sqrt{b}x) = \begin{cases} M(\sqrt{b}t,x)\cdot M(\sqrt{1-b}t,\dfrac{\sqrt{a}}{\sqrt{1-b}}\xi) & , \ b \neq 1 \\ M(t,x)\exp(\sqrt{a}t\xi) & , \ b = 1 \end{cases}$$

where $a \in C - \{0\}$ and $b \in C - \{0,1\}$. We take the branches of the square roots $\sqrt{a}$, $\sqrt{b}$ and $\sqrt{1-b}$ so that they have real values when $a > 0$ and $0 < b < 1$. The formula (6) leads us to the well known additive formula of the Hermite polynomials:

$$(6')\quad H_N(\sqrt{a}\xi + \sqrt{b}x) = \begin{cases} \sum_{n=0}^{N} \binom{N}{n} b^{n/2}(1-b)^{(N-n)/2} H_n(x)\, H_{N-n}(\dfrac{\sqrt{a}}{\sqrt{b}}\xi), & b \neq 1 \\ \sum_{n=0}^{N} \binom{N}{n} a^{(N-n)/2} H_n(x)\xi^{N-n} & , \ b = 1. \end{cases}$$

In the next section we will need the following formulas:

$$(7)\quad E^x\exp(t(\sqrt{a}\xi + \sqrt{b}x)) = M(i\sqrt{b}t,\frac{\sqrt{a}}{i\sqrt{b}}\xi) \ ,$$

$$(6'')\quad E^x H_N(\sqrt{a}\xi + \sqrt{b}x) = \begin{cases} (1-b)^{N/2} H_N(\dfrac{\sqrt{a}}{\sqrt{1-b}}\xi) & , \ b \neq 1 \ , \\ a^{N/2}\xi^N & , \ b = 1 \ . \end{cases}$$

and

$$(7'')\quad E^x(\sqrt{a}\xi + \sqrt{b}x)^N = (i\sqrt{b})^N H_N(\frac{\sqrt{a}}{i\sqrt{b}}\xi) \ .$$

2. Group $G(\sqrt{a},\sqrt{b})$. Let P be the linear space of all polynomials in L_2. Consider a family of operators $\{G(\sqrt{a},\sqrt{b})\}$ on P:

$$(G(\sqrt{a},\sqrt{b})f(\xi) \equiv E^x f(\sqrt{a}\xi + \sqrt{b}x).$$

Using the formulas (6") and (7"), we get

PROPOSITION.

$$(i)\quad G(\sqrt{a},\sqrt{b})\ x^N = (i\sqrt{b})^N H_N(\frac{\sqrt{a}}{i\sqrt{b}}\xi) \ ,$$

$$(ii)\quad G(\overline{a}, \overline{b})\ H_N(x) = \begin{cases} (1-b)^{N/2} H_N(\dfrac{\sqrt{a}}{\sqrt{1-b}}\ ) & , \ b \neq 1 \ , \\ a^{N/2}\xi^N & , \ b = 1 \ . \end{cases}$$

This proposition implies that the operator $G(\sqrt{a},\sqrt{b})$ is an onto map from P to P.

Let us consider some operators of G with special values of parameters and consider the images of $H_N(x)$ and x^N under these operators:

	$H_N(x)$	x^N	
	$\downarrow$	$\downarrow$	
$F_2 = G(i,\sqrt{2})$;	$i^N H_N(\xi)$	$(\sqrt{2}i)^N H_N(\frac{1}{\sqrt{2}}\xi)$	: Fourier-Wiener tr.
$S = G(1,1)$;	ξ^N	$i^N H_N(-i\xi)$	: S-transform
$G = G(i,1)$;	$i^N \xi^N$	$i^N H_N(\xi)$	: Gauss-transform

The operator $T = \exp(-|\xi|^2/2)\cdot G$ is called T-transform. The ∞-dimensional version of this T-transform plays an essential role in T. Hida's works (for example, see [2]).

In the theory of Unitary representations of ∞-dimensional motion group, the ∞-dimensional version of the transform F_2 behaves as a kind of Fourier transform ([4],[8]).

Take a, b, c and d in $R-\{0\}$, as $0 < b,d,bc+d < 1$. Then we have

(8) $G(\sqrt{a},\sqrt{b})\cdot G(\sqrt{c},\sqrt{d}) = G(\sqrt{ac},\sqrt{bc+d})$.

To see this, observe that

$$G(\sqrt{a},\sqrt{b})\cdot G(\sqrt{c},\sqrt{d})\ f(y) = G(\sqrt{a},\sqrt{b})E^x f(\sqrt{c}y + \sqrt{d}x) =$$

$$= E^{Y} E^x f(\sqrt{c}(\sqrt{a}\xi + \sqrt{b}y) + \sqrt{d}x) = E^Y E^x f(\sqrt{ac}\xi + (\sqrt{cd}y + \sqrt{d}x))$$

$$= E^z f(\sqrt{ac}\xi + \sqrt{bc+d}z) = G(\sqrt{ac}, \overline{bc+d}) f(y) \ .$$

This composition law is the same as the following law of matrices:

$$\begin{pmatrix} a & 0 \\ b & 1 \end{pmatrix}\cdot\begin{pmatrix} c & 0 \\ d & 1 \end{pmatrix} = \begin{pmatrix} ac & 0 \\ bc+d & 1 \end{pmatrix} , \ a,b \in C \text{ and } a \neq 0.$$

Then, by analytic continuation of parameters we get,

THEOREM. $\{G(\sqrt{a},\sqrt{b})\}$ is locally isomorphic to the matrix group $\left\{\begin{pmatrix} a & 0 \\ b & 1 \end{pmatrix};\ a,\ b \in C,\ a \neq 0\right\}$.

Now, we can define the inverse operators of F_2, S and G :

	$H_N(x)$	x^N	
	$\downarrow$	$\downarrow$	
$F_2^{-1} = G(-i,-\sqrt{2})$;	$(-i)^N H_N(\xi)$	$(-i\sqrt{2})^N H_N(\frac{1}{\sqrt{2}}\xi)$	:

$S^{-1} = G(1,-i)$; $\qquad 2^{N/2} H_N(\frac{1}{\sqrt{2}}\xi) \qquad H_N(\xi) \qquad : \; :\cdot:$

$G^{-1} = G(-i,-1)$; $\qquad (-i)^N \xi^N \qquad (-i)^N H_N(\xi)$:

Specifically, $S^{-1}f$ is denoted as :f: and is called a *renormalization* of f ([3],[5]). Consider the 1-parameter subgroup $\{L_u = G(1,\sqrt{u});\ u \in R\}$ in G and its infinitesimal generator.

$$\frac{d}{du}(L_u f)(\xi)\Big|_{u=0} = \frac{d}{du}\int_{-\infty}^{\infty} f(\xi+\sqrt{u}x)\,d\mu(x)\Big|_{u=0} = \int \frac{x}{2\sqrt{u}}\, f'(\xi+\sqrt{u}x)\,d\mu(x)\Big|_{u=0}$$

$$= \int f''(\xi+\sqrt{u}x)\,e^{-x^2/2}\,\frac{dx}{2\sqrt{2\pi}}\Big|_{u=0} = \frac{1}{2}\int \frac{1}{\sqrt{2\pi u}}\, f''(\xi+z)\,e^{-z^2/2u}\,dz\Big|_{u=0}$$

$$= \frac{1}{2} f''(\xi) .$$

That is, L_u describes the 1-dimensional heat propagation:

(9) $$L_u = \exp\left(\frac{u}{2}\frac{d^2}{dx^2}\right) ,$$

$$S = \exp\left(\frac{1}{2}\frac{d^2}{dx^2}\right) \quad \text{and} \quad :\ : = \exp\left(-\frac{1}{2}\frac{d^2}{dx^2}\right) .$$

3. 1-dimensional outline of Hida calculus. In this section we consider specially the operator S. For $f = \sum_{n=0}^{N} a_n H_n$ of L_2, $S(f) = \sum a_n \xi^n$. Set $F_0 = \sum \oplus C$ and identify F_0 with the image $S(P)$. Let us define a norm of $S(f)$ in F_0 as $\|S(f)\|_F \equiv \|f\|_{L^2}$. Take the completion F of F_0 with respect to the norm $\|\cdot\|_F$. Then L_2 and F are isomorphic. For $\zeta = \sum \zeta_n \xi^n$ and $\eta = \sum \eta_n \xi^n$ of F the inner product (ζ,η) is $\sum n!\zeta_n \bar{\eta}_n$. In this sense we write F as exp C and call it the *Fock space* of C.

Let us define some operators on L_2 and F. For the mononomial ξ^n of F, set

$$\partial\xi : \xi^N \longrightarrow N\xi^{N-1} ,$$

and set ∂_ξ^* the adjoint operator of ∂_ξ ,

$$\partial_\xi^* : \xi^N \longrightarrow \xi^{N+1} .$$

In this sense ∂_ξ and ∂_ξ^* are called the annihilation and the creation operators of the Fock space F. ∂_ξ^* can be written $\xi\cdot$, a product operator in F. Define a *diffential operator* and its adjoint in L_2:

$$\partial_x = S^{-1}\partial_\xi S, \quad \partial_x^* = S^{-1}\partial_\xi^* S$$

Let us consider a *product operator* $x\cdot$ in L_2. Recall the formula (4),

$$x\cdot H_N(x) = H_{N+1}(x) + N\cdot H_{N-1}(x) ,$$

then it is natural to define the *product operator* in L_2 as

$$x\cdot = \partial_x^* + \partial_x .$$

Now we obtain the notions of a kind of *differentiation* and *multiplication*. It is natural to require a notion of *Fourier transform* which exchanges the foles of the differentiation ∂_x and the multiplication $x\cdot$. Recently Professor H.H. Kuo defined a Fourier transform which satisfies this requirement [6].

The key relation is

$$:e^{xy}:_x = e^{xy}/(e^{-y^2/2}) = e^{xy}/(E^x e^{xy}) = \sum \frac{y^n}{n!} H_n(x) .$$

After this, we use the variable y as the variable of the Fourier images and η as the associated variable of y under the S-transform. First we have a proposition:

PROPOSITION. The linear extension of the transform $x^n \longrightarrow x^{n+1} - n\cdot x^{n-1}$ agrees with ∂_x^* on P.

PROOF. The generating function can be written $M(t,x) = \exp(-t^2/2) \sum \frac{t^n}{n!} x^n$. Under the transform in question M(t,x) is transformed to

$$\exp(-t^2/2) \sum \frac{t^n}{n!} (x^{n+1}-nx^{n-1}) = \exp(-t^2/2)(x\sum \frac{t^n}{n!} x^n - t\sum \frac{t^{n-1}}{(n-1)!} x^{n-1})$$

$$= x\cdot M(t,x) - t\cdot M(t,x) = \sum H_{n+1}(x)\frac{t^n}{n!} \quad . \quad \textit{q.e.d.}$$

Set $\theta_x(y) = :e^{ixy}:_y = \sum H(y)\frac{(ix)^n}{n!}$. Professor H.H. Kuo defines the dual Fourier transform $F^*\phi$ of the element ϕ of P as $E^y\phi(y)\phi_x(y)$. For example, $\phi(y) = \sum a_n H_{n+1}(y)$ is transformed to $(F^*\phi)(x) = \sum a_n(ix)^n$. Let us calculate the dual-Fourier images of operators ∂_y^* and $y\cdot$. Since $\partial_y^*\phi(y) = \sum a_n H_{n+1}(y)$, $(F^*\partial_y^*\phi)(x) = \sum a_n(ix)^{n+1}$. That is

$$F^*\partial_y^* = ix.$$

The operator $y\cdot$ operates as $y\cdot\phi(y) = (\partial_y + \partial_y^*)\phi(y) = \sum a_n(H_{n+1}(y) + n\cdot H_{n-1}(y))$. So $(F^*y\cdot\phi)(x) = \sum a_n((ix)^{n+1} + n(ix)^{n-1})$. That is $F^*y\cdot$ transforms x^n into $ix^{n+1}-inx^{n-1}$.

Then by the proposition, $F^* y\cdot = i\partial_x^*$. F^* exchanges the dual-differentiation ∂_x^* with the multiplication $x\cdot$.

The definition of the Fourier transform $\hat{\psi}$ of ψ of Professor Kuo is

$$\langle \hat{\psi},\phi \rangle \equiv \langle \psi, F^*\phi \rangle \text{ , for any } \phi \in P.$$

According to this definition, we get

THEOREM. $(\partial_x)\hat{} = -iy\cdot$ and $(x\cdot)\hat{} = -i\partial_y$.

The Fourier transform is defined on the dual space of P in the same manner as the Fourier transform in the theory of distributions. In the next section, we will treat the generalized functionals of Brownian motion. So, the definition of this Fourier transform suits our purpose.

Example. $F^*M(t,y) = \sum \frac{t^n}{n!}(ix)^n = e^{itx} = M(it,x)e^{-t^2/2}$.

Then

$$\begin{aligned} \langle \hat{M}(s,x), M(t,y) \rangle &= \langle M(s,x), F^*M(t,y) \rangle \\ &= \langle M(s,x), \exp(-t^2/2)M(it,y) \rangle \\ &= \exp(-t^2/2) \sum \frac{(it)^n s^n}{n!} = \exp(-t^2/2)e^{its} \\ &= \sum_{n=0} \frac{s^n}{n!} i^n \sum_{k=0} (-\frac{1}{2})^k \frac{t^{2k+n}}{k!} . \end{aligned}$$

That is $\hat{H}_n(x) = i^n \sum_{k=0}^{\infty} (-1)^k H_{n+2k}(y)/(2^k k!)$.

We get the following interesting relation between S-transform and T-transform:

THEOREM. $\hat{S\phi} = T\phi$.

PROOF. $SH_n(x) = i^n \sum_{k=0}^{\infty} \xi^n(-\xi^2)^k/(2^k k!) = i^n \xi^n e^{-\xi^2/2} = TH_n(x)$

Note. Writing down the Fourier transform directly in the form of integral as follows, we see that F^* is just the Fourier transform.

$$\begin{aligned} F^*\phi(x) = E^y\theta_x(y)\phi(y) &= \frac{1}{\sqrt{2\pi}} \int_{-\infty}^{\infty} e^{ixy} e^{y^2/2} \phi(y)\, e^{-y^2/2}\, dy = \\ &= \frac{1}{\sqrt{2\pi}} \int_{-\infty}^{\infty} e^{ixy}\phi(y)\, dy. \end{aligned}$$

We can easily get the inverse Fourier transform using the kernel $\overline{\theta_y(x)}$.

4. Relations with Hida's calculus. Let $S \subset L^2(R) \subset S^*$ be the Gel'fand triplet. Consider a positive definite function $C(\xi) = \exp(-\|\xi\|^2/2)$ on S. Associated with this function, there is a probability measure μ on S^*. Hida's calculus analyzes the space of square summable non-linear functionals of S^*, $(L^2) = L^2(S^*,\mu)$. Let us define the S-transform and T-transform of an element F of (L^2).

$$(SF)(\xi) = E^x f(x+\xi) = C(\xi)E^x f(x,e)^{<x,\xi>}, \quad \xi \in S$$

$$(TF)(\xi) = E^x f(x)e^{i<x,\xi>} \qquad \xi \in S$$

Let $\{e_n\}$ be a c.o.n.s. of $L^2(R)$ such that the elements $e_n \in S$. We can expand the element $x \in S^*$ as $x = \sum a_n e_n$. Then we can consider the function $F(x)$ of (L^2) as a function of infinite variables $F(a_1,a_2,\ldots)$. The variables a_n have the standard Gaussian law N(0,1) with respect to the measure μ and are independent of each other. By this reason, in Case F is a tame function we can apply the results or the simple extension of the results of 3.

Hida's idea is that, instead of the usual c.o.n.s. we can use

$\{ \frac{\chi_{\Delta t}}{\sqrt{\Delta t}} \}$ as an o.n.s. and consider the limit as $\Delta \to 0$, that is we consider $\{\delta_t; t \in R\}$ as a c.o.n.s.. In this case the extensions of the results of 3 is the following:

S-transform maps (L^2) into a space of (non-linear) functions on S. For example $\phi \in (L^2)$, such that $\phi(x) = H_n(<x,e_k>)$ -- recall that $<x,e_k>$ is a random variable distributed N(0,1), so 3 is directly applicable --

$$U_\phi = S(\phi) = <\xi,e_k>^n = \int_{-\infty}^{\infty}\cdots\int_{-\infty}^{\infty} e_k(t_1)e_k(t_2)\ldots e_k(t_n)\xi(t_1)\ldots.\xi(t_n)\, dt_1dt_2\ldots dt_n .$$

The norm of U_ϕ is

$$\|U_\phi\|^2 = n! \int_{-\infty}^{\infty}\cdots\int_{-\infty}^{\infty} |e_k(t_1)|^2\cdots|e_k(t_n)|^2 dt_1\cdots dt_n .$$

Under the transform S, the space (L^2) is transformed onto the direct sum

$$S(L^2) = \sum n!L^2(R)^{\hat{\otimes} n} = F ,$$

where $\hat{\otimes}$ means the symmetric tensor product. Professor Hida considers that for a good functional F in F *the differentiation of a time point* t must be obtained by

$$\lim_{|\Delta t|\to 0} \to \frac{d}{d\varepsilon} F(\S + \frac{\varepsilon\chi_{\Delta t}}{\sqrt{\Delta t}})$$

This is equal to the functional derivative $\frac{\delta}{\delta\xi(t)}$ in the theory of variational calculus. A difficulty now arises: A general element of F is not differentiable. There is a good way to avoid this difficulty. Let us follow the theory of distributions. Consider the triplet for any integer n:

$$S(R)^{\hat{\otimes} n} \subset L^2(R)^{\hat{\otimes} n} \subset S^*(R)^{\hat{\otimes} n} ,$$

and

$$E = \sum\sqrt{n!}S(R)^{\hat{\otimes} n} \subset F \subset \sum\sqrt{n!}S^*(R)^{\hat{\otimes} n} = E^* .$$

We consider E and E^* as topological linear spaces with the projective limit topology and the inductive limit topology respectively. Then $E \subset F \subset E^*$ becomes again a Gel'fand triplet. In the space E^*, we can define an operator $\partial_{\xi(t)} = \frac{\delta}{\delta\xi(t)}$ and its dual $\partial^*_{\xi(t)} = (\frac{\delta}{\delta\xi(t)})^*$ in the generalized sense. The inverse image $S^{-1}(E)$ is called the space of *testing functionals* and its dual $(S^{-1}(E))^* = S^{-1}(E^*)$ is called the space of *generalized Brownian functionals*. Now we obtain the *differential operators* and the *multiplication operators at* t as follows:

$$\partial_{x(t)} = S^{-1}\frac{\delta}{\delta\xi(t)} S ,$$

$$\partial^*_{x(t)} = S^{-1}(\frac{\delta}{\delta\xi(t)})^* S$$

$$x(t)\cdot = \partial_{x(t)} + \partial^*_{x(t)} .$$

Using the kernel $\theta_x(y) = :e^{ixy}:_y = S_y^{-1}(e^{ixy})$ we see that Kuo's Fourier transform $\hat{}$ can be defined in the same manner in the 1-dimensional case and we have

THEOREM.

$$\hat{\partial}_{x(t)} = -iy(t),$$

$$(x(t)\cdot)^\wedge = -i\partial_{y(t)} \quad \text{and}$$

$$\hat{S\phi} = T\phi .$$

Finally for a good function F, we can define an ∞-dimensional Laplacian Δ as

$$\Delta F(x) \equiv \frac{d}{du} E^\xi F(x + \sqrt{u}\xi)\,|_{u=0} .$$

For examples 1) $F_1(X) = \int_0^1 F(t)x(t)dt$,

$$\Delta F_1 = 0.$$

2) $F_2(x) = \int_0^1\int_0^1 F(t,s)x(t)x(s)dtds$ then

$$\Delta F_2 = \int_0^1 F(t,t)dt.$$

Related to this Laplacian, there are interesting works about ∞-dimensional Brownian motion and Harmonic functions ([1]).

REFERENCES

[1] Y. Hasegawa; Lévy's functional analysis in terms of an infinite dimensional Brownian motion I,II. To appear in Osaka Journal of Mathematics (1982).

[2] T. Hida; Analysis of Brownian functionals. Carleton Math. Lect. Note No. 13 2nd ed. (1978).

[3] T. Hida and L. Streit; On quantum theory in terms of white noise. Nagoya Math. Journal vol. 68 21-34 (1977).

[4] L. Streit and T. Hida; Generalized Brownian functionals and the Feynman integral. To appear in Stochastic processes and their applications (1982).

[5] N. Kono; Special functions connected with representations of the infinite dimensional motion group. J. Math. Kyoto Univ. vol. 6 61-83 (1966).

[6] I. Kubo and S. Takenaka; Calculus on Gaussian white noise. I-IV Proc. Japan Acad. I and II vol. 56A 376-380, 411-416 (1980)
III vol. 57A 433-437 (1981)
IV vol. 58A 186-189 (1982).

[7] H.H. Kuo; On Fourier transform of generalized Brownian functionals. Preprint (1981).

[8] P. Lévy; Problémes concrets d'analyse fonctionnelle. Gauthier-Villars 1951.

[9] A. Orihara; Hermite polynomials and infinite dimensional motion group. J. Math. Kyoto Univ. vol. 6 1-12 (1966).

SOME PROBABILISTIC PROBLEMS
IN THE SPATIALLY HOMOGENEOUS BOLTZMANN EQUATION

Hiroshi Tanaka

Department of Mathematics
Faculty of Science and Technology
Keio University, Yokohama, Japan

1. Introduction

1.1. The master equation approach to the spatially homogeneous Boltzmann equation initiated by Kac [1] and continued by McKean [3], Grünbaum [5] and others is briefly reviewed together with some new results on

(I) propagation of chaos (law of large numbers),
(II) fluctuation (central limit theorem).

We are interested in the time evolution of the velocities $X_1^{(n)}(t), \dots, X_n^{(n)}(t)$ of n particles moving in the space R^3 under certain binary interaction (collision). We assume that $(X_1^{(n)}(t), \dots, X_n^{(n)}(t))$ is a Markov process on R^{3n} with generator

$$(K_n\varphi)(x_1,\dots,x_n)$$

$$= \frac{1}{n}\sum_{1\le i<j\le n}\int_{(0,\pi)\times(0,2\pi)}\{\varphi(\dots,x_i',\dots,x_j',\dots)-\varphi(x_1,\dots,x_n)\}Q(x_i,x_j,\theta)\,d\theta\, d\epsilon\,,$$

where x_i' and x_j' are the post-collision velocities of the i-th and j-th particles with velocities x_i and x_j. If $S(x,y)$ denotes the 2-dimensional sphere with center $(x+y)/2$ and diameter $|x-y|$, the x_i' and x_j' are always on $S(x_i,x_j)$ or more precisely $S(x_i',x_j')=S(x_i,x_j)$. We now take a spherical coordinate system on $S(x_i,x_j)$ with north pole x_i and denote by θ (resp. ϵ) the colatitude (resp. longitude) of x_i'. The function $Q(x,y,\theta)$, which is determined by the interparticle (binary) potential, is assumed to be nonnegative and depend only on $|x-y|$, $x+y$ and θ. The forward equation

$$(1)\qquad \frac{d}{dt}\langle u(t),\varphi\rangle = \langle u(t),K_n\varphi\rangle, \quad \varphi = \text{(test) function on } R^{3n}$$

describing the Markov process $X^{(n)}(t)$ is called the n-particle master equation corresponding to the following spatially homogeneous Boltzmann equation

(2) $$\frac{\partial u}{\partial t} = \int_{(0,\pi)\times(0,2\pi)\times R^3} (u'u_1' - uu_1)Q(x,x_1,\theta)d\theta d\epsilon\, dx_1 ,$$

where $u = u(t,x)$, $u_1=u(t,x_1)$, $u'=u(t,x')$, $u_1'=u(t,x_1')$; x' and x_1' are the post-collision velocities, i.e., $(x,x_1) \rightarrow (x',x_1')$ by "collision"; the notation $\langle u,\varphi\rangle$ in general stands for the integral of a function φ with respect to a measure u. As in [7] we consider a weak version of (2);

(3) $$\frac{d}{dt}\langle u(t),\varphi\rangle = \langle u(t)\otimes u(t),K\varphi\rangle ,$$

or equivalently

(3#) $$\frac{d}{dt}\langle u(t),\varphi\rangle = \langle u(t)\otimes u(t),K^{\#}\varphi\rangle ,$$

where φ is a (test) function R^3 and

(4) $$(K\varphi)(x,x_1) = \int_{(0,\pi)\times(0,2\pi)} \{\varphi(x') - \varphi(x)\}Q(x,x_1,\theta)d\theta d\epsilon ,$$

$$(K^{\#}\varphi)(x,x_1) = \{(K\varphi)(x,x_1) + (K\varphi)(x_1,x)\}/2 .$$

By a weak solution of (2) we mean a probability measure solution of (3) (=($3^{\#}$)) .

1.2. <u>Propagation of chaos</u>. Let $\{u_n, n>1\}$ be a sequence of probability measures, each u_n being a symmetric probability measure on the n-fold product space $R^{3n} = R^3\times\ldots\times R^3$. Let u be a probability measure on R^3 . Then a sequence $\{u_n\}$ is said to be u-chaotic if

$$\langle u_n,\varphi_1\otimes\ldots\otimes\varphi_m\otimes 1\otimes\ldots\otimes 1\rangle \rightarrow \prod_{k=1}^{m}\langle u,\varphi_k\rangle \quad \text{as} \quad n\rightarrow\infty \quad \text{for any} \quad \varphi_1,\ldots,$$

$\varphi_m\in C_0(R^3)$, $m\geq 1$. The relation between the master equation (1) and the corresponding Boltzmann equation (2) was made clear by Kac [I] through the following propagation of chaos : <u>Let</u> $u_n(t)$ <u>be the solution of</u> (1) <u>with initial value</u> u_n <u>and assume that</u> $\{u_n, n>1\}$ <u>is</u> u-<u>chaotic</u>. <u>Then</u> $\{u_n(t), n>1\}$ <u>is also</u> u(t)-<u>chaotic where</u> u(t) <u>is the</u> (<u>weak</u>) <u>solution</u> <u>of</u> (2) <u>with initial value</u> u . We next introduce the normalized occupation number

$$\bar{X}_n(t) = \frac{1}{n}\sum_{k=1}^{n}\delta_{X_k^{(n)}(t)}$$

where δ_x denotes the δ-distribution at x . We can easily show that

$\{u_n\}$ is u-chaotic if and only if the law of large numbers holds for $\{u_n\}$ in the following sense:

$$\frac{1}{n}\sum_{k=1}^{n}\delta_{X_k^{(n)}} \longrightarrow u , \qquad n \to \infty \text{ (in probability)}$$

where $X^{(n)} = (X_1^{(n)},\dots,X_n^{(n)})$ is a u_n-distributed random vector. Therefore, since $X^{(n)}(t)$ is $u_n(t)$-distributed provided that $X^{(n)}(0)$ is u_n-distributed, the propagation of chaos is equivalent to the following <u>law of large numbers</u>:

$$(5) \qquad \overline{X}_n(0) \to u,\ \ n \to \infty \text{ (in prob.)} \Rightarrow \overline{X}_n(t) \to u(t),\ \ n \to \infty \text{ (in prob.)}$$

where $u(t)$ is the same as before.

The proof of the propagation of chaos was first given by Kac [1] for the case of 1-dimensional Kac's model of Maxwellian molecules; McKean [3] gave a beautiful proof for some special case including cutoff model of the Boltzmann equation of Maxwellian molecules. Murata [6] treated the 2-dimensional non-cutoff Maxwellian model. Grünbaum [5] discussed the case of a considerably wide (cutoff) class; his discussions covered the gas of hard spheres but under some assumption which was unverified though very believable. In §2 of this article the propagation of chaos will be proved in the following two cases.

(i) $\displaystyle\int_0^{\pi} Q(x,y,\theta)\,d\theta \le \text{const.}(1+|x|^2+|y|^2)$.

(ii) (Maxwellian type) $Q(x,y,\theta)$ is a function $Q(\theta)$ of θ alone satisfying $\displaystyle\int_0^{\pi}\theta^2 Q(\theta)\,d\theta < \infty$.

It is to be noted that the case (i) includes the gas of hard spheres ($Q(x,y,\theta) = \text{const.}|x-y|\sin\theta$) while the case (ii) includes the 3-dimensional Maxwellian molecules with the inverse 5-th power interparticle repulsive force (in such a case $Q(\theta) \sim \text{const.}\,\theta^{-3/2}$, $\theta \downarrow 0$) .

1.3. <u>Fluctuation</u>. Since the normalized occupation number $\overline{X}_n(t)$ is fluctuating about a solution $u(t)$ of the Boltzmann equation (2), the next problem is to study the asymptotic behavior of

(6) $$Y_n(t) = \sqrt{n}(\overline{X}_n(t) - u(t))$$

as $n \to \infty$. The case of McKean's 2-state model of Maxwellian moleclues was first discussed by Kac [2] and then by McKean [4] in detail. As found in heuristic discussion by [4] for the case of gas of hard spheres, the limit process of $Y_n(t)$ must be, in general, an infinite dimensional Ornstein-Uhlenbeck process. Rigorous discussions in the case of Kac's 1-dimensional model of Maxwellian molecules were given by Tanaka [7] (equilibrium case) from the point of view of a limit theorem on Markov processes taking values of tempered distributions. Non-equilibrium case was then treated by Uchiyama [8]. Recently, Uchiyama [9] discussed the equilibrium case of cutoff type including gas of hard spheres. In §3 of this article the fluctuation theory (=central limit theorem) will be discussed in the case (ii) (Maxwellian type) along the same lines as in [7]. The emphasis here is on the non-cutoff property.

Fundamentally our method is to derive appropriate convergences of Markov processes $\overline{X}_n(t)$ and $Y_n(t)$ knowing the convergence of their generators (a martingale problem approach will then be useful), except for the treatment of chaos propagation in the case (ii) where the cutoff approximation will be used. Proofs are only outlined; details will appear elsewhere.

2. Propagation of chaos

2.1. Case (i). Let $\xi_0=1$, $\xi_1=x$ and $\xi_k=|x|^k$ for $k\geq 2$ $(x\in R^3)$.

Theorem 1. The function $Q(x,y,\theta)$, depending only on $|x-y|$, $x+y$ and θ, is assumed to satisfy the condition (i) of §1. In addition, we assume that

(7) $K\varphi$ is continuous provided that φ is bounded and continuous.

Let u_n be the initial distribution of $X^{(n)}(\cdot)$ and assume that $\{u_n\}$ is a u-chaotic sequence satisfying

$$\langle u,\xi_6\rangle<\infty, \quad \sup_{n\geq 1}\langle u_n, \xi_6\otimes 1\otimes\cdots\otimes 1\rangle<\infty .$$

Then for any $\varepsilon>0$ and T $(0<T<\infty)$

(8) $$P\left\{\sup_{0\leq t\leq T}\rho(\overline{X}_n(t), u(t))>\varepsilon\right\}\to 0$$

as $n\to\infty$, where ρ is any metric on $\mathcal{M}$ (the space of probability measures on R^3) which gives the usual vague topology on $\mathcal{M}$.

Remark. $u(t)$ in (8) is the solution of (3) (with $u(0)=u$) whose existence and uniquencess are guaranteed by the following Arkeryd's result [10]: Under the same assumption on $Q(x,y,\theta)$ as in Theorem 1 except for (7) (which is unnecessary here), for any initial value $u(o) = u$ satisfying $\langle u, \xi_4\rangle < \infty$ there exists a unique solution $u(t)$ of (3) such that $\langle u(t), \xi_4\rangle$ is bounded on each finite t-interval. The solution $u(t)$ also satisfies $\langle u(t), \xi_k\rangle = \langle u, \xi_k\rangle$, $k = 0,1,2$.

The proof of the theorem is sketched here. Choose a sequence $\{f_k, k\geq 1\}$ in $C_0(R^3)$ such that $\|f_k\|_\infty \leq 1$ and the set of all (finite) linear combinations of f_k's is dense in $C_0(R^3)$, and set $\rho(u, \tilde{u}) = \sum_{k=1}^{\infty} 2^{-k}|\langle u-\tilde{u}, f_k\rangle|$ for $u, \tilde{u} \in \mathcal{M}$. We first consider the special case in which $u_n(\mathcal{X}_n) = 1$, $n>1$, where $\mathcal{X}_n$ is the ball in R^{3n} of radius cn , the constant c being independent of n . Let $\mathcal{M}_0$ be the set of $u \in \mathcal{M}$ such that $\langle u, \xi_2\rangle \leq c$ and W be the space (endowed with the Skorohod topology) of $\mathcal{M}_0$-valued right continuous paths with left limits. Then $\overline{X}_n(t)$ is regarded as a Markov process with sample path in W . Denote by P_n the probability measure on W induced by the process $\overline{X}_n(t)$. We can prove the following lemmas (1°-3°) in which T is an arbitrary positive constant.

1°. $E_n\{\rho(w(t_1),w(t_2))^2\rho(w(t_2),w(t_3))^2\} \leq \text{const.}\,|t_3-t_1|^2$ for $0\leq t_1< t_2<t_3\leq T$, where const. may depend on T . Therefore, $\{P_n\}$ is tight.

2°. $\sup_n P_n\{\sup_{0\leq t\leq T}\langle w(t), \xi_4\rangle > N\} \longrightarrow 0$ as $N \to \infty$.

3°. If P_∞ is any limit point of $\{P_n\}$, then

a) $\sup_{0\leq t\leq T}\langle w(t), \xi_4\rangle < \infty$, P_∞-a.s.,

b) $\langle w(t),\varphi\rangle - \langle w(0),\varphi\rangle - \int_0^t \langle w(s)\otimes w(s), K^{\#}\varphi\rangle ds = 0$, P_∞-as, $\varphi \in C_0(R^3)$.

Since $\overline{X}_n(0) \to u$ in probability, $w(0)=u$ (P_∞-a.s.). Therefore, Arkeryd's uniqueness result applied to 3° implies that $w(t)=u(t)$, $t\geq 0$, P_∞-a.s., i.e., $P_\infty = \delta_{u(\cdot)}$. This implies (8).

General case can be reduced to the spacial case by noticing that $u_n(\mathcal{X}_n) \to 1$ as $n \to \infty$ where $\mathcal{X}_n$ is defined as before choosing a constant $c > \langle u, \xi_2\rangle$.

2.2. Case (ii). We deal with this case by approximating $Q(x,y,\theta)$ by cutoff one. Let $Q_\varepsilon(\theta)=Q(\theta)$ (for $\varepsilon<\theta<\pi$) and $=0$ (for $0<\theta\leq\varepsilon$), and define $K^{(\varepsilon)}$ with $Q(\theta)$ replaced by $Q_\varepsilon(\theta)$ (cutoff) in the definition (4) of K . Let $u_\varepsilon(t)$ be the solution of

$$(3\varepsilon) \qquad \frac{d}{dt}\langle u(t),\varphi\rangle = \langle u(t)\otimes u(t), K^{(\varepsilon)}\varphi\rangle$$

with initial value u.

Theorem 2. (i) If $\langle u,\xi_2\rangle<\infty$, then $u_\varepsilon(t)$ converges weakly to some $u(t)$ (as $\varepsilon\downarrow 0$) which is a solution of (3) with initial value u. (ii) If $\langle u,\xi_2\rangle<\infty$ and if $\{u_n\}$ is a u-chaotic sequence satisfying

$$\lim_{n\to\infty}\langle u_n,\xi_2\otimes 1\otimes\ldots\otimes 1\rangle = \langle u,\xi_2\rangle ,$$

then $\{u_n(t)\}$ is also $u(t)$-chaotic and

$$\lim_{n\to\infty}\langle u_n(t),\xi_2\otimes 1\otimes\ldots\otimes 1\rangle = \langle u(t),\xi_2\rangle ,$$

where $u(t)$ is the solution of (3) constructed in (i).

3. Fluctuation

We consider only the case of non-cutoff Maxwellian type. Thus we assume that a function $Q(\theta)$ satisfying (ii) of §1 is given. We set

$$g(x)=(2\pi)^{-3/2}e^{-|x|^2/2}\ , \quad g=g(x)dx\ , \quad e_0(x)=\sqrt{g(x)}\ .$$

We also assume that the initial distribution of $X^{(n)}(\cdot)$ is the n-fold product $g^{n\otimes}$. In this case we have $u_n(t)=g^{n\otimes}$ and $u(t)=g$, and (for notational convention) it is better to modify the definition (6) of $Y_n(t)$ as follows.

$$Y_n(t) = \sqrt{n}\{\overline{X}_n(t) - g\}/e_0(\cdot)\ ,$$

i.e.,
$$\langle Y_n(t),\varphi\rangle = n^{-1/2}\sum_{k=1}^{n}\left\{\frac{\varphi(X_k^{(n)}(t))}{e_0(X_k^{(n)}(t))} - \langle e_0,\varphi\rangle\right\} .$$

The fluctuation theory is to study the asymptotic behavior of $Y_n(t)$ as $n\to\infty$. Note that $Y_n(t)$ is a Markov process on the state space

$$\left\{\eta\in\mathcal{S}'(R^3):\ \eta=\sqrt{n}(\overline{x}-g)/e_0(\cdot)\ ,\quad \overline{x}=\frac{1}{n}\sum_{1}^{n}\delta_{x_k},x_1,\ldots,x_n\in R^3\right\} .$$

We introduce some notation.

$$\hat{\varphi}(x,y) = \varphi(x') + \varphi(y') - \varphi(x) - \varphi(y)\ ,$$

$$Q[\varphi,\psi] = \frac{1}{4}\int_{(0,\pi)\times(0,2\pi)} \hat{\varphi}(x,y)\hat{\psi}(x,y)Q(x,y,\theta)d\theta d\epsilon \ ,$$

$$\varphi^{\#}(x) = \varphi(x)/e_0(x), \quad \tilde{\varphi}(x,y) = \widehat{\varphi^{\#}}(x,y) \ .$$

Let $F(\eta)$ be a function of the form

$$F(\eta) = f(\langle\eta,\varphi_1\rangle,\dots,\langle\eta,\varphi_m\rangle), \quad f\in C_0^{\infty}(R^3), \quad \varphi_1,\dots,\varphi_m\in\mathcal{S},$$

where $\mathcal{S}=\mathcal{S}(R^3)$, the space of rapidly decreasing C^{∞}-functions. Then the generator L_n of the Markov process $Y_n(t)$ is given by

$$L_nF(\eta) = \sum_{\alpha=1}^{m}\left\langle e_0\eta\otimes\left(\frac{e_0\eta}{\sqrt{n}} + 2g\right) , K^{\#}\varphi_{\alpha}^{\#}(x,y)\right\rangle\partial_{\alpha}f$$

$$+ \sum_{\alpha,\beta=1}^{m}\left\langle\left(\frac{e_0\eta}{\sqrt{n}} + g\right)^{2\otimes}, Q[\varphi_{\alpha}^{\#},\varphi_{\beta}^{\#}]\right\rangle\partial_{\alpha\beta}^2 f + R_n \ ,$$

$$R_n = \frac{1}{6n^2\sqrt{n}}\sum_{\alpha,\beta,\gamma=1}^{m}\ \sum_{1\le i<j\le n}\int_{(0,\pi)\times(0,2\pi)}(\tilde{\varphi}_{\alpha}\tilde{\varphi}_{\beta}\tilde{\varphi}_{\gamma})(x_i,x_j)\partial_{\alpha\beta\gamma}^3 fQd\theta d\epsilon \ ,$$

where the argument in $\partial_{\alpha\beta\gamma}^3 f$ is

$$\left(\langle\eta,\varphi_1\rangle + \frac{\kappa\tilde{\varphi}_1(x_i,x_j)}{\sqrt{n}},\dots,\langle\eta,\varphi_m\rangle + \frac{\kappa\tilde{\varphi}_m(x_i,x_j)}{\sqrt{n}}\right), \quad 0<\kappa<1 \ ,$$

and hence the limiting generator $L=\lim_{n\to\infty}L_n$ is given (at least formally) by

$$LF(\eta) = 2\sum_{\alpha=1}^{m}\langle e_0\eta\otimes g, K^{\#}\varphi_{\alpha}^{\#}\rangle\partial_{\alpha}f + \sum_{\alpha,\beta=1}^{m}\left\langle g\otimes g, Q[\varphi_{\alpha}^{\#},\varphi_{\beta}^{\#}]\right\rangle\partial_{\alpha\beta}^2 f \ .$$

Now the problem may be stated as follows: (a) Find a diffusion process $Y(t)$ with generator L on a suitable space of distributions. (b) Prove the convergence in the law sense of $Y_n(t)$ to $Y(t)$.

Linearized collision operator: If we introduce l.c.o. $\mathcal{L}$ by

$$\mathcal{L}\varphi(x) = e_0(x)\int_{(0,\pi)\times(0,2\pi)\times R^3} g(y)\tilde{\varphi}(x,y)Q(x,y,\theta)d\theta d\epsilon dy \ ,$$

L can be expressed as

$$\text{(9)} \qquad LF(\eta) = -\sum_{\alpha,\beta=1}^{m} (\mathcal{L}\varphi_\alpha, \varphi_\beta)_0 \partial^2_{\alpha\beta} f + \sum_{\alpha=1}^{m} \langle \eta, \mathcal{L}\varphi_\alpha \rangle \partial_\alpha f ,$$

where (,) denotes the usual inner product in $L^2(R^3)$.

Eigenfunctions of $\mathcal{L}$: For each integer $\ell \geq 0$ we choose $2\ell+1$ harmonic polynomials H_ℓ^m, $m=0, \pm 1, \dots, \pm\ell$ of degree ℓ so that the family

$$\left\{ S_\ell^m \equiv H_\ell^m \Big|_{S^2} \text{(spherical harmonics)}: \ m=0, \pm 1, \dots, \pm \ell \right\}$$

forms an ONS in $L^2(S^2)$, and set

$$e_{\underline{n}}(x) = c_{\underline{n}} e_0(x) L_n^{\ell+\frac{1}{2}}(|x|^2/2) H_\ell^m(x) ,$$

$$\underline{n} = (n, \ell, m), \quad n, \ell = 0, 1, \dots, \quad m = 0, \pm 1, \dots, \pm \ell ,$$

where

$L_n^{\ell+\frac{1}{2}}(t)$ = the associated Laguerre polynomial of degree n and order $\ell + \frac{1}{2}$,

$$c_{\underline{n}} = \left\{ \frac{n!\, \pi^{3/2}}{2^{\ell-1}\, \Gamma(n+\ell+\frac{3}{2})} \right\}^{1/2} .$$

Then $\left\{ e_{\underline{n}} : \underline{n} = (n, \ell, m) \right\}$ is a CONS in $L^2(R^3)$. It is known that $e_{\underline{n}}$'s are eigenfunctions of $\mathcal{L}$ ([11] [12]), i.e.,

$$e_{\underline{n}} = -\lambda_{\underline{n}} e_{\underline{n}} ,$$

where

$$\lambda_{\underline{n}} = 2\pi \int_0^\pi \left\{ 1 - (\cos\tfrac{\theta}{2})^{2n+\ell} P_\ell(\cos\tfrac{\theta}{2}) - (\sin\tfrac{\theta}{2})^{2n+\ell} P_\ell(\sin\tfrac{\theta}{2}) \right\} Q(\theta) d\theta$$

$$\geq 0 \quad \text{if} \quad 2n + \ell > 0 ,$$

$$\lambda_{(0,0,0)} = \lambda_{(0,1,m)} = \lambda_{(1,0,0)} = 0 \quad \text{for} \quad m = 0, \pm 1 ,$$

$P_\ell(t)$ being the Legendre polynomial of degree ℓ . We can prove that

$$\text{(10)} \qquad \lambda_{\underline{n}} \leq \text{const.}(2n + \ell)^2 .$$

Moreover, $e_{\underline{n}}$'s are also eigenfunctions of $\frac{|x|^2}{4} - \Delta$, i.e.,

(11) $$\left(\frac{|x|^2}{4} - \Delta\right)e_{\underline{n}} = (2n + \ell + \tfrac{3}{2})e_{\underline{n}} .$$

Spaces of distributions:

$$\|\varphi\|_\alpha = \left\|\left(\frac{|x|^2}{4} - \Delta\right)^{\alpha/2}\varphi\right\|_0 , \quad \alpha \in R$$

$$\left(= \left\{\sum_{\underline{n}} a_{\underline{n}}^2 (2n + \ell + \tfrac{3}{2})^\alpha\right\}^{1/2} \quad \text{for } \varphi = \sum a_{\underline{n}} e_{\underline{n}} \text{ by (11)}\right),$$

$\mathcal{S}_\alpha$ = the Hilbert space obtained by completing $\mathcal{S}$ with respect to $\|\cdot\|_\alpha$,

$\mathcal{S}_\alpha'$ = the dual space of $\mathcal{S}_\alpha$ $(\cong \mathcal{S}_{-\alpha})$.

Stochastic differential equation: Let $B(t)$ be a Brownian motion on $\mathcal{S}'$ determined by

$$E\left\{e^{i\langle B(t),\varphi\rangle}\right\} = e^{-t\|\varphi\|_0^2/2} , \quad \varphi \in \mathcal{S} , \quad B(0) = 0;$$

in fact $B(t)$ exists as an $\mathcal{S}_{3+\varepsilon}'$-Brownian motion $(\forall \varepsilon > 0)$. From the expression (9) of $\mathcal{L}$ it follows that the Markov process $Y(t)$ with generator L should satisfy the stochastic differential equation

(12) $$dY(t) = \sqrt{-2\mathcal{L}}\, dB(t) + \mathcal{L}\, Y(t)dt .$$

If we set $Y_{\underline{n}}(t) = \langle Y(t), e_{\underline{n}}\rangle$, then (12) yields

$$dY_{\underline{n}}(t) = \sqrt{2\lambda_{\underline{n}}}\, dB_{\underline{n}}(t) - \lambda_{\underline{n}} Y_{\underline{n}}(t)dt ,$$

where $B_{\underline{n}}(t)$'s are independent copies of 1-dimensional Brownian motion. Making use of the bound (10) for $\lambda_{\underline{n}}$ it can be proved that

$$\sum_{2n+\ell \le k} Y_{\underline{n}}(t)e_{\underline{n}} \rightarrow Y(t) \quad \text{as} \quad k \rightarrow \infty$$

uniformly on each finite t-interval in the space $\mathcal{S}_{3+\varepsilon}'$ almost surely for any $\varepsilon > 0$, and we can finally prove the following theorem.

<u>Theorem 3</u>. The Markov process $Y(t)$ with generator L and satisfying

$$E\left\{e^{i\langle Y(0),\varphi\rangle}\right\} = e^{-\left\{\|\varphi\|_0^2-(e_0,\varphi)_0^2\right\}/2}, \quad \varphi\in\mathcal{S}$$

exists as a diffusion process on $\mathcal{S}'_{3+\varepsilon}$ for any $\varepsilon>0$, and any finite dimensional distribution of $Y_n(t)$ as a process on $\mathcal{S}'_{3+\varepsilon}$ converges to the corresponding finite dimensional distribution of $Y(t)$ as $n\to\infty$.

It is to be noted that the SDE (12) has a solution $Y(t)$ which is continuous in $\mathcal{S}'_{3+\varepsilon}$, while the process $\sqrt{-2\mathcal{L}}\,B(t)$ is not always continuous in $\mathcal{S}'_{3+\varepsilon}$.

References

1. M. Kac, Foundations of kinetic theory, Proc. Third Berkeley Symp. on Math. Stat. and Prob., 3(1956), 171-197.
2. M. Kac, Some probabilistic aspects of the Boltzmann-equation, Acta Physica Austriaca, Suppl. X(1973), 379-400.
3. H. P. McKean, An exponential formula for solving Boltzmann's equation for a Maxwellian gas, J. Combinatorial Theory, 2(1967), 358-382.
4. H. P. McKean, Fluctuations in the kinetic theory of gases, Comm. Pure Appl. Math., 28(1975), 435-455.
5. F. A. Grünbaum, Propagation of chaos for the Boltzmann equation, Arch. Rational Mech. Anal., 42(1971), 323-345.
6. H. Murata, Propagation of chaos for Boltzmann-like equation of non-cutoff type in the plane, Hiroshima Math. J., 7(1977), 479-515.
7. H. Tanaka, Fluctuation theory for Kac's one-dimensional model of Maxwellian molecules, to appear in Sankhyā, 44, Series A, Part I (1982).
8. K. Uchiyama, Fluctuations of Markovian systems in Kac's caricature of a Maxwellian gas, to appear in J. Math. Soc. Japan.
9. K. Uchiyama, A Fluctuation problem associated with the Boltzmann equation for a gas of molecules with a cut-off potential, to appear.
10. L. Arkeryd, On the Boltzmann equation, Part I, II, Archive for Rational Mech. Anal., 45(1972), 1-16, 17-34.
11. C. S. Wang Chang and G. E. Uhlenbeck (1952), In "The Kinetic Theory of Gases", Studies in Statistical Mechanics, Vol. V, North-Holland, Amsterdam (1970).
12. C. Cercignani, Mathematical Methods in Kinetic Theory, Plenum Press, New York (1969).

UNILATERAL MODELS FOR STOCHASTIC LATTICE PROCESSES.

Dag Tjøstheim
Department of Mathematics
University of Bergen
5000 Bergen, Norway

1. Introduction.

Let $(\Omega,\mathfrak{F},P)$ be a probability space and Z the set of all integers. Denote by Z^n the regular cartesian lattice obtained by taking the product of n copies of Z. The purpose of this paper is to study a class of parametric models for a lattice process $\{F(x,\omega), x \in Z^n, \omega \in \mathfrak{F}\}$, where each $F(x,\cdot)$ is measurable with respect to $\mathfrak{F}$. To simplify our notations we will suppress the ω-dependence and write $\{F(x), x \in Z^n\}$ or simply $F(x)$.

In practice data on a lattice can arise in at least two ways. One possibility is lattice sampling of continuous data (e.g. satellite photographs), the other is by interpolation of irregularly spaced discrete measurements. Parametric models for such data could be used for information compression and image recognition. In the time domain the parameters of autoregressive (AR) models, for example, have been used (Tjøstheim 1981a) for feature extraction and wave form recognition in such diverse fields as seismic discrimination, speech recognition and EEG analysis. Time series models are unilateral in structure following the natural distinction between past and present. No such obvious ordering exists in the lattice case, and a priori it seems natural that a parametric model for $F(x)$ should contain neighboring values in all directions. However, as demonstrated by Whittle (1954) it is very hard to apply standard methods of statistical inference to such models.

These difficulties motivate the introduction of unilateral lattice process models, and these models are the topic of this investigation. A brief review of the representation theory of such models is given in Section 2. A theory of estimation is outlined in Sections 3 and 4. Some of the proofs will only be sketched. Full proofs will be published elsewhere.

2. Representation theory of unilateral models.

Let H be the Hilbert space of all complex-valued random variables having a second moment, and where the inner product between to random variables F and G in H is defined by $(F,G) = E\{F\overline{G}\}$. Let $\{F(x), x \in Z^n\}$ be a lattice process such that $F(x) \in H$ for $x \in Z^n$. The linear space $H(F)$ associated with $F(x)$ is defined as the subspace $H(F) \subset H$ obtained by taking the closure in H of the linear hull of the set of elements $\{F(x), x \in Z^n\}$. Clearly the Hilbert space $H(F)$ is separable.

In all of the following $\{F(x), x \in Z^n\}$ will be assumed to be zero-mean and weakly homogeneous; i.e.

$$E\{F(x+h)\overline{F(y+h)}\} = E\{F(x)\overline{F(y)}\} \tag{2.1}$$

for arbitrary $x, y, h \in Z^n$. Two main types of unilateral representations have been studied.

2.1. Half-space representations.

These types of representations were introduced by Whittle (1954) who considered the planar case and expressed $F(x_1,x_2)$ as an autoregression on $F(x_1,y_2)$ for $y_2 > x_2$ and $F(y_1,y_2)$ for $y_1 > x_1$ and y_2 unrestricted.

Helson and Lowdenslager (1958,1961) developed a mathematical theory for these representations in quite a general setting. Following their terminology S is a half-space (located at the origon) of lattice points if

A1: $0 \notin S$

A2: $x \in S$ if and only if $-x \notin S$, unless $x = 0$

A3: $x \in S$ and $y \in S$ imply $x+y \in S$,

such that $Z^n = S \cup (-S) \cup \{0\}$. This definition and much of the theory can be extended (Helson and Lowdenslager 1961) to the case where Z^n is replaced by the dual $\hat{K}$ of a compact abelian group K. The half-space S induces a linear order on Z^n by

$$y < x \quad \text{if} \quad x-y \in S \tag{2.2}$$

As is easy to check this ordering coincides with a lexicographic ordering of Z^n.

Assume that the spectral density $g(e^{i\lambda}) = g(e^{i\lambda_1},\dots,e^{i\lambda_n})$ of $F(x)$ exists and let $I = [-\pi,\pi]$. Helson and Lowdenslager (1958,1961) showed that

$$\int_{I^n} \ln g(e^{i\lambda})d\lambda > -\infty \tag{2.3}$$

is a necessary and sufficient condition for the spectral factorization problem to have a solution in the general lattice half-space case. The significance of the condition (2.3) for our purposes is that it guaranties existence of a Wold-type decomposition

$$F(x) = W(x) + \sum_{y\in S} b(y)W(x-y) \tag{2.4}$$

and a corresponding (usually infinite) recursively defined AR representation

$$F(x) - \sum_{y<x} a(x-y)F(y) = W(x) \tag{2.5}$$

where $\{W(x), x \in Z^n\}$ is a white noise process with $E\{W(x)\overline{W(y)}\} = \delta_x^y \sigma_W^2$, and where the ordering is defined by the half-space S . This recursive property in turn implies that the Jacobian J_W corresponding to a transformation from F-variables to W-variables is independent of the AR parameters. It is exactly the lack of this property which creates problems for the estimation of non-unilateral AR models.

In time domain the Wold decomposition is coupled with the concept of a purely non-deterministic (PND) process, which is defined in terms of the ordered chain of Hilbert spaces spanned by $\{F(s), s \leq t\}$. The definition of PND has been generalized in various ways to the random field case. Based on their definition of PND Kallianpur and Mandrekar (1981) obtain unilateral expansions different from those discussed in this paper.

2.2. Causal type (quadrant) representations.

Following the notation in Tjøstheim (1978), for $a,b \in Z^n$, $S[a,b]$ is defined by

$$S[a,b] = \{x = (x_1,\ldots,x_n) \in Z^n : a_k \leq x_k \leq b_k ; \quad k = 1,\ldots,n\} \tag{2.6}$$

and $S\langle a,b] = S[a,b] - \{a\}$. Moreover, we define $S[a,\infty] = \{x \in Z^n , x_k \geq a_k\}$ and $S\langle a,\infty] = S[a,\infty] - \{a\}$. The symbols $S[-\infty,b]$ and $S[-\infty,b\rangle$ are defined likewise. Corresponding to (2.5) we say that $F(x)$ has a unilateral expansion of causal type if

$$F(x) = W(x) + \sum_{y \in S\langle 0,\infty]} b(y)W(x-y) \tag{2.7}$$

with a corresponding recursively defined AR representation. In the planar case this means a representation using the lattice points of the first quadrant. The term "causal" has now come into common usage for these representations especially in the engineering literature.

The spectral condition (2.3) is necessary but not sufficient for a representation (2.7) to exist. A sufficient but not necessary condition is obtained (Rudin 1969, p.54, Tjøstheim 1978) by requiring that $g(e^{i\lambda})$ is bounded, positive and lower semi-continuous on I^n .

3. Theory of estimation.

We assume that a basic half-space (quadrant) has been chosen once and for all and that it is fixed. Following Whittle (1954) and Tjøstheim (1978) we will restrict ourselves to AR models. No doubt it will be possible to extend the theory to autoregressive-moving average (ARMA) models. On the other hand it is clear from Sections 2.1 and 2.2 that a large class of weakly homogeneous lattice processes can be approximated by unilateral AR models.

Using the notation defined after (2.6) we define a causal (quadrant-type) AR process of order $p = (p_1, \ldots, p_n)$ by

$$F(x) - \sum_{y \in S\langle 0,p]} a(y)F(x-y) = W(x) \tag{3.1}$$

for $x \in Z^n$, where $\{W(x), x \in Z^n\}$ is a weakly homogeneous white noise process.

It is clearly possible to find a half-space $S_{1+}(\infty)$ in Z^n such that $S\langle 0,\infty] \subset S_{1+}(\infty)$ and such that $S_{1+}(\infty)$ does not contain any $x \in Z^n$ with $x_1 < 0$. ($S_{1+}(\infty)$ may be taken to consist of all x with $x_1 > 0$; with $x_1 = 0$, $x_2 > 0$; $x_1 = x_2 = 0$, $x_3 > 0$; ... ; $x_1 = \ldots = x_{n-1} = 0$, $x_n > 0$). We let $S_{1+}(p) = S_{1+}(\infty) \cap S[-p,p]$ and define a half-space AR process of order $p = (p_1, \ldots, p_n)$ by

$$F(x) - \sum_{y \in S_{1+}(p)} a(y)F(x-y) = W(x) \tag{3.2}$$

with $x \in Z^n$. Clearly $S\langle 0,p] \subset S_{1+}(p)$.

A number of results will be common for the two models (3.1) and (3.2) To avoid too much repetition we will use the common symbol S_p for $S\langle 0,p]$ and $S_{1+}(p)$ in such situations. The symbol S_∞ is defined likewise. Similarly $d(p)$ will be used to denote the number of unknown AR parameters $\{a(y), y \in S_p\}$. It is easy to check that for $S_p = S\langle 0,p]$; i.e. model (3.1), we have

$$d(p) = \prod_{i=1}^{n} (p_i + 1) - 1 \tag{3.3}$$

whereas for $S_p = S_{1+}(p)$; i.e. model (3.2), we have

$$d(p) = \tfrac{1}{2}\left[\prod_{i=1}^{n} (2p_i + 1) - 1\right] \tag{3.4}$$

We assume that (3.1) and (3.2) can be inverted so that

$$F(x) = W(x) + \sum_{y \in S_\infty} b(y)W(x-y) \tag{3.5}$$

with $\sum_{y \in S_\infty} |b(y)|^2 < \infty$. If $A_0(z) = \{z : A(z) = 0\}$ is the zero set of $A(z) = 1 - \sum_{y \in S_p} a(y)z^y$, then a sufficient condition for stability is that $\bar{D}_n \cap A_0(z)$ is empty, where $\bar{D}_n$ is the closure of the open unit polydisc D_n in C^n. Many other sufficient conditions have been derived, especially for $n = 2$ (cf. O'Connor and Huang 1978 and references therein). It should be noted that in the engineering literature, $\Sigma|b(y)|^2 < \infty$ is usually replaced by $\Sigma|b(y)| < \infty$ corresponding to the emphasis on L^1-bounded signals.

3.1. Types of estimates.

Assume that we have observations of $F(x)$ for $x \in S[1,M]$, where $M_1 \geq p_1 + 1$ and $M_i \geq 2p_i + 1$; $i=2,\ldots,n$. We define estimates $\hat{R}(u,v)$ of $R(u,v) = E\{F(u)\overline{F(v)}\}$ by

$$\hat{R}(u,v) = \left(\prod_{i=1}^{n} M_i\right)^{-1} \sum_{x \in S[1,M-u+v]} F(x+u-v)\overline{F(x)} \tag{3.6}$$

for $u-v \in S_p$, with a similar definition for $u,v \in S_p$, and get the so-called Yule-Walker (YW) estimates $\{\hat{a}(y) , y \in S_p\}$ from (cf. Tjøstheim 1978)

$$\sum_{y \in S_p} \hat{R}(u,y)\hat{a}(y) = \hat{R}(u,0) , \qquad u \in S_p \tag{3.7}$$

By ordering the elements in S_p in a linear order we can write (3.7) as a matrix equation

$$\hat{R}_p \hat{a} = \hat{r} \tag{3.8}$$

where $\hat{R}_p$ is the $d(p) \times d(p)$ matrix and $\hat{a}$ and $\hat{r}$ are the $d(p)$-dimensional vectors obtained by using this ordering on $\hat{R}(u,y)$, $\hat{a}(y)$ and $\hat{R}(u,0)$ respectively.

Let

$$L(M,p) = \{x \in S[1,M] : x - y \in S[1,M] \text{ for } y \in S_p\} \tag{3.9}$$

Then the least squares (LS) estimates $a^*(y)$ of $a(y)$ are obtained by minimizing

$$\sum_{x \in L(M,p)} \left|F(x) - \sum_{y \in S_p} a(y)F(x-y)\right|^2 ; \tag{3.10}$$

i.e., $\{a^*(y) , y \in S_p\}$ is obtained from

$$\sum_{x \in L(M,p)} \left\{F(x)\overline{F(x-u)} - \sum_{y \in S_p} a^*(y)F(x-y)\overline{F(x-u)}\right\} = 0 , \quad u \in S_p . \tag{3.11}$$

If $M_i \to \infty$ for $i=1,\ldots,n$ then the difference between the two estimates $\hat{a}(y)$ and $a^*(y)$ becomes negligible in the limit, and thus the asymptotic theory is the same.

3.2. Consistency and asymptotic normality.

Weak consistency for model (3.1) was obtained in Tjøstheim (1978). For notational convenience we consider a sample region with $M_1 = M_2 = \ldots = M_n = T$; i.e. with $N = T^n$ observations altogether. We denote this region by $I(T)$.

Theorem 3.1: Let $\{F(x), x \in Z^n\}$ be a stable causal or half-space AR(p) model generated by a series of independent identically distributed random variables $\{W(x), x \in Z^n\}$. Assume that we have observed $F(x)$ for $x \in I(T)$. Then as $T \to \infty$, the vector $\hat{a} = \{\hat{a}(y), y \in S_p\}$ of YW (or LS) estimates defined by (3.8) converges almost surely to the vector $a = \{a(y), y \in S_p\}$ of AR parameters.

Proof: The assumption on $\{W(x), x \in Z^n\}$ means that $\{F(x), x \in Z^n\}$ is strictly homogeneous. Clearly the invariant sets of $\{W(x), x \in Z^n\}$ have probability measure 0 or 1. Using the stability, inverting in terms of $\{W(x), x \in Z^n\}$, we have that the shift operator of the $F(x)$-process agrees with that of the $W(x)$-process on the domain on which it is defined. Thus the invariant sets of $\{F(x), x \in Z^n\}$ have measure 0 or 1, and $F(x)$ is ergodic. Using the definition (3.6) of $\hat{R}(u,v)$ and the ergodic theorem for spatial processes (cf. Adler 1981, p.143) it follows that $\hat{R}(u,v) \xrightarrow{a.s.} R(u,v)$ as $T \to \infty$. It now follows from (3.6) and (3.7) that $\hat{a}(y) \xrightarrow{a.s.} a(y)$ for $y \in S_p$. ||

For real-valued causal models asymptotic normality was obtained in Theorem 8.1 of Tjøstheim (1978). Essentially the same proof can be carried through for the half-space case for a general linear ordering.

3.3. Determination of the order parameter p.

Up to now we have considered estimation theory for AR(p) lattice processes for a fixed p. In practice p is unknown and must be determined from the data. As a natural generalization of the criteria used in the time series case (see e.g. Hannan and Quinn 1979) we consider a procedure where an estimate $\hat{p}$ of p is obtained by choosing the q minimizing the criterion function

$$C(q) = \ln \hat{\sigma}^2(q) + N^{-1} f(N)\, d(q) . \tag{3.12}$$

Here q is allowed to vary in $S[0,K]$ for a fixed (independent of N) $K \in Z^n$. Furthermore, $N = \prod_{i=1}^{n} M_i$ is the total number of observations, while $\hat{\sigma}^2(q)$ is the residual variance for a fitted AR(q) model using LS estimates (YW estimates give same result); i.e.

$$\hat{\sigma}^2(q) = N^{-1} \sum_{x \in L(M,q)} \left| F(x) - \sum_{y \in S_q} a^*(q,y) F(x-y) \right|^2 . \tag{3.13}$$

The function $d(q)$ gives the number of estimated AR parameters and is defined in (3.3) and (3.4). Finally the function $f(N)$ determines the strength of the "penalty" term of (3.12). In the time series case $d(q) = q$ and $f(N) = 2$, $\ln N$, $2 \ln\ln N$ for the so-called AIC, BIC and LIL criteria, respectively.

It seems natural to introduce a partial ordering $\prec$ among the orders $q \in S[0,K]$ by

$$q \prec q' \quad \text{iff} \quad q_i \leq q_i' \qquad i=1,\ldots,n \ . \tag{3.14}$$

We need some lemmas. The recursive property obtained by concentrating on unilateral half-spaces and causal representations is vital for the first lemma.

Lemma 3.1: Let $\{F(x)\,, x \in Z^n\}$ be a stable causal or half-space AR(p) process with $p \prec K$ for some $K \in Z^n$. Let $q \in S[0,K]$ and let

$$\sigma^2(q) = \min_c E|F(x) - \sum_{y \in S_q} c(y)F(x-y)|^2 \tag{3.15}$$

If $p \prec q$, then $\sigma^2(p) = \sigma^2(q)$, whereas if $p \nprec q$, then $\sigma^2(p) < \sigma^2(q)$.

Proof: Due to stability we have $E\{Z(x)\overline{F(x-y)}\} = 0$ for $y \in S_K$ and thus

$$P_K F(x) = \sum_{y \in S_p} a(y)F(x-y) \tag{3.16}$$

where P_K is the projection operator on the subspace of $H(F)$ spanned by $F(x-y)$ for $y \in S_K$. From the definition of a projection operator we have

$$\begin{aligned} \sigma^2(p) = \sigma_W^2 &= E|F(x) - \sum_{y \in S_p} a(y)F(x-y)|^2 \\ &= \min_c E|F(x) - \sum_{y \in S_K} c(y)F(x-y)|^2 = \sigma^2(K) \end{aligned} \tag{3.17}$$

For $p \prec q \prec K$ it follows that $\sigma^2(p) = \sigma^2(q) = \sigma^2(K)$. Using the fact that $F(x)$ is recursively defined as in (3.1) or (3.2) it is not difficult to show that the variables $\{F(x-y)\,, y \in S_K\}$ are linearly independent. From the uniqueness property of the projection operator it follows that $\sigma^2(q) > E|F(x) - P_K F(x)|^2 = \sigma^2(p)$ for $p \nprec q$. ||

Using the same technique as in the proof of Theorem 3.1 it can be shown that the results of Lemma 3.1 imply that for $p \nprec q$,

$$\lim_{T \to \infty} \hat{\sigma}^2(p) < \lim_{T \to \infty} \hat{\sigma}^2(q) \tag{3.18}$$

almost surely. It is a consequence of (3.18) that if the factor $N^{-1}f(N)$ tends to zero as $N \to \infty$, then the criterion function $C(q)$ of (3.12) cannot have a minimum for a q such that $p \nprec q$ when $T = N^{1/n} \to \infty$, and the only possibility of making an error asymptotically is by choosing q such that $p \prec q$. We will examine this possibility closer.

Lemma 3.2: Let $\{F(x), x \in Z^n\}$ be a stable causal or half-space AR(p) model generated by a series of independent identically distributed random variables $\{W(x), x \in Z^n\}$. Assume that we have observed $F(x)$ for $x \in I(T)$. Then for $0 < v$ and $p+v < K$ we have

$$T^n \sigma_W^{-2} \left(\hat{\sigma}^2(p) - \hat{\sigma}^2(p+v)\right) \xrightarrow{d} U(p+v,p) \tag{3.19}$$

as $T \to \infty$, where $U(p+v,p)$ has a χ^2 distribution with $d(p+v) - d(p)$ degrees of freedom.

Proof: Let $\{a(y), y \in S_{p+v}\}$ be the AR coefficients of an AR(p+v) process and let a_1 be the d(p)-dimensional vector obtained by arranging $\{a(y), y \in S_p\}$ in an arbitrary linear order. Furthermore, denote by a_2 the $(d(p+v)-d(p))$-dimensional vector obtained by a linear ordering of the remaining elements of $\{a(y), y \in S_{p+v}\}$. Let $G = G(x,y)$ be the matrix of dimension $d(T,L) \times d(p+v)$ defined by $\{G(x,y) = F(x-y)\ ;\ x \in L(M,p+v),\ y \in S_{p+v}\}$, where $M = (T,\ldots,T)$ and $d(T,L)$ is the number of points in $L(M, p+v)$. The columns of G are ordered consistently with the ordering of a_1 and a_2, and the rows are ordered in an arbitrary linear order. Let F be the vector obtained by ordering $\{F(x), x \in L(M, p+v)\}$ in the same way as the rows of G and let W be defined analogously using $\{W(x), x \in L(M,p+v)\}$. Then the defining equation of $F(x)$ can be written as a regression

$$F = [G_1\ G_2] \begin{bmatrix} a_1 \\ a_2 \end{bmatrix} + W = Ga + W$$

where $a_2 = 0$ if $F(x)$ is AR(p). The LS estimate $a^* = \{a^*(y), y \in S_{p+v}\}$ can now be written

$$a^* = (G'\,\overline{G})^{-1} G'\,\overline{F} \tag{3.20}$$

where G' denotes transposed, and where the recursive definition of $F(x)$ and the stability assumption guaranties the existence of $(G'\,\overline{G})^{-1}$ with probability one. According to Theorem 3.1, $T^{-n} G'\,\overline{G} \xrightarrow{a.s.} R_{p+v}$ as $T \to \infty$, where R_{p+v} corresponds to the matrix R_p of (3.8). Let

$$Q = \sum_{x \in L(M,p+v)} \left|F(x) - \sum_{y \in S_{p+v}} a(y)F(x-y)\right|^2 = (F-Ga)'\,\overline{(F-Ga)}\ . \tag{3.21}$$

Now assume $a_2 = 0$ and denote by $Q(p)$ the minimum of Q under this restriction. Using classical regression methods it follows

$$Q(p) = T^n \hat{\sigma}^2(p+v) + a_2^{*\prime} A_{22}^{-1} \overline{a_2^*} \tag{3.22}$$

where A_{22} is the $(d(p+v)-d(p)) \times (d(p+v)-d(p))$ lower right corner submatrix of $(G'\bar{G})^{-1}$. On the other hand $Q(p) = T^n \hat{\sigma}^2(p)$ and thus

$$T^n \sigma_W^{-2} \left(\hat{\sigma}^2(p) - \hat{\sigma}^2(p+v)\right) = \sigma_W^{-2} T^{n/2} a_2^{*\prime} (T^n A_{22})^{-1} T^{n/2} \overline{a_2^*} \quad . \tag{3.23}$$

Here

$$T^n (G'\bar{G})^{-1} \xrightarrow{a.s.} R_{p+v}^{-1} = \begin{bmatrix} R^{11} & R^{12} \\ R^{21} & R^{22} \end{bmatrix} \tag{3.24}$$

and thus $T^n A_{22} \xrightarrow{a.s.} R^{22}$. Since, using the analog of Theorem 8.1 of Tjøstheim (1978),

$$T^{n/2} a_2^* \overset{d}{\to} N(0, \sigma_W^2 R^{22}) \tag{3.25}$$

if $a_2 = 0$, it follows that the right hand side of (3.23) converges in distribution as $T \to \infty$ towards a χ^2 distribution with $d(p+v) - d(p)$ degrees of freedom. ||

Theorem 3.3: Let $\{F(x), x \in Z^n\}$ be a stable causal or half-space AR(p) process generated by a series of independent identically distributed random variables $\{W(x), x \in Z^n\}$. Assume that we have observed $F(x)$ for $x \in I(T)$, and that the vector q minimizing $C(q)$ of (3.12) over $S[0,K]$ is used as an estimate $\hat{p}$ of p. If $p < K$ and the function f of (3.12) is such that $N^{-1} f(N) \to 0$ and $f(N) \to \infty$ as $N \to \infty$, then we have that $P[\hat{p} \neq p] \to 0$ as $T = N^{1/n} \to \infty$.

Proof: From the comment after Lemma 3.1 it follows that it is sufficient to consider the case $p < \hat{p}$. Let $\hat{p} = p+v < K$, where $0 < v$. Then from (3.12)

$$C(p+v) = C(p) + \ln\left[\hat{\sigma}^2(p+v)/\hat{\sigma}^2(p)\right] + N^{-1} f(N)\left(d(p+v) - d(p)\right). \tag{3.26}$$

But

$$N \ln\left[\hat{\sigma}^2(p+v)/\hat{\sigma}^2(p)\right] = T^n \ln\left[1 - \hat{\sigma}^{-2}(p)\{\hat{\sigma}^2(p) - \hat{\sigma}^2(p+v)\}\right] \tag{3.27}$$

and by Taylor expanding the logarithm and using the fact that $\hat{\sigma}^2(p) \xrightarrow{a.s.} \sigma_W^2$, we have that the difference (cf. Shibata (1976) for the time series case) between $N \ln\left[\hat{\sigma}^2(p+v)/\hat{\sigma}^2(p)\right]$ and $-N \sigma_W^{-2}\left(\hat{\sigma}^2(p) - \hat{\sigma}^2(p+v)\right)$ converges to zero in probability as $T \to \infty$. Using Lemma 3.2 and the fact that $f(N) \to \infty$ as $T \to \infty$ it follows that

$$\lim_{T\to\infty} P\left(C(p+v) < C(p)\right) = \lim_{T\to\infty} P\left(U(p+v,p) > [d(p+v) - d(p)] \cdot f(N)\right) = 0 \tag{3.28}$$

where $U(p+v,p)$ is the χ^2 distributed variable given in (3.19). ||

It follows from this theorem that the BIC and LIL criteria are weakly consistent since for those $f(N)$ is given by $\ln N$ and $2 \ln \ln N$, respectively, while the AIC criterion is not. This does not necessarily mean that the AIC criterion is inferior to the BIC and LIL criteria. The somewhat limited relevance of consistency results of this kind for lattice processes should be borne in mind, since many AR representations will be infinite, and what we really have is an approximation problem.

The order determination criteria discussed here could be used in combination with the AR spectral formula to obtain AR spectral estimates for lattice processes as demonstrated in Tjøstheim (1981b).

4. Processes generated by lattice martingales.

The estimation theory established in the preceding section has been established under the assumption that the generating variables $\{W(x), x \in Z^n\}$ are identically and independently distributed. It has been shown in the time series case (Hannan 1973) that the independence assumption may be relaxed, and that it suffices to assume that the generating variables constitute martingale differences of a special type. It will be the purpose of this section to indicate an extension of some of these results to causal AR(p) lattice processes. Proofs will only be sketched.

4.1. Lattice martingales and innovations.

The concept of spatial martingales on R_+^2 has been treated in papers by Cairoli and Walsh (1975) and Wong and Zakai (1976). A lattice martingale concept on Z^n can be introduced quite analogously.

Let $(\Omega, \mathcal{F}, P)$ be a probability space and let $\{\mathcal{F}_x, x \in S[a,b]\}$ be a family of sub σ-algebras of $\mathcal{F}$. The σ-algebra $\mathcal{F}_x$ can be thought of as being generated by $\{W(y), y < x\}$ where $<$ is the partial order (3.14). For $t \in Z$, let

$$\mathcal{F}^i(t) = \bigvee_{x: x_i \le t} \mathcal{F}_x \tag{4.1}$$

and assume that the family $\{\mathcal{F}_x, x \in S[a,b]\}$ satisfies

B1: If $x < y$, then $\mathcal{F}_x \subset \mathcal{F}_y$.

B2: The operation of taking conditional expectation with respect to the σ-algebras $\mathcal{F}^i(t)$ commutes and for a bounded random variable $F \in (\Omega, \mathcal{F}, P)$

$$E\{F|\mathcal{F}_x\} = E\Big\{\cdots E\{E\{F|\mathcal{F}^1(x_1)\}|\mathcal{F}^2(x_2)\}\cdots|\mathcal{F}^n(x_n)\Big\} \tag{4.2}$$

for $x = (x_1,\dots,x_n) \in S[a,b]$.

The commutativity condition B2) represents a relatively strong restriction. It implies (Cairoli and Walsh 1975) that

$$\mathcal{F}_x = \bigcap_{i=1}^{n} \mathcal{F}^i(x_i) \tag{4.3}$$

The second order version of B2) has been used as a basic condition in Tjøstheim (1976,1978) and Kallianpur and Mandrekar (1981).

Let $\{\mathcal{F}_x , x \in S[a,b]\}$ be a system of σ-algebras satisfying B1) and B2) . A process $\{G(x) , x \in S[a,b]\}$ is a lattice martingale with respect to $\{\mathcal{F}_x , x \in S[a,b]\}$ if

C1: $G(x)$ is measurable with respect to $\mathcal{F}_x$.

C2: For each x , $E|G(x)| < \infty$.

C3: For each $x < y$, $E\{G(y)|\mathcal{F}_x\} \overset{a.s.}{=} G(x)$.

In all of the following we will assume that $\{F(x) , x \in Z^n\}$ is a stable causal-type AR(p) process as defined in (3.1), so that $F(x)$ can be inverted and represented as a linear process as in (3.5) with $S_\infty = S\langle 0,\infty]$, and such that $\mathcal{F}_x^{(F)} = \mathcal{F}_x^{(W)} = \mathcal{F}_x$, where $\{\mathcal{F}_x , x \in Z^n\}$ satisfies B2) . (The condition B1) is automatically satisfied.) Moreover, we assume that the following lattice innovation condition is fulfilled

$$E\{W(x) | \bigvee_{i=1}^{n} \mathcal{F}^i(x_i-1)\} \overset{a.s.}{=} 0 \tag{4.4}$$

Due to the linear process representation (3.5) this is equivalent to assuming

$$W(x) \overset{a.s.}{=} F(x) - E\{F(x) | \bigvee_{i=1}^{n} \mathcal{F}^i(x_i-1)\} \tag{4.5}$$

With these assumptions it is not difficult to show that $\{G(x) = \sum_{y \in S[1,x]} W(y) , x \in S[1,\infty]\}$ is a lattice martingale.

4.2. Consistency and asymptotic normality.

The following theorem is in some respect a generalization of Theorem 3.1.

Theorem 4.1: Let $\{F(x) , x \in Z^n\}$ be a stable and causal AR(p) process such that the coefficients $\{b(y) , y \in S\langle 0,\infty]\}$ of the linear process expansion (3.5) satisfy $\sum_{y \in S\langle 0,\infty]} |b(y)| < \infty$. Let the generating process $\{W(x) , x \in Z^n\}$ be a strictly homogeneous process satisfying the innovation condition (4.4) and the conditions $E|W(x)|^4 < \infty$ and

$$E\{|W(x)|^2 \mid \bigvee_{i=1}^{n} \mathcal{F}^i(x_i-1)\} \overset{a.s.}{=} \sigma_W^2 \tag{4.6}$$

for $x \in Z^n$. Assume that we have observed $F(x)$ for $x \in I(T)$. Then as $T \to \infty$, the vector $\hat{a} = \{\hat{a}(y), y \in S\langle 0,p]\}$ of YW (or LS) estimates defined by (3.8) converges almost surely to the vector $a = \{a(y), y \in S\langle 0,p]\}$ of AR parameters.

Outline of proof: As in the proof of Theorem 3.1 it is sufficient to prove that $\hat{R}(u,v) \xrightarrow{a.s.} E\{F(u)\overline{F(v)}\} = R(u,v)$ for arbitrary $u,v \in Z^n$. Since $\{F(x+u)\overline{F(x+v)}, x \in Z^n\}$ is strictly homogeneous for fixed $u,v \in Z^n$, it follows from the ergodic theorem that $\hat{R}(u,v)$ converges almost surely towards a random variable $Y(u,v)$, say. To identify $Y(u,v)$ with $R(u,v)$ it is sufficient to prove that $\hat{R}(u,v) \xrightarrow{P} R(u,v)$. This can be done by extending the arguments of Hall and Heyde (1980,p.184-187) to the lattice case ‖.

When it comes to asymptotic normality we assume that the lattice process $\{F(x), x \in Z^n\}$ is real-valued and that the conditions of Theorem 4.1 are fulfilled. Then $\hat{a} \xrightarrow{a.s.} a$ and reasoning as in Section 8 of Tjøstheim (1978) and neglecting edge effects asymptotic normality of $\{\hat{a}(y), y \in S\langle 0,p]\}$ will result if we can prove asymptotic normality of

$$J_T^{(m)} = T^{-n/2} \sum_{x \in I(T)} \sum_{u \in S\langle 0,p]} r(u)W(x) \sum_{y \in S[0,m]} b(y)W(x-u-y) \tag{4.7}$$

as $T \to \infty$. Here $\{r(u), u \in S\langle 0,p]\}$ are arbitrary real numbers and m is a fixed point in Z^n. The coefficients $b(y)$ $(b(0) = 1)$ are those appearing in the linear process representation (3.5) of $F(x)$.

A proof of asymptotic normality of $J_T^{(m)}$ can be pieced together by observing that

$$H(x) = \sum_{u \in S\langle 0,p]} r(u)W(x) \sum_{y \in S[0,m]} b(y)W(x-u-y)$$

constitutes the martingale elements of a lattice martingale $G(x) = \sum_{y \in S[1,x]} H(y)$ and by adapting the martingale central limit theorem (cf. Hall and Heyde, 1980, p.51-63) to the present situation. The martingale property of $G(x)$ is easy to obtain, but the extension of the martingale central limit theorem requires some nontrivial changes of the one-dimensional proof and will be presented in a separate publication.

References.

1. Adler, R.J. The Geometry of Random Fields, New York, Wiley 1981.

2. Cairoli, R. and Walsh, J.B. Stochastic integrals in the plane, Acta Math., 134 (1975), pp. 111-183.

3. Hall, P. and Heyde, C.C. Martingale Limit Theory and Its Application. New York, Academic Press, 1980.

4. Hannan, E.J. The asymptotic theory of linear time-series models. J.Appl. Prob., 10 (1973), pp. 130-145.

5. Hannan, E.J. and Quinn, B.G. The determination of the order of an autoregression, J. Roy. Statist. Soc. Ser.B, 41 (1979), pp. 190-195.

6. Helson, H. and Lowdenslager, D. Prediction theory and Fourier series in several variables, Acta Math., 99 (1958), pp. 165-201.

7. Helson, H. and Lowdenslager, D. Prediction theory and Fourier-series in several variables II, Acta Math., 106 (1961), pp. 175-213.

8. Kallianpur, G. and Mandrekar, V. Nondeterministic random fields and Wold and Halmos decompositions for commuting isometries. Tech. Rep. 2, Center for Stochastic Processes, Department of Statistics, University of North Carolina (1981).

9. O'Connor, B.T. and Huang, T.S. Stability of two-dimensional recursive digital filters, IEEE Trans. Acoust. Speech, Signal Processing, ASSP-26 (1978), pp. 550-560.

10. Rudin, W. Function Theory in Polydiscs. New York, Interscience-Wiley 1969.

11. Shibata, R. Selection of the order of an autoregressive model by Akaike's information criterion, Biometrika, 63 (1976), pp. 117-126.

12. Tjøstheim, D. Spectral representations and density operators for infinite-dimensional homogeneous random fields, Z. Wahrscheinlichkeitstheorie und Verw. Gebiete, 35 (1976), pp. 323-336.

13. Tjøstheim, D. Statistical spatial series modelling, Adv. Appl. Prob. 10 (1978), pp. 130-154.

14. Tjøstheim, D. Multidimensional discrimination techniques-theory and application. NATO Advanced Study Institute on Identification of Seismic Sources-Earthquake or Underground Explosion. E.S. Huseby and S. Mykkeltveit eds., D. Reidel Publishing Company,(1981a), pp. 663-694.

15. Tjøstheim, D. Autoregressive modelling and spectral analysis of array data in the plane, IEEE Trans. Geoscience Remote Sensing, GE - 19 (1981b), pp.15-23.

16. Whittle, P. On stationary processes in the plane, Biometrica 41 (1954), pp. 434-449.

17. Wong, E. and Zakai, M. Weak martingales and stochastic integrals in the plane, Ann. Probability, 4 (1976), pp. 570-586.

RANDOM WALKS AMONG RANDOM SCATTERERS

S. R. S. Varadhan

Courant Institute of Mathematical Sciences

New York University, New York, N. Y. 10012, U. S. A.

We consider a lattice Z^d of vectors in R^d with integral coordinates and a random subset $S \subset Z^d$. The distribution of the random subset S is assumed to be invariant with respect to translations in Z^d and ergodic. This random subset has the interpretation of the sites at which scatterers are located. A particle starts from the origin at time 0 and moves in a random direction. The direction could be any one of the 2d possible directions with equal probability. It covers one unit per unit time and continues in a straight line motion until it reaches a site that is occupied by a scatterer. Then the particle picks a new direction, again uniformly and randomly from among the 2d possible directions. It is further assumed that new direction is picked statistically independently of everything else. In other words the motion of the particle consists of uniform motion along any of the 2d possible axes directions with change of direction occurring randomly in the manner described whenever the particle passes through a site that is a member of the randomly chosen set $S \subset Z^d$.

Under mild regularity conditions we prove a functional central limit theorem for the position at time n of the particle. It is important to note that the random set S, stays fixed forever.

Themethod of proof consists of viewing the problem slightly differently. The particle is moving randomly in a random universe and its motion of course is controlled by the universe. One can pretent that the particle does not move at all but only that the universe slides around it. Since we want to keep track of the motion let us consider a state space consisting of the pair S and v where S is any subset of Z^d and v is any one of the 2d directions along the axes. We can define a Markov chain whose state space is $\Omega \times V$ where Ω is the set of all possible subsets of Z^d and Vis the set of v's. One has a natural Markov chain on $X = \Omega \times V$ where if $0 \notin S$ then the chain moves from (S,v) deterministically to $(S-v,v)$. Here $S-v$ is the set obtained by translating S by $-v$. If $0 \in S$ then from (S,v) the state moves to $(S-v',v')$ where v' is chosen from among the members of V with probability $1/2d$ for each one. If P is any translation invariant measure on Ω then $P \times \mu$ is an invariant measure on X for the Markov chain, where μ is the uniform distribution on the set V of directions. The central limit theorem we are after then takes the usual form of studying $f(x_1) + \ldots + f(x_n)$ where $x_1,\ldots,x_n,\ldots$ is the Markov chain on X that we just described with a stationary distribution $P \times \mu$ and $f(x)$ is the vector valued function $f: \Omega \times V \to R^d$ defined by $f(S,v) = v$.

Although the problem now is the central limit theorem for additive functionals of Markov chains we have the complication that the Markov chain is infinite dimensional and is barely ergodic with no mixing properties. However one can use martingale methods developed in [1] to study this problem and obtain functional limit theorems under very mild regularity assumptions on the statistics P of our random set S. The details of the proof will appear elsewhere.

[1] G. Papanicolaou, D. Stroock and S. R. S. Varadhan, Martingale Approach to Some Limit Theorems, in: Statistical Mechanics, Dynamical Systems, Duke Turbulence Conference Proceedings, Duke University Mathematics Series, Vol. 3, 1977.

Acknowledgement.

This work was supported in part by the National Science Foundation, Grant MCS 8117526.

Malliavin's calculus in terms of generalized Wiener functionals

S. Watanabe
Department of Mathematics, Kyoto University

The present work was inspired by the talk of Professor H.Kuo given at the conference in which he discussed the problem how to give a mathematical meaning to what is called Donsker's δ-function. It is defined formally as

$$\delta_{t,x}(w) = (2\pi)^{-1}\int_{-\infty}^{\infty} e^{i\xi(w(t)-x)}\, d\xi$$

where $w(t)$ is a sample path of one-dimensional Wiener process. It is obvious that we cannot realize $\delta_{t,x}(w)$ as an ordinary Wiener functional (i.e. a measurable function on the Wiener space) and Kuo's idea was to use Hida's theory of generalized Brownian functionals.

Here we discuss a similar problem of defining composite functions of Schwartz's distributions and a class of Wiener functionals in a more general way. A composite function thus obtained is no longer a Wiener functional in general but it can be realized as a what we call generalized Wiener functional. In this connection, Professor Hida [2] already introduced the notion of generalized Brownian functionals and our notion is similar to that of Hida in the sense that our space of generalized Wiener functionals is also defined as a dual space of certain space of test Wiener functionals. This space of test functionals is somewhat different from that of Hida, however, and we choose it to be more convenient for our purposes. In this connection, the work of Professor Meyer given also at the conference is very important in defining and analyzing the space of test functionals. Also, we prefer a path space formulation rather than a white noise formulation because our interests are most in those functionals obtained by Ito's calculus, stochastic integrals or solutions of stochastic differential equations.

Now we can define composite functions of Schwartz's tempered distributions and a class of Wiener functionals as generalized Wiener functionals. In doing this, we shall see that we are doing essentially the same thing as a part of Malliavin's calculus as discussed in e.g. Malliavin [5], Ikeda-Watanabe [3] and Stroock [8] : that is, we can rewrite some part of Malliavin's calculus in the context of generalized Wiener functionals.

Let $\{W_0^r, F, P^W\}$ be the standard r-dimensional Wiener space: W_0^r is the Banach space $\{ w \in C([0,T] \to R^r);\ w(0) = 0 \}$ with the norm $\|w\| = \max_{s\in[0,T]}|w(s)|$, P^W is the standard Wiener measure and F is the completion of the Borel σ-field on W_0^r. Here $T > 0$ is arbitrary but fixed. Let H be the Hilbert subspace of W_0^r formed of all $w=(w_\alpha(t))_{\alpha=1}^r$ such that $w_\alpha(t)$ is absolutely continuous with square-integrable derivative and endowed with the Hilbertian norm $|w|_H^2 = \Sigma_\alpha\int_0^T|\dot{w}_\alpha(t)|^2dt$. A measurable function defined on the space $\{W_0^r, F, P^W\}$ is called a Wiener functional and two Wiener functionals are identified whenever they coincide almost everywhere. The real L^p-space $L^p(W_0^r,P^W)$ of Wiener functionals is denoted simply by L^p, $p \geq 1$. A real-valued function $F(w)$ on W_0^r is <u>called a smooth functional</u> if it is expressed as $F(w) = f(w(t_1),w(t_2),\ldots,w(t_n))$, $w \in W_0^r$, for some n, $0<t_1<t_2 \ldots <t_n$ and $f \in C^\infty(R^n)$ such that f and all of its derivatives are of polynomial growth order. The totality of smooth functionals is denoted by $\underline{S}$. Obviously, $\underline{S} \subset L^p$ for any $1 \leq p < \infty$ as spaces of Wiener functionals. For $F \in \underline{S}$, we have

$$F(w+h) = F(w) + F'(w)[h] + \frac{1}{2}F''(w)[h,h] + \ldots + \frac{1}{n!}F^{(n)}(w)[h,h,\ldots,h] + o(\|h\|^n)$$

and a symmetric n-multilinear form $F^{(n)}(w)[h_1,h_2,\ldots,h_n]$ on W_0^r is determined from this for each $w \in W_0^r$. It is called the n-th <u>Frechet derivative of</u> F at w. Its restriction to $H \hookrightarrow W_0^r$ is a symmetric n-multilinear form on H which we call the n-th <u>H-derivative of</u> F at w and denote by $D^nF(w)$. It is clear that $D^nF(w) \in H^*\otimes H^*\otimes\ldots\otimes H^*$ for any $w \in W_0^r$ (the Hilbert space formed of all n-multilinear forms V on H with finite Hilbert-Schmidt norm $|V|_{HS}^2 = \sum_{i_1,\ldots,i_n=1}^{\infty} V[h_{i_1},\ldots h_{i_n}]^2$, $\{h_i\}$ being an orthonormal basis of H).

For $F \in \underline{S}$, we set

$$LF(w) = \text{trace } D^2F(w) - F'(w)[w]$$

and call it the <u>Ornstein-Uhlenbeck operator</u>. It is a linear and symmetric operator from $\underline{S}$ into $\underline{S}$: $(LF,G)_{L^2} = (F,LG)_{L^2}$ for any $f,g \in \underline{S}$. Following Meyer [6], we set

$$\|F\|_{p,k} = (\|F\|_p^p + \|LF\|_p^p + \ldots + \|L^kF\|_p^p)^{\frac{1}{p}}, \quad F \in \underline{S}, \quad 1 \leq p < \infty,\ k = 0,1,2,\ldots$$

where $\|\ \|_p$ is the L^p-norm. These norms constitute a system of compatible norms on $\underline{S}$.

DEFINITION 1. $\underline{D}_{p,k}$ = the closure in L^p of $\underline{S}$ under the $\|\ \|_{p,k}$-norm.

Clearly if $1 \leq p \leq q < \infty$,

$$\begin{array}{ccccccccc}\cdots \hookrightarrow & \underline{D}_{p,k+1} & \hookrightarrow & \underline{D}_{p,k} & \hookrightarrow \cdots \hookrightarrow & \underline{D}_{p,0} & = & L^p \\ & \cup & & \cup & & \cup & & \cup \\ \cdots \hookrightarrow & \underline{D}_{q,k+1} & \hookrightarrow & \underline{D}_{q,k} & \hookrightarrow \cdots \hookrightarrow & \underline{D}_{q,0} & = & L^q.\end{array}$$

DEFINITION 2. $\underline{T} = \bigcap_{1 \leq p < \infty, k=0,1\ldots} \underline{D}_{p,k}$.

Thus, $\underline{T}$ is a complete countably normed space. The following two lemmas are due to Meyer [6].

LEMMA 1. For any $1<p<\infty$ and $k=0,1,\ldots$, there exists a constant $C_{p,k}>0$ such that

$$\|F\cdot G\|_{p,k} \le C_{p,k}\|F\|_{2p,k}\|G\|_{2p,k} \quad \text{for every } F,G \in \underline{\underline{S}}.$$

COROLLARY 1. $\underline{\underline{T}}$ is an algebra.

COROLLARY 2. For any bounded set $B \subset \underline{\underline{T}}$ and a sequence $F_n \in \underline{\underline{T}}$ such that $F_n \to 0$ in $\underline{\underline{T}}$, $GF_n \to 0$ in $\underline{\underline{T}}$ uniformly in $G \in B$, i.e. $\sup_{G\in B}\|GF_n\|_{p,k} \to 0$ as $n\to\infty$ for any p,k.

LEMMA 2. For any $1<p<\infty$ and $k=0,1,\ldots$, there exists a constant $C_{p,k}>0$ such that

$$\| |D^kF|_{HS}\|_p \le C_{p,k}\|F\|_{p,k} \quad \text{for every } F \in \underline{\underline{S}}.$$

Shigekawa [7] defined the space $H(p_0,p_1,\ldots,p_k)$ of Wiener functionals for $k=0,1,\ldots$, $1\le p_i<\infty$, which coincides with the closure in L^{p_0} of $\underline{\underline{S}}$ under the norm $\|F\|_{p_0} + \||DF|_H\|_{p_1} + \ldots + \||D^kF|_{HS}\|_{p_k}$. Note that for $F \in H(p_0,p_1,\ldots,p_k)$, the weak derivatives D^iF, $i=1,2,\ldots,k$, are naturally defined as $H^*\otimes\ldots\otimes H^*$-valued Wiener functionals. (H^* is identified with H in a usual way and then $|\ |_{HS} = |\ |_H$.)

COROLLARY $\underline{\underline{T}} \subsetneq H(p_0,p_1,\ldots,p_k)$ for any $k=0,1,\ldots$ and $1\le p_i<\infty$.

DEFINITION 3. $\underline{\underline{T}}'$ = the dual space of $\underline{\underline{T}}$ i.e. $\Phi \in T'$ if and only if Φ is a real continuous linear functional on $\underline{\underline{T}}$. We call $\Phi \in T'$ a generalized Wiener functional.

It is well known that $T' = \bigcup_{\substack{1<p<\infty \\ k=0,1,\ldots}} (D_{p,k})'$. We always identify $(L^2)'$ with L^2 in the usual way. Then, for $p>2$, we have

$$\underline{\underline{T}} \subsetneq L^p \subsetneq L^2 = (L^2)' \subsetneq (L^p)' = L^{p/p-1} \subsetneq \underline{\underline{T}}'.$$

In particular, $L^p \subset \underline{\underline{T}}'$ for every $p>1$. We denote by $\langle\ ,\ \rangle$ the canonical bilinear form on $\underline{\underline{T}}'\times\underline{\underline{T}}$. Clearly $\langle\Phi,F\rangle = E(\Phi(w)F(w))$ if $F \in \underline{\underline{T}}$ and $\Phi \in L^p \subset T'$ (E is the expectation on the Wiener space).

We shall introduce the following concepts of convergence for a sequence in $\underline{\underline{T}}'$: the first two are standard in the theory of topological vector spaces.

DEFINITION 4. Let Φ_n, $\Phi \in \underline{\underline{T}}'$, $n=1,2,\ldots$.

(i) We say that $\Phi_n \to \Phi$ weakly if $\langle\Phi_n-\Phi,F\rangle \to 0$ for every $F \in \underline{\underline{T}}$ as $n\to\infty$.

(ii) We say that $\Phi_n \to \Phi$ strongly if $\sup_{F\in B}|\langle\Phi_n-\Phi,F\rangle| \to 0$ for any bounded set $B \subset T$ as $n \to \infty$.

(iii) We say that $\Phi_n \to \Phi$ *-strongly if, for some p $(1 \le p < \infty)$ and k $(k=0,1,\dots)$, $\Phi_n, \Phi \in (\underline{D}_{p,k})'$ and $\|\Phi_n - \Phi\|_{-p,-k}$ $(:= \sup_{F \in \underline{D}_{p,k},\ \|F\|_{p,k} \le 1} |\langle \Phi_n - \Phi, F \rangle|) \to 0$ as $n \to \infty$.

Clearly, we have the following implication: *-strongly $\Rightarrow$ strongly $\Rightarrow$ weakly. Note also by the general theory ([1]) that T is sequentially weakly complete: for $\Phi_n \in T'$, $n=1,2,\dots$. if $\langle \Phi_n, F \rangle$ is a Cauchy sequence for every $F \in \underline{T}$, then there exists a unique $\Phi \in \underline{T}'$ such that $\Phi_n \to \Phi$ weakly.

Let $S = S(R^d)$ be the Schwartz space of rapidly decreasing C^∞-functions on R^d and $S' = S'(R^d)$ be the Schwartz space of tempered distributions on R^d. Let $F(w) = (F^1(w), F^2(w), \dots, F^d(w))$ be a d-dimensional Wiener functional and consider the following assumptions on F:

(A1) $F^i \in \underline{T}$, $i=1,2,\dots,d$.

(A2) If we set $\sigma(w) = (\sigma^{ij}(w))$ where $\sigma^{ij}(w) = \langle DF^i(w), DF^j(w) \rangle_H$, then for almost all w (P^W) $\sigma(w)$ is strictly positive definite and, setting $\sigma^{-1}(w) = (\gamma^{ij}(w))$, $\gamma^{ij} \in L^p$ for all $1 \le p < \infty$.

THEOREM. Suppose F satisfy the assumptions (A 1) and (A 2). Then there exists a mapping $S' \ni T \to \hat{T} \in \underline{T}'$ with the following properties:

(i) if $T = f(x) \in S$ $(\subset S')$, then $\hat{T} = f(F(w)) \in \underline{T}$ $(\subset \underline{T}')$,

(ii) if $T_n \to T$ in S' then $\hat{T}_n \to \hat{T}$ in $\underline{T}'$ *-strongly.

Furthermore, a mapping from S' into $\underline{T}'$ with the above properties is unique and is necessarily linear.

Proof. The proof is essentially Malliavin's calculus. First, note that if $T \in S$ then $\hat{T}$ is uniquely determined by (i). Note also that, for every $T \in S'$, there exists a real α and a sequence $f_n \in S$ such that $T \in S_{-\alpha}$ and $\|T - f_n\|_{-\alpha} \to 0$ ($S_{-\alpha}$ is the Hilbert space which is the completion of S under the norm $\|f\|_{-\alpha} = \|(-\Delta + |x|^2)^{-\alpha} f\|_{L^2(R^d)}$, $f \in S$ (cf.[4]).) Next, we choose an integer $m > 0$ such that $S_{m-\alpha} = (-\Delta + |x|^2)^{-m}(S_{-\alpha}) \hookrightarrow C_\infty$ where C_∞ is the completion of S under the norm $\|f\|_\infty = \max_{x \in R^d} |f(x)|$. Therefore, if we set $(-\Delta + |x|^2)^{-m} f_n = \phi_n$ and $(-\Delta + |x|^2)^{-m} T = \phi$, then $\phi_n, \phi \in C_\infty$ and $\|\phi - \phi_n\|_\infty \to 0$.

By a chain rule involving the Ornstein-Uhlenbeck operator L, we have ([3])

$$(\partial_i \psi)(F) = \Sigma_{k=1}^d \gamma^{ik} \{ L(F^k \psi(F)) - \psi(F) LF^k - F^k L(\psi(F)) , \quad \psi \in S .$$

Combining this with the symmetry of L, we see easily that, setting $(-\Delta + |x|^2)^m \psi = \theta$,

$$\langle \theta(F), G\rangle = \langle \psi(F), \ell(G)\rangle \qquad G \in \underline{T}$$

where $\ell(G) \in \underline{T}$ is of the form $\ell(G) = \Sigma_{i_1,\dots,i_j} H_{i_1}(L\dots(L(H_{i_{j-1}} L(H_{i_j} G)))\dots)$ with $H_{i_k} \in \underline{T}$ which are polynomials in γ^{ij}, F^i and LF^i. Since the operator L and the multiplication by an element in $\underline{T}$ are bounded operators $\underline{D}_{p',k'} \to \underline{D}_{p,k}$ provided $k' \geq k+1$ and $p' \geq 2p$ (cf. Lemma 1), we can find p ($1 \leq p < \infty$) and $k \in \{0, 1, \dots\}$ such that

$$\sup_{G \in \underline{T},\, \|G\|_{p,k} \leq 1} \|\ell(G)\|_{1,0} := C < \infty \text{ (note that } \|\ \|_{1,0} \text{ is just } L^1\text{-norm).}$$

Now we can estimate as follows: $\sup_{\|G\|_{p,k} \leq 1} |\langle f_n(F) - f_{n'}(F), G\rangle| =$

$$\sup_{\|G\|_{p,k} \leq 1} |\langle \phi_n(F) - \phi_{n'}(F), \ell(G)\rangle| \leq C\|\phi_n - \phi_{n'}\|_\infty \to 0, \text{ as } n,n' \to \infty .$$

This implies that $\hat{T} \in (\underline{D}_{p,k})'$ exists and $\|f_n(F) - \hat{T}\|_{-p,-k} \to 0$ proving that $f_n(F) \to \hat{T}$ *-strongly in $\underline{T}'$. $\hat{T}$ is uniquely determined from T and is independent of a particular choice of a sequence f_n. Indeed, if f'_n is another sequence, we have $\sup_{\|G\|_{p,k} \leq 1} |\langle f_n(F) - f'_n(F), G\rangle| \leq C\|\phi_n - \phi'_n\|_\infty \to 0$ as $n \to \infty$ where $\phi'_n = (-\Delta + |x|^2)^{-m} f'_n$. Now the mapping $T \to \hat{T}$ is established. The above argument shows in fact that the mapping $S_{-\alpha} \ni T \to \hat{T} \in (\underline{D}_{p,k})'$ is continuous and the property (ii) is obvious from this. The uniqueness and the linearity of the mapping is also obvious in the above proof. Q.E.D.

PROPOSITION 1. If $T \in S'$ is defined by a continuous function $T(x)$ of polynomial growth order, then $\hat{T} = T(F(w))$.

Proof We can choose $f_n \in S$ such that $|f_n(x)| \leq b(1+|x|^a)$ for some positive a and b independent of n and $f_n(x) \to T(x)$ at every x as $n \to \infty$. Then $f_n(F) \to T(F)$ in L^2 and hence $f_n(F) \to T(F)$ *-strongly in $\underline{T}'$. On the other hand, it is clear that $f_n \to T$ in S' and hence $f_n(F) \to \hat{T}$ *-strongly in $\underline{T}'$. This proves that $T(F) = \hat{T}$.

DEFINITION 5. For $T \in S'$, $\hat{T} \in \underline{T}'$ in the theorem is denoted by $\hat{T} = T(F) = T(F(w))$. It is called the composite of $T \in S'$ and the Wiener functional F.

Now we discuss the dependence on a parameter. The parameter may be any multidimensional one but we assume it real just for the simlicity of notations. Proofs are provided by more or less the same arguments as above.

PROPOSITION 2. Let $I=(a,b)$ be an interval and $F(w)$ be a d-dimensional Wiener functional satisfying the assumtions (A1) and (A2). Then we have the following.

(i) If $\alpha \in I \to T_\alpha \in S'$ is continuous (continuously differentiable), then $\alpha \in I \to T_\alpha(F) \in \underline{\underline{T}}'$ is continuous *-strongly (resp. continuously diffentiable *-strongly). In particular, for every $G \in \underline{\underline{T}}$, $\alpha \in I \to \langle T_\alpha(F), G\rangle$ is continuous (resp. continuously differntiable and

$$\left\langle \frac{dT_\alpha}{d\alpha}(F), G\right\rangle = \frac{d}{d\alpha}\langle T_\alpha(F), G\rangle \quad).$$

(ii) If $\alpha \in I \to T_\alpha \in S'$ is continuous then for every $G \in \underline{\underline{T}}$,

$$\left\langle \left(\int_I T_\alpha \, d\alpha\right)(F), G\right\rangle = \int_I \langle T_\alpha(F), G\rangle \, d\alpha$$

where $\int_I T_\alpha d\alpha \in S'$ is defined by $\langle \int_I T_\alpha d\alpha, \phi\rangle = \int_I \langle T_\alpha, \phi\rangle d\alpha$, $\phi \in S$.

Next, let $T \in S'$ and F_α, $\alpha \in I$, be a family of d-dimensional Wiener functionals satisfying the assumptions (A 1) and (A 2). We set $\langle DF^i_\alpha, DF^j_\alpha\rangle_H = \sigma^{ij}_\alpha$, $\gamma^{ij}_\alpha = (\sigma^{-1}_\alpha)^{ij}$ and assume that $\{\gamma^{ij}_\alpha\}_{\alpha \in I,\ i,j=1,\dots,d}$ is a bounded set in L^p for every $1 \le p < \infty$.

PROPOSITION 3. Under the above assumption, if furthermore $\alpha \in I \to F_\alpha \in \underline{\underline{T}}^d$ is continuous,(continuously differentiable) then $\alpha \in I \to T(F_\alpha) \in \underline{\underline{T}}'$ is continuous *-strongly (resp. continuously differntiable *-strongly and

$$\frac{d}{d\alpha}\langle T(F_\alpha), G\rangle = \sum_{i=1}^d \left\langle \frac{\partial T}{\partial x_i}(F_\alpha), \frac{dF^i_\alpha}{d\alpha} G\right\rangle \quad).$$

Finally, the existence of smooth densities for the laws of a class of Wiener functionals can be discussed, in this context, as follows. Suppose that a d-dimensional Wiener functional $F(w)$ satisfy (A 1) and (A 2). Let δ_x , $x \in R^d$, be the Dirac δ-function at $x: \langle \delta_x, \phi\rangle = \phi(x)$, $\phi \in S$. Then $\delta_x(F) \in \underline{\underline{T}}'$ is defined by the theorem. Since $x \to \delta_x \in S'$ is clearly C^∞, $p(x) = \langle \delta_x(F), 1\rangle$ is also C^∞ and $D^\alpha_x p(x) = \langle (D^\alpha_x \delta_x)(F), 1\rangle = (-1)^{|\alpha|}\langle (D^\alpha \delta_x)(F), 1\rangle$ by Prop. 2 (i). (Note that the constant functional $1 \in \underline{\underline{T}}$.) Also it is clear that $\int_{R^d} \phi(x)\delta_x(\ )dx = \phi(\ )$ for $\phi \in S$ and hence by Prop. 2 (ii),

$$\int_{R^d} \phi(x) \langle \delta_x(F), 1\rangle dx = \langle \phi(F), 1\rangle = E(\phi(F(w))) \quad ,$$

that is, $\int_{R^d} \phi(x)p(x)dx = E(\phi(F(w)))$. Thus $p(x)$ is the C^∞-density of the law of F.

More generally, we see in the same way that C^∞-function $\langle \delta_x(F), G\rangle$ is a version of $E(G(w) \mid F(w) = x)p(x)$ for every $G \in \underline{\underline{T}}$.

REFERENCES

[1] I.M.Gelfand and G.E.Shilov: Generalized functions, Vol.2, Function and generalized function spaces, Academic Press, 1966.

[2] T.Hida: Analysis of Brownian functionals, Carleton Mathematical Lecture Notes, 13, Carleton Univ., 1978.

[3] N.Ikeda and S.Watanabe: Stochastic differential equations and diffusion processes, North-Holland/Kodansha, 1981.

[4] K.Ito: Stochastic analysis in infinite dimensions, Stochastic analysis, Academic Press, 1978, 187-197.

[5] P.Malliavin: C_k-hypoellipticity with degeneracy, Stochastic Analysis, Academic Press,1978, 199-214, 327-340.

[6] P.A.Meyer: Some analytical results on the Ornstein-Uhlenbeck semigroup in infinitely many dimensions, A note distributed at IFIP/ISI Working conference on the theory and applications on random fields at Bangalore, 1982.

[7] I.Shigekawa: Derivatives of Wiener functionals and absolute continuity of induced measures, J.Math.Kyoto Univ. 20, 1980, 263-289.

[8] D.W.Stroock: Malliavin calculus and its applications, Stochastis integrals, Lecture Notes in Math. 851, Springer 1981, 394-432.

Lecture Notes in Control and Information Sciences

Edited by A. V. Balakrishnan and M. Thoma

Vol. 22: Optimization Techniques
Proceedings of the 9th IFIP Conference on Optimization Techniques,
Warsaw, September 4–8, 1979
Part 1
Edited by K. Iracki, K. Malanowski, S. Walukiewicz
XVI, 569 pages. 1980

Vol. 23: Optimization Techniques
Proceedings of the 9th IFIP Conference on Optimization Techniques,
Warsaw, September 4-8, 1979
Part 2
Edited by K. Iracki, K. Malanowski, S. Walukiewicz
XV, 621 pages. 1980

Vol. 24: Methods and Applications in Adaptive Control
Proceedings of an International Symposium
Bochum, 1980
Edited by H. Unbehauen
VI, 309 pages. 1980

Vol. 25: Stochastic Differential Systems – Filtering and Control
Proceedings of the IFIP-WG7/1 Working Conference
Vilnius, Lithuania, USSR, Aug. 28 – Sept. 2, 1978
Edited by B. Grigelionis
X, 362 pages. 1980

Vol. 26: D. L. Iglehart, G. S. Shedler
Regenerative Simulation of Response Times in Networks of Queues
XII, 204 pages. 1980

Vol. 27: D. H. Jacobson, D. H. Martin, M. Pachter, T. Geveci
Extensions of Linear-Quadratic Control Theory
XI, 288 pages. 1980

Vol. 28: Analysis and Optimization of Systems
Proceedings of the Fourth International Conference on Analysis and Optimization of Systems
Versailles, December 16–19, 1980
Edited by A. Bensoussan and J. L. Lions
XIV, 999 pages. 1980

Vol. 29: M. Vidyasagar,
Input-Output Analysis of Large-Scale Interconnected Systems – Decomposition, Well-Posedness and Stability
VI, 221 pages. 1981

Vol. 30: Optimization and Optimal Control
Proceedings of a Conference Held at Oberwolfach, March 16–22, 1980
Edited by A. Auslender, W. Oettli, and J. Stoer
VIII, 254 pages. 1981

Vol. 31: Berc Rustem
Projection Methods in Constrained Optimisation and Applications to Optimal Policy Decisions
XV, 315 pages. 1981

Vol. 32: Tsuyoshi Matsuo,
Realization Theory of Continuous-Time Dynamical Systems
VI, 329 pages, 1981

Vol. 33: Peter Dransfield
Hydraulic Control Systems – Design and Analysis of Their Dynamics
VII, 227 pages, 1981

Vol. 34: H.W. Knobloch
Higher Order Necessary Conditions in Optimal Control Theory
V, 173 pages, 1981

Vol. 35: Global Modelling
Proceedings of the IFIP-WG 7/1 Working Conference Dubrovnik, Yugoslavia,
Sept. 1–5, 1980
Edited by S. Krčevinac
VIII, 232 pages, 1981

Vol. 36: Stochastic Differential Systems
Proceedings of the 3rd IFIP-WG 7/1 Working Conference
Visegrád, Hungary, Sept. 15–20, 1980
Edited by M. Arató, D. Vermes, A.V. Balakrishnan
VI, 238 pages, 1981

Vol. 37: Rüdiger Schmidt
Advances in Nonlinear Parameter Optimization
VI, 159 pages, 1982

Vol. 38: System Modeling and Optimization
Proceedings of the 10th IFIP Conference
New York City, USA, Aug. 31 – Sept. 4, 1981
Edited by R.F. Drenick and F. Kozin
XI, 894 pages. 1982

Vol. 39: Feedback Control of Linear and Nonlinear Systems
Proceedings of the Joint Workshop on Feedback and Synthesis of Linear and Nonlinear Systems
Bielefeld/Rom
XIII, 284 pages. 1982

Vol. 40: Y.S. Hung, A.G.J. MacFarlane
Multivariable Feedback: A Quasi-Classical Approach
X, 182 pages. 1982

Vol. 41: M. Gössel
Nonlinear Time-Discrete Systems – A General Approach by Nonlinear Superposition
VIII, 112 pages. 1982

Vol. 42: Advances in Filtering and Optimal Stochastic Control
Proceedings of the IFIP-WG 7/1 Working Conference
Cocoyoc, Mexico, February 1–6, 1982
VIII, 391 pages. 1982

Lecture Notes in Control and Information Sciences

Edited by A. V. Balakrishnan and M. Thoma

Vol. 43: Stochastic Differential Systems
Proceedings of the 2nd Bad Honnef Conference
of the SFB 72 of the DFG at the University of Bonn
June 28 – July 2, 1982
Edited by M. Kohlmann and N. Christopeit
XII, 377 pages. 1982.

Vol. 44: Analysis and Optimization of Systems
Proceedings of the Fifth International
Conference on Analysis and Optimization of Systems
Versailles. December 14–17, 1982
Edited by A. Bensoussan and J. L. Lions
XV, 987 pages, 1982

Vol. 45: M. Arató
Linear Stochastic Systems
with Constant Coefficients
A Statistical Approach
IX, 309 pages. 1982

Vol. 46: Time-Scale Modeling of Dynamic Networks
with Applications to Power Systems
Edited by J. H. Chow
X, 218 pages. 1982

Vol. 47: P. A. Ioannou, P. V. Kokotovic
Adaptive Systems with Reduced Models
V, 162 pages. 1983

Vol. 48: Yaakov Yavin
Feedback Strategies for Partially
Observable Stochastic Systems
VI, 233 pages, 1983

Vol. 49: Theory and Application of Random Fields
Proceedings of the IFIP-WG 7/1
Working Conference
held under the joint auspices of the
Indian Statistical Institute
Bangalore, India, January 1982
Edited by G. Kallianpur
VI. 290 pages. 1983